PHILOSOPHY IN AMERICA
AN AMS REPRINT SERIES

THE PUBLIC LIFE OF

THOMAS COOPER

1783-1839

AMS PRESS

NEW YORK

*Steel Engraving of Thomas Cooper
taken from his Lectures on Political Economy London, 1831*

THE PUBLIC LIFE OF

THOMAS COOPER

1783-1839

By

DUMAS MALONE, PH.D.

*Associate Professor of History in the
University of Virginia*

*This Essay was Awarded the John Addison Porter Prize,
Yale University, 1923*

NEW HAVEN: YALE UNIVERSITY PRESS
LONDON: HUMPHREY MILFORD
OXFORD UNIVERSITY PRESS
MDCCCCXXVI

Library of Congress Cataloging in Publication Data

Malone, Dumas, 1892-
    The public life of Thomas Cooper, 1783-1839.

    (Philosophy in America)
    Reprint of the ed. published by Yale Univer-
sity Press, New Haven.
    Bibliography: p.
    Includes index.
    1. Cooper, Thomas, 1759-1839.   2. United
States—Politics and government—1783-1865.
3. Statesmen—United States—Biography.
I. Title.
E302.6.C7M2   1979   973.5′092′4 [B]   75-3122
ISBN 0-404-59117-5

TO
MY FATHER AND MOTHER

CONTENTS

ILLUSTRATIONS

PREFACE

IT is my hope that this study of the career of Thomas Cooper may contribute something to a better understanding of the many important political, economic, and intellectual movements in which he participated, and that it may be of interest for its own sake. Cooper is significant because of the part he played in public affairs during an important English decade and a critical American generation, and is extraordinarily interesting as a person. As its title indicates, this volume describes his public life and does not claim to be a personal biography. None the less, I have incorporated the more important personal material that I have discovered, and I hope that the picture of the man himself is not obscured by the minute historical details with which a monograph inevitably abounds. I should not like my readers to miss seeing him. It seems improbable that they will, because his personality and his public activities are inseparable.

Never the holder of an office that enabled him directly to determine state policy, Cooper sought to affect the course of events by agitation and the exertion of his influence upon important statesmen, and to facilitate the "march of mind" by educational activities of various kinds. He was preëminently a controversialist and, in the larger sense, an educator. In South Carolina he took full advantage of his strategic position in the state college, but in most cases his prominence and influence were chiefly due to the versatility of his mind and the aggressiveness of his nature. His failures are in part attributable to the fact that he so frequently attempted the impossible, but even more to temperamental limitations. His remarkably extensive and diverse writings are much more important than his official activities and have received correspondingly large attention in this study. I have not included them in the title because I have felt myself unqualified to discuss the more technical philosophical, scientific, and legal treatises, and because I have described most of the other writings—political, economic, theological, and personal—in connection with the various movements and controversies of which they form a con-· stituent part.

Cooper's name has been frequently mentioned in general historical works and monographs, particularly in connection with the political campaign of 1800 and the nullification controversy in South Carolina; his educational activities and religious disputes during his later years have been in part described by local writers; and his contributions to science and philosophy have received respectful recognition in the historical literature of those subjects; but no one has hitherto investigated his career as a whole, or any part of it in detail. I find it difficult to explain the long neglect of him. It has been suggested to me by others that the highly controversial character of his life and the general opinion that his influence was primarily destructive may have deterred the timorous. His personal papers have not been preserved,[1] and prospective biographers may have been dismayed by the necessity of recovering by indirect means the personal details of his history. In my own effort to reconstruct the story of his career, I have found it necessary to pursue an itinerary almost equivalent to his own, and the picture of the man which has at length appeared is a mosaic

[1] See the Bibliographical Note.

of innumerable tiny stones, many of which have been found in unexpected literary quarries.

In general, I have tried to depict Cooper as his contemporaries saw him, and have endeavored to provide a correct historical background and to estimate his significance in any particular circumstance. I have not been able to consider all the far-reaching implications of his teachings and cannot claim to have attained technical mastery of all the movements in which he played a part. I could easily spend many years more in trying to orientate and interpret him, but it seems desirable to present the facts as I have found them in order that they may be available to others. It would be impossible to characterize so long and varied a career in a phrase, or to summarize it in a paragraph, and I shall attempt neither here. Suffice it to say that Cooper seems to have been, through all his wanderings and despite apparent inconsistencies, a passionate advocate of political and intellectual freedom against tyranny in any guise, and an enthusiastic promulgator of what he believed to be the truth. The story of his innumerable controversies is a significant part of the larger history of his day; his letters to Jefferson, Madison, Van Buren, Nicholas Biddle, James H. Hammond, Mahlon Dickerson, and others of his contemporaries constitute a fascinating commentary upon his times; and the prophetic utterances with which all his writings abound reveal some of the hopes which animated the forward-looking minds of his age.

My attention was first attracted to Thomas Cooper in the seminar of Professor Allen Johnson of Yale University in the history of American polity, and my investigations were begun at his suggestion and carried through under his constant encouragement. His wise and friendly counsel was given me freely from the inception of the work in 1920 until its completion as a doctoral dissertation along the lines of the present volume in 1923, and it is only because of his absence from the country that I have failed to secure his advice in regard to its final form. Of the many persons who have assisted me by valuable suggestions during the course of my investigations and have given me access to materials of which I might otherwise not have known, I wish to express special appreciation to the following: Professor H. M. Ellis of the University of Maine, Former Provost Edgar F. Smith of the University of Pennsylvania, Mr. A. S. Salley, Jr., secretary of the Historical Commission of South Carolina, and Professors Yates Snowden and Edwin L. Green of the University of South Carolina. For courtesies shown me in the use of the historical materials of which they are custodians, I am particularly indebted to Mr. John C. Fitzpatrick and Miss Emily Mitchell of the manuscripts division of the Library of Congress, Mr. Ernest Spofford of the Pennsylvania Historical Society, Miss Ellen Fitzsimmons of the Charleston Library Society, Mr. Stanley Jast and Mr. John H. Swann of the Free Reference Library of Manchester, as well as to various officials and attendants of the libraries of Yale University, the University of South Carolina, the College of Charleston, and the University of Virginia, the Virginia State Library, the Chetham Library, Manchester, and the British Museum. Professor William E. Dodd of the University of Chicago has cheered me with many words of encouragement, and Professor Charles M. Andrews of Yale University, the editor of the series in which this volume appears, has increased my already great personal obligations to him by giving me invaluable counsel in the final preparation of the manuscript for publication.

In the notes I have indicated my indebtedness to a number of writers who have treated of various aspects of Cooper's career and of certain movements in which he participated, although in no instance have I depended upon a secondary source. I have made some changes in the spelling, punctuation, and capitalization of the shorter quotations from contemporary writings, but have left the longer quotations in their original form.

DUMAS MALONE.

The University of Virginia,
March 15, 1925.

PART ONE: ENGLAND

CHAPTER I

MANCHESTER BEGINNINGS, 1783-1791

DURING Thomas Cooper's old age in South Carolina one of his admirers claimed, with greater enthusiasm than accuracy, that he was famous on two continents. By that time England had doubtless forgotten him and he did not lack for critics to assert that even in America he had gained not fame, but infamous notoriety. In his native land he was never famous and was only temporarily notorious. England relinquished without protest this immature philosopher of revolution and unsuccessful advocate of reform, and it is improbable that even his more notable American exploits as Republican agitator and pioneer of nullification and secession aroused much interest among his former countrymen. Of his career as judge, scientist, educator, religious controversialist, and universal scholar, they knew little and probably cared to know nothing more.

Englishmen have been even more indifferent to his early than to his later life. They have not pried into obscure local records to ascertain the sources of his greatness, nor sought to recall anecdotes indicative of budding genius. Although he himself was fully aware of his public significance, he seems to have regarded the personal background of his life as unimportant. Fugitive and incidental references to his career in England are to be found in his later writings, but these are almost silent in regard to his personal life before he became a public figure. The story of his early years must be pieced out with fragments.

He was born in Westminster, October 22, 1759, the son of Thomas Cooper, who was entitled to bear heraldic arms and seems to have been a man of means.[1] The family fortunes permitted of the son's being sent to Oxford, and he was able subsequently to make large investment in an industrial enterprise in Lancashire. During most of his life in England he seems to have felt free to devote himself largely to scientific and intellectual pursuits and to the public weal, without serious concern about finances; and later references to a once-adequate fortune,[2] which we know was largely lost at Manchester, indicate that until disaster met his firm he occupied a position of financial independence. He doubtless gained something by his exertions as a barrister and manufacturer and is said to have acquired a considerable fortune by his first marriage, but he probably got something besides his name from his father.

In February, 1779, at the age of nineteen, he was matriculated at Oxford from University College, where he seems to have been in residence earlier. He never took a degree from the university, although from a statement made by him many years later we are led to conclude that he took the necessary examinations, which he described as easy.[3] According to the family tradition he

1 Jos. Foster, *Alumni Oxonienses*, 1715-1886, I, 294. By far the best account of Cooper's life in England which has yet appeared in print is H. M. Ellis's ''Thomas Cooper—A Survey of His Life,'' *South Atlantic Quarterly*, XIX, 24-42. The collection of letters from Cooper's descendants made by the late Colyer Meriwether and preserved in the library of the University of South Carolina is the best source as regards family traditions. For incidental references in Cooper's own writings which indicate a relatively high economic and social position during his youth, see *Emporium of Arts and Sciences*, new series, II, 402, and *Port Folio*, 4 series, I, 397-8.

2 *Cf*. Philadelphia *Aurora*, April 25, 1800.

3 ''Letter to a Friend on University Education,'' Sept. 15, 1814, *Port*

refused to sign the Thirty-Nine Articles, which we can well believe. A later sympathetic commentator upon the career of a fellow free-thinker may have reflected his own feelings when he suggested that Cooper, like Shelley, must have found "the dry, inquisitive, pedantic despotism of Oxford intolerable."[4] Such may well have been the case, especially since there was no apparent aesthetic compensation. The physical charms of the city of colleges seem to have left no impress upon a nature which was largely devoid of aesthetic appreciation. His protest, whether explicit or implicit, must have been that of the utilitarian, not that of the romanticist.

Either while at Oxford or before he went there he gained a thorough grounding in the classics which, despite his scientific bent and utilitarian philosophy, he always emphasized as of fundamental importance in education.[5] It was perhaps while he was at Oxford, however, that the interest in science which was to remain with him throughout life was first aroused. It is said that he wished to become a physician and studied law only because of his father's persuasion. During the hot summer of 1780 he attended anatomical lectures in London, and he afterwards took a clinical course at the Middlesex

Folio, 3 series, V, 352. If he was speaking with strict accuracy when he said he passed "five and thirty years ago," this must have been in 1779. He was married August 12, 1779, so one would assume that he took the examinations before that time, although it is not impossible that he may have remained in residence after his marriage. The statutes did not forbid. He spoke elsewhere of the long vacation of 1780, *Emporium*, new series, II, 430. There is no certainty that he remembered his dates accurately and the whole matter is confused. The records of the college give no further information.

4 "Dr. Thomas Cooper," London *Reasoner and Theological Examiner*, IX, 242; an article written in 1850, doubtless by one of the editors of this organ of free-thinkers.

5 See his "Letter to a Friend on University Education," *Port Folio*, 3 series, V, 349-59; and numerous references in letters to Jefferson about the University of Virginia and in addresses as president of South Carolina College.

hospital and for anatomical information even observed veterinary dissections in St. John's, Clerkenwell.[6] He attended the patients of a Manchester physician under direction after he had taken up his residence in the community, and had the reputation there of being a good practical chemist.

It was probably his interest in chemistry which led him to become a member of the firm of Baker, Teasdale, Bridges and Cooper, calico-printers, at Raikes, near Bolton and about ten miles from Manchester.[7] Printing was begun in 1780, five years before Cooper was certainly a resident of the community. He may have been a non-resident member of the firm from the beginning. His most active interest seems to have been manifested in 1790 and thereafter. He claimed later that he was one of the three men who introduced the bleaching process of Berthollet into Manchester in that year and with the assistance of another devised a new method of producing the necessary oxymuriatic acid. He said that he used this with perfect success in his own establishment and that this chemical improvement saved a million sterling to English bleachers and calico-printers.[8] He was probably a useful partner when other interests did not distract him. The firm did a considerable business and it was probably due to no negligence of his that it fell with a crash in 1793, in a time of great depression.[9] The story of his losses was current during the first decade of his residence in America, but in time he could safely claim

[6] *Emporium*, new series, II, 430; E. F. Smith, *Life of Robert Hare*, pp. 58-61.

[7] John Graham, History of Printworks in the Manchester District from 1760 to 1846, p. 416. Folio manuscript, Manchester Reference Library, the only available work and not entirely reliable as to dates.

[8] *Port Folio*, Feb. 1817, 4 series, III, 194; *Emporium of Arts and Sciences*, new series, I, 159-60.

[9] See below, pp. 71-2.

and receive credit here for great practical knowledge of manufacturing processes.

The register of alumni of Oxford states that in 1787 he became a barrister-at-law from the Inner Temple, but his name does not occur on the list of graduates. A number of references indicate that he traveled the northern circuit, which included Lancashire. He has left a story of a trumped-up case at the Lancaster assizes in which Boswell, whom he regarded as the greatest fool he ever knew, was made the butt of ridicule.[10] He seems to have been nominally a barrister from 1787 to 1790, although even then his pursuits were chiefly literary, philosophical, and scientific.[11] In America he was regarded as very learned in the law, as he undoubtedly was, and he made elaborate and valuable suggestions about legal education, as became his reputed omniscience.

At the beginning of his career in this new industrial region in the north, he was a prosperous citizen, doubtless without a premonition of that failure in practical affairs which was persistently to disturb although rarely to distress his life. Several years before he came to Lancashire he was married in St. George's Parish, Hanover Square, Middlesex, with Alice Greenwood, who before her death in Pennsylvania in 1800 was to bear him five children.[12] By 1785 he was living south of Manchester at Woodheys, Altringham, Cheshire; later he removed to Lever Hall, Bolton, where he could keep his eye upon the

10 "Judge Cooper's Table-Talk," E. A. and G. L. Duyckinck, *Cyclopaedia of American Literature*, 1855, II, 333.

11 Joseph Priestley, *Theological and Miscellaneous Works*, XIX, 504.

12 The marriage was on August 12, 1779. John H. Chapman, ed., *Register Book of Marriages belonging to the Parish of St. George, Hanover Square, in the County of Middlesex*, I, 303. Dr. J. M. Baldy of Philadelphia, a descendant, gave the information about the children of this marriage in a letter to Colyer Meriwether, July 15, 1897. Meriwether Collection, University of South Carolina library.

dye-works. If we may accept the description by which South Carolinians have long recalled him, his personal appearance must have astounded all the communities in which he lived almost as much as his versatility amazed them. It is said that he was less than five feet tall, and that his massive head dominated a tapering figure, making him look like nothing so much as a wedge with a head on it.[13] Another way of saying that in him the intellectual was supreme. The face itself was clean-cut and he must have given an impression of extraordinary vigor and vivacity.

Although destined to become in another generation a veritable hot-bed of reform movements, Manchester was at this time noted for conservatism.[14] After the failure of their hopes of Stuart restoration in 1715 and 1745, the principal inhabitants had in time become reconciled to the Hanoverians, who had shown no great desire to extend popular rights or to innovate in religious matters. Until the outbreak of the French Revolution, there was little clash of parties and relative calm prevailed. "Jacobites and Hanoverians, Churchmen, and Dissenters, lived together in tolerable harmony, smoking their pipes and drinking their ale in peace and quiet converse about the progress of their new machinery and the widening prospects of manufactures and trade."[15] In this complacent and unsuspicious community, Thomas Cooper first shed the light of his radical philosophy among the intelligentsia; here at first he gained general commenda-

[13] J. Marion Sims, *The Story of My Life*, pp. 82-3. Sims graduated at South Carolina College in 1832. For a steel engraving of Cooper, taken from his *Lectures on Political Economy*, 2d ed., see frontispiece. For a very striking silhouette from life, taken from Wm. H. Brown's *Portrait Gallery of Distinguished American Citizens*, 1846, p. 81, see below, p. 256.

[14] Archibald Prentice, *Historical Sketches and Personal Recollections of Manchester*, ch. I; *cf.* James Wheeler, *Manchester: Its Political, Social and Commercial History*, part I, ch. III.

[15] Prentice, *Historical Sketches*, pp. 1-2.

tion for his humanitarian zeal, then aroused fiercest hostility as he raised the banner of reform.

Most of the members of the Manchester Literary and Philosophical Society were doubtless men of conservative temper, but it was their avowed purpose to stimulate inquiry and discovery.[16] Possibly unaware of his irrepressible radicalism, they could have had little but admiration for the erudite young visitor who read them in 1783 a ponderous but innocuous essay on the history of physiognomy.[17] They elected him to honorary membership a month later[18] and, presumably because he had now become a resident of Lancashire, transferred him to the list of ordinary members in 1785.[19] Within a few months he was elected one of the vice-presidents,[20] and he continued such until his indignant withdrawal in 1791 from an organization which professed regard for learning but was unwilling to express its sympathy with Joseph Priestley, whom Cooper regarded as the learned victim of the fanatical ignorance of the Birmingham mob.[21] Lines of political and ecclesiastical cleavage were not sharply drawn at first, and Cooper was associated in this learned society with Thomas Walker, Samuel Jackson, James Watt, Jr., and others later to be identified

[16] "A Short Account of the Institution and Views of the Literary and Philosophical Society, Manchester," appendix II, *List of Members and Officers*, pp. 47-8.

[17] "Observations respecting the History of Physiognomy," *Memoirs* of the Manchester Literary and Philosophical Society, III, 408-62.

[18] Nov. 12, 1783, R. Angus Smith, "A Centenary of Science at Manchester," *Memoirs*, 3 series, IX, 436.

[19] Dec. 21, 1785, *ibid.*, p. 418; *List of Members and Officers*, p. 20.

[20] There were four vice-presidents and these served as members of the committee on papers. Cooper was one of these, 1786-91, and during the last two years his was the first name of the four. *List of Members and Officers*, pp. 10, 44; *Memoirs*, 3 series, IX, 400.

[21] See below, pp. 30-1.

with him in the ill-fated movement for parliamentary reform.[22]

Cooper's contributions to the deliberations of the society were copious and diverse. Some of them were printed in its *Memoirs,* and he himself committed to the public a volume containing essays which the society heard but did not publish and others which his colleagues in learning may have inspired and may have read but did not hear. Few in our day have shaken the dust from Cooper's *Tracts, Ethical, Theological and Political,*[23] or have traced his thought through the yellowish pages of the *Memoirs.* Few will do so because of the intrinsic merit of the writings. These are pompous in their display of learning and daring in their expression of opinions then regarded as radical, but they are neither original nor profound. Their significance lies primarily in their indication of tendencies of thought, and in their revelation of the spirit and point of view of their enthusiastic author.

We can readily detect within these writings that intellectual audacity and willing belligerency which were ever characteristic of their author, yet at no time during his later years did he appear so disinterested. His earliest utterances, radical as they were, breathed the calm and quiet of the secluded study and the confidence of the disinterested seeker after eternal truth. Freedom of inquiry, as the *sine qua non* of social progress, he advocated throughout his long life, but at no time with such winsomeness as here.

Nowhere in all Cooper's writings is there so charming or naïve an expression of independence as in the note of dedication to his *Tracts.*[24] He presented his essays to one

22 *List of Members and Officers.*

23 Vol. I, published 1789; note of dedication dated Dec. 1, 1787.

24 Addressed to the Rev. J. Barwis, perhaps a former teacher, Niton, Isle of Wight.

who held opinions, he dared suppose, for the most part in perfect opposition to his own; and stated that if conformity of opinion were necessary to a dedication, his work must remain ungraced with the name of any of his friends, with all of whom at some time or other he had had the good fortune to differ widely in sentiment on points of literary controversy. Elsewhere he said that he was prepared to make no apology for advancing unpopular opinions, but that by right he was entitled and by duty he was compelled to communicate to others such truth as he had arrived at by careful inquiry.[25] The important thing was that opinions be well presented; if they were false, an answer would be required and the adoption of truth would be accelerated.[26] He felt that nothing had been so harmful to man as the opinion that it was inexpedient to publish sentiments of supposed bad tendency. To this he attributed "the infamous and tyrannical interference of the civil power in matters of mere controversy," and he hoped that the day was not far distant when it would be considered an axiom that actions alone, and not opinions, were the proper objects of the interference of magistrates.[27] Little did he foresee how his own experiences were destined to belie the hopes of these untroubled years!

He had supreme confidence in the ultimate triumph of truth. His favorite maxim, which he first quoted here, was *"Magna est veritas et praevalebit."*[28] As he expressed it elsewhere, "Truth, whenever it be thoroughly discussed will never fail to come like tried gold out of the fire: with Ajax, it requires nothing but daylight and fair play."[29] Equally refreshing, if to the cynic equally unwarranted, is his assertion that he is not concerned whether his own opinions shall or shall not prevail, that

---

[25] *Tracts,* p. xi.   [26] *Ibid.,* pp. 169-77.   [27] *Ibid.,* p. 177.
[28] *Ibid.,* p. 176.   [29] *Ibid.,* p. xiv.

he will be equally satisfied whether they be the truth or shall produce it.

To an emphasis upon freedom of thought and speech, which was to characterize his whole career and was destined to make him a boon intellectual companion of Thomas Jefferson, Cooper conjoined in his political philosophy an emphasis upon the freedom and prime importance of the individual member of society. Later experiences in France and America were to bring their disillusionments, but he began his career as an ardent advocate of the rights of man. Driven on by the logic of his original assumption of natural equality, he came to advocate during his last years in England unrestricted manhood suffrage[30] and even to assert the doctrine of the essential political equality of women with men.[31] His first concern was, however, to state the principles of civil liberty and fearlessly to proclaim doctrines of justifiable revolution.

If we may judge from his *Propositions respecting the Foundation of Civil Government*,[32] the first general statement of his political faith, he had slight interest in governmental organization. His concern was rather to declare, with confident dogmatism, that government had originated in the consent of the people, to point out the rights remaining with the people which might not be infringed upon, to emphasize the responsibility of the government to the people and the right of the latter to alter the government at their will. His interest was not in orderly and efficient administration, but in the liberty of the individual. The presumption was against the gover-

[30] ''Propositions respecting the Foundation of Civil Government,'' *Reply to Burke's Invective*, 1792, p. 106 n.

[31] *Ibid.*, pp. 98-9 n.

[32] Read before the society, March 7, 1787; published in the *Memoirs*, III, 481-509; also with his *Reply to Burke's Invective*, 1792, with several additional footnotes, and republished in Columbia, S. C., 1826.

nors, the limitations of whose authority were emphasized. His fear was of tyranny and oppression, not of revolution and anarchy.

In this writing, indeed, the right of revolution is strongly emphasized. Almost a fourth of his propositions bear directly upon the rightful power of the people to change their government,[33] and half of these refer to the use of force.[34] He warned all would-be revolutionists that the evil results of forcible action might exceed the good, but felt that the evil was likely to be temporary and the good permanent. Nor did he think there was likely to be violent action on light ground. So he looked to the future with calm confidence; the coming convulsions had for him no terrors. "The structure of political oppression . . . begins now to totter: its day is far spent: the extension of knowledge has undermined its foundations, and I hope the day is not far distant when in Europe at least, one stone of the fabric will not be left upon another."[35]

Although nothing loath to assume full responsibility for the expression of bold sentiments, Cooper claimed no originality for the political opinions proclaimed by him in these early years. Indeed, by reference and quotation he indicated the sources whence his ideas came. There is little in his doctrine of revolution which is not implicit or explicit in Locke, and numerous parallelisms indicate his primary indebtedness to the philosopher of the Glorious Revolution of 1688.[36] His more immediate inspiration came, however, from a senior contemporary, with whom he was destined later to live on terms of greatest per-

[33] Propositions VI, XXI, XXIX-XXXIV.

[34] Propositions XXX, XXXII-XXXIV.

[35] *Memoirs*, III, 509.

[36] *Cf.* Proposition I, 4, 6, with Locke, *Treatises on Civil Government*, II, 114-66; Proposition I, 9, with II, 176, 185, 196; Propositions XVI, XVII, with II, 95-9; Proposition XXV, with II, 122; Proposition VI, with II, 149; Propositions XXI, XXIX-XXXIII, with II, 221 ff.

sonal as well as intellectual intimacy. He was a disciple of Joseph Priestley in political philosophy, as in metaphysics, theology, and chemistry. He later described Priestley's well-known *Essay* as "the first plain, popular, brief and unanswerable book on the principles of civil government,"[37] and specially commended the passage which suggested to Jeremy Bentham his famous formula of the greatest good for the greatest number.[38] Cooper's utilitarianism seems to have come direct from Priestley; in their revolutionary doctrines, both master and disciple were essentially Lockian.

Of the other chief English philosophers of revolution in his day, Cooper gave mild approval to Dr. Richard Price[39] and expressed indiscreet enthusiasm for Thomas Paine,[40] so he may be regarded as a promulgator of the doctrines of the revolutionists. The point of view of these thinkers has been aptly characterized by the great historian of English thought in the eighteenth century, in words particularly applicable to their less conspicuous associate who was destined to engage in violent controversy with Edmund Burke:

Priestley and Bentham, not less than Rousseau and his followers, altogether ignore the historical method in politics. They are absolutely indifferent to that conception of the continuity of the social organism which supplies the vital element in Burke's teaching. They reject all "prescription" as equivalent to blind prejudice. They propose to reform society anew, without refer-

[37] Cooper, "Of Dr. Priestley's Political Works and Opinions," appendix 3, *Memoirs of Dr. Joseph Priestley*, 1806, II, 354; referring to Priestley's *Essay on the First Principles of Civil Government*, 1768.

[38] *Ibid.*, II, 352; Priestley's *Essay*, p. 5; *cf.* Leslie Stephen, *History of English Thought in the Eighteenth Century*, II, 62, 126. Note, however, that Stephen grants priority to Francis Hutcheson.

[39] *Memoirs of Priestley*, II, 358.

[40] *Reply to Burke's Invective*, pp. 67, 75 n.

ence to the special traditions and beliefs by which it has hitherto been bound together.[41]

As a philosopher of materialism, Cooper has in our day been granted an honorable place in the history of American thought,[42] although few of his contemporaries in the United States relished or even tolerated his teachings. It has been pointed out that his materialism became more thoroughgoing in his last years, because of French influences, and that his first tract on the subject is not a good sample of his mental furniture.[43] It is significant chiefly in its anticipations, controversial as well as philosophical.

The fundamental ground of his position was the dependence of the psychical upon the physical.[44] He approached the subject from the point of view of physiology rather than metaphysics, of which he was ever suspicious and scornful. He was convinced that mental phenomena are dependent upon and result from the physical organization of the brain, without the assistance of an immaterial principle, and sought to demonstrate the impossibility of the doctrine of an immaterial, immortal soul.[45] He believed not only that the soul did not exist previous to the body, but that it could not exist after the body was destroyed, because with the body must go the brain which is the source of ideas. He was equally as dogmatic as radical, going so far as to say that there was "the same proof for the truth of the doctrine of *materialism,* as that gold is heavy, ink black, water fluid, or any other indubi-

[41] Leslie Stephen, *History of English Thought in the Eighteenth Century,* II, 253.

[42] I. Woodbridge Riley, *American Philosophy, the Early Schools,* bk. V, ch. V.

[43] *Ibid.,* pp. 414-15.

[44] "Sketch of the Controversy on Materialism," read before the society, Jan. 17, 1787, but published independently by Cooper in *Tracts,* pp. 167-303.

[45] *Ibid.,* pp. 178, 189 ff.

table assertion.''[46] It is easy to see why the holder of such doctrines later got into so much trouble in South Carolina! It is to be noted, however, that he claimed that his position was perfectly consistent with a belief in a future state of retribution and the doctrines of Christianity and that all the materialists with whom he was acquainted were Christians.[47] References to Hartley and Priestley may have brought some slight reassurance in eighteenth-century England, but they availed naught in nineteenth-century South Carolina, where the Presbyterian clergy instinctively perceived in the materialism of the president of the state college a denial of all supernaturalism.

In his ethics, he again shocked the orthodox by asserting that individual interest is the ultimate motive of action.[48] He claimed that ultimate self-interest would not clash with religion and virtue, although if it should, self-interest must prevail for anything else would be absurd. In theology, he showed himself a determinist both in regard to man and God,[49] and an Unitarian.[50] In one who was by temperament an individualist and a revolutionist, the doctrine of necessity seems inconsistent with his practice. He certainly did not meekly acquiesce and accept practical conditions as he found them. He was less critical of himself than of his opponents and in practice followed his temperament rather than a consistent theory of submission. In one sense at least his determinism was significant: he went forth to battle in entire confidence;

[46] *Ibid.*, p. 206.

[47] *Ibid.*, pp. 225, 283; *cf.* p. 293, where acceptance of immortality upon scriptural authority is indicated.

[48] ''Essay on Moral Obligation,'' *Tracts*, pp. 1-122. An able and learned discussion. For Cooper's own position, see pp. 86 ff. He rejected both external authority and innate ideas and stood with the empiricists, Locke and especially Hartley.

[49] ''Whether the Deity be a Free-Agent,'' *Tracts*, pp. 123-165. See especially pp. 133 n., 151, 163.

[50] ''A Summary of Unitarian Arguments,'' *ibid.*, pp. 465-526.

none of the Calvinists whom he later derided was more convinced of his predestination to salvation than was Cooper of the necessary correctness of his own opinions. He felt that he was highly reverent of God in attributing His actions to some motive which operates necessarily, namely, the communication of the highest possible degree of happiness.[51] Religion in the personal sense, however, probably meant very little to Thomas Cooper. The God he worshipped was Truth and his creed was Freedom. Brought up in the Establishment, he abhorred its mysteries as he deplored its connection with the state. Perhaps through the influence of Priestley, he gave nominal adherence to Unitarianism as the most rational and comprehensible theological system. He argued that the Unitarian position was both acceptable to reason and consistent with the Scriptures, and attempted an impossible harmonization of reason and authority.[52] He was not yet ready to go the full length of historical criticism, although he refused to be convinced by texts which pointed toward doctrines regarded by him as absurd and contradictory. Probably his professions of loyalty to the Scriptures were only for the sake of argument, for he always applied reason as the ultimate test. He was proceeding logically to a rejection of all external authority, as his clerical foes at this time and subsequently did not fail instinctively to perceive.

Trinitarian dogma he regarded as contradictory and meaningless, a mere juggling with words with consequent confusion. He insisted that words be used in their commonly accepted meaning and argued that, in such case, there could not be three persons who were both the same

---

[51] *Ibid.*, p. 164.

[52] *Ibid.*, p. 466. He naïvely assumed that it would be impossible for the Scriptures to set forth absurd and contradictory doctrines.

and different.[53] He defended Unitarianism on historical, rational, and scriptural grounds,[54] but we may be sure that his own acceptance of it was due to his finding it relatively comprehensible. All mystery was to him abhorrent; he would turn the bright light of truth into every department of human life and thought, whatever the consequences. The dim religious light brought no peace to his restless soul, and it was ever incomprehensible to him why so many men loved to loiter in the shadows which he was so passionately seeking to dispel. There is no indication that he ever appreciated the difficulties and dangers involved in the substitution of a rational for what he regarded as an irrational doctrinal position, or the essential worth of the religion which so many men enjoy despite a crude or inadequate theology. His hope was in the emancipation of the intellect; he realized neither the dangers of such emancipation nor the relative unimportance of the purely intellectual in matters of religion. It is not surprising that many simpler, less rational and less ruthless natures should have regarded him as heartless and irreverent.

He little thought, however, to confuse or distress the common man; in theology, as elsewhere, he spoke for freedom and individualism against tyranny and mechanical conformity. The existing situation he found depressing, but of the future he was confident. "There is no doubt, but truth will in the end prevail. At present, indeed, it is in theological as in political matters, not the weight of argument, but the number of voices that carry the day. Ecclesiastical, however, as well as political tyranny seems on the decline, and it is the duty of every friend of mankind to exert his endeavours unceasingly to hasten their downfall."[55]

[53] *Ibid.*, p. 475.
[54] *Ibid.*, pp. 499 ff.   [55] *Ibid.*, p. 526.

Disillusioning experiences of later years served considerably to modify Cooper's political philosophy in the direction of conservatism, but in metaphysics, ethics, and theology time served but to carry him further toward materialism, utilitarianism, and complete rejection of authority. His writings at Manchester[56] clearly indicate the path his mind was to follow, and they serve to explain at the outset much of the controversy in which he was later involved. With all their cold intellectuality, these essays reveal the combative temper of the man and his passion for truth and freedom. He was not long to content himself with being a closet-philosopher; throughout life he was to be a crusader for the principles in which he strongly believed. He first spoke to the learned of Manchester in the name of truth and freedom, then rushed forth to make vigorous assault upon some of the more flagrant tyrannies with which eighteenth-century England abounded.

The public might have been enlightened on who knows what other abstruse philosophical matters had not Cooper been lured from the quiet paths of abstract thought. He was correcting the tracts meant for a second volume of essays when the subject of the slave trade began to be agitated, and, while his health permitted, he employed the whole of his leisure during the winter of 1787-1788 not ineffectually to excite the attention of his fellow citizens to that "infamous and impolitic traffic."[57] Party lines seem not to have been drawn in Manchester on this question and the best elements of the population

---

[56] Two other essays, "Observations on the Art of Painting among the Ancients," *Memoirs*, III, 510-97; and "On Identity," *Tracts*, pp. 305-464, may be mentioned but seem not to merit discussion here.

[57] *Tracts*, p. viii.

supported the reform which the young radical championed.

His writings against the slave trade, which were published first in a local paper[58] and then in pamphlet form in the autumn of 1787,[59] preceded the more general local movement, if they did not initiate it. In December, as one of the leaders, he was writing to assure the conservatives that no specific plan of abolition was being advocated, that the difficulties which were involved were fully recognized, and that only a general campaign of publicity was being launched.[60] Perhaps it was this moderation, which one would not expect in Thomas Cooper, that secured for the movement such general support.

That Cooper should have been interested in so significant an humanitarian enterprise is not at all surprising. Thomas Walker, the most conspicuous of the Manchester reformers and his intimate associate, said later that he was a man "whose time and whose labours were ever at the command of the injured and the unfortunate; whose talents and whose learning, which were very considerable, were uniformly devoted to the great interests of mankind."[61] Cooper's humanitarianism was to be tempered somewhat by realism in later years. Occasionally even he came to terms with his environment. In South Carolina he owned slaves and accepted African slavery as an institution. He was then fighting against other tyrannies, but tyranny of some sort he was ever attacking, and he was always happiest in pleading the cause of a group which he regarded as oppressed.

When he wrote his *Letters on the Slave Trade* he was unquestionably opposed to slavery as a tyrannical and

---

[58] Wheeler's Manchester *Chronicle*, file for 1787 not preserved.
[59] *Letters on the Slave Trade.* A supplement was published in 1788.
[60] Dec. 3, 1787, Manchester *Mercury*, Dec. 11, 1787.
[61] *Review of Political Events in Manchester*, 1794, p. 55.

inhumane institution.[62] The stirring and graphic details with which he enlivened his descriptions of the sufferings of the unfortunate negroes were taken somewhat uncritically from other writers,[63] and his elaborate calculations of the loss of life show lack of scientific precision;[64] but he clearly manifested profound human sympathy and by his extensive and arduous investigations sufficiently demonstrated his zeal. He placed the entire discussion on a high moral plane by urging that the negroes be regarded as men, not brutes, and by insisting that the English had no right to condone cruelty for the sake of financial gain.[65]

His personal contributions to the cause consisted of money as well as time. He and his wife were among the chief subscribers,[66] and the fact that the cost of publishing his pamphlets was met from the general contributions need be no reflection upon his zeal.[67] He was one of the committee appointed at the first general meeting to conduct the business of the society which had been formed,[68] and the success which marked the efforts to secure signatures to the petition which was forwarded to parliament

[62] *Cf.* the quotation from Cowper on the title page:

> ''I would not have a Slave to till my ground,
> To carry me, to fan me while I sleep,
> And tremble when I wake, for all the wealth
> That sinews bought and sold have ever earn'd.''

[63] The Quakers, Clarkson, Wesley, and others.

[64] One calculation is marred by an error which should have been obvious, *Letters*, p. 25; *Supplement*, pp. 3, 4. His estimate of importations is far too high, and his conclusions in regard to the total loss of life seem fantastic, *Supplement*, pp. 41, 44.

[65] *Letters*, appendix, pp. 29-34.

[66] *Cf.* subscription lists, Manchester *Mercury*, Dec. 11, 1787, Jan. 15, Dec. 23, 1788.

[67] Announcement of expenditures, *ibid.*, Dec. 23, 1788. The total cost of pamphlet and supplement was *c.* £50.

[68] Dec. 27, 1787, (Manchester) Society for the Purpose of Effecting the Abolition of the Slave Trade, Manchester *Mercury*, Jan. 1, 1788.

in February, 1788, was doubtless in considerable part due to his writings and personal efforts.

This petition asked for investigation and condemned the principle and practice of the slave trade.[69] Thomas Walker stated that the more than ten thousand signers comprised the first in property, consequence, and reputation in the community.[70] The committee of subscribers who reported in December, 1788, felt that the sentiment which had been aroused throughout the nation against the traffic in slaves might be attributed to the activity and example of Manchester, and viewed the delay of decision on this question with less uneasiness because in Manchester all political distinctions had vanished before the consideration of the subject.[71]

It was claimed as late as February, 1792, when a petition to which Cooper's name was appended was forwarded to parliament, that unanimity on this subject persisted.[72] None the less, the movement failed of immediate results, as is well known. Despite the efforts of Pitt, Wilberforce, Clarkson, and others, no remedial action was taken and the legal suppression of the trade did not come until two decades later, when Cooper was concerned with other matters in Pennsylvania. Meanwhile, questions of religious and political reform had aroused the attention of the citizens of Manchester and the boasted unanimity was irretrievably lost.

The beginning of violent strife of parties, which was to continue until the advocates of reform were completely silenced and the city was delivered over to their enemies, came in 1789 with the discussion of the repeal of the Test and Corporation Acts,[73] when the alarm of the Church-

[69] Ibid., Jan. 8, 12, Feb. 5, 1788.
[70] Ibid., March 25, 1788.   [71] Ibid., Dec. 23, 1788.
[72] Ibid., Feb. 11, 18, March 10, 1792.
[73] Prentice, Historical Sketches of Manchester, ch. I; Walker, Review of

men was comparable to that manifested by them in the days of Sacheverell, and when Cooper advocated religious tolerance with an intolerance equal to their own. Aroused by the activity of the Dissenters of the district,[74] a group of members of the Established Church prevailed upon the boroughreeve and constables to call a meeting early in 1790 in defense of the standing order and the "salutary" existing laws.[75] It was claimed by the opposition that the meeting was not a public one in the accepted sense, that no discussion was allowed, and that resolutions were passed without a division. A protesting group, among whom were George Lloyd as chairman, Thomas Walker, Thomas Cooper, and Samuel Jackson, met at the Bull's Head Inn and drew up strong resolutions.[76] An exchange of heated communications between the rival chairmen followed, Lloyd claiming that neither his own applications to be heard nor those of Cooper for him had been heeded, and declaring that the presumption was against the party which denied discussion and was guilty of such high-handed and irregular procedure.[77]

The day after the much-discussed Manchester meeting, a meeting of Protestant Dissenters over which Cooper presided was held at Warrington. Such prominence in ecclesiastical gatherings was not customary with him later. He could not be accurately described as a profoundly religious man even at this time, but he was always an implacable foe of any sort of ecclesiastical

---

Political Events in Manchester, pp. 11 ff. Motions of repeal made by Beaufoy were defeated in the Commons, March 28, 1787, and May 8, 1789, *Parliamentary History*, XXVI, 780-832; XXVIII, 1-41; and Fox's motion of repeal was defeated, March 2, 1790, *ibid.*, XXVIII, 387-452.

[74] Meetings were held at Warrington, Jan. 6, 1790, Manchester *Mercury*, Jan. 19; and at Manchester, Jan. 18, *ibid.*, Jan. 19. Cooper may have been present at some one or all of these, but no mention was made of him in the newspapers.

[75] Feb. 3, *ibid.*, Feb. 2, 9.

[76] *Ibid.*, Feb. 9.   [77] *Ibid.*, Feb. 23, March 2.

tyranny and anything which even approximated an established church. His choice as chairman can be explained but hardly justified; as a presiding officer he did not prove eminently successful. Two of the dissenting groups, the Baptists and Independents, withdrew, leaving him with the Presbyterians. The memory of his association with the Calvinists must have amused him in later years, despite the slenderness of his sense of humor. The seceders suspected the chairman and the Presbyterians of more far-reaching designs than the repeal of the Corporation and Test Acts. Burke, whom Cooper accused of getting his information from one Samuel Fletcher, stated in the house of commons that the moderate men left the meeting because it avowed violent intentions, such as the removal of the liturgy from the church and the abolition of tithes.[78] As if in anticipation of the future, Cooper hurled at Burke a flaming letter,[79] and emptied the vials of his wrath upon Samuel Fletcher. Fletcher and the seceders had their word in the newspapers,[80] and from various unchristian paragraphs we can reconstruct the story of the unedifying occasion.

The Baptists and Independents, who sought merely the repeal of the two objectionable laws, wanted the assembly to declare against any more radical action and to this the chairman, supported by the Presbyterians, objected. When questioned as to what other steps were intended, Cooper replied that there was "the greatest need for hypocrisy in the business," and stated that it was neither reasonable nor scriptural to make their intentions known, "using our Saviour's words, *I have yet many things to*

---

[78] Debate of March 2, 1790, *Parliamentary History*, XXVIII, 437-8.

[79] "To the Right Honourable Edmund Burke," March 4, 1790, London Library *Pamphlets*, XVIII, no. 16.

[80] Manchester *Mercury*, March 9, April 6, 1790.

say unto you, but ye cannot hear them now." Opinions differed as to whether or not this quotation was irreverent; Cooper thought not. He said that for a mere repeal of the Corporation and Test Acts he would not give a brass pin's head, a nip of straw, or some other such trifle of which his memory was later uncertain. He later stated that he objected to the passage of any resolution which would limit future action by implying that the two acts in question were the only grievances of which the Dissenters had reason to complain. He himself deemed the repeal of other penal laws of greater consequence. The benefit of the Toleration Act did not extend to Dissenters who disbelieved in the Trinity, with whom he vociferously identified himself. To an Unitarian who did not mean to serve any of the offices to which the Corporation and Test Acts applied, the mere repeal of these laws was in his opinion worthless.

While his desire to remove all restrictions from Unitarians was natural and commendable, Cooper's controversial manners in this instance were far from good. He reflected upon Fletcher's truthfulness and integrity and spoke with horror of the "wild insanity" of his religion, and he wrote contemptuously to the distinguished Burke. This statesman did not deign to reply, although he was to make most uncomplimentary reference to Cooper in due time.[81] Fletcher made heated rejoinder and said, among many other things, that the chairman of the meeting was no more entitled to the name Christian than was a follower of Mahomet. He was referring to Cooper's rejection of the doctrine of the Trinity. We are more inclined to deny the name Christian to the Manchester reformer because, whatever other virtues he may have had, in controversy certainly he had not charity.

His activities against ecclesiastical privilege served to

[81] See below, p. 42.

draw Cooper closer to Joseph Priestley, in whose works we now begin to find references to him. From the distinguished Unitarian clergyman we learn that Cooper was sent to London as a delegate from the Dissenters of a northern county,[82] and that he and Walker were to dine with him in Birmingham and discuss the removal of religious disabilities.[83] This same year Priestley, with other distinguished men of science, recommended his disciple to the Royal Society, but Cooper was rejected by a majority vote when one-third would have been sufficient.[84] Priestley said that the king's two librarians and many church dignitaries came to vote against him. Several well-known scientists together with a number of Cooper's associates in the Manchester Literary and Philosophical Society added their signatures to a second recommendation, but he was rejected by a much greater majority than before.[85]

Priestley, who was surprised and indignant at this rejection, attributed it entirely to the opposition of vested interests, ecclesiastical and political. He stated that Cooper's knowledge of chemistry and philosophy far exceeded his own, that his high abilities had been shown by his publications and were generally recognized, and that, indeed, if the clergy had looked through the three kingdoms they could not have found an abler man to put an affront upon. The Birmingham philosopher cherished his resentment until he and his disciple

---

[82] *Theological and Miscellaneous Works*, XIX, 221.

[83] John T. Rutt, *Life and Correspondence of Joseph Priestley*, II, 58.

[84] *Theological and Miscellaneous Works*, XIX, 220-1, 221 n. In addition to Priestley, the following recommended Cooper: Mr. Kirwan, later to be president of the Royal Society of Ireland, James Watt, Dr. Crawford, and Dr. Watson.

[85] *Ibid.*, XIX, 504. Among others, Matthew Boulton, Josiah Wedgewood, and Sir G. Staunton added their signatures.

together sought a land where they felt such mistakes would not occur.[86]

Meanwhile Cooper, undaunted by the failure of his efforts against the slave trade and ecclesiastical privilege, had turned his attentions more directly to parliamentary reform. English reformers had found considerable ground for discouragement during the eighties, but the centenary celebrations of 1788 had stimulated them to renewed activities, and the French Revolution served to give the reform movement a new zeal and dynamic.[87] It is true that developments across the channel frightened conservatives into even more pronounced reaction, but until November, 1790, when Burke's *Reflections* were published, revolutionary France stimulated more than she alarmed. The enthusiasm which was engendered expressed itself most significantly in the activities of societies of reformers. The movement for reform was definitely checked by the spring of 1792, when on April 30 the proposal of Charles Grey was so coolly received and on May 21 the first proclamation against sedition was issued. With the sedition proclamation, indeed, the process of repression began.

Cooper came into the movement for parliamentary reform through the Manchester Constitutional Society, an organization in which, next to Thomas Walker, he was probably the leading spirit.[88] The Church and King Club,

[86] Rutt, *Life of Priestley*, II, 119 n.

[87] George S. Veitch, *The Genesis of Parliamentary Reform*, ch. V.

[88] Walker, *Review*, pp. 11 ff.; Blanchard Jerrold, "Thomas Walker the Elder," *The Original*, bk. I, p. 81. No list of charter members has been found, but Cooper's intimate association with Walker and his group leaves little room for doubt that he was a member of the society from the beginning. He was probably interested in parliamentary reform as early as 1783, for in several lists of his works he is credited with a pamphlet, *Arguments in Favor of a Reform in the Representation of the People,* published that year. We have not yet found a copy of this, but the arguments doubtless recur in his later writings which are accessible.

which was termed by some wit the "Tythe and Tax Club," had been organized in defense of the Test and Corporation Acts and had celebrated in March, 1790, as it did annually thereafter, the "glorious decision" of the house of commons against religious innovation.[89] This organization of conservatives also opposed all attempts at political reform, regarding promulgators of "wild theories and seditious doctrines respecting the rights of man" as enemies of the constitution, and would-be reformers of parliament as audacious and baneful disturbers of the public peace. In the beginning of October of the same year, the Manchester Constitutional Society was formed to oppose the doctrines of the conservative club and to establish liberal principles of government.

The first statement of political principles made by the society[90] might have been taken bodily from Cooper's *Propositions,* and he probably played a significant part in the work of formulation. It asserted that the authority of governors can be derived only from the consent of the governed; that the happiness of the people ought to be the sole end and aim of civil government; and that every officeholder is ultimately responsible to the people for the complete discharge of the duties of his office. The reformers claimed, as Cooper himself had done, that "actions only, and not opinions, are the proper objects of civil jurisdiction."[91] They asserted that laws or statutes could be enacted only by the consent of a majority of the people, either given expressly or "by means of a full, fair and adequate representation." Then followed the statement that the defective state of the representation of England and the extended duration of parliaments re-

---

[89] Manchester *Mercury,* March 9, Feb. 19, 1791; March 10, 1792.
[90] Walker, *Review,* p. 17 n.; Manchester *Chronicle,* March 5, 1791.
[91] *Cf. Tracts,* p. 179.

quired a speedy and effectual reform. To this the attention of the society was to be particularly directed.

Their campaign, like that of the other societies, was to
be one of publicity with the intent to enlighten.[92] The
absence of an adequate newspaper medium hampered
them during 1791, and no detailed account of their activity during that year remains.[93] The election of Thomas
Walker to be boroughreeve in 1791 probably did not
bring about even the temporary ascendancy of his group,
but the reformers gained from it a greater opportunity to
express themselves on public questions. At a public meeting in April they secured the passage of resolutions
strongly protesting against war with Russia and making
appeal to parliament against it.[94] When the conservative
group in turn protested against what they claimed was
interference with the executive power, Walker submitted
the question of the constitutionality of the resolutions to
Cooper and two other men learned in the law. Cooper,
who had supported the resolutions in the first place, ably
defended them on the ground of the right of petition.[95]
He was destined to be even more conspicuous later for
his hostility to foreign wars.

Their enthusiasm for the French Revolution gave occasion to the strongest expression of disapproval of the
reformers. They celebrated the anniversary of the taking
of the Bastile by a dinner at the Bridgewater Arms. In
order to prevent animosity it was requested by the six
stewards, of whom Cooper was one, that no matters of
English political concern should be introduced and that
no cockade or other badge be worn such as might give

[92] *Cf.* the resolutions calling for the publication of the principles of the
society in the chief papers of England, Manchester *Chronicle*, March 5, 1791.

[93] For 1792, the Manchester *Herald* gives much fuller information.

[94] April 19, 1791, Manchester *Chronicle*, April 23.

[95] *Ibid.*, May 7, 14.

offense to those who had not the same feeling toward the revolution.[96] The enemies of the society went so far as to distribute a highly inflammable handbill in which the suggestion was made that it would be an admirable expression of English spirit to pull down the house over the heads of the diners, and that their brains would be much improved if mingled with brick and mortar.[97] No actual riot took place, however, such as occurred in Birmingham on the same day. Probably this was because Walker as boroughreeve had large control over the police. It is reported that the dinner was one of great unanimity and conviviality and that the spirit of the occasion was heightened by toasts and songs which glorified democracy and predicted the downfall of despotism.[98] Repression had not yet chilled the enthusiasm of the advocates of the rights of man.

The destruction of Dr. Priestley's church and personal property by rioters in Birmingham called forth from the Manchester Constitutional Society a tribute of respect and sympathy which sounded a characteristic note of injured virtue.[99] When Samuel Jackson, a member of the reform group, moved that the Literary and Philosophical Society make similar expression, the matter was postponed and on November 4 letters of resignation were received from Jackson, Cooper, Thomas Walker, and

---

[96] Manchester *Chronicle*, July 2; Walker, *Review*, p. 22 n.

[97] Walker, *Review*, p. 23.

[98] The following song may be regarded as typical:

"The French no more, in stupid joy,
Torment the air with 'Vive le Roi'—
A nobler wish expands the mind—
Let Justice live—and live Mankind."
Manchester *Chronicle*, July 16, 1791.

[99] Sept. 13, 1791, *ibid.*, Oct. 22. For an account of the riot, see Priestley's "Appeal to the Public on the Subject of the Riots in Birmingham," *Theological and Miscellaneous Works*, XIX, 345 ff.

James Watt, Jr.,[100] who was later to be associated with Cooper in his stirring experiences in France. This circumstance marks the further development of Cooper's friendship with Priestley, and indicates his alienation from the distinctively intellectual group and his complete identification with the advocates of reform.

Among the many famous and notorious persons whom Cooper met during his enthusiastic English years and with whom he carried on vivacious conversation and correspondence was Horne Tooke. A year before the organization of the Manchester Constitutional Society, he had been present at a meeting of the Revolution Society in London and had supported Tooke in a motion to deny membership to peers unless they should enter without their titles and with only their family names. Although the motion was not put, Cooper rejoiced that so important a question had occupied the time of the meeting "instead of stupid songs, unmeaning toasts, and drunken bumpers," and that aristocracies had had this intimation that the people had lost neither their sense nor their spirit.[101]

During the winter of 1792, Cooper was to make it a custom to dine with Tooke, and two of his letters written to Tooke during the summer of 1791 were introduced as evidence in the trial of this notorious agitator for treason three years later.[102] The Manchester Constitutional Society, which had already expressed public approbation of

---

[100] *Memoirs,* 3 series, IX, 173; *cf.* Priestley, *Theological and Miscellaneous Works,* XIX, 503.

[101] Letter to Walker, Nov. 5, 1790, Jerrold, "Thomas Walker the Elder," *Original,* pp. 81-2.

[102] T. B. and T. J. Howell, *A Complete Collection of State Trials,* XXV, 120-2. The first letter is undated, the second is dated August 29, 1791. For interesting comments upon Tooke, see two letters from Cooper to John Fellows of New York, written in 1829, *Athenaeum,* April 16, 1898.

the writings of Thomas Paine,[103] had requested Cooper to prepare an abridgement of the *Rights of Man*. He sent this abridgement to Tooke for suggestions. The latter, with characteristic carelessness, made no reply and Cooper later asked him to burn the preface which he had sent with the abridgement. Manchester developments by this time doubtless counseled prudence.

In his first letter, Cooper stated that things were going on well at Manchester, that the Constitutional Society met "numerously and with a proper spirit," and that every possible exertion was being made by the aristocracy against them. In his second letter, he was somewhat less optimistic. Thus he acknowledged the receipt of an address which Tooke had sent him for insertion in one of the Manchester newspapers, and stated that he approved of much of it and would gladly circulate it if he could, but that he could not. Walker had submitted it to Wheeler, the more moderate of the Manchester publishers, but he had declined to publish it because of the danger of prosecution. These circumstances had led the reformers to decide to set up a paper of their own, which would be at first gently, but always decidedly, democratic and not so pestered with "Presbyterian nonsense."

It was not until the following spring that the Manchester *Herald*, published by Matthew Falkner, a member of the society, made its first appearance.[104] It continued to advocate the cause of the people, with considerable assistance from Thomas Cooper, until its dissolution a year later. Two other reform societies were established in Manchester in May and June, 1792, the Patriotic Society

---

[103] Resolutions of May 3, 1791, Manchester *Chronicle*, May 7.

[104] March 31, 1792; see the statement to the public in the issue of that date; *cf.* Walker, *Review*, p. 25. In the biographical sketch of Cooper in Fred Leary's (Manchester) *Directory of 1788*, pp. 48-9, it is stated that he was the editor. At any rate, he made a number of communications, as will appear.

and the Revolution Society.[105] The local movement for reform was not yet checked when Cooper, thrilled with hopes of a new international order,—a fraternity of free peoples,—bore a message of good will to the foes of tyranny in France. With his communication with the Jacobins, he ceased to be a local figure and gained for the moment national notoriety.

[105] For the official statements of their principles, see Walker, *Review*, pp. 34-7 n.

CHAPTER II

REVOLUTION AND REACTION, 1792-1794

THAT revolutionary France should have been included in the itinerary of Thomas Cooper's life is not surprising. Political excitement ever delighted him and, whether by fortune or design, he ever found it. That he could have been content with second-hand knowledge of the thrilling developments in France when it was possible for him to witness them and perhaps to participate in them, is inconceivable. He himself said that when his friend from Manchester, James Watt, son of the inventor, went to Paris on business in the spring of 1792, he accompanied him for pleasure.[1] We may be sure, however, that it was not conventional amusement primarily that he sought; he meant to be a first-hand observer of the revolution.

He did not approve of all that happened in France after his departure, and during his most conservative days in America stated that he returned from Paris disgusted, but such letters of his as remain from this visit indicate that he enjoyed himself immensely. He is reported to have said during his old age in South Carolina that his weeks in Paris were the happiest of his entire life: he laughed more than he ever did before or afterwards and in each month he lived a year; every energy of his mind was called out and every moment was engaged; important events unceasingly occurred and inces-

---

[1] Cooper, *Reply to Burke's Invective*, p. 7; Samuel Smiles, *Lives of Boulton and Watt*, p. 408.

santly occupied the mind. This we learn from fragments of his table-talk, memoranda of which were taken by a friend and disciple.[2] Not an entirely reliable source doubtless as regards details of fact, but in this instance probably accurate enough as to general impressions.

By March, 1792, Cooper and Watt were in France and in April they received a request from the Manchester Constitutional Society to communicate with the patriotic societies of France with a view to establishing a correspondence for the benefit of common humanity. Although they did not go in the first place as official emissaries, as their critics claimed, the request from Manchester was not so accidental as they themselves later implied. The matter of corresponding with the French had been agitated in the Manchester Constitutional Society before they left, and before they reached Paris they had written to ask that they be commissioned as its delegates.[3] Thus they sought an introduction into revolutionary circles. Although correspondence with the Jacobins had already been begun by the Revolution Society in London, the delegation of Cooper and Watt gained for their own society notoriety and called forth most bitter comments from English conservatives.[4]

In due time the delegates from Manchester appeared among the Jacobins. We should like to believe the story of the delivery of their address as we have it from a later day. It is said that Cooper told Robespierre that he had written an address which Watt had translated, and that he asked the Jacobin leader to deliver it for him, as he spoke French badly. This Robespierre promised to do.

[2] "Memoranda of the Table-Talk of Judge Cooper," made by D. J. McCord and published in E. A. and G. L. Duyckinck's *Cyclopaedia of American Literature*, 1855, II, 332-3.

[3] Watt to Thomas Walker, postscript by Cooper, March 6, 1792, Jerrold, "Thomas Walker the Elder," *Original*, bk. I, p. 83.

[4] *Cf.* Veitch, *Genesis of Parliamentary Reform*, pp. 130, 189 ff.

At the club, however, when the crowd called for the speech of Citoyen Gouappè, which had been formally announced, Robespierre refused to budge. Whereupon Citoyen Gouappè, after a remonstrance, said, "Citoyen Robespierre, vous êtes un coquin!" and with that mounted the platform and delivered the address, which was received with great enthusiasm![5] A good story, at any rate.

From more sober and authoritative accounts we learn that certain deputies of the constitutional society of Manchester, presented by Robespierre, obtained entrance to the meeting of April 13, and that an address from them was there delivered.[6] This was probably prepared by Cooper originally, although perhaps he did not deliver it. It began with the reassuring statement that despite the concert which was being formed among the despotic powers of Europe against the cause of liberty and the rights of man, there were men everywhere who were interested in the French cause, which was the cause of all mankind. The light thrown by the French on "the true principles of politics and the natural rights of man" should teach that the time had come to banish national prejudice, which was largely the creation of despots, and to recognize universal brotherhood. The Manchester society requested amicable communication and correspondence with the idea of ultimate federation among European patriotic societies. "Our society will be happy to join its efforts to yours in propagating those important principles of liberty, which alone can fix on a firm and immovable basis, the empire of peace and the happiness of mankind." Congratulations were presented the

5 "Table-Talk," Duyckinck, *Cyclopaedia*, II, 332.

6 F.-A. Aulard, *La Société des Jacobins, Recueil de Documents* (referred to hereafter as *Jacobins*), III, 496, 499; Cooper, *Reply to Burke's Invective*, appendix, pp. 85-6.

Jacobins for having been termed "the most determined
enemies of arbitrary power," and they were exhorted to
proceed in their philanthropic exertions and to continue
to merit the execrations of tyrants and the benedictions
of the human race.

The spokesman of the Jacobins in reply paid eloquent
tribute to the English for the sublime example they had
afforded the universe in the Glorious Revolution of 1688,
and stated that the proposal of an alliance of nations and
the establishment of one human family was highly agreeable.[7] "Already," he said, "the English flag, united and
entwined with the three-coloured flag of France, and the
thirteen stripes of the brave Americans is suspended
from the roofs of almost every patriotic society in
France." The Society of the Jacobins, in the name of all
the patriotic societies of France, bound itself to the Manchester society by an inviolable promise. In a letter, international good will was reiterated and the triumph of justice and humanity was confidently predicted.[8]

Two days after their appearance before the Jacobins,
Cooper and Watt participated in the well-known fête of
the soldiers of Château-Vieux. The Swiss regiment of
that name had been sent to the galleys for insubordination, and in December, 1791, the assembly had refused to
pardon them. None the less they were later conducted to
Paris by Callot d'Herbois, a retired actor, and introduced
to the assembly on April 12, 1792.[9] A fête was organized,
dedicated to liberty.

In the session of the Jacobin club on April 14, M. Tal-
lien asked for the fête the three flags which hung in the

---

[7] M. Carra, the vice-president; Cooper, *Reply*, appendix, pp. 86-8; Aulard,
Jacobins, III, 500-502.

[8] Cooper, *Reply*, appendix, pp. 88-9; *cf.* Aulard, *Jacobins*, III, 507.

[9] J. R. Macdonald, "The Legislative Assembly," *Cambridge Modern
History*, VIII, 226.

hall.[10] Upon his expressed desire that each of these be borne by a citizen of the nation which it represented, the deputy of the constitutional society of Manchester offered himself and was accepted as bearer of the British flag. The Jacobin records do not state whether this deputy was Cooper or Watt. It is a matter of no vital importance which one bore the flag or whether they bore it together; the action was unquestionably concurred in by both.

The description of this occasion, given by Burke about a year later when speaking upon a motion relating to seditious practices, indicates the conservative reaction and protest:

Messrs. Cooper and Watt had presented an address, and carried the British colors in a procession, and on what occasion? The most infamous that ever disgraced the name of government. A set of soldiers had been tried by a court martial, and condemned to the gallies. These were fit men for the republicans of Paris. They might be useful—though bad soldiers, they might be good murderers. They were released in contempt of the Assembly then sitting, brought to Paris, and paraded in triumph through the hall. On this detestable occasion, Mr. Cooper and Mr. Watt carried the British colors. They were locked in the fraternizing embrace. They received the fraternizing kiss. They went from the Hall of the Assembly to the Hall of the Jacobins, where they kissed the bloody cheek of Marat, the iron cheek of Pluto instead of Proserpine.

What ardent transports thro' their bosoms ran,
Clasp'd in th' embrace of the godlike man![11]

Cooper himself viewed the occasion quite differently. In a letter to Thomas Walker he gave a glowing description of the fête and extolled it as a meeting of two hundred thousand sober, orderly, and at the same time enthusias-

10 Aulard, *Jacobins*, III, 503.
11 Feb. 28, 1793, *Parliamentary History*, XXX, 552.

tic citizens, "the first festival truly civic that Europe has seen."[12] The official organ of the Manchester reformers doubtless reflected their attitude in giving a detailed and sympathetic description.[13]

The Jacobins had given the delegates from Manchester a cordial invitation to attend their meetings and of this they took due advantage. Cooper was convinced that amidst all their noise, impetuosity, irregularity, long-windedness, and impatience of contrariety of opinion, there was much important discussion, much eloquence, acuteness, and effect.[14] It was natural that one who so distrusted all rulers should have been specially impressed with their watchfulness of the men in power. "They are," he said, "the governors of the governors of the kingdom."

Before the Manchester delegates left France, relations between them and Robespierre apparently became strained, although we do not vouch for the accuracy of the stories which gained currency. Cooper is said to have stated many years later that spies were set upon them, but that he and his companion found out who they were, invited them regularly to dinner and always got them drunk.[15] He associated chiefly with the Brissotines and one evening tried to gain their support in the matter of a contemplated insult of Robespierre at the club. This he hoped would result in a brawl, in which Robespierre and his supporters would be "broken up." He himself would have greatly liked it, he claimed, but the Frenchmen would not risk it. It is said that Robespierre later denounced both Cooper and Watt. According to one

12 April 25, 1792, Jerrold in the *Original*, pp. 85-6.
13 Manchester *Herald*, April 28, May 5, 1792. No further details are given about Cooper.
14 Letter to Walker, April 25, 1792, *Original*, pp. 84-6.
15 "Table-Talk," Duyckinck, *Cyclopaedia*, II, 332.

story, he accused them at the club of being secret emissaries of Pitt, whereupon Watt sprang into the tribune and eloquently and persuasively defended himself, and presumably his companion as well.[16] It may well be that Watt fled the city because he felt his life unsafe; and whether for safety or not, Cooper returned to England in May,[17] never to return to distracted France. At home he found that Burke had attacked him in the house of commons and that the reformers were being forced upon the defensive.

The debate of April 30, which gave occasion to Burke's attack upon Cooper, grew out of the announcement of Charles Grey that he would introduce, at the next session, a motion for parliamentary reform.[18] He spoke in the name of the Society of the Friends of the People, an organization of moderate reformers who advocated freedom and greater frequency of elections and more equal representation.[19] They declared that they sought to avert from Great Britain such convulsions as had occurred in France and that they would resist all efforts to promote confusion or even to secure improvement of conditions by ''unconstitutional and irregular courses.'' Pitt deliberately precipitated a general discussion and, by voicing the unwarranted suspicion that the movement for

---

[16] Smiles, *Lives of Boulton and Watt*, pp. 414-5. In his table-talk, Cooper refers to the denunciation, but does not give these graphic details, for which we do not vouch.

[17] His *Reply to Burke's Invective* was probably written late in May, 1792, and in this he states that he returned to England two weeks before, p. 3. The first letter to Walker bears the date March 6, so it seems probable that he was in France a little more than two months, although in his table-talk (Duyckinck, II, 332) he speaks of having been there four months.

[18] For the debate, see *Parl. Hist.*, XXIX, 1300-41. For a discussion of its significance in the history of the reform movement, see Veitch, *Genesis of Parliamentary Reform*, pp. 198 ff.

[19] For their ''Declaration,'' see *Parl. Hist.*, XXIX, 1303-4 n.; for their ''Address to the People of Great Britain,'' see *ibid.*, XXIX, 1305-10 n.

reform was but the preliminary to an attempt to overthrow the whole system of government,[20] endeavored to
discredit the reformers and alienate from them the aristocratic Whigs, thus dividing the opposition to his ministry.[21] The conservatives took up the cry of alarm which
he raised and forced the reformers to defend themselves
against the charge that they were in sympathy with
revolutionists.[22] Under these circumstances a radical like
Cooper could expect no mercy from the conservatives and
little defense from the reformers.

Burke, like Pitt, opposed reform and agitation, but he
was more specific in his attacks upon alleged revolutionists.[23] In the course of his speech, he paid his respects
to Paine's *Rights of Man,* which he termed a most infamous libel upon the constitution of the country, tending
to subvert and overturn it. He felt sure that there was
no one in the house who was the avowed friend of despotism, and that there was nothing like a conspiracy against
the privileges of the people. On the other hand, he felt
safe in saying that there were those in the country who
were the avowed enemies of the constitution. Upon the
cry that he name his men, he stated that those clubs and
societies who recommended Paine's book were openly
hostile to the constitution. Also, there were men in England who did not scruple to enter into alliance with the
Jacobin club of Paris, a set of the worst traitors and

[20] For Pitt's speech, see *ibid.,* XXIX, 1302-12.

[21] W. T. Laprade, in his ''England and the French Revolution,'' Johns
Hopkins University *Studies in Historical and Political Science,* series
XXVII, discusses Pitt's political tactics fully and suggestively. See *ibid.,*
ch. III, especially pp. 55-9.

[22] Among the members of the Society of the Friends of the People who
spoke were Thomas Erskine and Richard Sheridan, see *Parl. Hist.,* XXIX,
1327-30, 1333-5. Fox, who was not a member of the society and who did
not think the time advantageous for a discussion of reform, none the less
supported Grey; see *ibid.,* XXIX, 1312-17.

[23] *Ibid.,* XXIX, 1317-24, especially 1322-3.

regicides that had ever been heard of. Agents had been
sent to enter into a federation with that iniquitous
organization, and those agents were men of some consideration in the country. He named Thomas Cooper and
James Watt and read the address presented by them to
the Jacobins. This he regarded as proof that there were
English clubs which bound themselves to approve of the
conduct of those regicides and to act in concert with them.
He named Thomas Walker in this connection and said
that the Manchester worthies undertook to represent all
England. He asserted that the gentlemen favoring reform, in order to succeed must unite themselves with
some of the worst men in the kingdom.

The advocates of moderate reform could not well rally
to the defense of the supposed revolutionaries from Manchester. Indeed, they felt it necessary to relieve themselves of the odium which attached itself to men who
corresponded with the French and advocated the doctrines of Thomas Paine, and the discussion served to
draw a sharp line of demarcation between the moderates
and the radicals. Sheridan, it is true, commended Walker,
whose advocacy of reform had led him to sign the society's resolution, and who was "a man of sense, character, and opulence." He also had the pleasure to know
Thomas Cooper, and thought that his correspondence
with the French might be as easily explained as Burke's
correspondence with Americans during the Revolution.[24]
Such an attitude, however, was exceptional. Erskine took
pains to declare that Cooper and Watt had nothing whatever to do with the Friends of the People, and even so
genuine a reformer as he seems to have regarded their
point of view as improper.[25] The charge that the associa-

[24] *Ibid.*, XXIX, 1334.
[25] *Parliamentary Register*, XXXII, 483 (not *Parl. Hist.*). It should be

tion originated in the societies of Manchester and Sheffield and that it adopted the "pernicious" doctrines of
Paine was strongly denied by William Baker.[26]

The name of Cooper was actually proposed for membership in the Society of the Friends of the People, presumably before the debate in parliament had advertised
him so unpleasantly, but certain members, of whom
Baker was one, stated privately that they would renounce
all connection with the organization if he were admitted.
At the meeting of May 19, his name was voluntarily withdrawn by the original proposer, before any public objection had been made.[27] It was his association with the
Jacobins which was principally objected to, for five members withdrew on June 4, because of the continuance in
the organization of John Cartwright, who as secretary of
the Society for Constitutional Information had carried
on correspondence with the French, an action which the
seceding group regarded as indistinguishable from that
of Cooper.[28] Baker, one of the five, explained his action
in a speech at the county meeting of Hertfordshire somewhat later, and by his references to Cooper caused that
gentleman to write a heated letter of rejoinder.[29] In this
he made spirited defense of his actions in France and
referred sarcastically to the horror which his presence
in the Friends of the People would have caused his easily-
affrighted critic.

Meanwhile, the Manchester Constitutional Society had

noted that Erskine later acted as counsel for Paine and Walker when they
were tried on charges, respectively, of libel and sedition.

[26] *Parl. Hist.*, XXIX, 1339.

[27] *Proceedings of the Society of the Friends of the People in 1792*, p. 50.

[28] *Ibid.*, p. 48. The five were John Russell, William Baker, J. C. Curwen,
Dudley North, and J. Courtenay. It should be noted that the Friends of the
People officially declined correspondence and denied connection with the
Society of Constitutional Information, *ibid.*, pp. 25-34, 49 ff.

[29] Manchester *Herald*, August 4, 1792. The letter is dated July 19 and
was sent originally to the London *Morning Chronicle*.

defended itself against the charges made by the opponents of reform, and not denied by the moderate group, that it was revolutionary. Following the address to the Jacobins and the attack of Burke upon Cooper and Watt, and to some extent upon Walker, the society was "brought very conspicuously before the public," and "became the object of much conversation and calumny." By publishing, on May 8, the text of the address to the Jacobins and the reply to it, they sought to give accurate information as to what had actually occurred.[30] The members thought it necessary also, in order to prevent mistake and misrepresentation, to publish a week later a declaration which disclaimed any intention to overthrow the British constitution.[31] They avowed their aim to be the restoration of "the constitution to its original purity, by removing the corruptions and abuses that deform it, and which render its practice at perpetual variance with its applauded theory." Far from seeking to arouse sedition, they claimed they were solicitous to remove the danger of it and to secure the tranquillity of the nation.

They tried also to speak reassuringly in regard to their attitude toward France. They openly rejoiced that the revolution had effected the emancipation of millions from slavery and caused the renunciation by the French of schemes of ambition and conquest, but declined to express approbation of all the measures which the latter had adopted and expressed regret at such calamities as had occurred. They denied holding the opinion that a similar revolution was necessary in Great Britain. So far as correspondence with the French was concerned, however, they yielded nothing to parliamentary clamor. They would not yet surrender hope of the establishment

30 Cooper, *Reply to Burke's Invective*, appendix, pp. 85-9.
31 Walker, *Review*, pp. 25-30.

of an international fraternity of free peoples. Such was also the attitude of the Society for Constitutional Information of London. This organization, after the reception of Cooper and Watt had been announced to it by the correspondence of these gentlemen, sent an appreciative letter to the Jacobins which they published in England, May 18. They referred to the delegates from Manchester as "worthy gentlemen" and as "united with our society." The expressions of international good will which this letter contained we may be sure met with Cooper's full approval, for he himself published a copy of it in connection with his reply to Burke,[32] although the royal proclamation against sedition had then been issued.

Cooper claimed that he was surprised to learn upon his return from France that his actions had received so much attention. Burke's "ridiculous fears and intemperate invectives" he said he would not have heeded, but a pack of parliamentary orators had taken up the hue and cry so he felt compelled to justify his conduct and intentions. The tone of his *Reply to Burke's Invective*,[33] however, is not that of reluctant controversy. His pamphlet of some eighty pages remains as a monument to his own power of invective and his early passion for democracy. With this daring venture in controversy he ceased to be a novice and became a veteran.

Although Cooper claimed that his conduct in France required no defense he did not neglect his opportunity to

[32] *Reply*, pp. 90-1. Cooper may have been a member of this society, although verification is lacking.

[33] Manchester, 1792. There were two London editions, 1792 and 1793. The pamphlet was probably written in May, and possibly between May 21 and 25, since it refers to the proclamation of sedition of the former date and displays ignorance of the debate which occurred upon the latter, *ibid.*, p. 66. It was certainly written before August 10, for it refers to the king of France as still in power, *ibid.*, p. 6. The first announcement of its publication was in the Manchester *Herald*, August 18.

make one.[34] He described the Jacobin club as a society whose standing in France showed that they could not be traitors, and the relations of the king of France with whom made absurd the charge that they were regicides. He and Watt were not sent expressly to enter into a federation with them, he declared, although he saw no reason for objection if they were. Nor did the Manchester society bind itself to a general approbation of the conduct of the Jacobins except to join with them in their efforts to propagate the principles of liberty. He denied that he and Watt undertook to represent all Englishmen or to speak in their name, and that they were sworn into a federation.

A correspondence between societies of different nations for the advancement of political knowledge Cooper regarded as not reprehensible but highly expedient.[35] The effort to further international brotherhood, as against that of courts and ministers to foster an artificial discord and enmity, he thought most commendable. In his own behalf and in behalf of the British patriotic societies, he disavowed all revolutionary intention.[36] He declared that he and all his political friends felt that under existing circumstances no one could be justified in asking for more than reform in representation and limitation of the duration of parliaments. He agreed with Burke that the burden of proof rested upon those who would destroy the frame of a country's government, and himself favored amendation of the present system rather than revolution, "of which the evil would be grievous, extensive and inevitable."

So far as theory went, however, he admitted a much more radical position. He devoted some fifty pages[37] to a bitter indictment of "privileged orders," which in a

34 *Reply*, pp. 5-8.   35 *Ibid.*, pp. 8 ff.
36 *Ibid.*, pp. 14 ff.   37 *Ibid.*, pp. 17-66.

newly-formed state, he said, would be considered as "incumbrances, absurd and useless, dangerous and unjust." He admitted that in England privileged orders were at their best and did not seek to overthrow what he considered probably the best system in Europe.[38] None the less, it would have been only natural for less careful readers of his pamphlet to adjudge him a violent opponent of even the English system, which he by no means neglected to criticize.

The likelihood of misunderstanding was increased by the tone of Cooper's polemic and by numerous remarks of his which were almost certain of misrepresentation. He quoted Lafayette's saying, "For a nation to change the form of its government, it is sufficient that she wills it,"[39] then remarked upon the danger and difficulty of such change because of the opposition of privileged orders. As a true friend of the people, he desired peaceable reformation lest oppression lead to revolution in the end. His position here was sane, but popular interpretation almost certainly emphasized the word revolution and passed by his qualifying statements. Indeed, despite all his words of reassurance, there was considerable ground for suspicion that although he was at present advocating reformation he had no insuperable aversion to revolution as a last resort. A further ground for criticism was his unqualified endorsement of Thomas Paine.[40]

That he might be accused of libel against the constitution he fully realized, but he was confident that his conduct was not and had not been seditious and was quite willing, as indeed he always was, to take a chance in

[38] *Ibid.*, p. 66.   [39] *Ibid.*, p. 61.

[40] *Ibid.*, pp. 67, 75 n. Cooper in this work showed an extensive acquaintance with the writings of radicals and reformers. He stated that he considered the works of Milton, Harrington, and Sydney as both less profound and less popular than those of Paine, Sieyès, Barlow, Oswald, and Mirabeau; *ibid.*, p. 17 n.

order to establish fuller freedom of speech upon political questions. He felt that tender concern for the British constitution was carried to excess.

In the fashionable System of political Botany, it [the constitution] is a Sensitive Plant, shrinking from the slightest breath of enquiry; and therefore strongly fenced round from too close an Inspection, with the thorns and briars of the Law; while the Attorney General, like the Angel of Punishment at the Gate of Paradise, guards the entrance into this holy ground, and brandishes an *ex officio* Information to strike terror into the heart of each bold intruder. We are required to take upon trust the mysteries of this far-famed Constitution, . . . and we are taught to know that in Politics as in Religion, where Reason ends, Faith begins.[41]

He admitted being a heretic or, as Burke said, an atheist in politics in the sense that he believed only upon conviction and was convinced only upon inquiry. He could not conceive what a constitution was good for whose principles would not bear examination, nor how a country could be free where men were punished for peacefully endeavoring to point out the errors and defects of the government. And he made a sharp distinction between one who incited revolt and one who incited inquiry.

The tone of Cooper's reply cannot be said to be calm, dispassionate, or judicial. He loosed upon his critics a torrent of argument and in his denunciation of Burke in particular lashed himself into a very fury of invective. He spoke of that gentleman's "gross blunders and obvious misrepresentations" and stated that his character was at too low an ebb for one to derive much credit from his abuse. He said that he would endeavor to show that Burke was probably mistaken in supposing that he and Watt were the worst men in the kingdom while he him-

41 *Ibid.*, pp. 67-8.

self was alive to make the assertion. Accusations against
his associate and himself he referred to as "mere Burk-
isms, assertions without proof and invective without
argument," and one charge he termed a "flagrant un-
truth," which Burke was called upon to contradict or
prove, if he had any character of veracity to lose.[42]

His contempt was expressed most fully perhaps in the
following impatiently vehement passage:

> But what must be the Complexion of that Man's mind, who
> can be irritated to a degree of political Insanity at these expres-
> sions of Friendship and Benevolence towards our Neighbours
> and Fellow Creatures? Who sickens at the Thought of perpetual
> peace and fraternal Union between rival Nations. Who entertains
> no Sentiments of Compassion, but for the rich and the great, the
> Kings, and the nobles of the earth! Who can contemplate with-
> out emotion, the prospect of Bloodshed and Devastation among
> Millions of the devoted Victims of Pride and Despotism, and
> who bewails with a feminine Lamentation, the loss of a nick-
> name or a Gewgaw, the broken play things of a puerile Nobility!
> Who seems to regard the *people* as fit only for the Goad, and the
> Whip, and the Spur; for Labour without Intermission, in Peace;
> for slaughter without Commiseration, in War—And who, blas-
> pheming against human nature itself, impiously terms the great
> Mass of Mankind, *the Swinish Multitude!*[43]

Cooper bitterly resented Burke's expression, "swinish
multitude," and referred to it no fewer than eleven times
despite his statement that he would have little to say
about it. But it is doubtful if Burke's original remark
deserved such invective. He had been speaking of the
fact that the nobility and clergy had kept learning in
existence, and expressed the fear that, in an age of revolution, "along with its natural protectors and guardians"
learning would be "cast into the mire and trodden under

the hoofs of a swinish multitude.''[44] That there is danger of such a fate for learning in times of revolution no one can justly deny, and Cooper distorted the emphasis when he detached this one phrase from its setting and scornfully rang the changes upon it throughout his reply. He was not fair to his distinguished critic in describing him as ''that inveterate enemy of human kind,''[45] yet there can be no doubt but that Burke distrusted the people, in whom his less distinguished opponent had greatest confidence. The measure of Cooper's indignation was the measure of his democracy.

His confidence in the people, if somewhat naïve and not wholly warranted by human experience, is nevertheless stimulating and refreshing. In contempt of Burke, he appealed to the people whom he himself regarded as the only class in the community worth appealing to.[46] He was not prepared to believe that public spirit and independence were exclusively confined to the rich. On the contrary, he almost suspected that it was no easier for a very rich man to be a thorough patriot than for the proverbial camel to go through the eye of a needle. He realized the poor man's temptation to sacrifice his opinions for bread, but felt that when the poor did yield it was primarily because of want and ignorance, which should be done away with. He had supreme faith that if confidence were shown in the people they would gain a due sense of dignity and justify the expectations which were entertained of their good conduct.[47]

In his verbal assault upon the citadel of privilege he showed himself relentless toward him whom he regarded as one of its chief defenders. Burke, he said, stood revealed by his own words as ''the public professor of political turpitude, the systematic opponent of every spe-

[44] *Reflections on the Revolution in France*, 1790, p. 117.
[45] *Reply*, p. 70.   [46] *Ibid.*, p. 13.   [47] *Ibid.*, pp. 70-1.

cies of reform, and in love with the very sinfulness of sin"; unblushingly he obtruded himself "on the disgusted eye of the public, in all the nakedness and deformity of political vice."[48]

No one can justly claim that Cooper was fair to Burke. He felt, to be sure, that Burke had been grossly unfair to him and certainly he regarded him as the implacable foe of his own dearest political principles and all the reform movements in which he so ardently believed. He wrote in the spirit of heated controversy, not in the calm, dispassionate spirit of the detached historian or philosopher. He was not attempting to give a full and well-rounded interpretation of Burke for the benefit of coming generations. Of that he would have been incapable. Rather was he endeavoring to overthrow this gigantic obstacle to reform and the rights of the people. He wrote as a propagandist of freedom, not as a scholarly interpreter of the period of the French Revolution.

The picture which he gave of Burke's place in English politics is obviously inaccurate and he utterly failed to appreciate the deeper motives of the man. If Burke was incapable of appreciating the things which Cooper held dearest, so was Cooper incapable of a proper evaluation of those held dearest by Burke: order, reverence, heredity, prescription, tradition, property, necessity for continuity in institutions. Cooper greatly underestimated the importance of Burke's contributions to political philosophy, scorning his "discourses of political mysticism," and his magnifying of difficulties. To the profundity of Burke's position he did not penetrate. He instinctively perceived the essential clash between Burke's philosophy and his own, and hastened to join battle, without any regard to comparative standing in the political world, taking advantage of all the tricks of the game he knew.

[48] *Ibid.*, pp. 82-3.

In considering the respective positions and attitudes
of the two men, one is reminded of Burke's own picture
of the grasshoppers and the cattle, whereby he sought to
contrast the prevailing spirit of content in England with
the critical and contentious spirit of a small but violent
minority.

Because half a dozen grasshoppers under a fern make the field
ring with their importunate chink, whilst thousands of great
cattle, reposed beneath the shadow of the British oak, chew the
cud and are silent, pray do not imagine, that those who make the
noise are the only inhabitants of the field; that, of course, they
are many in number; or that, after all, they are other than the
little shrivelled, meagre, hopping, though loud and troublesome
insects of the hour.[49]

Cooper would doubtless have resented being called an
insect and would certainly have objected to other implications of the figure, but no one else would have admitted
more readily that he was not of the dumb driven cattle.
Perhaps he would have preferred Socrates' designation
and termed himself a gadfly, whose God-given function
was to sting the patient herd and arouse it from its ignorant complacency.

Burke did not condescend to reply to the bitter attack
which had been made on him, nor even to refer to it when
he paid his compliments to Cooper in the house of commons upon a later occasion.[50] He preferred to ignore the
importunate chink of this particular grasshopper. The
reformers themselves greeted the pamphlet with great
enthusiasm. Cooper's Manchester associates specially
commended this "masterly work" to the attention of the
public, and other societies thanked him for his "noble
exertions" and his "manly and spirited defense" of the

[49] *Reflections*, 1790, pp. 126-7.
[50] Feb. 28, 1793, *Parl. Hist.*, XXX, 552; Walker, *Review*, p. 25.

cause of liberty.[51] At frequent celebrations he was honored by laudatory toasts, and songs were sung and toasts
were drunk defiantly to the "swinish multitude."[52]

Perhaps the pamphlet reached the leaders more than
the common people whose claims the author had presented so passionately. Writing later, during the most
conservative period of his life, Cooper said that in this
particular case Sir John Scott (later Lord Eldon), the
attorney-general, made a distinction of which he had no
right to complain when he said to him, "Continue if you
please to publish your reply to Mr. Burke in an octavo
form, so as to confine it probably to that class of readers
who may consider it coolly: so soon as it is published
cheaply for dissemination among the populace, it will be
my duty to prosecute."[53] In 1792, the author probably did
complain of this restriction, but he did not disregard the
warning and was not prosecuted for sedition.

The first proclamation against sedition, which was
issued May 21, 1792, was the opening salvo in the campaign of repression.[54] The language of the proclamation
itself and the discussion in the commons leave little doubt
that a weapon had been forged for use against the
patriotic societies.[55] The "wicked and seditious writings," the publication, dispersal and commendation of
which were objected to, obviously included the works of
Paine which Cooper and his associates were praising so

[51] Resolutions of the Manchester Constitutional Society, Sept. 25, 1792,
Manchester *Herald*, Sept. 29; Sheffield Society for Constitutional Information, Oct. 10, 1792, *ibid.*, Oct. 27; London Revolution Society, Nov. 14,
1792, *ibid.*, Nov. 24; Southwark Society of the Friends of the People, Nov.
28, 1792, *ibid.*, Dec. 8.

[52] *Ibid.*, Sept. 22, Nov. 10, Dec. 1, 1792.

[53] Cooper, *Institutes of Justinian*, 1812, p. 630.

[54] *Annual Register*, XXXIV, part II, appendix to chronicle, 192-3; *Parl.
Hist.*, XXIX, 1476-7; Walker, *Review*, pp. 30-2.

[55] For the debate, see *Parl. Hist.*, XXIX, 1477-1514. An amendment by
Grey was defeated without a division, *ibid.*, XXIX, 1487-9.

highly; and there could have been no uncertainty about the reference to "suspected correspondence with foreign parts with a view to forwarding seditious purposes." Warnings and exhortations against riots and tumults were nominally directed to both conservative and radical groups, but the latter had ground for suspicion that officers of the law would not be impartial; and the charge to magistrates to make inquiries and reports in the matter of "wicked writings" threatened to limit that freedom of speech upon which the propagation of doctrines of reform depended.

Some objection to the system of espionage was made in parliament and it was claimed that the proclamation was unnecessary and would arouse groundless suspicion and alarm, but sentiment was overwhelmingly favorable to the policy of the government. It was generally asserted by its supporters that the proclamation was directed against the patriotic societies and was not designed, as some claimed, to discredit and divide the Friends of the People and thus check the movement for parliamentary reform.[56] That the tide of conservatism was rising and that the action of the government served further to accentuate the distinction which had already been drawn between the moderates and the radicals must, however, have been apparent to all.

Cooper was not slow to manifest that resentment of this action which was to be expected of him. In his reply to Burke he said that while he was writing what might have been considered a libel against the government, "the name of our gracious Sovereign (if public construction be well-founded) has been most impudently and atrociously perverted to the base purposes of *calumny* and *falsehood* against Mr. Watt and myself, in the late

[56] Besides Grey, Fox made this claim, *ibid.*, XXIX, 1509-12.

Proclamation.''[57] His feeling was that if the correspondence alluded to in the proclamation were really seditious the law would already have set to work against it, and that the endeavor was being made to inflame the public against lawful actions and against persons of unblemished character acting from the best intentions. Far from denying the correspondence with which he himself had been concerned, he asked the public to judge it for itself. Then, in open defiance of the advocates of repression, he predicted that at no far-distant time the people would regard it as an honor conferred upon him and Watt that public report had connected their names on this occasion with that of Thomas Paine. Apparently he had not yet seen the text of the proclamation and was not familiar with the nature of the debate upon it, else he would not have thought the action so specifically directed against himself and Watt. The reference in the proclamation to correspondence with foreign parts was general, and neither his name nor that of his companion was mentioned at any time during the debate. Probably no member of parliament took him as seriously as he took himself.

Through the columns of the Manchester *Herald,* which was the official organ of the reformers in that city and of which he was later reported to have been the editor, he attacked the proclamation more directly.[58] Here he deplored the action of the government as quite unnecessary and declared that the proclamation would be productive of the very disorder and discontent which it was designed to allay. Its great defect as he saw it was that it was so

[57] *Reply,* pp. 66-7.

[58] June 2, 1792; also given by Walker, *Review,* pp. 40-2 n. The communication was signed ''Sydney,'' the pen-name used by Cooper in an address in the same paper, Dec. 10, 1792, and attributed to him by Walker, *ibid.,* p. 55. An entire paragraph of the communication of June 2, is almost identical with a paragraph in the *Reply to Burke's Invective.*

general, that it proceeded by hints and insinuations rather than by specific citation of offenses and would thus certainly engender public suspicion. He went so far as to say, "I hope the advisers of this indiscreet measure will shortly be impeached for promoting a proclamation so flagrantly calculated to excite jealousies and alarms among the people, where none existed before." He made the characteristic charge that the whole effort to check public discussion was due to the concern of the rulers lest their own conduct be exposed, and said that they led one to suppose they loved darkness rather than light because their deeds were evil.

The action of the government seems to have been due to hysteria and, in part, to the deliberate purpose of Pitt to win over the conservative Whigs by appealing to their fears.[59] It seems unquestionably to have been ill-advised.[60] Neither the foreign nor the domestic situation warranted such infringement upon individual liberty in the name of national security and public order. The patriotic societies rightly insisted upon the legitimacy of international correspondence in time of peace, and although somewhat restrained by prudence continued to communicate with France during the summer and autumn of 1792. British opinion at this time was not favorable to revolution and the fears of the government were not well founded. The devotion of the vast majority of the people to the constitution and orderly government under it was recognized by even the more hysterical advocates of repression, and appreciation of the situation was expressed repeatedly in the debates in the house of commons. The patriotic

[59] Laprade, in his "England and the French Revolution," p. 60 (Johns Hopkins *Studies*, series XXVII), says, "His purpose was primarily to promote party defection among the Whigs, and only secondarily, if at all, to check the propaganda of the reformers." War psychology, however, doubtless played its part then, as it has since.

[60] *Cf.* Veitch, *Genesis of Parliamentary Reform*, pp. 208 ff.

societies had declared that they sought only parliamentary reform and that by legal means. There was no sufficient justification for the persistent disbelief of their avowals and the wholesale association of them with Thomas Paine. Even those who like Cooper publicly praised him offended in words, not actions; they incited criticism, not revolt. Patient tolerance of such men would doubtless have been the part of wisdom then, as it so generally has been in Great Britain. In this instance the threatening gesture of the government served, in Manchester at least, not to discourage but to stimulate suspicion and disorder, so there was loss not only to liberty but also to public peace.

A meeting to address the king on the proclamation was planned by the conservatives of Manchester for June 4, and during the three days previous to this date an address urging abstention from the meeting was distributed by members of the opposing group.[61] Although the constitutional society by official action severely criticized the proclamation much as Cooper did, it claimed that its primary object was to avoid the violence and disorder which might result from the bringing together of a crowd of individuals of differing shades of opinion. By emphasizing their desire to preserve peace and harmony the reformers thought to answer the "calumnies" of their enemies. At the same time, however, they laid themselves open to the charge of disloyalty to the king, for June 4 was the birthday of George III and the meeting was designed to express loyalty to him at the same time it voiced approval of the action of the government.[62]

Whether as a direct result of the meeting or not, there was rioting in Manchester upon the evening of the king's

[61] Walker, *Review*, pp. 35-9.

[62] *Cf.* communication describing the happenings at Manchester, London *Morning Herald*, June 7, 1792.

birthday.[63] The crowd which had gathered to see some
"illuminations" in St. Ann's Square became disorderly,
attacked several peaceful spectators, and attempted with
uprooted trees to batter down the doors of two chapels
of Dissenters. The cry, "Church and King—Down with
the Rump," which was raised by the rioters further indicates the coincidence of the lines of political and ecclesiastical demarcation.

Before reports of this disorder could have reached
Paris, the tribulations of their friends in Manchester
were discussed among the Jacobins. In consequence of
the denunciation of Cooper and Watt in parliament and
reports of their subsequent persecution, the club voted
to send a letter of consolation and encouragement, but
later decided not to write to the Manchester society since
no official notice of their persecutions had been received.
At the meeting of June 4, Oswald, an Englishman, urged
that a letter of sympathy be sent. He deplored bondage
to etiquette when their friends were in such danger, and
drew a lurid, and so far as our information goes, an extravagant picture of the perils to which the former Manchester representatives were exposed:

MM. Cooper and Watt, endowed the one and the other by an
ardent and patriotic spirit, have exposed to the greatest dangers
their fortune and even their life, to bind together the bonds of
friendship between the two nations. M. Cooper, pursued by
ministerial informers, perhaps languishes today in a dungeon,
perhaps even a multitude, misled by the agents of a perfidious
ministry, deliver to the flames the house of our friend; his fortune is ruined, perhaps his blood flows, and you have calmly
voted that it is not necessary to write a word of consolation to
your Manchester friends![64]

63 Walker, *Review,* pp. 39-40.
64 Aulard, *Jacobins,* III, 653.

In the discussion which followed divergent views were expressed, but the order of the day was voted without acceding to Oswald's request. The prevailing opinion seems to have been that the information concerning the alleged persecutions, being based on newspaper reports and vague rumors, was too unofficial to justify definite action by the Jacobins. This attitude seems now to have been sane and wise, and it need not indicate lack of sympathy.

Sympathy with the struggle of their French friends against despotism continued to be manifested by Cooper and his associates during the summer and autumn of 1792. The direful threats made against the revolutionists by the Duke of Brunswick in his manifesto of July 25, aroused the indignation of the English reformers, who doubtless joined with Cooper in approving of the suspension of Louis XVI on August 10. A narrative of the events and circumstances of this suspension, written immediately afterwards by J. B. d'Aumont, was sent him by its author for publication in order that false reports current in England might be corrected. In publishing the pamphlet, Cooper stated that he did not doubt the fidelity and correctness of the account, so we may assume that he regarded the French king as guilty of treachery to his people and approved of his removal.[65] We should expect Cooper to have rejoiced in the attempted overthrow of the hereditary system in a land where he must have regarded it as particularly useless and dangerous.

[65] *Narrative of Proceedings relative to the Suspension of the King of France*, Manchester, 1792. Since it was announced in the Manchester *Herald* as late as Oct. 27 that the pamphlet was in press, it probably appeared too late to be of influence in England. Cooper added a few explanatory footnotes to the above narrative and published in connection with it Condorcet's *Reflections on the English Revolution of 1688, and that of the 10th of August, 1792,* together with an address of the National Assembly which set forth the motives which induced that body to suspend the king and call a national convention.

The Manchester reformers had probably learned of the September massacres by the twelfth of the month, but their zeal for the cause of the revolutionists does not seem to have been lessened thereby. Announcement was made on that date of a meeting of the "friends of human liberty" at Bull's Head Inn on the eighteenth to start a subscription for the relief of "brethren" in France who were suffering the calamities of war as the result of a "cruel combination of despots" against dawning liberty.[66] By this time, though, the forces of order showed themselves well organized and expressed their national patriotism with extravagant fervor. Alarmed at the conduct of a set of "daring miscreants" whose avowed purpose was to assist the "French savages" and introduce unspeakable calamities in happy and prosperous England, one hundred and eighty-six keepers of inns and alehouses signed a declaration that they would offer no further hospitality to clubs hostile to the most excellent British constitution.[67] Walker attributed this action to a visit made the innkeepers and publicans by a tax-gatherer and some other persons who advised them for their own good not to allow meetings of reform societies in their houses. Whether to save their licenses or not, the innkeepers denied themselves the custom of the three societies of reformers,[68] which met during the following autumn, winter, and spring under conditions of relative security at the home and warehouse of Thomas Walker.

By giving official expression to its continued sympathy for the French, the Manchester Constitutional Society became more than ever an object of suspicion to panic-stricken English conservatives. It subscribed to an ad-

[66] Walker, *Review*, pp. 41-4; Manchester *Herald*, Sept. 15, 1792.

[67] *Ibid.*, pp. 42-3 n.; Manchester *Chronicle*, Sept. 15, 1792.

[68] Constitutional, Patriotic, and Reformation. The two latter were organized May 24 and June 6, 1792, respectively, *ibid.*, pp. 34-7 n.

dress of friendly encouragement which was sent to France by the London Corresponding Society late in September,[69] and joined with several English societies in a strongly pro-revolutionary address which was read in the Convention November 7.[70] The latter condemned the repressive policy of the British government at the same time it expressed sympathy with the French in their resistance to foreign invaders. There is, however, no sufficient reason to believe that the society to which Cooper belonged shared the hope which the Society for Constitutional Information voiced later in the same month that revolutionary developments might take place in England itself.[71]

In the speech of the king at the opening of parliament on December 13, it was asserted that seditious practices had been renewed more openly of late and that the consequent tumult and disorder had necessitated the interposition of a military force in support of civil magistrates.[72] The reference was to the royal proclamation of December 1, calling forth the militia.[73] In the debate upon the royal message in the house of commons it was stated that the fright of the government grew out of the alleged effect of radical sentiments, especially those of Paine, upon the lower classes, the dangerous topics discussed in the meetings of the reform societies, the correspondence between these societies and France; the late French decree offering aid to all peoples who sought assistance to obtain freedom; and the apparent determination of the

[69] Sept. 27. *Annual Register* (edition of 1821), XXXIV, 70-2; *cf.* Veitch, *Genesis of Parliamentary Reform*, pp. 220-2. This address was originally prepared for presentation to the Legislative Assembly, but the Republic was declared shortly before its adoption.

[70] *Collection of Addresses transmitted by certain English Clubs and Societies to the National Convention of France*, pp. 6-8.

[71] Nov. 28. *Ibid.*, pp. 11-14.   [72] *Parl. Hist.*, XXIX, 1556-7.

[73] *Annual Register*, XXXIV, part II, State Papers, 196-7.

French to aggrandize their territories.[74] The enfeebled opposition protested against the calling forth of the militia at a time when there was no insurrection, but the action of the ministry was approved by the customary majority.

Before the debate in parliament took place, Cooper violently protested against the royal proclamation on the ground that it was the preliminary to war with France, as indeed it was. A meeting was to be held in Manchester December 11 to address the king on the proclamation, and in the hope of influencing this gathering Cooper published a strong address against war.[75] From the "unrequested interference in Dutch politics," the royal proclamation, and other actions of the government he concluded that it was determined upon war, to which it would proceed as soon as it felt sure of public approbation. In this he was probably not far from the truth,[76] but he took no account of the practical problems of international politics. He considered the whole question largely in the abstract and opposed this particular war more because of his theoretical objections to all war than because of the specific issues involved. He did not mention the French or their cause. Perhaps his sympathy for them had ebbed somewhat, but at least he did not want Great Britain to fight against them.

He opposed war on the ground that the value of property would be thereby decreased, that taxes would be

[74] *Parl. Hist.*, XXX, 1-80; see especially, pp. 42-9 (Dundas) and pp. 51-5 (Burke).

[75] Cooper's address, which was signed "Sydney" and printed privately by the author and his friends, was dated Dec. 10, 1792. It is quoted in part by Walker, *Review*, pp. 50-5, as from Cooper.

[76] Laprade, "England and the French Revolution," pp. 79-82, Johns Hopkins *Studies*, XXVII, upholds this position. The more conventional emphasis upon Pitt's efforts to maintain peace is given by J. H. Rose, *William Pitt and the Great War*, ch. 3, and William Hunt, in the *Political History of England*, X, 337-44.

increased and trade curtailed, that prosperity would be imperiled, and that the small manufacturer and the worker in particular would be injured. He alluded to the "calumnies" to which the "friends of the people" were constantly exposed, but declared that they entertained "no personal enmities, no aversion but to the enemies of the people, and no disrespect of the constitution, but where it has become hostile to the rights of the people." He urged that the meeting request the king "to remove from his councils all ministers hostile to the peace of the country, and take such measures as are most effectual to prevent the dangers of impending war."[77]

At least one society of reformers in addition to his own approved highly of Cooper's arguments and suggestions. The London Constitutional Society, on December 14, ordered that his address be published in the newspapers and that one hundred thousand copies be printed by the society and distributed to correspondents in Great Britain and Ireland.[78] At the meeting of the following week, however, the secretary reported that he had offered the address to the *Morning Chronicle* and the *Morning Post* and that both had refused to print it. The latter expressed sorrow that self-preservation would not permit the publication of "this excellent paper, drawn by a masterly hand," which they wished to see in the possession of every Englishman, and asserted that after the verdict against Paine proprietors of newspapers feared to insert anything except "fulsome panegyrics on a depraved legislature and hungry court minions," for anything else was likely to be termed a libel. As late as June of the following year, a man was arrested in Manchester on the

[77] Walker, *Review*, p. 55.

[78] "Proceedings of the Constitutional Society" (London), Dec. 14, 21, 1792, *Second Report of the Committee of Secrecy of the House of Commons*, appendix C; *Annual Register*, XXXV, appendix to chronicle, 77-8.

charge of distributing the address, which was then unofficially termed seditious, but no action was taken against either the distributor or the author.[79] Probably the paper had little circulation elsewhere.

If Cooper's arguments had any influence upon local opinion it was by way of stimulating opposition to his own position and to his group. The meeting at Manchester was, according to an account which doubtless was not unbiased, "a more respectable and numerous meeting than ever was remembered on any former occasion" and it proceeded to commend the government and all its works.[80] It resulted in the forming of an association to preserve the happy existing order against the efforts of "levellers" and "republicans" and to support the executive power in counteracting all attempts at treason and sedition. The large committee which was appointed to carry the resolutions into effect included the borough-reeve and constables, and in due time it offered a reward of ten guineas to informers of sedition. In none of these actions could the reform societies have found much occasion for rejoicing, and the riot which occurred the same evening disclosed to them even more convincingly the dangerous ebbing of their fortunes.

During the autumn the two conservative papers had teemed with inflammatory paragraphs against the "Jacobins" and "equality incendiaries," who were deceiving the working people, they said, and leading them to believe that all things would soon be held in common and that they would not have to work any longer.[81] One pertinent question doubtless gave many influential citizens pause, "What would become of the manufacturers of this town,

79 See below, p. 70.

80 Manchester *Chronicle*, Dec. 15, 1792.

81 Wheeler's *Chronicle* and Harrop's *Mercury; cf.* Walker, *Review*, pp. 45-8, for quotation from the latter, Dec. 4.

and its neighbourhood, were all men upon an *equality?*"[82] The reform societies did not meekly submit to misrepresentation, but in a handbill distributed early in December answered the charge that they were "levellers."[83] They denied that they contended for equality of wealth and insisted that they sought equality of rights before the law, in elections, and in the exercise of talents. They claimed that they did not urge that all men be perpetually equal, for God and nature had forbidden this, but that all mankind should "start fair in the race of life."

This clash of hopes and fears, appearing here by no means for the first time in England and destined to reappear many times in imperfect human society, expressed itself in Manchester in something more than an exchange of rallying cries and epithets. The meeting of December 11 was held at noon and it was soon reported that there would be a riot that night. According to one report, "the unthinking and imprudent part of the populace" "got plenty of liquor," and it was perhaps because of this fact that rumor was proved veracious.[84] The booksellers Falkner and Birch, publishers of the *Herald,* had gained the ill will of the foes of sedition because the reformers were accustomed to resort to their shop for news and because their paper was sympathetic with the latter group. A mob which raised the shout, "Church and King,—Damn Tom Paine," and which was probably little discouraged by officers of the law, attacked the shop and house and smashed the windows. The following evening, Walker's

[82] Editorial in the *Chronicle,* Dec. 1. The hostility of this paper to the reformers greatly increased during 1792; *cf.* its reply to the charge of changing sides, Oct. 27.

[83] Walker, *Review,* pp. 46-8 n.

[84] *Ibid.,* p. 59. Walker gives his own account of the events and quotes letters from two observers, *ibid.,* pp. 55-70. An account, less critical of the rioters and officials of the law, is given in the London *Morning Chronicle,* Dec. 13-15, 1792.

house, where the constitutional society had just met, was attacked several times and had many windows broken. Walker finally dispersed the crowd by firing over their heads, and the next day saved himself by expostulation. For his escape from molestation, Cooper was probably indebted to the ten miles which separated his home near Bolton from Market Square.

In various letters to the press after the event, Walker sought to absolve the "friends of the people" from all charge of tumult and sedition, and to show that their efforts were all directed to the promotion of prosperity and happiness.[85] Certain insinuations made by him regarding the instigation and ulterior purpose of the disorder and the excessive prudence of the guardians of the law led to an indecisive controversy with the borough-reeve and constables. By this time few in Manchester were open to conviction on any partisan question. The citizenry were divided into two sharply distinguished factions, of which the larger had the sympathy, if not the backing, of the officials of the law.

In a discussion in the house of commons, December 17, Grey and Fox sought to explain the disorder in Manchester and the earlier riot in Birmingham on the ground of religious rather than political antagonism.[86] Invective against Dissenters, libelous in its character, had gone unpunished, they claimed, and had done more to cause disaffection and disorder than had the activities of the reformers. Grey stated that the destruction of the houses of Cooper and Walker was reported, thus indicating the association of these two men in the public mind. William Windham, defending the government, said that no partiality had been shown and that the indignation against Walker was due rather to his political than religious

85 *Review*, pp. 67-86.
86 For the entire discussion, see *Parl. Hist.*, XXX, 128-37.

opinions. He felt that "it was natural and even justifiable for men to feel indignation against those who promulgated doctrines, threatening all that was valuable and dear in society; and if there were not means of redress by law, even violence would be justifiable."[87] Walker's heated rejoinder to this at a considerably later date[88] doubtless brought little conviction of error to the advocates of repression, and the address in justification of their conduct and aims, issued by the three reform societies of Manchester on December 20,[89] probably brought little reassurance to a government whose fear of sedition had become hysterical. Although the harassed societies stated that they would continue to meet, peaceably but firmly, to carry forward their avowed objects, this was their last public act.

The English reformers in general were doubtless unwilling to approve of the Reign of Terror in France, and with the outbreak of war between that country and their own in February, 1793, correspondence with the revolutionists became impracticable, as well as undesirable. By this time, if not earlier, Cooper ceased to sympathize with the revolutionists, of whom he had once hoped so much. Early in 1794, after his return from a prospecting trip to the United States, he severely criticized the French and contrasted them with the Americans who were now holding out to him the hand of hope.[90] He said that, highly as he approved of much of the political theory which the French had adopted, he could not approve of the "ferocious injustice of many of their practices." He spoke specifically of their court procedure, their actions against the interests of property, their sup-

[87] *Ibid.*, XXX, 135.   [88] *Review*, 1794, pp. 87-92.
[89] *Ibid.*, pp. 92-5, an address inspired by Fox's speech in the course of the debate of Dec. 13.
[90] *Some Information respecting America*, pp. 75-7. See below, pp. 75 ff.

pression of freedom of speech and action, their delight in executions, and their animosity to the English.

All these circumstances, much as I admire the many great qualities of the French nation, would excite me to shun the society of the present generation of that country. They are a wonderful people; but in my opinion rather to be admired at a distance, than fit for a peaceable man to reside among. . . . I look for happiness amid the attachments of friends and kindred; where the obligations of private society shall be inviolable; where I may talk folly and be forgiven; where I may differ from my neighbour in politics and religion with impunity; and where I may have time to correct erroneous opinions without the orthodox intervention of the halter or the guillotine. Such times may and will come in France, but I fear not before the present race shall die away.

He thoroughly approved of the revolution while it was passing through its more theoretical stages and sought the overthrow of ancient despotism in the name of the natural rights of man, but disapproved of the injustices which marked the course of destruction and the new tyranny which replaced the old. It was in the name of the rights and liberty of the individual that he first supported the revolution and then protested against it. In the end, he disapproved of conservative, aristocratic England and turbulent, radical France for essentially the same reason. In neither land could one be truly free.

The coercion of radicalism in England continued with increasing rigor. On February 28, in the commons, Sheridan moved a committee of inquiry into reports of sedition, but the motion was finally lost without a division.[91] In his speech in opposition to it, Burke made reference to Cooper and Watt by name.[92] He claimed that an English

[91] For the whole debate, see *Parl. Hist.*, XXX, 523-57.
[92] *Ibid.*, XXX, 552.

faction was trying to force the nation into an alliance with France, but made specific reference only to correspondence and activities prior to the outbreak of war. Among other things, he spoke of the address of Cooper and Watt to the Jacobins and more particularly of their participation in the fête of the soldiers of Château-Vieux, and of the subscription opened in Manchester for the widows of the Marseillois who fell on August 10.

There is no reason to believe that the Manchester reformers were active, much less seditious, after December 20, 1792, when they published their last address. Unable to meet at public houses, all three organizations took advantage of Walker's hospitality until June, 1793, when legal proceedings against some of their members began. In March of that year, Falkner and Birch discontinued the *Herald* and fled before the storm.[93] A handbill surrounded by a border of black described the death of "Monsieur Herald" as due to six mortal wounds, that is, six indictments, and not to the earlier assault and battery.[94] Cooper and Walker were named as among the pall-bearers.

Rumors that charges of high treason had been preferred against Walker became current, and he finally succeeded in forcing an actual trial in April, 1794, when he was accused of unlawfully trying to overthrow the constitution and government of the kingdom and of speaking seditious words against the king.[95] Erskine served as counsel and Cooper, then returned from his visit to

[93] Leary, (Manchester) *Directory of 1788*, biography of Matthew Falkner, p. 45.

[94] C. H. Temperley, *Dictionary of Printers and Printing*, p. 775 n. It will be remembered that the office of the publishers had been attacked on December 11.

[95] *The Trial of Thomas Walker* gives a full account with the indictment, testimony, speeches, etc. Appendices I-XI show Walker's efforts to secure a trial. *Cf.* Howell, *State Trials*, XXIII, 1055-1166.

America, was instrumental in bringing about the indictment and conviction of a perjurer who bore false testimony against his friend.[96] By the acquittal of Walker the
conduct of the entire group of reformers was cleared of
all charge of sedition. Before his case could be brought
up, proceedings were begun against various individuals,
all of whom were acquitted save one.[97] Benjamin Booth,
upon the testimony of Dunn the perjurer, was convicted
of "damning the king," but he was later pardoned. There
were no proceedings against Cooper. Booth was arrested
in June, 1793, charged with having distributed a seditious
paper on the subject of war signed "Sydney."[98] This was
Cooper's address, now in a new edition. No indictment
was preferred on this ground, however, so Cooper cannot
be said to have been directly involved in any prosecution.
It is hard to see how he could have escaped, unless it were
because of his impending emigration, if his conduct had
not been legally unexceptionable.

So far as the Manchester reformers were concerned,
the fears of the government seem to have been unjustifiable. Without inquiring into the question whether parliamentary reform at this time would or would not have
been perilous, we can say that Cooper and his friends
advocated a legitimate measure in a legitimate way. More
lawlessness was manifested by their local enemies than
by themselves, and the essential correctness of their conduct after war had begun was indicated by the failure of
the proceedings against them. The prosecutions themselves were a mistake. They served only to bring unde-
served and unnecessary inconvenience and suffering
upon earnest and patriotic men and to embitter their

[96] *Trial of Walker*, p. 105; *Review*, p. 89 n.

[97] *Trial of Walker*, appendices XIII-XX. William Paul, Samuel Jackson, James Cheetham and Oliver Pearsall were acquitted.

[98] *Trial of Walker*, appendix XIX; Walker, *Review*, p. 96.

lives. In the case of Cooper, the result of the whole political development was to drive him from England, where he might have served usefully as a citizen, to another land. One of his friends urged that he bear with his countrymen a few years more and remain to help "stem the torrent of folly."[99] Perhaps he might have done so had he not been one of those who cannot rest from travel.

It seems improbable that the failure of Cooper's firm played any direct part in causing his emigration. When he sailed for America in August, 1793, Baker, Teasdale, Bridges, and Cooper were at least solvent, but in November, when he was yet exploring the United States, a sale of the property of the firm was announced "by order of the trustees."[100] Apparently there was not technical bankruptcy, but a sale was forced by the creditors. The long lists of bankrupts in the newspapers and numerous references there to economic distress indicate that 1793 was a bad year, especially among calico-printers.[101] It was generally felt that the stagnation of trade was due to the war, and it was said that the large unemployment led many to join the army. Cooper's forebodings about the results of war were to this extent justified, but probably he had not reckoned on the loss of his own fortune. He seems to have saved something from the wreckage, for he had means to invest in a land scheme in Pennsylvania

[99] Felix Vaughan, writing after Booth's conviction. Jerrold, "Thomas Walker the Elder," *Original*, pp. 86-7.

[100] The first announcement of the sale was made in the Manchester *Chronicle*, Nov. 9, 1793, and numerous announcements were made early in 1794; *cf.* an announcement of a meeting of the creditors, Manchester *Mercury*, Feb. 25, 1794. Part of the sale seems to have been made by the firm itself, *ibid.*, March 4. The name of the firm has not been found on any list of bankrupts during the period and the term "bankrupt" was not used in any of the advertisements.

[101] *Cf.* a communication to the Manchester *Chronicle*, April 20, 1793; Jno. Reilly, *History of Manchester*, pp. 279-80; Prentice, *Historical Sketches*, p. 22.

and was able at least to establish his family comfortably there.[102] His days of financial independence, however, were over; and financial necessities were destined in America somewhat to restrict his freedom of action and at times even to teach him prudence.

The end of the first great period in the life of Thomas Cooper found him disillusioned and somewhat baffled, momentarily defeated, but not yet discouraged. He had not found among his own countrymen or among the seemingly more congenial spirits across the channel that concern or reverence which he himself so strongly felt for eternal truth. Free inquiry was discouraged, his own convictions were misinterpreted, reform was blocked by what he regarded as stupid conservatism or perverted to intolerable anarchy and tyranny, human interest was flagrantly belittled or disregarded. So this knight-errant of freedom and humanity turned toward a new land, where, as fate would have it, he was to struggle against one tyranny or another for almost half a century.

102 See below, p. 80.

PART TWO: PENNSYLVANIA

CHAPTER III

ENGLISH REFUGEES AND AMERICAN FEDERALISTS, 1794-1799

To the liberty-loving spirit of Thomas Cooper reactionary England had become a veritable house of bondage, and revolutionary France, however admirable in republican theory, was best observed from afar. America appeared as a land of promise. He had no thought to pause and rust unburnished; it was not yet too late to seek another world. He first came to the United States, not as an immigrant or a political adventurer but as a visitor and investigator, seeking first-hand acquaintance with the land which he hoped would serve him and his persecuted English friends as a haven of refuge and would offer free play to talents now unappreciated.

In August, 1793, when he was not yet thirty-four years old, he embarked for America in company with two of Joseph Priestley's sons and a portion of his own family, and in February of the following year he left New York to return to England to fetch the rest of his family to what he now judged to be in reality as well as reputation a land of freedom.[1] During this visit he spent a considerable time in New York and even longer in Pennsylvania, and made a prospecting trip into the regions of the upper Susquehanna where ultimately he settled.[2] Information

[1] *Some Information respecting America* (referred to hereafter as *America*), preface; Rutt, *Life of Priestley*, II, 205.
[2] *America*, letter IV.

about other regions of the country he gained largely through personal conferences with representatives of the various sections which the presence of the federal government at Philadelphia made possible.[3] No section escaped his consideration, and upon what he regarded as adequate information he based his conclusion that America was preferable to both England and France,[4] that Pennsylvania was the most attractive of the states, and that for him and his friends the counties of Northumberland, Luzerne, and Northampton offered the most fruitful promise.[5] The regions where slavery prevailed he dismissed from consideration as unsuitable to himself and others of like convictions, little dreaming, we may be sure, that the last years of his life were to be spent in the state which, most completely of all, was committed to the system of African slavery, and that he himself was to become one of the staunchest defenders of South Carolina and her social and political philosophy.

Upon his return to England he was pressed by so many inquiries respecting the state of society, the means of living, and the inducements to settle in America, that he determined to reply in print to the questions which had been put to him most frequently.[6] In 1794 there appeared, from the press of London and Dublin, his *Some Information respecting America,* a volume which may be regarded as the forerunner of the interminable procession of books, pamphlets, and newspaper articles which during the forty-five years of his life in the United States was to issue from his restless pen. He himself declared the work to be plain, incomplete, and in no sense entertaining, but there is value for the historian in the recorded observations of a highly intelligent foreign visitor

3 *Ibid.*, preface.　　　　4 *Ibid.*, pp. 52-5, 75-80.
5 *Ibid.*, letter I.　　　　6 *Ibid.*, preface.

who admitted, however, a certain predilection for the country of which he wrote.

Its government, indeed, he described with enthusiasm and adopted somewhat prematurely as his own:

There is little fault to find with the government of America, either in principle or in practice: we have very few taxes to pay, and these are of acknowledged necessity, and moderate in amount: we have no animosities about religion; it is a subject about which no questions are asked: we have few respecting political men or political measures: the present irritation of men's minds in Great Britain, and the discordant state of society on political accounts is not known there. The government is the government *of* the people, and *for* the people.[7]

In his optimistic description of American political democracy he anticipated the greater part of Lincoln's famous saying. He described the differences between the Federalists and Anti-Federalists in the way which has become conventional and remarked upon the greater moderation of political controversy in America than in England.[8] He gave no marked indication of his own political preferences. He and his companion bore letters of introduction to John Adams from Priestley the elder,[9] who was on most friendly terms with the former minister to England, and doubtless had no foreboding of the painful alienation which was to come. Joseph Barnes, who for many years corresponded with his patron, Thomas Jefferson, gave each of them a letter of introduction to him.[10] The references which this made to democracy and suffering for the cause of freedom must have strongly commended the visitors to the secretary of state, who was so soon to retire from this position to form a political group

[7] *Ibid.*, pp. 53-4.   [8] *Ibid.*, pp. 67-9.
[9] Priestley, *Letters to the Inhabitants of Northumberland*, 1801, p. 48.
[10] August 17, 1793, Jefferson Papers (Library of Congress), XCI.

in opposition to aristocracy and repression. Mutual appreciation might easily have been anticipated but it was yet unexpressed.

The general commendation of the state of society in America which Cooper gave was somewhat surprising as coming from a man of learning, but was entirely natural in a strong utilitarian and passionate lover of freedom. He described the life in the large towns as being very similar to that in the towns in England, while life in the settled country he regarded as preferable in America, because of the absence of rich proprietors and great lords and because of the prevalence of moderate holdings and general prosperity. The great advantage and attraction of America, as one who had recently suffered financial reverses saw it, was "the total absence of anxiety respecting the future success of a family."[11] Here also, in the country at least, a man was appreciated rather for what he was than for what he seemed. A false step was not irretrievable, and every employment had room for industry. He spoke to his English friends as one who already regarded himself as an American, "In fine, *ours* is a rising country. I am sorry to say it, but I fear *yours* is a falling country."[12]

His optimism extended even to the future of learning and literature. The people were not ignorant, newspapers and book-societies abounded, and though learning in the European sense was uncommon, good sense and some reading were universal. There was yet no distinct literary class, but America had already produced men of great distinction and would certainly produce more. He remarked upon the inadequacy of libraries, which he was later to bemoan, and recognized that since the war the Americans had been more absorbed in the improvement of their pockets than their minds, but confidently pre-

[11] *America,* p. 52.   [12] *Ibid.,* p. 57.

dicted that the new generation would devote itself more than had the old to literature, philosophy, and the arts.[13] Here a man of science and learning, such as he admitted himself to be, might well hope to be both serviceable and conspicuous.

American opportunities commended themselves no less to the sons of Joseph Priestley. The eldest and youngest of these accompanied Cooper on his visit of observation and the second, William, after a stay in France, determined also to go to the United States. It was primarily on their account that Priestley the elder decided to emigrate. After the riot in July, 1791, had caused him to remove from Birmingham, he had been in somewhat uncertain status and his situation in England became increasingly unpleasant, even though it was not hazardous. The hostility to him prevented his placing his sons to advantage in their native land and when they felt impelled to seek their fortunes elsewhere he determined to join them.[14] The personal intimacy between him and Cooper had not been so great in England as it was later to become in America, where they were to keep their books and apparatus under the same roof and, certainly by 1799 and possibly even earlier, were to live together; but close kinship of spirit had manifested itself long before they left England and in the entire emigration project Cooper was associated with the Priestleys. His arguments and representations probably did much to overcome the reluctance of the older man.

It seems unlikely that when Dr. and Mrs. Priestley landed in New York, June 4, 1794, Thomas Cooper with his wife and younger children landed with them;[15] and

[13] *Ibid.*, pp. 64-6.

[14] Priestley, *Memoirs*, I, 118-20, 125-6; Rutt, *Life of Priestley*, II, 118-19, 170-1, 223, 238. He went first to London, and in December, 1791, succeeded to Price's pulpit at Hackney.

[15] *Memoirs*, I, 163; Rutt, II, 234 n. There is no mention of Cooper in the

apparently he had no share in the expressions of regret at the departure of the more venerable and more lovable man from England,[16] or in the enthusiastic welcome which he received in America. Priestley's progress from New York through Philadelphia to Northumberland was almost triumphal. The clergy were generally suspicious[17] and William Cobbett stated with malice aforethought that Washington refused to see him for fear of displeasing the British,[18] but several officials did him honor[19] and he was showered with resolutions from democratic, anti-British, and learned societies.[20] Cooper probably landed at some other time during the summer and proceeded more directly to his new home. He was yet an inconspicuous man and until the campaign of 1799 and 1800 gained notice chiefly through his association with Priestley.

During their visit to America, or perhaps even earlier, Cooper and Joseph Priestley, Jr., had formed the project, with other Englishmen, of fathering an English settlement in America.[21] This they proposed to establish on Loyalsock Creek in Pennsylvania, about fifty miles north of the town of Northumberland. The settlement was not to be confined to any particular class of men, religious or political, but was meant simply to be a rallying point for English immigrants, who it was thought would be happier in a society of an accustomed kind than if scattered through the country. According to the younger Priestley, the original projectors reserved only a few shares for themselves and paid the full price for these.

letters written by Priestley and his wife in description of the voyage, and in one of these the statement is made that the only other woman cabin passenger was from France. Rutt, II, 231; cf. 229-30, 235-7.

[16] *Memoirs*, II, appendix 6, ix-x; Rutt, II, 212-22, 225 n.

[17] Rutt, II, 263.   [18] *Porcupine's Works*, 1801, I, 139.

[19] Rutt, II, 234 n.

[20] *Memoirs*, II, appendix 6, x; Rutt, II, 241-2, 247-55, 261-2.

[21] Rutt, II, 238-9 and note; *America*, pp. 73 n., 74-5.

Cooper was enthusiastic for the project when he wrote his *America,* which apparently had as an object the encouragement of settlers, but the scheme fell through. Young Priestley regarded this as fortunate, for he felt that, owing to the erroneous ideas held by the English immigrants and their ill-adaptation to wilderness life, "the projectors would most probably have been subject to still more unfounded abuse than they have been, for their well-meant endeavours to promote the interests of their countrymen."[22]

Dr. and Mrs. Priestley went to Northumberland because it was the town nearest the proposed settlement, and when the project failed remained there because they liked the locality.[23] A distinguished French visitor who saw it in 1795 was far from enthusiastic about the village, stating that it contained about one hundred houses and was undoubtedly the worst-built town he and his traveling companions had yet seen. Of its future development, however, he was hopeful.[24] Cooper's family[25] probably arrived about the same time as the Priestleys. By spring he was engaged in clearing and preparing for cultivation a tract of some hundred acres which he had bought, and ill-adapted as he was to a retired rural life, is reported to have said that he preferred his present mode of living to any other.[26] At his trial for sedition in 1800, he stated that his practice was his principal means

[22] Rutt, II, 239 n.   [23] *Memoirs,* I, 126-7, 165.

[24] La Rochefoucault Liancourt, *Travels through the United States,* I, 69.

[25] The children of Thomas Cooper and Alice Greenwood numbered five certainly: Charles, who left no children; Eliza, who married Dr. Joseph Manners of Clifton, N. J.; John, later a judge, who married Mary Spering and left many descendants; and two other sons of whom there is no record. Information gained from a letter of Dr. J. M. Baldy, Meriwether Collection, University of South Carolina. Since Cooper referred to his large family (*America,* preface), it may be assumed that three or more children were living at the time of his emigration.

[26] La Rochefoucault Liancourt, *Travels,* I, 76.

of support, certain sources of income in England having failed him.[27] Presumably he began the practice of law immediately upon his settlement in Northumberland, although his income from this source could hardly have been sufficient to support him at the beginning. He stated later that he frequently acted as consulting physician, although he made it a custom to accept no fees for medical services.[28] He had studied anatomy in England and in due time ranked high as a chemist, so was doubtless well qualified to practice medicine, although as yet without a medical degree.

Though he was suspected, a few months after his arrival, of aiming at a seat in Congress,[29] there is nothing to show that he played any active part in public affairs during his first years in America. Perhaps he deliberately held aloof as long as possible, as Priestley claimed he himself did. Doubtless the two Englishmen spent much time in reading, scientific experiment, and philosophical and theological discussion. Priestley's wife died in September, 1796,[30] and Cooper may have taken up his residence with him following that event. He was certainly living with him in 1799.[31] Writing in defense of himself in that year, Priestley stated, in disproof of the charge that he was in straitened circumstances, that his house, which was completed in 1797, was superior to any in the county, and outside Philadelphia was surpassed by few in the state, while his library and philosophical apparatus were much more valuable than the house and were supe-

27 *An Account of the Trial of Thomas Cooper*, p. 50; Wharton, *State Trials*, p. 677.

28 Letter to the trustees of the University of Pennsylvania, August 4, 1818, printed in E. F. Smith's *Life of Robert Hare*, pp. 58-61.

29 La Rochefoucault Liancourt, *Travels*, I, 76.

30 Rutt, II, 354.

31 At the time of the publication of his own *Political Essays*. *Memoirs of Priestley*, I, 200-1.

rior to anything of the kind in America.[32] The facilities
for study and investigation which were open to Cooper,
then, were unexcelled in America, if not superior to anything the country afforded. We may imagine him, in the
quiet and leisure which must have been afforded by an
outlying Pennsylvania village, luxuriating in learning.
Here he must have stored in his capacious intellectual
treasure-house many a gem of philosophy, science, and
even literature—for he did not yet despise the poets,
playwrights, and novelists—with which, at a later day,
the eyes of the unlearned were to be dazzled.

Judging from the enthusiastic support given the cause
of Jefferson afterwards by Northumberland County, the
community at this time must have been not unfavorably
disposed toward fugitives from English persecution.
Apparently the inhabitants were friendly and respectful
to the refugees, whether or not they were capable of fully
appreciating their services to science and freedom. Unitarianism was undoubtedly foreign to the religious
thought and practice of the community, and the newcomers never regarded it as possible to establish a distinct Unitarian congregation. Priestley accordingly held
religious services every Sunday, first at his own residence
and later in a neighboring schoolroom,[33] and these Cooper
probably attended. His respect for Priestley was unbounded, and while he was even now regarded by his
friend as an unbeliever,[34] he tolerated a religious faith
and practice which had in them so little of mystery and
no order of priesthood.

Priestley seems to have adopted a deliberate policy of
avoiding all political discussion and controversy,[35] but
however desirous of political obscurity he may have been,

[32] Letters to the Inhabitants of Northumberland, I.
[33] Memoirs, I, 191.   [34] Rutt, II, 231, 295.
[35] Ibid., II, 378; Letters to the Inhabitants of Northumberland, passim.

his reputation prevented his long remaining unmolested. The glad shouts of welcome which he received from the anti-British groups and the men of learning were soon more than matched by the contemptuous invective of that arch-enemy of Jacobinism, William Cobbett (Peter Porcupine), who launched a scurrilous pamphlet on Priestley's emigration within a month of the arrival of the venerable philosopher at his hoped-for haven of refuge.[36] From that time forward the baying of the Federalist pack was never long silenced. Before many months they raised the cry against Cooper also, but for the present he was safe in his covert at Northumberland.

Cobbett described the circumstances of the riot in Birmingham and the subsequent award of damages to Priestley in such a way as to justify the rioters and imply that Priestley did not suffer. He ridiculed the addresses to him upon his arrival, as being from "several societies of scoundrels, under various denominations."[37] He referred with alarm to his French citizenship, belittled his scientific attainments, and asserted that he meditated violence against the American commonwealth and the government of England. Contemptuous references to Priestley recurred in Cobbett's pamphlets and in his *Porcupine's Gazette* whenever there was the slightest pretext.[38] In the spring of 1797, Priestley preached a sermon in Philadelphia urging charity for poor emigrants, which was ridiculed by Cobbett in a characteristic pamphlet. A few weeks later, in a letter to a friend in

[36] *Observations on Priestley's Emigration.* This was first published in August, 1794, went through at least four editions in Philadelphia, and was published in Liverpool and in several editions in London. See *Porcupine's Works,* I, 151-215.

[37] *Porcupine's Works,* I, 121.

[38] *Cf. ibid.,* VI, 411-12; VII, 149-50; IX, 388-410; and Priestley, *Letters to the Inhabitants of Northumberland,* VI.

England, the distressed old man complained of this abuse:

The writer of that scurrilous pamphlet on my emigration now publishes a daily paper, in which he frequently introduces my name in the most opprobrious manner, though I never take the least notice of him; and have had nothing to do with the politics of the country; . . . He, every day, advertizes his pamphlet against me, and after my name adds, "commonly known by the name of the firebrand philosopher." He also publishes a periodical pamphlet called the Political Censor, in which he never fails to mention me in a similar manner.[39]

He later complained of an even more derogatory expression, for Cobbett had said, "I hope I shall see the malignant old Tartuff of Northumberland begging his bread through the streets of Philadelphia, and ending his days in the poorhouse, without a friend to close his eyes."[40]

Not until 1798, however, was Priestley goaded to make public rejoinder to the strictures of Cobbett. During that summer two letters which had been found by the British upon a Danish ship were published, first in England and then in America. One of these was addressed to Priestley from Paris by a former parishioner, J. H. Stone, and the other was enclosed for delivery to "M. B. P.," who was later revealed as Benjamin Vaughan, a former member of parliament but now a refugee in America. These led to the charge in England that Stone and Priestley were apostates, while Cobbett charged them with being spies in the interest of France. Since Stone described with great satisfaction the progress and prospects of the French in their struggle against the British, the irritation of the British press was natural; and a contemptu-

[39] To Rev. T. Lindsey, April 30, 1797. Rutt, II, 377-8.
[40] *Letters to the Inhabitants of Northumberland*, p. 2.

ous reference to President Adams naturally offended patriotic Americans.

Upon the publication of Stone's letters, first in *Porcupine's Gazette*[41] and successively in Federalist papers throughout the country, Priestley sent Cobbett a letter of explanation and defense, claiming that he was in no sense responsible for the sentiments of his correspondent.[42] Cobbett forthwith issued a pamphlet[43] with intent to prove that "this Apostle of Sedition," wherever he went, was still hostile to all lawful power and still an admirer of the "woeful revolution in France," that he still maintained implacable hatred for Great Britain and wished her revolutionized and ruined. He claimed that Priestley was responsible for the sentiments expressed in the letters until he should disavow them and the friendship of Stone. Priestley had fallen into an embarrassed and degraded situation in America, he said, and for his future home and fortune looked to France. His guilt in this particular instance was apparent to all who were "uncorrupted by the base and despicable principles of the Priestlean school."[44]

Cooper would have borne such attacks much less patiently, for even Priestley said that his feelings might be "something too quick."[45] Probably he was already growing restless. And if the enthusiastic observer of American life was not yet willing to retract his assertion that there was greater moderation in American political controversy than in English, there were experiences yet in store for his revered friend and himself which would necessitate a reconsideration of his hasty earlier generalization. In the bitter political controversy of the late years of the

[41] *Porcupine's Works*, IX, 224-45.
[42] *Ibid.*, IX, 247-8; *cf. Letters to the Inhabitants of Northumberland*, V.
[43] *Ibid.*, IX, 245-78.   [44] *Ibid.*, IX, 278.
[45] *Letters to the Inhabitants of Northumberland*, p. 48.

administration of John Adams, he himself was to play a rôle which could by no stretch of the imagination be termed one of moderation.

The attacks upon Priestley by Cobbett and the Federalist press would have been enough to force the English refugee and his disciple into the camp of Jefferson, but probably they would have arrived there in any case. Priestley indeed had known Adams in England and received from him several expressions of appreciation immediately following his own arrival in Philadelphia.[46] The lectures of the Unitarian divine in that city in 1796 were faithfully attended by the vice-president, and were dedicated to him;[47] but by the following spring a coolness had developed between the two men.[48] This was aggravated by the silence with which Adams treated the application which Priestley and Cooper made, in August, for the appointment of the latter as agent of the United States before the board of commissioners in Philadelphia, by virtue of article six of the treaty of amity and commerce with Great Britain.[49] Cobbett and other Federalist writers later explained the hostility of Cooper and Priestley to Adams on the ground of the disappointment of their hopes of political preferment, declaring that when they failed to be rewarded by a government which they had honored by their immigration, and were denied

[46] *Account of the Trial of Cooper*, appendix 6. For the association of Adams with Priestley in England, see the former's *Works*, III, 396, 397, 420.

[47] *Discourses relating to the Evidences of Revealed Religion*, pp. iii-vii. Adams was rather fearful lest the dedication to him would get him the character of a heretic, but at this time unquestionably approved of Priestley. *Works*, I, 488; *cf.* Rutt, *Life of Priestley*, II, 336.

[48] Priestley to Rev. T. Belsham, Jan. 11, 1798, Rutt, II, 391.

[49] See below, pp. 104-8. For the letters of Priestley and Cooper, see *Account of the Trial of Cooper*, pp. 5-7; Wharton, *State Trials*, 661. Adams said he made no reply because he never answered letters of solicitation, *Works*, IX, 13.

an opportunity to exert their eminent talents in official position, they turned with bitterness upon the administration! With the candidacy of McKean, an "avowed friend of France," for governor of Pennsylvania in 1799, the "emigrated philosophers" looked with confidence to him, and that they might have ground for pretension, "zealously, ably and efficaciously" supported his cause.[50]

This explanation of the political attitude of Priestley and Cooper in the controversial years 1799 and 1800, given by their political foes, is upon its face neither accurate nor just. There is no sufficient reason to question the oft-repeated statement of Priestley that he refrained from politics and political discussion as long as possible. He was not even naturalized. Appreciating and reciprocating the early cordiality of Adams, he relied upon it in making an application for his friend which he thought entirely defensible, for, although Cooper had favored Jefferson's candidacy for the presidency in 1796 and made no effort to disguise his political sentiments, party lines were not yet sharply drawn and Priestley thought him eminently qualified for the position.

Even the frankly hostile Cobbett admitted that Priestley's letter to Adams and that of Cooper which accompanied it had in them nothing that was demeaning, but breathed as independent a spirit as letters on such a subject possibly could.[51] Priestley stated frankly that he and his friend were described as democrats and were studi-

[50] Cobbett, reply to Priestley, April 30, 1800, *Porcupine's Works*, XI, 395-434. See below, pp. 104-8. Cobbett claimed that Priestley sought the chaplaincy of Adams's first congress and wanted the treasurership of the mint, even if he did not actually apply for it. The latter did get a few votes in the election of chaplain of the house of representatives, but was not actually nominated. *Annals of Congress*, 5 Cong., I, 635. The charge of aggressive seeking of office by Priestley seems preposterous.

[51] *Porcupine's Works*, XI, 400; *cf.* Priestley, *Letters to the Inhabitants of Northumberland*, pp. 44-9.

ously represented as enemies of government, but claimed that they had been persecuted for being friends of American liberty and that their preference for the government of the United States had brought them hither. He thought Cooper's politics no ground for objection to his appointment and vouched for his unquestionable ability and his fidelity to his trust. Cooper's accompanying letter stated that the objection mentioned by his proposer might reasonably be deemed of weight, but that he saw no impropriety in the application.

It is not unreasonable to suppose that the rejection of this application caused the Northumbrians to be less favorably disposed to President Adams than they had been formerly. Meanwhile, Jefferson was beginning to manifest appreciation of Priestley, somewhat cautiously it may be at first, but with increasing enthusiasm. Thus began a thoroughly natural friendship between men of essentially similar opinions and many common interests, for Jefferson was highly appreciative of science and, indeed, of all sorts of learning and was even freer than Priestley in his religious views. As they became more intimate, the older man several times expressed to certain of his correspondents the pious hope that Jefferson was not, after all, an unbeliever.[52] Jefferson, on his side, lamented the small consideration which Cooper had given the piedmont of Virginia and the Shenandoah Valley when seeking a location for himself and Priestley.[53] Jefferson's friendship for the old chemist did not burst into full flower before the fateful election year, 1800, by which time unmistakeable evidence had been given of political loyalty to himself. The intimacy with the

[52] Rutt, II, 373, 511.

[53] Jefferson to Priestley, Jan. 18, 1800, Jefferson Papers, CVI; *cf.* a more general statement of regret in a letter to Tench Coxe, May 1, 1794, *Writings* (Ford), VI, 508.

younger and more impetuous man, which was to continue
so many years and be marked by such a splendid display
of learning on the part of both, came only after the death
of Priestley, when the mantle of Jefferson's friendship
fell from his shoulders upon those of Cooper. But even
before the alienation from Adams, Priestley, and perhaps
Cooper also, had begun to feel the kindly beams of Jefferson's beneficence and this alone would perhaps have
been sufficient to lure them into his political fold.

Apart from any and all of these considerations, however, Priestley and Cooper could by no show of logic have
been other than opponents of the naturalization, alien,
and sedition laws against which, after 1798, the artillery
of the Republicans was chiefly directed. The author of a
sermon in behalf of poor emigrants would naturally have
opposed any stringent limitations upon the naturalization of newcomers to America. Priestley, never having
been naturalized, was himself an alien, and both he and
Cooper thought there was real danger of his being
ordered from the country.[54] Pressure seems to have been
brought to bear upon the president to use the Alien Act
against him. Priestley himself said that the secretary of
state and other officers of the government favored his
deportation, but that in his opinion Adams revolted
against it.[55] In view of the old friendship, perhaps, the
president even warned Priestley to be on his guard. It
was because of his supposed danger, due to current mis-

[54] Rutt, II, 454.

[55] Pickering's hostility to the Northumbrians seems, however, not to have
manifested itself until after they had begun to exert themselves politically.
After the republication in the *Aurora*, July 12, 1799, of Cooper's letter of
June 29, to the readers of the Sunbury and Northumberland *Gazette* (see
below, pp. 101-3), the secretary of state wrote Adams: ''Cooper has taken
care to get himself admitted to citizenship. I am sorry for it; for those who
are desirous of maintaining our internal tranquility must wish them both
[Cooper and Priestley] removed from the United States.'' Adams, *Works*,
IX, 6. Adams's feeling in regard to Priestley would doubtless not have

understanding, that the latter wrote in 1799 his *Letters to the Inhabitants of Northumberland.*[56]

The Sedition Act would naturally have been opposed on general principles by both these protagonists of free speech. The limitations which this law placed upon discussion of the conduct of public officials were offensive to Cooper in theory and galling in practice. The cause for which he fought with consistent zeal and even with heroism throughout his long and not entirely consistent career was freedom of speech. He burned incense at no religious shrine perhaps, but before the altars of Freedom and Truth he did devoutly worship. Since he held that truth was impossible of attainment without freedom of inquiry and discussion there was no conflict of allegiance. No party group which favored interference with what was to him the most sacred of the rights of man could have commanded his support. Here, then, is a sufficient explanation of his political alignment.

Priestley first broke his silence on subjects of political controversy with a paper entitled *Maxims of Political Arithmetic,* which was published in the *Aurora* in February, 1798.[57] A year later Cooper departed from the policy of prudent silence, which must have so fretted his impetuous and controversy-loving spirit. In the spring of 1799, in order to relieve the editor of the Sunbury and Northumberland *Gazette,* who was publishing a work of Priestley's, he assumed temporarily the editorship of that paper and was responsible for it from April 20 through June 29.[58] Except for two replies to one of his own essays,

been fully appreciated by that gentleman. He wrote Pickering, August 13, 1799: "I do not think it wise to execute the alien law against poor Priestley at present. He is as weak as water, as unstable as Reuben, or the wind. His influence is not an atom in the world." *Ibid.,* IX, 14.

[56] See below, pp. 106-8.   [57] Feb. 26, 27.

[58] *Political Essays,* 1st ed., preface.

all the letters and miscellaneous articles which appeared during the period were either composed or selected by him.

There can be no doubt but that he added vigor to this hitherto obscure local paper. He himself stated that his writings "occasioned much conversation—some blame, and some praise," and that a corrected edition of his newspaper essays was called for. A volume entitled *Political Essays* accordingly appeared shortly thereafter, and a second edition issued from the press early in 1800. This provided Jeffersonian ammunition of the first order and assured Cooper's prominence in the Republican campaign. The publication of these essays in pamphlet form led to the charge of duplicity against him; this led to his abusive language against John Adams, and this in turn to his trial for seditious libel. So with the writings in the Sunbury and Northumberland *Gazette,* his first active American campaign began. The days of obscurity and insignificance were over; for no considerable period during the next forty years was the name of Thomas Cooper, whether of Northumberland, Carlisle, Philadelphia, or Columbia, unknown to the American public.

His attitude and the character of his political opinions at this juncture were admirably described by him in the preface to the first edition:

I hope they [the essays] will afford some proof that I remain in this Country what I was in Europe, a decided opposer of political restrictions on the Liberty of the Press, and a sincere friend to those first principles of republican Government, the Sovereignty of the people and the responsibility of their servants. Having adopted these opinions on mature consideration, and the fullest conviction, I shall retain and profess them; but I am sorry to say they are likely ere long to become as unfashionable in this Country as in the Monarchies of Europe.

In this, as well as in later arguments and activities during the campaign which ended with the victory of Jefferson, he was thoroughly consistent with his professions and actions while in Europe. He was running true to form as a member of the opposition. The hopeful enthusiasm of his earliest American days had given way, not to unmitigated pessimism to be sure, but to direful forebodings. Tyranny had raised its ugly head, and a watch-dog of democracy and freedom could but sound the alarm and seek to arouse the complacent and unsuspicious populace.

Oddly enough, the first note sounded by him was one of conservatism. He deplored the opposition to the assessed taxes which had appeared in the neighboring county of Northampton, and rejoiced that there had not been a similar "misguided opposition to the laws" in Northumberland.[59] He took a strong stand in support of obedience to law, pointing out that "there must be an end to all government if laws enacted by constitutional authority are to be violently opposed wherever they are disliked." He approved of the principle of taxation adopted in this case, as fairest in its operation and most favorable to the poor, because the proportion of the tax increased with the wealth and ability of the taxpayer. Throughout his American career he consistently favored undisguised direct taxation and opposed such methods of indirection as involved deception of the ignorant populace. Furthermore, even in his wildest moments, he retained that respect for law which he had brought with him from England and which radically differed from the prevailing feeling of Pennsylvania democrats. It was on

[59] "On the Assessed Taxes," April 20, 1799, *Political Essays*, pp. 3-4. In July, 1798, Congress had levied a direct tax upon lands, houses, and slaves; and in Pennsylvania, in the absence of any considerable number of slaves, the tax fell largely upon houses and lands. Chief objection was made to the house-tax and to the irritating conduct of the assessors in measuring and counting the windows to determine the value of a house. The most serious

this point that he afterwards broke with the extreme wing of his party in its attack upon the judiciary.

In his "Observations on the Fast Day," he sounded a note of hysteria, although he followed good democratic precedent.[60] In the appointment by the president of April 25 as a day of general fasting, he perceived the tendency to join politics and religion and to commence in America an alliance between church and state. He stated that he had no objection to religious acts which were voluntary and sincere. "But," he said, "I hope we shall never be drilled into them, or compelled to wheel to the east, or wheel to the west in religious discipline at the direction of any *man* whatever." He regarded devoutness, kindness, and benevolence as highly desirable, but was decidedly averse to "political religion."

This hysterical outburst drew forth a rejoinder from the wife of Joseph Priestley, Jr., in which Cooper's argument was completely demolished.[61] Because of the slight predilection of the people for religion and the strength of sectarian rivalry in the United States, Mrs. Priestley had little fear of religion's being made an instrument of state intrigue in this country. Cooper's whole argument, indeed, was based upon unfounded fears of the alliance of church and state. He had brought with him to America the point of view of English dissent and seems to have failed to appreciate how different American religious conditions were from those in England. In view of the actual situation, his fears seem fantastic and

opposition came in the well-known Fries's rebellion, which occurred in the most eastern counties. Echoes of opposition, however, were heard in Northampton. *Cf.* McMaster, *History of the People of the United States*, II, 434-9.

[60] April 27, 1799, *Political Essays*, pp. 5-7. *Cf.* McMaster, *United States*, II, 283 ff., for attacks on the fast day of May 9, 1798; and *Aurora*, April 30, 1799, and thereafter, for attacks on the fast day of April 25, 1799.

[61] Signed "E. P.," *Political Essays*, pp. 7-10.

chimerical. A later writer to the *Gazette* remarked in jocular fashion that the readers of the paper had been amused, if not edified, by Cooper's observations on fasting.[62] Apparently these were not taken very seriously.

He was much more in line with justifiable Republican criticism of the administration and made a genuine contribution to the political philosophy of the party in his attacks on the efforts which were being made to muzzle the press and destroy its freedom. He published an extract from a speech of Erskine's on the doctrine of libel,[63] with an introduction by himself, published an essay on the Sedition Act,[64] and in the second edition of the *Essays* added a more philosophical discussion of the freedom of the press.[65] In the introduction to Erskine's speech, he stated that the time *might* come in America when every one who was minded to address the public on political questions would find it worth while to become acquainted with the law of libel, and in the essay on the Sedition Act, he took the position that the time *had* come through the passage of that law. In both writings he pointed out, doubtless not without self-consciousness, that the ablest and most fearless writers would be most likely to suffer the penalties of laws restricting freedom of discussion, and asserted that from the "collision of opinion" all human improvements in metaphysics, morals, government, and religion had proceeded.

He specifically objected to the Sedition Act on the

[62] "On Political Nicknames," signed "Countryman," *ibid.*, p. 17.

[63] *Ibid.*, pp. 11-13. Erskine in defense of an English publisher, Stockdale, who was prosecuted for publishing observations by Rev. Mr. Loggan of Leith on the trial of Hastings.

[64] *Ibid.*, pp. 13-17.

[65] "On the Propriety and Expediency of unlimited Enquiry," *ibid.*, 2 ed., pp. 59-88. Part I by E. P. (Mrs. Joseph Priestley, Jr.), preface and part II by Cooper. The final arguments were largely taken from the preface to his *Tracts, Ethical, Theological and Political*, 1789.

ground that it was unconstitutional; on the ground that it required for the vindication of an alleged offender legal proof of his charges, which might be almost impossible to give even though the facts were notorious; and, most of all, because it involved the indictment of *opinion,* of which there was no infallible criterion. He saw in the act the well-known expedient of a bad government to shield itself from criticism, and regarded it as highly improper and most indelicate that such a law had been passed by the party in power and that its enforcement had been left in the hands of partisans of the administration.

Cooper's entire treatment of the doctrine of the freedom of the press was broadly philosophical in tone, as befitted a disinterested seeker after truth, with only slight indication of personal pique against the administration; and in its scope far surpassed current Republican arguments, such as appeared in the party press and reflected the much narrower point of view of immediate political opposition. He opposed restriction, not primarily because it had been adopted as an administration measure, but because he felt it to be essentially incompatible with that freedom of inquiry, which throughout his life he consistently advocated as the *sine qua non* of all intellectual and social progress. His concern was not merely for freedom in America, where the absence of it so hampered the furthering of the Republican cause, but for freedom everywhere, because everywhere it was a supreme desideratum.

He insisted that he was concerned in this discussion, not with the private conduct of individuals and the question of slander, but with freedom of inquiry into public measures and the conduct of public men, in which the public had an indubitable interest. He was opposed here, as always, to secrecy and mystery, whether in church or state. "The more we understand of the science of government," he said, "the less necessity we find for governmental secrets. State-craft and priest-craft are fond of hidden mysteries: they delight in their esoteric and exoteric doctrines and measures; but hidden motives are always suspicious in a republican government. In such a government, so far as we have experienced, secrecy is the child of misconduct and the parent of mischief."[66] As usual, he was suspicious of rulers and regarded unrestrained discussion of measures of government as the only adequate safeguard against tyranny.

The advocates of restriction of speech had said much about the hopeless ignorance of the people and the necessity of preventing appeals to their prejudices. Cooper took the high ground that only by discussion and the diffusion of knowledge could ignorance be overcome and prejudice eradicated. He was confident that if the people were enabled to read and incited to think they would cease to be "Mr. Sedgwick's ignorant herd or Mr. Burke's swinish multitude." Not every blacksmith could become a Newton, to be sure, and the necessity of human labor would remain; but the means of knowledge should be put within the power of every man, and no station in society should necessarily imply such unremitting labor as to deny some leisure to utilize these means. "The country where this unremitting labor is necessary to the customary subsistence of any class of the community, is a bad one; in some shape or other there is despotism in it. The country where every man and woman cannot read and write, has reason to complain of its rulers."[67]

He felt that the western insurrection and the riots in Northampton, of which so much had been made by the advocates of restriction, would never have occurred if reasoning and argument had sufficiently preceded military force.

[66] *Political Essays*, 2 ed., pp. 78-9. [67] *Ibid.*, p. 84.

It is the general diffusion of knowledge—it is free discussion, that eradicates the prejudices of the people: . . . people will be governed by their passions, if they are not governed by their reason. . . . If the complaints of the multitude, be they well or ill founded, are forcibly suppressed, there is danger: for people will think, though they may be prohibited from speaking; and sometimes they will act: but in nine cases out of ten, let the ebullitions of political opinion evaporate as they arise, and they will not acquire force enough to justify apprehension.[68]

In such expressions as these Cooper appears at his best, and Jeffersonian campaign literature contains no finer statement of democratic idealism or of the desirability of freedom of discussion.

In due time Cooper was to gain a considerable fame in America as an economist. Imbued with the doctrines of Adam Smith and the classical school and familiar with the writings of the physiocrats, he began at Northumberland to preach *laissez-faire* and the superior importance of agriculture over commerce. This he did in part for purposes of general enlightenment, for he deplored the ridicule which the "conceited and ignorant" partisans of the day had cast upon the economists and felt that no man should pretend to be a legislator who had not read Adam Smith and the most important of the French writers.[69] He felt keenly the lack of public documents and European collections, but doubtless thought that even such scattered facts and statistics as he could bring together would serve a purpose of general illumination in a region so innocent of the light of economic truth. His two essays entitled "Political Arithmetic" had, however,

[68] *Ibid.,* pp. 84-5.

[69] *Ibid.,* 1 ed., p. 49. He showed prophetic foresight in the matter of the development of economics, as in so many other things. Thus he said, "I have long wished that the scattered facts of political economy and statistics, young as these sciences are, were collected and compared, that we might get at the important inferences they afford." *Ibid.,* p. 43.

a more important immediate political purpose, because in them he attacked both directly and indirectly the policy of the government and did further service to the Jeffersonian cause.[70]

He specifically objected to the efforts of the government to protect foreign commerce, the value of which he estimated as being less than the expense of supporting it. The exports of the United States consisted of articles of the first necessity, he said, and they would be carried away in foreign vessels if American were not available. "Thus the only part of our commerce really defended by the American ships of war is the *carrying trade*." For the benefit, not of the farmer or mechanic but primarily of British agents in commercial towns, he asserted, heavy taxes were levied upon the entire community and a navy was created which would lead the nation to greater belligerency and even war.[71]

In general he objected to foreign commerce because he thought agriculture and internal commerce of far greater importance.[72] He was convinced that until the home territory of a country was intensively cultivated and fully peopled foreign commerce was a losing concern, and that the support of the latter by prohibitions and bounties and the protection of it by wars and navies was "egregious folly and gross injustice." He was not in favor of pro-

[70] *Ibid.*, pp. 39-56. The first of these is signed "Back Country Farmer" and the second, "T. C.," but the inclusion of the first in his successive volumes indicates his authorship. The two essays represent identically the same point of view and the second is considerably the more extended and may be said to include the arguments of the first.

[71] *Ibid.*, pp. 39-42.

[72] *Ibid.*, p. 43. He recognized that his point of view was in general that of Arthur Young and of Priestley, with whom he had doubtless often discussed these matters. His originality, in so far as he was original, lay in the first case in his application of Young's arguments to American conditions and in the second in his greater elaboration. *Cf.* Priestley, "Maxims of Political Arithmetic," *Aurora*, Feb. 26, 27, 1798.

hibiting foreign commerce, but opposed the protection of speculation. If merchants should choose to invest their capital in so precarious a business, he felt that they should do so at their own risk as other adventurers did. He was passionately opposed to any policy which was likely to lead to war, and felt that the peace and prosperity of the country would be sufficiently guaranteed by the fostering of agriculture and the improvement of internal communication.

If wars are necessarily attendant upon commerce, it is far wiser to dispense with it: to imitate the Chinese and other nations who have flourished without foreign trade: your commodities, the nations who want them will fetch away:—If they will go to China for tea cups, they will come to America for Bread. . . .

If any profession is to be fostered, let it be the Tiller of the Earth, the fountain head of all wealth, and all power, and all prosperity. Improve your roads, clear your rivers, cut your canals, erect your bridges, facilitate intercourses, establish schools and colleges, diffuse knowledge of all kinds; agricultural, veterinary, statistical. No fear but if you will raise produce and people they will find their market. It will soon be discovered what articles are wanted, what are the most profitable, and such will be supplied. On this simple plan of *home defence,* how is war possible? Who would or could invade you? But on the system of foreign Commerce, a smuggling merchant may involve you in dispute, and render peace and happiness insecure: on that system sooner or later, war, taxes, debts and despotism are inevitable.[73]

[73] *Political Essays,* pp. 55-6. It should be noted that Cooper opposed commerce chiefly because he regarded it as a breeder of war. He was an agrarian, but not a foe of the security-holding class, as Charles A. Beard claims the Republicans in general were (*Economic Origins of Jeffersonian Democracy*). He was rather a consistent advocate of *laissez-faire* and an implacable foe of militarism and despotism.

Cooper's attack upon foreign commerce, together with the earlier and briefer discussion of the same subject by Priestley, attracted the notice of Jefferson, who expressed full approval of them both. Thus he wrote Priestley early in 1800, with that appreciativeness which did so much to retain for him the loyalty of his supporters, "The papers of Political Arithmetic both in yours and Mr. Cooper's pamphlets are the most precious gifts that can be made to us; for we are running navigation-mad, and commerce-mad, and navy-mad, which is worst of all. How desirable it is that you could pursue that subject for us."[74] A few weeks later, Jefferson forwarded to a political lieutenant in Virginia, for distribution to the county committees of the state, a dozen copies of Cooper's papers on "Political Arithmetic," which had been printed separately as well as in the second volume of his *Essays*. Jefferson's own connivance was to be kept secret, lest a "handle" be made of his advocating views which, none the less, he was "anxious should be generally exhibited."[75]

In the last issue of the *Gazette* during his editorship, Cooper made an indirect though scarcely veiled attack upon the administration and the Federalists,[76] which was little marked by a spirit of fairness. He supposed himself the occupant of the presidential chair and outlined the policies which he would pursue to increase the power of the executive at the expense of the rest of the country,

[74] Jan. 18, 1800, *Writings* (Ford), VII, 406; Rutt, *Life of Priestley*, II, 435.

[75] Jefferson to Philip Norborne Nicholas, March 23, 1800, *Writings* (Ford), VII, 439. For the correspondence between Cooper and Jefferson in regard to the protection of commerce, when this had become to the latter a practical as well as a theoretical question, see below, pp. 190-2.

[76] June 29, 1799, *Political Essays*, pp. 31-9. We have not considered several essays which are of minor or purely local significance. For the reaction of the secretary of state to this address, see Adams, *Works*, IX, 5-6.

thus giving a summary of the policies which he actually opposed. He said that he would undermine the constitution by extending the powers of the federal courts and officials and encroaching upon the states; that he would restrict the liberty of the press by laws against libel and sedition; and that he would impress the idea that the opponents of governmental measures were enemies of the country. He would treat with derision and abhorrence the doctrines of the rights of man and the sovereignty of the people, especially by seizing upon every fault and folly of the French to bring these doctrines into disrepute. He would appoint to office only those men whose opinions conformed with his own, and would multiply grades and distinctions in society. He would gain over the clergy and acquire a reputation for sanctity by an outward expression of religious sentiments, by declamations against infidels and atheists, and by frequent appointment of days of humiliation and prayer. He would cultivate moneyed men by preferring mercantile interests to agriculture, and by catering to the bankers. "But the grand engine, the most useful instrument of despotic ambition would be a standing army." He would invent reasons for one, if none existed. For the same reason, he would encourage naval armament. This would enable him to gain over adherents by offices and contracts, would provide greater opportunities for aggressive action than would the army and, at the same time, would win him the support of the mercantile interests.

Thus Cooper more than insinuated that the actions of the Federalists had been directed toward strengthening the executive power rather than advancing the interests of the people. He manifested indirectly his own acceptance of the chief principles of the Jeffersonian party and his implacable hostility to despotism in any guise. He opposed most strongly of all the attitude of the government toward its critics.

The doctrine of *confidence* in the executive has been urged in this country with almost as much perseverance as by the friends of Mr. Pitt in England. . . . Fair, open, decent and argumentative opposition to the measures of the prevailing party has been constantly treated . . . as evidence of disaffection, of designs hostile to the union, of preference to French interests, and enmity to our country: and this in terms of gross, persevering, and most ungentleman-like abuse.[77]

Thus he took strongest ground on the most significant part of the Jeffersonian program, the vindication of the right of opposition.

Though the publication of his *Political Essays* unquestionably gained for Cooper a position of local political prominence and a certain amount of recognition by the Republican partisans of the state, it was several months yet before he began to figure with any prominence in the columns of their chief organ, the Philadelphia *Aurora,* and it was not until 1800 that he became in the eyes of the Republicans a conspicuous champion, and in the eyes of the Federalists a notorious demagogue.

In the state election in Pennsylvania in 1799, he participated to the extent of issuing in September an address to the electors of Northumberland county,[78] in which he advocated the election of Thomas McKean, the chief justice of the state and the Republican candidate for governor, over James Ross, the Federalist candidate. He compared the two parties in much the same way as formerly, in order to show that the Republicans were the true friends of the people, and compared the two candi-

[77] *Political Essays,* pp. 37-8.
[78] Philadelphia *Aurora,* Sept. 11, 1799. Presumably copied from the Sunbury and Northumberland *Gazette,* but without such indication.

dates to show that Ross might do for a king, but that
McKean had a record of devotion to republican principles. Whether it was in part due to the efforts of Cooper
or not, McKean was elected governor, and his majority
in Northumberland was overwhelming.[79] Meanwhile, a
paragraph in the *Aurora* indicated that Cooper's reputation was becoming ponderous:

> A poor devil of a *Sophist* has attacked the celebrated *Thomas
> Cooper* in a long winded essay in Fenno's paper—some one
> talked of an ant tickling the posteriors of an elephant.[80]

A very much more serious attack appeared in the
Reading *Weekly Advertiser* of the same date, October 26.
Following the republication of Cooper's address to the
readers of the Sunbury and Northumberland *Gazette*,[81]
a communication to the Reading paper gave a perverted
account of the applications of Cooper and Priestley to
Adams, seeking to show that the address of the former
was due to a desire to revenge himself upon the president, who had rejected his application. The communication stated that Cooper had assured Adams that, although he had been called a democrat, his real political
sentiments were such as would be agreeable to the president, and it added further that Priestley in his letter
assured Adams of the pliability of Cooper's democratic
principles. It claimed that Adams rejected the application
with disdain, being greatly surprised that any one should
think of the appointment of an Englishman to such an
important office.[82] Cooper's revengeful address was

[79] Official returns, *Aurora*, Dec. 24, 1799: Northumberland County,
McKean 2997, Ross 637.

[80] Oct. 26, 1799. The attack referred to has not been found in the numbers of Fenno's *Gazette of the United States* which are available.

[81] Presumably in the *Political Essays*.

[82] This account must have been based upon information given by the
administration, for the interpretation was essentially that of Adams himself.

termed by this writer a "cunning and insidious" production, and he was described as excelling or equalling Porcupine in impudence. He and Priestley were called upon to deny the story.

A reply from Cooper was not long in coming. On November 2, he issued a handbill in which he quoted the communication from the Reading paper, published the letters of application, described the circumstances, and commented very vigorously upon the charges which had been made.[83] His remarks about the president led in due time to his indictment. He appealed to the public to judge whether his application and letter to John Adams were not entirely manly, whether there was anything in them of vanity or servility. "Do not these letters take for granted that I am a democrat, though not a disturber of all government; and that what I am I shall remain, even though it be deemed a *reasonable objection to my appointment?* Is this, or is this not, adhering to my principle, whatever becomes of my interest?"

He made an unqualified denial of the charge that his address proceeded from motives of revenge, declaring that two years elapsed from the date of the letters before he wrote anything on the politics of the country, and that when he did write he did not recollect the letters. He felt that he was justified in taking any fair means to improve his position, but stated that not even the "prudence of middle age" would make him sacrifice his principles. He said that no office for which he was eligible in America could recompense him for the offers he rejected in its

Writing Pickering, August 13, 1799, he said: "Both [Cooper and Priestley] made apologies for his reputation as a democrat, and gave intimation of a reformation." Adams had no thought of intrusting so important a work to a foreigner and, according to his custom, did not answer the letters of solicitation. *Works*, IX, 13.

[83] *Account of the Trial of Cooper*, pp. 4-7; Wharton, *State Trials*, pp. 660-2 n.

favor,[84] and stated that it was not in the power of promises or threats, of wealth or poverty, to extinguish the political enthusiasm which had actuated his conduct for twenty years. The writ against Cooper for libel against the president in the above broadside was not issued until the spring of 1800, so this matter may be postponed until we treat of the events of that time.[85]

Meanwhile, Priestley, having allowed the "low scurrility" of Cobbett to pass unnoticed for five years, and having written only one political article[86] during that time, had come to feel the necessity of vindicating his character and conduct, and for this reason wrote his *Letters to the Inhabitants of Northumberland.*[87] He was fearful of action against himself under the Alien Act, having been informed that he was particularly watched and threatened. Cobbett had been very successful in creating sentiment hostile to him, he said, so he wanted to tell what he was, what he had done, and what he thought about the government, in order that his accusers might be better informed. He said later that his letters were not without good effect in making clear his position, to his neighbors at least, and in bringing about a change in public opinion which rendered him safe from the threat of prosecution. He confessed by this time, however, that party violence in America was greater than anything he had ever known in England.[88]

These letters give an authoritative statement of Priestley's position, but it seems undesirable to go into a general discussion of them here. There are certain references

---

[84] Apparently before he left England. The exact nature of these we have not yet determined.

[85] See below, pp. 118 ff.

[86] "Political Arithmetic," *Aurora*, Feb. 26, 27, 1798; reprinted at the end of his *Letters*, pp. 81-96.

[87] 2 edition, Philadelphia, 1801. 1 edition, apparently 1799.

[88] Rutt, II, 425, 432-3, 435.

to Cooper, however, which are worthy of consideration. Thus in speaking of the prejudice which existed against himself because of his being regarded as an enemy of the United States, he intimated that Cooper had been involved in this prejudice because of association with him.[89] He stated that while he approved of Cooper's *Essays,* he was in no sense their patron and had done practically nothing to further their circulation.[90] Regarding the application to Adams, he said that it was not intended as an affront to the president, for whom he had always had high esteem, and involved no dereliction of principles on Cooper's part.[91] Adams had just entered into office and had done nothing to offend persons of Cooper's political principles. He thought Cooper well qualified for the office because of his knowledge of English law and English commerce, as well as because of his acknowledged ability and activity. He thought that he was giving Adams an opportunity to show liberality by appointing a person of different political principles, to a position which was judicial in character and essentially non-political. The appointment would have pleased Priestley, for whom the president had always expressed much esteem and whom he had honored with correspondence and intercourse.

Priestley felt that, high as was Adams's position, he should for the sake of an ancient friendship and for simple justice have interposed to prevent so shocking a misinterpretation of the letters to him. If the writers had not retained copies of them, they would have been disgraced and Cooper would have been ruined because his livelihood depended upon his character. Writing after Cooper's trial, he said, "And surely if under such a provocation a few intemperate expressions dropped from a

89 *Letters,* II.   90 *Ibid.,* pp. 19-20.
91 *Ibid.,* pp. 47-9. Apparently written after Cooper's trial.

man whose feelings may be something too quick, they should have been overlooked.''[92]

An opportunity to condemn the federal judiciary, display his learning, justify emigration and at the same time serve the Jeffersonian cause, came to Cooper in the autumn of 1799. Isaac Williams, a citizen of the United States, had been tried in the federal district court of Connecticut on the charge of accepting a commission in a French armed vessel and serving there against Great Britain, with whom the United States was at peace, and had been convicted in September, 1799.[93] Williams claimed in his defense that he had duly become a citizen of France, but Chief Justice Ellsworth expressed the opinion that no citizen of the United States could throw off his allegiance without the consent of Congress. There was considerable interest in the case because the question of the right of expatriation was involved, and the denial of this right reflected upon immigrants to the United States, including Cooper, many of whom were very prominent in the councils of the Republican party.

In a series of essays in the *Aurora* during December, 1799, and January and February, 1800, Cooper discussed the question with great display of erudition, and argued in favor of the right of expatriation.[94] He took up the history of the question, beginning with classical times and quoting from Plato, Ovid, Cicero, Justinian, and others of lesser fame; stated and discussed the opinions of the writers on natural law, citing Grotius, Hennecius, Vattel, and others equally unknown to the layman; traced the development of English precedent, taking several shots at Coke; and arrived finally at the conclusion that with the growth of republicanism the right of expatriation was becoming more and more generally recognized,

[92] *Ibid.*, p. 48.   [93] Wharton, *State Trials*, pp. 652-8.
[94] Dec. 7, Jan. 21, 24, 25, Feb. 14.

and that, with very trifling exceptions, a man had the right to leave one country and take up residence in another whenever he felt it to be to his interest to do so. He considered the right of expatriation a characteristic of republican principles, and its abrogation, of despotic ones. He felt that successive revolutions had overthrown the doctrine of perpetual allegiance, and that considerations of individual interest and the utilitarian foundation of all valid law and morality were sufficient to outweigh mere precedent.

In setting forth his doctrine of justifiable revolution and emigration, Cooper elaborated upon the brief statements made by him in his *Propositions*,[95] which, as we have shown, go back ultimately to John Locke. He believed that man entered society to benefit his condition and that if the society in which he lived should not satisfy his legitimate wants, he could not be expected to remain in it. He claimed that the doctrine of perpetual allegiance was directly opposed to all revolutions, such as that against the Stuarts and that of the Americans against George III. The sentiment of patriotism Cooper valued little, but he felt that a citizen should be attached to a government by ties of interest. A state, he said, should not be a prison. A man was not to blame for having been born in a country, so could not be said to have consented to its conditions. Bad governments should be deserted and discouraged, good ones encouraged by immigration to them. Cooper rejected all external authority and expressed his utilitarian position with what some must have regarded as startling frankness:

There is no rule of right, no criterion of morality, but what is coincident with the good of mankind. That course of conduct

[95] *Propositions respecting the Foundation of Civil Government*, 1787, XVII; see above, pp. 12-15.

which promotes it, is right, is virtue; that which opposes it is wrong, is vice. That is just, that is right, that *ought* to be, and that only, which from reasoning or experience can be shown conducive to the happiness of the species.[96]

In his own emigration from England and his successive migrations in America, he acted upon the convictions expressed in these essays. Whenever he felt it to be to his interest to move, he did so. Nor can any valid objection be raised to such an attitude. One misses, however, the sense of local attachment and the affection for a place where a man was born or has long resided. The roots of Cooper's life never sank deep into any soil, although he seems to have had many strong personal attachments. But as his mind roamed restlessly through all ages and all learning, so was even his body restless. In mind, he was ubiquitous; in body, itinerant.

It is to be noted that other democratic writers attacked the opinion of the chief justice.[97] Reference was made in the Federalist press to "this herd of revilers," and among them was singled out for special attack, "Thomas Cooper of Northumberland, of restless memory."[98] Cooper referred to this attack by "one of Mr. Fenno's dull declaimers," and spoke of "the characteristic scurrility of the essay mongers of that paper."[99] Perhaps the thing which most irritated him was the charge that he either did not understand or had misrepresented the Latin quotations of which he had made such grand display. This charge he indignantly denied.

[96] *Aurora*, Jan. 25, 1800.

[97] Wharton, *State Trials*, pp. 655-8 n., traces the history of the question at issue, and refers to certain specific attacks upon Ellsworth's opinion. He says that "Mr. Cooper's fertile mind was exhausted" in this crusade.

[98] *Gazette of the United States*, Dec. 20, 1799, communication signed "Civis."

[99] *Aurora*, Jan. 24, 1800.

CHAPTER IV

REPUBLICAN POLITICS AND SEDITIOUS LIBEL, 1800

THE year 1800, when Federalist and Republican were locked in deadly struggle, was perhaps the most memorable of all the four-score years passed by Thomas Cooper upon earth. For sheer excitement, the year 1792, when he came into personal contact with the French Revolution and engaged in heated controversy with Burke, was comparable, but his own position was less conspicuous; and for national notoriety, the year 1827, when in South Carolina he daringly voiced sentiments of disunion, was equally notable, but there was then no tragedy of immediate martyrdom. In 1800, excitement and notoriety were combined with tragedy and triumph, and during this fateful twelvemonth he laid the enduring foundations of the most important of his American friendships, that with Thomas Jefferson.

By spring he had been singled out from the Republican mass as a leader sufficiently conspicuous to be deserving of constant abuse in the Federalist press. A writer to the Philadelphia *Gazette* in March said that the Jacobins had committed the whole of their electioneering concerns to Cooper for England, Callender for Scotland, and Duane for Ireland;[1] and another, having observed this reference

---

[1] Communication signed "Yankey," Philadelphia *Gazette*, March 11, 1800. James Thomson Callender, editor of the Richmond *Examiner*, was born in Scotland. William Duane, editor of the *Aurora*, the most important

to "the three Foreign Emissaries, who, under the Chief Juggler," had "at length obtained the entire management of the Jacobin puppets," proceeded to enlighten the public with further details:

> With respect to the organization of their political plan, it commenced by a subdivision of their business in detail, into three Grand Departments. Callender takes the southern, Duane the eastern, and Cooper, with Priestley for his aid major, has the whole of the Jacobin interest of the western country under his immediate controul; all the doings of these three *chiefs of division,* are subject to the controul of the Chief Juggler and his select council.[2]

Cooper and the two major agitators with whom he was associated were described as "the spurious offspring of our former taskmaster"; he was repeatedly termed a "fugitive Englishman," and was mentioned with Priestley, "that journeyman of discontent and sedition." Thus did the Federalists seek to stigmatize the Jeffersonian movement as un-American.

The prominence of Cooper was not due primarily to his discussion of expatriation nor to his *Political Essays,* either of which would have entitled him to be identified with the philosophers of the movement rather than with the agitators, but to his attack upon John Adams and, more immediately, to the conspicuous part played by him in the clash between William Duane, editor of the *Aurora,* and the United States senate.[3] Although the latter epi-

Jeffersonian organ, was born in the province of New York, but was of Irish parentage and before his final settlement in Philadelphia in 1795, had spent most of his life in Ireland and other parts of the British empire.

2 Communication signed "A Federal Republican," Philadelphia *Gazette,* March 12, 1800. Jefferson, of course, was the "Chief Juggler."

3 McMaster, *United States,* II, 462-5, gives an excellent brief account of the episode, although he shows no knowledge of the letter from Cooper to Jefferson which gives the plan of procedure followed by Duane. The story

sode partook of the character of *opera bouffe* in the end,
since Duane defied the senate and dared that august body
to capture him, it attracted national attention; and
Cooper, who with A. J. Dallas, later to be secretary of
the treasury under Madison, declined to serve as counsel
for Duane under the conditions laid down by the senate,
came in for the most violent abuse by the Federalist
press.

The affair began in February with an attack by Duane
on the electoral count bill introduced by James Ross, the
recently defeated Federalist candidate for governor of
Pennsylvania, which Duane interpreted as being part of
the scheme to secure the electoral vote of the state for the
Federalists by fair means or foul.[4] In his attack on the
bill, Duane condemned the caucus which had framed it and
other caucuses as well. The ire of the senate was aroused
and a committee of privileges declared that he had made
"false, defamatory, scandalous and malicious" assertions, "tending to defame the senate" and bring it into
disrepute, and that his publication of February 19 was
a "high-handed breach of the privileges" of the house.
It was therefore resolved that he be ordered to attend
at the bar of the senate, where he should have the opportunity to make any possible defense of his conduct.[5]

From a letter of Cooper to Thomas Jefferson,[6] we learn
just how Duane's procedure was planned with a view to
various possible contingencies. This letter not only dis-
closes the knowledge that Jefferson had of the plan of

can be recovered from the *Aurora*, March 21-28, 1800. *Cf.* Cooper's own discussion of the case in his *Essay on the Constitution*, 1826, pp. 39-40.

[4] See especially, *Aurora*, Feb. 19, 1800. The bill was favored by the
Federalists, *cf.* Philadelphia *Gazette*, Jan. 1, 1800.

[5] March 14, 1800. Entire report published in *Aurora*, March 17.

[6] Jefferson Papers, CXXI. This letter bears no date other than "Sunday
Evening," but in the original index is placed at March 23, 1800, that is,
the day before Duane addressed his letter to the vice-president.

campaign against the body over which he officially presided, but marks also the beginnings of his closer association with Cooper. Henceforth the Northumbrian was
an honored co-worker.

Duane, Dallas, and Cooper met on the day of the letter
to Jefferson and determined upon a course of action. It
was decided that Duane should address a letter to the
vice-president, asking that he be permitted counsel and
the right to summon witnesses. This letter he duly sent.
His hope was that this request would be denied, in which
case he would have strong ground for refusing to appear
before the senate. Lacking this denial, however, Duane
appeared, in accordance with the plan agreed upon for
this contingency, stated that he was dubious of the jurisdiction of the senate and of the exact legal status of the
case, and asked that he might advise with counsel. Upon
his retirement, the senate provided for the hearing of
testimony and for the attendance of Duane or his attorney to hear and cross-examine.

Duane then addressed letters to Dallas and Cooper
asking them to serve as counsel for him. They were
already acting as such informally. Both declined to serve
and the entire correspondence was duly published in the
partisan newspapers.[7] Dallas said that the senate had
already decided that the publication was false, malicious,
etc., and a breach of the legislative privileges of that
body; that counsel could not well deny the existence of
facts already examined and established by the senate;
and that there could be no inquiry into the jurisdiction of
the senate, or justification of the publication by proving
the truth of its charges. Hence he felt that he would be
unable to render any service to his client and that he
would find his position degrading to his profession and to
himself.

[7] *Aurora,* March 27, 1800; Philadelphia *Gazette,* March 27, 1800.

Cooper's reply was similar, but more violent in tone. He stated that he had every inclination to render service to Duane and his cause, but that he would not degrade himself by appearing before the senate with their gag in his mouth. The senate resolution, he said, was meant to preclude all argument on the jurisdiction of that body and all proof which might be offered in justification of Duane's assertions—wisely from the senate's point of view, for otherwise the system of caucuses would be exposed. The tribunal had prejudged the case, had dictated the mode of defense, had forbidden entrance upon the unanswerable part of the vindication, and would hear no objection to its jurisdiction. So he felt that his attendance would serve no purpose, but would tend to disgrace both his client's cause and his own. His final words breathe a spirit of profound democratic despondency: "Where rights are undefined, and power is unlimited—where the freedom of the press is actually attacked, under whatever intention of curbing its licentiousness, the melancholy period cannot be far distant when the citizen will be converted into a subject!"

The remaining developments are amusing to contemplate. Duane addressed a letter to the president of the senate, enclosing his correspondence with Dallas and Cooper.[8] Finding himself deprived of professional assistance, under the restrictions adopted by the senate, he declined any further attendance upon the body and left them to pursue such measures as they might deem proper. They voted him guilty of contempt, and a warrant for his arrest was issued,[9] but he followed the plan which had been originally devised for this contingency and avoided the sergeant-at-arms. Cooper had suggested that if apprehended he should resist by making applica-

---

[8] Published in *Aurora*, March 27, 1800.
[9] *Ibid.*, March 31, 1800.

tion for an *habeas corpus,* but Duane was sufficiently elusive to make such action unnecessary. Meanwhile, a vigorous remonstrance[10] was framed by his friends and presented to the senate on May 10. Even the Federalists felt that matters had gone too far and with the reading of the remonstrance the case ended. The editor of the *Aurora* and his counsel had every reason to exult when the senate was shown to be so impotent, despite its high-sounding declarations. But the elation of Cooper at least was considerably restrained by the difficulty in which he now found himself. His trial for sedition began within three weeks' time and was doubtless a direct result of the Duane episode.

The Federalist writers now took up their cudgels against the three offending democrats, who were termed by one writer "three foreign, mercenary cailiffs," fugitives from their own country, known only by turbulence and mischief in this, "wandering vagabonds who should be hooted away with hisses and curses."[11] The Philadelphia *Gazette* described Duane's refusal to appear at the bar of the senate as a "daring act of defiance," and commented upon the "impudent" letters of his counselors.[12] "Mr. Dallas," said the editor, "declined appearing as his counsel for the same motives which are adduced by one Cooper (a creature not known to our courts) whose letter, for its impudence, we publish." According to the *Gazette,* the refusal of these gentlemen to appear was due to their inability, because of the limitations imposed, to defend Duane by insulting the senate, a thing which would have afforded great opportunity for their talents. The senate had "warded off the curse of listening to the

10 Published in *Aurora,* March 28, 1800. No signatures yet, however.

11 Philadelphia *Gazette,* March 29, 1800. Dallas was born in the British West Indies.

12 *Ibid.,* March 27, 1800.

noisy nonsense of these wordy lawyers.'' Referring more specifically to Cooper, the *Gazette* continued: ''The letter from Cooper is insulting to the senate, and degrading to the American people. We forbear to animadvert on its contents, in the hope that severer notice will be taken of its insolence.''

In the same issue there was a communication addressed ''To Tom Cooper,'' the writer of which asserted that the virulence of Cooper's impudent letter was accounted for by his fear lest he should be whipped back to his cotton manufactory at Manchester.[13] But Cooper, he said, was too well known in England to be desirous of returning to his native land, and was too notoriously infamous to expect any mercy from the advocates of truth and justice in America. He spoke of Cooper's talents for cunning, his malignity and baseness, and described him as a canting English Jacobin, trying to arouse the mob in Duane's favor.

Subsequent editorials and communications dilated upon the character of the persons involved, and of the supporters of the *Aurora* in general, who were spoken of as persons of foreign extraction, fugitives from justice, etc. It was argued that the petition asking the senate to reconsider its resolutions against Duane was an effort to array the people against the government. ''A worthless fellow from a foreign nation, aided by fellow exiles, has dared, in his own cause, to issue a proscription of the senate of the United States, in the shape of a petition. It remains to be seen whether our government, our safety, and our happiness, are to be subverted by such men as the Irish and English fugitives—Duane and Cooper!''[14] It is worthy of note that Cooper was attacked

[13] Signed ''Anti-Jacobin,'' Philadelphia *Gazette*, March 27, 1800.
[14] *Ibid.*, March 28, 1800, *cf.* March 29.

most vigorously of the three and that his name generally came first when the three were mentioned.

The sanest of the many critics of Cooper's letter described his final sentence as "a curious specimen of Jacobinic logic" and stated that his doctrine was that the freedom of the press should be *unlimited,* while the powers of the government to punish abuses of that freedom ought to be *limited* and *restrained*.[15] This writer claimed that if the Jacobins should have their way, any individual might treat all officers of government with contempt, while the hands of the latter would be tied and they would have to submit to unbounded licentiousness. Further, Cooper implied that citizens of a free state were not *subjects*. But all citizens were subjects, the only difference being between the governments to which they were subject. The writer asserted that the Jacobins were trying to place individual citizens above the laws, and that if their doctrines should prevail, civil commotions would inevitably result and, in consequence, much liberty now enjoyed would be lost. There was no danger of monarchy, he said, except as resulting from such anarchy as the Jacobins sought. It is only fair to say that Cooper always opposed lawlessness. The restrictions to which he objected were those on freedom of discussion. On the other hand, when embroiled in political controversy, he frequently lost his grip on himself, made extravagant assertions, and descended to the level of sheer demagoguery. He loved liberty not unwisely, we feel, but at times certainly, too well.

It was no accident that the trial of Thomas Cooper for seditious libel against the president of the United States followed close upon the heels of the controversy between Duane and the senate, in which he had played so conspicuous a part. The Federalist administration could not

---

[15] *Ibid.*, April 26, 1800, copying from the *Commercial Advertiser*.

discipline Duane, but it could discipline his adviser. The statements about John Adams, which formed the basis for the indictment of the Republican writer, had been made the previous autumn in the handbill which he had published November 2, 1799, in reply to the attack upon him and his application to Adams for office.[16] The writ against him, however, was not issued until April 9, 1800, more than five months later, by which time he had become sufficiently prominent to be deserving of the attention of the federal judiciary. The trial occurred on April 19, and on May 1 he was sentenced to spend six months in prison and pay a fine of four hundred dollars. The issue was between free speech and justifiable criticism of the administration on the one hand, and the alleged abuse of freedom of speech, and seditious criticism on the other. The Federalists unquestionably gloated over the apparent discomfiture of their redoubtable critic, but Cooper accepted the challenge without hesitation and regarded himself as a martyr to the cause which was of all causes dearest to his heart.

In his comments upon the president, he was charged with having violated the Sedition Act, which prohibited "false, scandalous and malicious writing" against the government, Congress or the president, with the intent to defame them and bring them into contempt or disrepute.[17] In attempting to justify his apparent inconsistency, in opposing so strongly in 1799 the man to whom he had applied for office two years before, he had referred to objectionable actions on the part of the administration subsequent to his application, such as neither he nor his venerable friend Priestley had anticipated. They had not

16 Reading *Weekly Advertiser*, Oct. 26, 1799. See above, pp. 105-6.

17 The passages cited in the indictment are printed in *An Account of the Trial of Thomas Cooper, of Northumberland: on a charge of libel against the President of the United States*, 1800, pp. 6-7, and in Wharton, *State Trials*, pp. 659-62 n.

expected Adams to turn out so badly. He said that when he applied for office the country was not saddled with the expense of a permanent navy nor threatened under the auspices of the president with the existence of a standing army; its credit was not reduced so low that it was forced to pay eight per cent upon loans in time of peace; and the president had not projected embassies to such despotic governments as Prussia, Russia, and the Sublime Porte.

These statements were unquestionably intended to reflect upon the wisdom of the administration, but the repressive power of the federal courts would probably never have been exercised against Cooper had he not coupled with them certain more derogatory remarks about the president himself. Thus he stated that in 1797 Adams, who had just entered into office, "was hardly in the infancy of political mistake: even those who doubted his capacity thought well of his intentions"; and he spoke of the "unnecessary violence of official expression" which might justly have provoked a war with France. His most extravagant condemnation was vented upon the action of the president in the case, notorious at the time, of Jonathan Robbins, alias Thomas Nash. The British claimed that the latter was a deserter from one of their men-of-war, and charged him with having committed murder upon the vessel. On their representation, President Adams, acting upon what he felt to be his duties under the recent treaty with Great Britain, communicated to Judge Thomas Bee of the district court of South Carolina his "advice and request" that the accused be delivered up. After a hearing, Judge Bee complied with the request, and Nash was condemned by a British court-martial and hanged. Cooper, with the rest of the Republicans, took the position that the accused was really Robbins, a native American who had been forcibly impressed by the British and "delivered up with the advice and consent of Mr. Adams to the mock trial of a British court-martial." He asserted that the president had endeavored to influence a court of justice and characterized his action as "a stretch of authority which the monarch of Great Britain would have shrunk from; an interference without precedent, against law and against mercy!" In the cold light of history, the action of Adams seems to have been entirely justifiable, and Cooper's invective appears to have been a bit of sheer demagoguery, but his position was in full accord with that of the most distinguished Republicans.[18]

On April 10, the day following the issue of the writ, Cooper appeared before Judge Peters and was confronted with his handbill. He gave bail for appearance at the next court, a thousand dollars himself and a like sum by Israel Israel, a prominent Democrat. Two days later the indictment presented by William Rawle, United States attorney for the district of Pennsylvania, was found a true-bill by the grand jury. Cooper made a plea of not guilty and asked that subpoenas be issued to President Adams, Secretary of State Timothy Pickering, Jacob Wagner, clerk in Pickering's office, Thomas Pinckney, Congressmen John Davenport, Robert Goodloe Harper, Albert Gallatin, and others. Dallas was present as a friend of the accused and made certain suggestions regarding the subpoenas.

Justice Chase presided during the trial, and when the case was called on April 16, announced that a subpoena

---

[18] See Wharton, *State Trials*, pp. 392-457, for the entire controversy. Chief Justice Marshall and Justice Chase both approved the action of the president, and felt that he had not infringed upon the judiciary. The arguments of the opposition were presented by Senator Charles Pinckney of South Carolina and, it is said, by Madison, although the articles attributed to him have not been preserved. Gallatin was among those in the House who voted against approving the action of the president.

to the president would be an impropriety, hence had not
been issued. Cooper's general policy seems to have been
to delay the trial and to vex the prosecution as much as
possible. In this instance, he asked and secured postponement in order to secure official copies of certain of
Adams's speeches. When the court reassembled on April
19, he stated that he had not been able to secure these,
and after reflecting upon the obstructive tactics of the
executive and his underlings, asked for further postponement. Judge Chase regarded the grounds as insufficient,
and then Cooper presented as a further reason for delay
his inability to secure the attendance of other witnesses,
whose testimony he claimed was indispensable. None of
the distinguished men who had been summoned had at
that time appeared, although several of them did appear
later. One Federalist congressman said that so many
members of Congress were summoned that it was necessary for that body to adjourn in order that they might
attend.[19] Since Cooper did not avail himself of their testimony when they did appear, it was claimed by the Federalists that he was merely trying to postpone the trial.[20]
They said they were summoned in the expectation that
they would not come, and that their unexpected appearance defeated the trick. The effort to have the president
subpoenaed the Federalists also regarded as a device to
delay procedure.

It seems probable that such was Cooper's purpose, but
Chase could not be hoodwinked. He granted a slight delay
for preparation, then proceeded with the case. In the
absence of certified copies of Adams's speeches, he allowed Cooper to read from newspapers anything that he
wished, although the judge stated that this was not legal

[19] John Rutledge, Jr., *Annals of Congress*, 6 Cong., p. 930.
[20] Arguments of Rutledge and of Robert Goodloe Harper, *ibid.*, pp.
935-6.

evidence. The Federalists regarded this action as generous on Chase's part and asserted that Cooper was permitted to carry before the jury all the evidence he cared to adduce.

The position of the prosecution was stated by Rawle.[21] The prisoner had published a false, scandalous, and malicious attack on the president with the intent to excite the hatred and contempt of the people against him. It was not endurable that "foul and infamous falsehoods" against the president of the United States should be uttered and published with impunity, and an example should be made of Cooper to deter others. One peculiarity in the manner of this publication was that the writer did not, as was generally the case, shelter himself behind a fictitious name, but boldly took advantage of his own personal and professional standing to disseminate his opinions. "Such conduct must have arisen from the basest motives." The jury should judge whether such conduct did not endanger the security of the country.

The only witness called was one for the prosecution, John Buyers of Sunbury, a justice of the peace.[22] He testified that Cooper came to his house on December 6, 1799, showed him the handbill, pointed out his name, and said that he was the author of the paper. He said that this might save Buyers trouble at another time, and Buyers stated to the court that he knew very well what Cooper meant. On cross-examination, Cooper brought out the fact that he and Buyers had frequently joked each other on political subjects. It is evident that his action was one of bravado, and it seems highly probable that he anticipated prosecution and made no effort to avoid it,

---

[21] *Account of the Trial of Thomas Cooper,* pp. 15-16; Wharton, *State Trials,* pp. 662-3.

[22] *Account of Trial,* p. 17; Wharton, p. 663.

being perfectly willing that his should be made a test case.

Cooper served as his own counsel. He examined no witnesses, although he had opportunity to do so. He read several passages from Adams's speeches to prove that the statements made by him were true, thus seeking to disprove the charge that they were false and scandalous. He also sought to show that his motives were not malicious, but honest and fair, his criticism being the entirely legitimate expression of dissatisfaction with the party in power. He claimed that he had not endeavored to bring the president into contempt and disrepute because he had examined only his *public* conduct, with no imputation of improper motives. On the contrary, he had ever attributed honesty to Adams, even when he had strongly disapproved of his measures. He felt that his position as defendant was peculiarly difficult, because of the fact that the court officials were all appointees of the president whose conduct had been attacked. He acknowledged that there should be a certain degree of confidence in the executive, but upheld with characteristic vigor the freedom of the press and the right of opposition.

But this confidence ought not to be unlimited, and need not be paid up in advance; let it be earned before it is reposed; . . . It cannot be exacted by the guarded provisions of Sedition Laws, by attacks on the Freedom of the Press, by prosecutions, pains, and penalties on those which boldly express the truth, or who may honestly and innocently err in their political sentiments.— Let this required confidence be the meed of desert, and the public will not be backward to pay it.

But in the present state of affairs, the Press is open to those who will praise, while the threats of the Law hang over those who blame the conduct of the men in power . . . That conduct which will not bear investigation will naturally shun it; and whether my opinions be right or wrong. . . . I cannot help thinking that they would have been better confuted by evidence and argument than by indictment.[23]

In order to prove that his statements about Adams were true, Cooper took them up specifically, thus putting on record a criticism of the administration in general. He went into the question of the army and navy, the sending of embassies to autocratic European powers, the extravagant financial policy of the government, the violent expressions of the president against the French, and, most vigorously of all, the case of Robbins. He probably never hoped for acquittal, although his procedure was no less vigorous on that account, and he seems to have done everything possible to delay the trial and vex the prosecution. He doubtless expected considerable publicity for his case, so his defense was probably designed in large measure to accumulate Republican campaign ammunition. He felt that his criticisms of Adams were perfectly legitimate, and doubtless many of them were. But it was absurd for him to claim that he had not tried to bring Adams into contempt and disrepute; that was his primary object before the trial and during it, the point being, of course, that he felt that he had a perfect right to do so. In his defense, he appealed not so much to the court as to the American electorate. His willingness to be offered as a sacrifice indicated either an unusual political partisanship or an heroic devotion to the cause of freedom of speech, or both.

United States Attorney Rawle claimed that the accused had not established the truth of his charges, and replied to him point by point.[24] He contended, furthermore, that there was clear evidence of intent to defame. Cooper's argument, he said, had as its object not so much the con-

[23] *Ibid.*, p. 19; Wharton, p. 665.
[24] *Ibid.*, pp. 35-42; Wharton, pp. 668-70.

vincing the jury of the truth of his earlier statements against Adams as the further reflection upon him. This point seems to have been well taken.

The charge of Judge Chase to the jury was later severely criticized by Cooper, who claimed that he argued the case against him.[25] Although the general conduct of the case by the judge who was so much more severe upon Callender has been described by at least one subsequent commentator as moderate,[26] Cooper's objection to the summing up seems justifiable. After a preliminary discussion of the necessity of a government's protecting itself against libel and checking the licentiousness of the press, Chase proceeded to say that the task of the prosecution was to prove, first, that the traverser did publish the matters contained in the indictment, second, that he did publish with the intent to defame.[27]

The publication, he said, was not even denied. The traverser went to the house of a justice of the peace with the paper, in an indecent and outrageous manner, the more outrageous if the matter was a joke, as was implied. "This conduct showed that he intended to dare and defy the government, and to provoke them, and his subsequent conduct satisfied my mind that such was his disposition." Nor, thought the presiding judge, could there be any question as to Cooper's motives; he had boldly avowed his desire to censure the conduct of the president, which he thought deserved it. The qualifying expressions, such as his recognition of the president's honesty and good intentions, carried in every case a sting. His charges, if true, would destroy all public confidence in the president. Chase went particularly into the case of Jonathan Robbins, seeking to show that the action of Adams was in

25 See address to Chase, *Account of Trial*, pp. 58-64.
26 Wharton, p. 679 n.
27 *Account of Trial*, pp. 42-50; Wharton, pp. 670-7.

exact accord with his legal obligation under the British treaty, and that the charge of interference with the judiciary was without foundation. He said that the charge that the president was trying to create a standing army betrayed egregious ignorance, for there was no standing army and there could not be under the constitution because of the temporary character of appropriations.

Chase certainly did his best to damn Cooper completely when he said, "Take this publication in all its parts, and it is the boldest attempt I have known to poison the minds of the people."[28] He stated that the traverser should be acquitted if he had proved the truth of every charge—after the presiding judge had already stated his opinion that he had not; or if the publication should be adjudged to have been made without malice or intent to defame—after the above statement from himself. A verdict of guilty was inevitable. Cooper had certainly violated the Sedition Act as currently interpreted. The wisdom of that law, however, is another question. And so is its constitutionality.

After the jury had rendered the verdict of guilty on April 19, Chase expressed the desire to hear anything the prisoner might have to offer on the point of the mitigation of the fine and in extenuation of his punishment, and asked specifically for a statement of his circumstances. Cooper was brought again before the court on April 30, and made a statement. This he did, he said, not for the purpose of deprecating any punishment the court might think proper to inflict, but to prevent accidental or apparent harshness of punishment for want of information in his power to give.

[28] In Cooper's note in the *Account of the Trial*, he emphasized the position that it was not only the right, but the duty of a citizen to expose the chief magistrate when the latter adopted measures inconsistent with the public interest. See especially p. 42 n.

For this reason, therefore, and that the court may not be misled, I think it right to say, that my property in this country is
moderate. That some resources I had in England, commercial
failures there have lately cut off: that I depend principally upon
my practice: that practice, imprisonment will annihilate. Be it
so. I have been accustomed to make sacrifices to opinion, and I
can make this. As to circumstances in extenuation, not being conscious that I have set down aught in malice, I have nothing to
extenuate.[29]

Judge Chase expressed the suspicion that Cooper's
fine might be paid by the party with which he was identified, and stated that if he thought it would be, he would
impose the limit that the law allowed. If, however, it
should fall upon Cooper alone he would take his circumstances into account.

Cooper indignantly repudiated the suggestion that he
was or had ever been supported by a party. He said that,
in this instance, he wrote entirely from his own suggestions. Offers of assistance had been made to him in the
matter of the expected fine and these he had neither accepted nor rejected. If the fine imposed should be beyond
his ability to pay, he would accept these offers without
hesitation, but if the fine should be within his circumstances, he would pay it himself. The following passage
indicates the independence of action which he claimed:

Sir, I solemnly aver, that throughout my life, here and elsewhere, among all the political questions in which I have been
concerned, I have never so far demeaned myself as to be a party
writer. I never was in the pay or under the support of any party;
there is no party in this, or any other country, that can offer me
a temptation to prostitute my pen. If there are any persons here
who are acquainted with what I have published, they must feel
and be satisfied that I have had higher and better motives, than
a party could suggest. I have written, to the best of my ability,

29 *Ibid.*, p. 50; Wharton, p. 677.

what I seriously thought would conduce to the good of mankind. The exertions of my talents, such as they are, have been unbought, and so they shall continue; they have indeed been paid for, but they have been paid for by myself, and by myself only, and sometimes dearly. The public is my debtor, and what I have paid or suffered for them, if my duty should again call upon me to write or act, I shall again most readily submit to. I do not pretend to have no party opinions, to have no predilections for particular descriptions of men or of measures; but I do not act upon minor considerations; I belong here, as in my former country, to the great party of mankind.[30]

This appears to have been a thoroughly sincere statement, and it seems safe to say that Cooper was never in a primary sense a place-hunting politician and that he belonged to a higher order than such Republican writers as Callender and Duane. He never entirely lost his youthful ideal of truth and the betterment of humanity.

Judge Peters, who sat upon the bench with the more notorious Chase, said, after hearing Cooper's statement, that the court had nothing to do with parties but should consider only the prisoner's circumstances. Peters differed from Chase on several points and did not arouse the resentment of Cooper as did the presiding judge. On this particular occasion, Chase felt that time should be taken for consideration. On May 1 the prisoner was brought again before the court and sentenced to pay a fine of four hundred dollars and to be imprisoned for six months, and was required, at the end of that period, to find surety for good behavior, himself in one thousand dollars and two sureties in five hundred dollars each.[31]

There is strong reason to believe that the trial of Cooper was marked by greater moderation and fairness than were most of the trials under the Sedition Act. In the debate on this law in the house of representatives in

[30] *Ibid.*, pp. 50-1; Wharton, p. 678.   [31] *Ibid.*, p. 52; Wharton, p. 679.

January, 1801, Chase's conduct in this case was strongly
defended by several Federalist congressmen. Thus John
Rutledge, Jr., of South Carolina, said that the trial was
"one of the fairest and most deliberate that ever was
had," as the many members of Congress who attended
could testify.[32] The strongest expressions in favor of
Chase's conduct were made by Robert Goodloe Harper
who said, "Greater latitude of indulgence could not possibly be given in making a defense, than was given to
this person."[33] The attacks made by the Republicans
upon Chase's conduct in this particular case were feeble,[34] and it was not mentioned in the subsequent articles
of impeachment of that justice.[35] The crux of the matter
is not so much the conduct of Chase upon the bench,
which except for the summing up seems to have been
fair, nor the dilatory tactics and demagogic utterances
of Cooper, but the justification or lack of justification of
Republican opposition to the Sedition Act. From this
point of view, one need not depart from conventional
historical interpretation and can say that Cooper's
actions and procedure must on the whole be justified.

The account of the successive events of the trial appeared day by day in the Philadelphia press. The administration papers described it more fully than did the
Aurora, which said little while the trial was going on,
probably because of the danger of Duane's own position.
The Federalist chorus of abuse was somewhat restrained
during the trial, although the tone of the accounts of the
proceedings was always hostile. Following the verdict,
however, the chorus began to swell, and after the verdict
exultation was unrestrained. Sarcastic reference was

[32] *Annals of Congress*, 6 Cong., p. 930.
[33] *Ibid.*, p. 937.   [34] *Cf. ibid.*, p. 922.
[35] *Annals of Congress*, 8 Cong., 1st session, pp. 1237-40. There are references in the articles to the trials of Fries and Callender.

now made to "the noted Cooper," and "the seditious convict." Following the sentence, one paper reported that a subscription was being taken to pay the fine of Cooper, Callender, and other "Jacobin liars," thus explaining in a measure Chase's suspicions.[36] When the continued imprisonment of the redoubtable foe of Federalism was assured, the same paper commented satirically and exultingly upon the opportunities which the "wight of Northumberland," now held in "durance vile," would have to ruminate upon liberty.[37]

The most violent and at the same time the most interesting of the paeans of victory sounded over the incarcerated Republican bears the title *Prison Eclogue* and describes a dialogue, in Vergilian style, between Priestley and Cooper in the latter's cell.[38] In this work, which contains deprecatory insinuations against various other Democratic leaders besides the two exiles from England, Priestley is represented as congratulating Cooper upon his great opportunities, now that he is in prison, for contemplation and unlimited libellous writing. Here he may not only court the imprisoned muses, but give his pent-up spleen its utmost scope, dip his adventurous pen in ranker gall and make the freedom of the press still felt. Cooper himself expresses gratitude that he now may libel and blaspheme at will, and that his application to President Adams for a place has at last been granted!

The public comments of the Republicans upon the trial were, from the very nature of the case, more restrained. The precarious situation of the editor of the *Aurora* caused him to be unusually discreet. Thus he stated, after the verdict had been rendered, that he had studiously

[36] Philadelphia *Gazette*, April 25, 1800.

[37] *Ibid.*, May 8, 1800.

[38] Written by Mr. Dennie, a native of New England, and sent to Cobbett in London, who republished it in the *London Porcupine*, Nov. 1, 1800, and subsequently in *Porcupine's Works*, XII, 114-8.

refrained from the insertion of any article which might be construed as intended to influence the proceedings while the trial was going on, especially since he felt that Cooper needed no apologia. "We did not think that a character distinguished thro' a very active and conspicuous life, for supereminent talents and disinterestedness, the devotion of a rich genius and a competent fortune to the cause of truth and liberty stood in need of any vindication."[39] So the *Aurora* refrained from remarking upon the verdict, knowing that notes had been taken by a gentleman for the benefit of the public.[40] It felt it necessary to say no more than that the Republicans might be assured that they would have every reason to be satisfied with the effect of "this most singular trial" on the mind of the public, and with the whole tenor of Cooper's conduct on that occasion.[41] From a former client and a chief advocate of the principles of the Republican party this seems rather mild, but Duane's own perilous position is doubtless a sufficient explanation.

A more intimate friend, in a personal letter, spoke without restraint. Priestley wrote an old friend that Cooper had gained great credit by the trial, that he would doubtless be a rising man in the country, and that his trial had been the last blow to the Federalist party, which was now broken up.[42] A staunch Democrat from the Old Dominion who has not figured hitherto in our narrative gave strong private and public evidence of his disapproval of the proceedings and of his sympathy for

[39] April 25, 1800. Cooper's fortune was hardly "competent" at this time.

[40] Presumably these notes formed the text for *An Account of the Trial of Thomas Cooper*, Philadelphia, April, 1800. The preface, notes, and appendix were written by Cooper, but he stated that the work was not printed for him, despite the statement on the title page.

[41] *Cf.* also, May 13, 27; and "Letters of William Duane," Mass. Hist. Soc. *Proceedings*, XL, 260.

[42] Rev. T. Lindsey, May 29, 1800, Rutt, II, 436.

Cooper. Senator Stevens Thomson Mason of Virginia, writing to James Monroe, expressed deep concern at the suppression of political inquiry by the Federalists, who were well aware that the conduct of John Adams could not stand scrutiny, and stated that he would send Monroe a copy of Cooper's trial, which he described as ''a most cruel and abominable persecution.''[43] Not only so, but he attended the prisoner at the bar of the court, and greeted him with ''a fraternal hug and a most hearty congratulation'' immediately the sentence was pronounced. The Philadelphia *Gazette* reminded its readers that the same General Mason had sheltered Callender while the latter was on his travels *incognito* and had kindly interposed to relieve him from the natural course of justice when he had been taken up as a footpad.[44] The anti-British sentiments of Cooper commended him greatly to the Irish. At the anniversary festival of the Columbian Order of St. Tammany, on May 12, where a toast was also proposed to ''Brother William Duane,'' Cooper was acclaimed ''the man of universal science and liberty, suffering for truth under perversion of power.''[45]

One scene of violence resulted from the trial, in which Cooper's son, who seems to have inherited his father's impetuosity, was the most prominent figure. This was the son who later as a midshipman at Annapolis caused his father grave concern because of intemperance. Thomas Cooper, Jr., a youth of not more than eighteen years, resentful of the repeated attacks on his father in the Philadelphia *Gazette,* both during and after the trial, fell

[43] April 29, 1800, Monroe Papers (Library of Congress), VIII, 1061. Mason was the man who created such an uproar by publishing the text of Jay's treaty in the *Aurora*, contrary to the senate's action in forbidding publication.

[44] April 25, 1800.

[45] *Aurora*, May 14, 1800; *cf.* rejoinder, Philadelphia *Gazette*, June 3, 1800.

upon Andrew Brown, its publisher, and did his filial duty by chastising him. Later, in a letter to the *Aurora*,[46] he stated that Brown's strictures had tended to influence the minds of the jury as well as the public against his father, and that though he had transgressed the law and could not legally defend his action, he was convinced that he had punished Brown no more than he deserved. According to young Cooper's account of subsequent developments, Captain McEuen of *McPherson's Blues,* which was apparently a Federalist organization,[47] seized him by the hair, struck him repeatedly while others held him, scratched him on the face, and when told that he was Cooper's son, he or some one else said that he should be beaten the more on that account.

While the apostle of liberty was beginning his term of imprisonment, a movement was begun among his Federalist friends at Northumberland to obtain a pardon from the president. These men, with whom Cooper said he had always lived on friendly terms despite political differences, circulated a petition in his behalf. In a communication to the *Aurora*,[48] Cooper thanked his friends for their kindness, and said he had repeatedly heard that the remission of his sentence was generally expected in Northumberland. He said that he was not so attached to his new lodgings but that he would be glad to quit them with propriety, but added: "I am of opinion with Mr. Adams that 'repentance should precede forgiveness,' and until I receive myself, and hear that Dr. Priestley has received a satisfactory acknowledgement from Mr. Adams of the impropriety of his conduct to us, I may be

[46] May 9, 1800. The letters from Cooper's descendants from which our information about his children has been gained contain no reference to this son by name. Presumably he was one of the two unnamed sons about whom nothing was known. For the latter history of this youth, see below, pp. 167-8 n.

[47] *Cf. Aurora,* June 14, 1800.   [48] May 17, 1800.

turned out from hence, but I will not leave the place
under the acceptance of a favor from President Adams.''
He went on to say that he would not be ''the voluntary
cats-paw of electioneering clemency,'' that the sudden
conversion of the Federalists to moderation was suspicious, and that he hoped the Republicans would be on
guard against their insidious designs.

He was determined that as much Republican capital as
possible should be made out of his punishment. An account of his trial, based upon notes taken in shorthand by
one who attended, was announced for sale at the office of
the *Aurora,* May 14. The preface, notes, and appendix
were written by Cooper, but he insisted that the account
of the trial itself was not written for him, as was erroneously stated on the title page.[49] Nevertheless, he vouched
for its essential accuracy, thought useful lessons might
be learned from it, and doubtless rejoiced that Republican campaign literature was to this extent enriched
through his agency.[50]

He was permitted to serve out his term without inter-
ruption, and came out of prison early in October, to
plunge again into political controversy. While in prison,
where his abnormally active mind was free to roam at
large according to its wont, he relieved the tedium of
confinement by beginning a work in which the bankruptcy
law of America was compared with that of England.[51] In
the preface of this treatise, which issued from the Philadelphia press in 1801, he stated that the compilation
originated from the desire of being engaged in some professional pursuit during the latter months of ''a tedious
imprisonment to which I had the honour of being sentenced for exposing some few among the errors of a

---

[49] *Account of Trial,* p. 64.   [50] *Ibid.,* preface.
[51] *The Bankrupt Law of America, compared with the Bankrupt Law of England.*

weak, a wicked and a vindictive administration.'' During
his imprisonment he doubtless received numerous visits
from his friends and political associates,[52] and in the
abundant leisure which was afforded him meditated upon
ways and means to advance the cause of liberty.

By October 10, when he sent a fiery communication to
one of the Federalist papers, he was a free man. One
morning shortly before this date, Hall the marshal called
on him and told him that his term of confinement was
ended and that he was free to leave the prison.[53] Cooper
answered that he had not yet paid his fine, but expected
to do so that day. The marshal said that was no matter;
he might pay it when convenient. So they went out
together and met Israel Israel, the Republican sheriff of
Philadelphia who had befriended Cooper before. In the
street a letter containing a draft for four hundred dollars drawn on Abel Humphrys at two months was delivered to him. Humphrys, according to Cooper a bitter
English Federalist, refused to discount this, but upon the
application of Israel to Stephen Girard, the latter dis-
counted it without charge. It is not clear whether the
money was owed Cooper or whether he received it as an
honorarium from some Republican source. The failure
to secure a receipt from the marshal caused him much
trouble later when he sought the repayment of his fine.

The return to freedom could not have been very jubi-
lant or triumphal, because Mrs. Cooper had died a few
days before the release of her husband.[54] To this grief
was added the derangement of personal and professional
affairs. We know little of the inner side of Cooper's life

[52] Cf. his ''Table-Talk,'' Duyckinck, Cyclopedia of American Literature,
II, 333.

[53] Cooper to Senator Mahlon Dickerson, March 13, 1830, American Historical Review, VI, 733. He did not then remember the exact date of his
discharge.

[54] Bankrupt Law, preface.

during these days. Probably the "seditious convict" returned home for a few days to greet the remaining members of his own household and to seek counsel and comfort from his old friends, the Priestley's, with whom he had been living before his imprisonment. But he could not have lingered long in Northumberland for, whether from insensibility to grief, excessive ardor of political passion, or the desire to leave himself no time to brood over personal misfortune, he immediately rushed headlong into the political conflict, and left a plain trail through the newspapers of the period.

In the first place, he had a score to settle with C. P. Wayne, the editor of the Federalist *Gazette of the United States*, who from the vantage point of his Philadelphia office had been heaping maledictions upon the head of the helpless prisoner, who had been unable to "repay insolence by personal chastisement." Since he had been bound over to good behavior for twelve months and two of his friends had joined him to give surety, he could not take personal action even upon his release, but he could and did write a vigorous letter of expostulation in which he made threats of future vengeance.[55] Certain of his friends of Irish extraction, however, who labored under no such limitations, attacked the offending editor in his office, although with little injury to him.[56] The Federalist press played up the incident as an "United Irish Riot" and an exemplification of "Jacobin Liberty of the Press." One of the rioters was Dr. James Reynolds, who had been implicated in an earlier riot in the city[57] and

---

[55] *Gazette of the United States*, Oct. 11, 1800, letter dated Oct. 10.

[56] *Ibid.*, Oct. 13, 1800; Philadelphia *Gazette*, Oct. 13, 1800.

[57] He was tried with Duane and others, Feb. 21, 1799, for his connection with a riot in St. Mary's church-yard; see report of the trial, *Duane Pamphlets* (Library of Congress), LVI, 4; Wharton, *State Trials*, pp. 343-88. He was presumably Irish or of Irish sympathies, and cannot be identified with the James Reynolds of the Hamilton-Reynolds affair.

who accompanied Cooper to New York late in October, perhaps to aid him in the mission of law enforcement which drew him there.

Shortly after his release from prison, Cooper learned that his own strictures upon John Adams had been more than matched by the scathing words of Alexander Hamilton in his famous letter concerning the public conduct and character of the president.[58] The remarks of the former secretary of the treasury were no less damning and were far more likely to bring the chief magistrate into contempt and disrepute than were the more incidental remarks of Cooper, who had sought primarily to justify himself against a man who he felt had played him and Dr. Priestley false in the revelation of private and confidential correspondence. Hamilton, without any fear of prosecution we may be sure, had deliberately framed an indictment of the entire public career of John Adams and had discussed the limitations of the president's personality in most ruthless fashion. He had gone so far as to speak of "the unfortunate foibles of a vanity without bounds and a jealousy capable of discoloring every object,"[59] of the "disgusting egotism, the distempered jealousy and the ungovernable indiscretion of Mr. Adams's temper,"[60] and of the "desultoriness of his mind."[61] He had described him as an ordinary man who dreamed himself to be a Frederick and through vanity refrained from counseling with his ministers,[62] had stated that he was liable to paroxysms of anger which deprived him of self-command and had led him to humiliate most if not all of his ministers and many distinguished members of Congress,[63] and had declared that so great and intrinsic were

---

[58] *Works of Alexander Hamilton* (Lodge edition), VI, 391-444.
[59] *Ibid.*, VI, 396.   [60] *Ibid.*, VI, 402.
[61] *Ibid.*, VI, 423-4.   [62] *Ibid.*, VI, 419.
[63] *Ibid.*, VI, 429.

the defects of his character that he was unfitted for the office of chief magistrate.[64]

There can be little doubt but that the prosecution of Alexander Hamilton for seditious libel against the president would have been quite as justifiable as was that of Thomas Cooper,[65] but only an audacious man would have regarded it as even a remote possibility or would have thought of the threat of it as an expedient political manoeuvre. The erstwhile English reformer was nothing if not bold; one who had in earlier years denounced and defied Edmund Burke[66] was not afraid to threaten even the redoubtable Hamilton. It is not certain that he had seen the whole of the letter of the most distinguished member of the Federalist party when he formed his plan against him,[67] but he had learned what its general character was and had recognized it as an instrument supplied as by Providence for his hand.

The story of Cooper's efforts to obtain an impartial administration of justice can be pieced out with fragments culled from the contemporary newspapers.[68] He and Dr. Reynolds went to New York late in October. Their visit was greeted with contemptuous comment in the Federalist press. The New York *Gazette,* for example, thus remarked upon it:

[64] *Ibid.*, VI, 392. For strictures upon Adams's public conduct, see in addition, VI, 410, 413.

[65] *Cf.* the statement of McMaster, *United States*, II, 506-7: "Had Thomas Cooper, or James Thomson Callender, or William Duane put forth a pamphlet half as savage, he would in a few days have been safely lodged in jail. And so would Hamilton have been had the Sedition Law been passed for an honest purpose, and not to meet a party need."

[66] See above, pp. 45-53.

[67] Extracts from it were published in *Aurora*, Oct. 22, 25, 1800.

[68] The account here given essentially reproduces that given by the present writer in the *Amer. Hist. Rev.*, XXIX, 76-81, under the title "The Threatened Prosecution of Alexander Hamilton under the Sedition Act by Thomas Cooper."

The famous Thomas Cooper is in town—Dr. Reynolds accompanies him through the streets. A precious pair! It is said Cooper has come on for the purpose of commencing a prosecution against General Hamilton, for a lible on the President!!! Cooper has an experimental knowledge of the nature of the sedition act, and would willingly see it put in force against one of the best friends of the government.[69]

The *Gazette* also stated that Cooper had called at its office and purchased a copy of Hamilton's letter, but indignantly denied that any conversation had been had with him. Perhaps this was the first copy of the entire letter which Cooper had seen.

Meanwhile, a Republican mass-meeting had been held at Lovett's Hotel on October 27, "to congratulate Thomas Cooper, Esquire of Northumberland, on his emerging from *Chase's* repository of republicans," and toasts had been drunk to him, to the Irish, to Dr. Reynolds, and to William Duane.[70] Cooper was here described as "the conspicuous victim of the sedition law, the friend of science, and the able advocate of universal liberty." The Federalist Philadelphia *Gazette* commented sarcastically upon the meeting,[71] but the *Aurora,* whose editor had been toasted and whose republicanism was unreserved, had an editorial of almost a column a few days later on Cooper's mission.[72] To this mission it gave unqualified approval, saying that Hamilton would have no cause to complain after his prosecution of Frothingham,[73]

[69] Quoted in Philadelphia *Gazette,* Nov. 1, 1800.

[70] *Aurora,* Nov. 5, 1800.   [71] *Ibid.,* Nov. 4, 1800.

[72] *Ibid.,* Nov. 7, 1800.

[73] David Frothingham, convicted Nov. 16, 1799, on a charge of libel against Hamilton, and sentenced to pay a fine of $500 and be imprisoned for six months. He had charged Hamilton with an attempt to buy the *Aurora,* and had insinuated that he had received "secret service money of the king of Great Britain" for this purpose. Wharton, *State Trials,* pp. 649-51.

and that the Federalist party must swallow to the very dregs the cup they had administered to others. The *Aurora* was fearful lest the district attorney of New York would reject Cooper's advances, but felt that the temple of justice should be open to all. It declared that thanks were due "the respectable and much injured Thomas Cooper, for the noble and spirited firmness" which he had displayed in urging Hamilton's prosecution.

For the moment, however, the would-be prosecutor was foiled; he had hoped to see Hamilton in New York, but found that he had departed for Albany. Nothing daunted, he sent Hamilton the following extraordinary letter, which one Philadelphia paper published under the heading "Precious Letter from a very modest Man"[74] and of which another said, "A more preposterous affectation of regard for character . . . is not to be met with in the annals of Jacobinism."[75]

I came to New York for the purpose of asking Gen. Hamilton, in person, whether he was the author of an attack on the character of President Adams, which bears his name; and to say that I mean to use that information for the purpose of instituting against you, Sir, a prosecution under the detestable act of Congress, commonly known by the name of the *"Sedition Law."*

Under this law, passed through the influence of a party, of which you are (and I think justly) regarded as the head, I have suffered six months tedious imprisonment, and I have paid a fine of 100 dollars.[76] I therefore have a right to retaliate: I have a right to try the experiment, whether *Republicanism* is to be the victim of a law, which *Aristocracy* can break through with impunity. There have been many petty offenders in this respect among what is called the Federal party; but I have nothing to

---

[74] *Gazette of the United States*, Nov. 20, 1800.
[75] Philadelphia *Gazette*, Nov. 19, 1800, quoting the entire letter.
[76] Misprint for 400 dollars.

do with the Fenno's,[77] the Wayne's,[78] and the Journeymen of
Federalism. You are worth trying the experiment upon. Your
energy and your talents have rendered you a conspicuous object
of praise and blame.

I therefore have determined that in one way or other you shall
be brought before the public on this account; and I did so far
calculate on your character as to suppose, that you would not
deny what you have already written and sanctioned with your
name. I expect by your answer (directed to me at Lancaster,
Pennsylvania) the same information which I should have hoped
for personally. I came to town last night between 7 and 8 and
sent to you immediately. I write this hastily at eight this morning to send by the stage. I shall purchase your pamphlet at
Lang's, but make no use of that opportunity of prosecution till
I hear from you, which I expect by return post. The answer, I
have no doubt, will be such as becomes your character.

If the writer of this letter seriously expected a reply
from its recipient, the subsequent course of events must
have grievously disappointed him. Hamilton did not
deign to answer it and apparently turned it over immediately to the Albany *Register* for publication. From this
paper it was duly copied by both the Federalist and Republican press[79] and it was much commented upon both at
the time and subsequently,[80] so Cooper had at least the
satisfaction of gaining considerable publicity for himself
and of advertising further the inconsistency of the party
of the administration. But he was denied an extended
controversy such as he had probably hoped for. Hamilton
would engage in conflict on no such terms, or perhaps

[77] John Ward Fenno, editor of the *Gazette of the United States*, 1798-
1800.

[78] C. P. Wayne, Fenno's successor. See above, p. 137.

[79] *Cf. Aurora*, Nov. 20, 1800.

[80] *Cf. Gazette of the United States*, Nov. 24, 1800, copying about two-
thirds of a column from the New York *Gazette;* and Nov. 25, editorial
paragraph.

did not care to match pens with this particular antagonist on any terms whatsoever.

Meanwhile, the challenger had returned to Pennsylvania. Whether or not he went to Lancaster to lend a hand in the political affray at the state capital, as he seems to have intended, we do not know. Late in December, he was writing from Northumberland to the *Aurora* to explain to all anxious Democrats why Alexander Hamilton was still at large. Personal affairs, after his long neglect of them, had demanded his undivided attention, and well indeed they might. There were doubtless many personal readjustments which had to be made, as a result of his domestic tragedy and his long absence because of imprisonment. While he was making them, presidential electors were chosen, and the necessity for further campaigning against the Federalists was for the time removed.

In later years he looked back with satisfaction upon his activities in the campaign of 1800, and his sufferings for the sacred cause of freedom of speech, and he later gave Alexander Hamilton words of praise which he denied John Adams. For the moment, however, his vanity, which was excessive, was wounded by Hamilton's contemptuous disregard of him. Apparently he had disquieted that distinguished gentleman not at all. Whatever his motives may have been in the first place, he had proceeded in entire seriousness and deadly earnestness, and it seems unlikely that he found any amusement in the final developments, as another man might well have done. The *Aurora* published his letter on the last day of the year. He had doubtless delivered himself of it with all the solemnity which befitted such an epilogue.

The melancholy occasion which called me to Northumberland has hitherto prevented my noticing the conduct of Gen. *Hamil-*

ton. To the letter I sent him to Albany, I have received no answer; and I have sufficient reason to believe it was published by himself. I shall be grossly deceived if this will not furnish an additional reason to his friends to mistrust his judgement.

To Gen. *Hamilton* I owe no account of my future proceedings: but the public may desire, why this conspicuous offender against the *Sedition Law*—this Arch-defamer of our first magistrate, should not be called to account?—If this favourite law of the anti-republicans cannot protect the character of Mr. Adams—if General Hamilton, the vindictive prosecutor of Frothingham, may sin against the Sedition Law, and against the President with impunity, while republicans alone are subjected to its penalties —if no Attorney General is *directed* to prosecute, and the keen-eyed zeal of Judge Chase himself is closed upon the offence— what are we to think of the motives which produced this federal safeguard?

From any prosecution of mine general Hamilton is *now* safe. While there was a chance of Mr. Adams or Mr. Pinckney being called to the presidency, the experiment was worth trying,— whether the conduct of federal judges, and a federal jury, and a federal president towards general Hamilton, would have been similar to that which republicans have experienced, whose prosecution was directed by Mr. Adams, and conducted under the mild auspices of his honor Judge Chase!

But the hopes of aristocracy are no more! Neither the manageable Mr. Pinckney, nor the unmanageable Mr. Adams, is called to the presidency; and how either would have behaved on the conviction of general Hamilton, cannot now be ascertained. I have no motive to proceed. Nor will I contaminate the administration of Mr. Jefferson by promoting the operation of a law, which he would disdain to use against the most virulent of his opponents.

Even were this not the case, I should have relinquished the prosecution of general Hamilton, after the ignorance he has shewn of what was due his own character, and to mine. I lament that a man who might have rendered himself highly useful and truly estimable, should not only degrade himself by gross violations of moral propriety, but become at length so insensible as he appears to be, to the dictates of common politeness. The experiment I wished to make was worth making. I thought Gen. Hamilton was an object worthy of the experiment. I was mistaken: no man has the character sufficient for the purpose, who from ignorance or irritation, from pride or peevishness, can put off the character of a gentleman.

This episode probably played no significant part in determining the outcome of the campaign of 1800, but it may at least be regarded as a most delightful bit of political irony. It is surprising that it should have entirely escaped the attention of biographers of Hamilton and writers on the period. It was certainly well advertised at the time. Harrison Gray Otis, in a speech on the Sedition Law in the house of representatives in January, 1801, replying to the contention of Albert Gallatin that the failure of the magistrates to notice Hamilton's pamphlet indicated partizanship in the enforcement of the act, reminded the Pennsylvanian that in this particular case whatever designs the government may have had were anticipated by the eagerness of Democratic zeal.[81] Any interference with the plans of the "Northumbrian apostle of liberty" who rode post to New York to apply the law with his own hands, would have been most unseemly!

Cooper's absorption in the proposed indictment of Hamilton and in personal affairs at Northumberland delayed his participation in the bitter controversy over the method of choosing presidential electors in Pennsylvania.[82] Ultimately he burst into violent expression on the subject, thus bringing to a fitting close his activities in the campaign of 1800. The state legislature had neg-

---

[81] *Annals of Congress,* 6 Cong., p. 958.

[82] An account of this controversy is given by Channing, *History of the United States,* IV, 234-5. See Pennsylvania *House Journal,* 1800-01, pp. 40 ff., 48 ff. We have not had access to the *Senate Journal.* For the final act, see *Aurora,* Nov. 21, 1800. This paper in general gives the discussions in the assembly in fuller form than they are given in the *Journal.*

lected to provide for any method of choosing electors, and when it met in November, 1800, the deadlock between the Republican house of representatives and the Federalist senate, which had prevented earlier action, continued. By that time, it was too late to provide for election by the people, so the question was the method of choice by the assembly. The final outcome was the choice of eight Republican and seven Federalist electors, although this did not accurately represent the ratio between the two parties. The *Aurora* reckoned this as being eleven to four instead of eight to seven.[83]

The columns of the *Aurora* during November and December, 1800, fairly teemed with editorials and communications in which the villainy of the Federalist majority in the senate was emphasized. Cooper did not get into the fight until the end of December, and then he attacked not the action of the state senate primarily, but the constitution of that body. The *Aurora* on the first day of the new year published an address of about fifty inhabitants of Northumberland County to their neighbors and fellow-citizens in regard to the senate of Pennsylvania, and a form of petition addressed to the two houses of the legislature. Cooper's name was first on the list of signers, and the address, which bears many marks of his views and style, was later acknowledged by him as his composition. It began, after an introductory paragraph, by propounding the question, "In the legislative system of Pennsylvania, of *what use is the senate?*" This inquiry had been suggested by the obstinate opposition of that body to the known wishes of the majority of the people. Two members had successfully resisted and checked the popular desire.[84] Doubt of the usefulness of the senate, it was

[83] Nov. 15, 17, 1800.

[84] The senate had rejected by a vote of 13 to 11 the proposal of the house that electors be chosen by joint-ballot. *House Journal*, 1800-01, p. 22; list of yeas and nays in *Aurora*, Nov. 15, 1800.

said, had long been felt by the signers—it would probably have been accurate to say, by Cooper; the rest of the group were doubtless much more exercised over the immediate controversy than over the general question. "We have for some time had reason to doubt whether the machine of government (to use the metaphor of the illustrious Franklin) can proceed more efficaciously, for having one horse to draw before,[85] and two to drag behind."[86]

The greatest objection to the senate, according to Cooper, was its unresponsiveness to changes in public sentiment because of the length of the term of office, which was four years, a fourth of the body being elected each year. He felt that experience had "added more facts in support of that grand result of all political history— the basis of all republican government—that *power entrusted for too long a period will certainly be abused.*" He did not deny that a second deliberative assembly might sometimes be of use, but he could see no reason why the senate should have an *absolute negative* upon the acts of the representatives—perhaps he favored a suspensive veto—or why senators should be elected for four years instead of one. He deplored the American propensity to imitate and adopt the complex forms and antirepublican maxims of the corrupt system of Great Britain. Perhaps his experiences in conjunction with Duane were responsible for the intimation that the United States senate might be used by analogy to strengthen the argument. He felt that the senatorial doctrine of privilege was derived from the impure source of British aristocracy and was at open hostility with freedom of speech and trial by jury.

It was suggested in the address that citizens of the county hold meetings and sign and transmit to the legislature petitions similar to the one attached. In the peti-

---

[85] House.   [86] Senate and governor.

tion the recent misunderstanding between the two houses was deplored, and the length of the senatorial term was assigned as one of its chief causes. Annual election was recommended, and the assembly was requested to take constitutional measures to remedy the evil.

The chief significance of Cooper's action in this matter lies in the fact that later, after he had become a judge, he opposed the calling of a constitutional convention for the purpose of changing the manner of electing state senators and limiting the powers of the upper house. The senate was at that time a bulwark against the violent attacks of the more extreme Democrats upon the judiciary. Cooper's identification with the more conservative faction laid him open to the charge of inconsistency, and his unfortunate address of 1800 was produced in justification of the charge.[87]

Throughout the campaign of 1800, however, he was a consistent Democratic-Republican, a member of the opposition, clamoring for freedom of speech and the responsibility of public servants. By his political writings, his association with Duane against the United States senate, his own martyrdom for the cause of the party, and his energetic actions after his release from prison, he made himself a conspicuous figure. By the Federalists he was regarded and described as an infamous demagogue, by the Republicans he was hailed as martyr and apostle. Few Republicans did so much to set forth the political philosophy of the party, and if the rank and file could not appreciate the extraordinary intellectual endowments of the man as their leaders came in due time to do, they liked to speak òf him as a man of science and learning and to claim him as their own.

His high standing among his fellow Republicans was indicated by various toasts offered to him at party gath-

87 See below, ch. VI.

erings. Thus at a festival held in Philadelphia early in January, in celebration of the favorable commencement of the century and the success of Republican efforts, Dr. Reynolds in the chair, a volunteer was offered to "Thomas Cooper of Northumberland—May his talents, his services and his sufferings, be long and gratefully remembered."[88] At the various dinners on March 4, in celebration of the inauguration of Jefferson, toasts were drunk to him and to other sufferers under the Sedition Act.[89] He was coupled with Lyon, Callender, and Duane, to all of whom he was far superior, and apparently his sufferings under this law served most to arouse sympathy and enthusiasm for him. Another toast coupled his name with that of Priestley, and intimated that his greatest service had been with his pen.[90]

The one-time English reformer may not have been fully appreciated even by his co-laborers, but he had run true to form, and in some part through his efforts the party of opposition had been able to secure the reins of government. With his party, he was shortly to come into a position of responsibility with large opportunities for constructive service. It remained to be seen whether he was to prove a constructive force, who had hitherto been essentially critical and destructive, whether he was to remain true to his democratic principles when confronted with the practical problems of government.

[88] Jan. 3, 1801, *Aurora*, Jan. 6.   [89] *Ibid.*, March 10, 12, 1801.
[90] *Ibid.*, March 9, 1801.

CHAPTER V

THE LUZERNE CLAIMS, 1801-1804

THE years between the accession of Jefferson to the presidency and the removal of Cooper to a new field of labor in South Carolina in 1820, were the most conservative of his entire career. The inauguration of a Republican president brought no immediate break, however, in the life and activities of one who had hitherto been ever a member of the party of democracy. One writer has attributed Cooper's subsequent alienation from the more radical of his former associates to his dissatisfaction with the political rewards which came to him.[1] At this time, however, he sought no federal office, but expressed contentment with a promised appointment to the state judiciary.[2] For reasons which will appear, this appointment did not come as soon as had been expected, but within a few months he was made a member of the very important Luzerne commission, upon which he was to do genuinely constructive public service, and his loyalty to the Republican cause in Pennsylvania was not for some years called into question.

During the spring of 1801, he gave clear indication of his continued political intimacy with William Duane by serving as counsel for the editor of the *Aurora* several times in April and May.[3] Associated with him in the first

---

[1] Wharton, *State Trials*, p. 681.

[2] Cooper to Jefferson, March 17, 1801, Jefferson Papers, CX.

[3] Seven men charged with an assault on Duane, May 15, 1799, were

case were A. J. Dallas and Mahlon Dickerson, later to be senator from New Jersey and the most consistent advocate of the repayment of Cooper's fine.[4] Every time Duane appeared in court apparently he had as counsel such of these three men as were available. Cooper delayed his departure for Luzerne in order to serve him in May,[5] and by his activities in the Hollingsworth case[6] incurred the animosity of the prosecutor who later charged him with having brought about the intoxication of one of the witnesses. Cooper's letter of denial, sent from Wilkes-Barre in November, 1802,[7] showed that the alienation between the editor of the *Aurora* and his former counsel, due to the waning democratic ardor of the latter, had certainly not then come.

Cooper's most amazing action during the first year of the Jeffersonian régime was his candidacy for the position of chief clerk of the Pennsylvania senate, the very body whose usefulness he had so recently questioned. His action was the more surprising because he was then engaged in his work as Luzerne commissioner, and successful candidacy for an unimportant clerical post could have added nothing to his dignity and usefulness. The

brought up for trial in the mayor's court, April 27, 1801, and judgment was given in Duane's favor, May 7. His counsel were A. J. Dallas, Cooper, and Mahlon Dickerson. *Aurora*, April 28, May 8, 1801. The case against Duane instituted at the desire of the senate was called up May 12, 1801, when his counsel, Cooper and Dickerson, secured postponement. *Aurora*, May 14. This suit was dismissed Oct. 14, 1801. *Aurora*, Oct. 17.

[4] See below, pp. 374-5.

[5] Duane to Jefferson, June 10, 1801, Mass. Hist. Soc. *Proceedings*, 2 ser., XX, 266.

[6] Levi Hollingsworth prosecuted Duane for an alleged libel, bringing suit in a federal court on the ground that the defendant was a British subject, as the court ruled. *Aurora*, May 19, 25, 1801.

[7] For the letter of Hollingsworth to Duane in which this charge was made, see *Aurora*, Nov. 13, 1802. He did not mention Cooper by name, but Cooper in his reply stated that the charge was directed against him. *Aurora*, Nov. 23.

ranks of the Republicans in the senate had been rein-
forced as a result of the last election and he perhaps
counted on partisan support, but his criticism had been
directed against the senate as an institution, not merely
against its Federalist members, so his application was
highly presumptuous as well as undignified. It met the
fate it so richly deserved. Speaker Samuel Maclay of
Northumberland presented his petition, but it commanded only one vote in addition to his own.[8] Perhaps
Cooper cherished some resentment at this cavalier treatment, but at any rate there was now nothing to prevent
his complete devotion to a matter of far greater importance and one which was worthy of his abilities.

Until the decision against Connecticut by the Decree
of Trenton in 1782, that state had claimed, under the
terms of her charter from Charles II, the land in the
Wyoming valley which had been largely settled by her
citizens.[9] Settlement in this region had been fostered by
the Susquehanna Company, which had existed since
1753[10] and had purchased the land from the Indians and
disposed of it in turn to settlers, without having, however, any title from the colony of Connecticut or from
the crown. The Decree of Trenton[11] affirmed the title of

---

[8] Cooper's petition was presented Dec. 8, 1801. Pennsylvania *Senate Journal*, XII, 20. George Bryan was elected, Dec. 9, by a vote of 20 to 2. Those
voting for Cooper were Maclay and Robert Whitehill of Cumberland, *ibid.*,
XII, 25-6.

[9] We have discovered no satisfactory account of the Wyoming controversy,
but the chief materials necessary for one are contained in William H.
Egle's ''Documents relating to the Connecticut Settlement in the Wyoming
Valley,'' *Pennsylvania Archives*, 2 series, XVIII. (This we shall refer to
hereafter as *Wyoming Documents*.) The best brief account which we have
found is contained in Cooper's own ''Observations on the Wyoming Controversy,'' *Aurora*, March 17, 1802. For developments before the Revolution,
see L. H. Gipson's *Jared Ingersoll*, ch. XI; and J. T. Adams's *Revolutionary New England*, pp. 204, 260-1, 413.

[10] Minutes, *Wyoming Documents*, pp. 1-123.

[11] *Ibid.*, p. 629.

Pennsylvania to both soil and jurisdiction, but did not deal with the question of private title to the soil, and this continued a subject of controversy for a couple of decades. There were Connecticut settlers upon the land and the Susquehanna Company continued to exist and encouraged them to stand up for their rights. Meanwhile, Pennsylvania settlers had come in, some of them with titles from the state.

A law confirming the titles of the Connecticut settlers who had been resident in the region at the time of the Decree of Trenton or earlier, had been passed by the Pennsylvania legislature in 1787,[12] but this had been first suspended[13] and then repealed,[14] the legislature having thus shown itself vacillating and indecisive in policy. The opinion of Cooper as expressed in 1802, almost a year after his appointment as Luzerne commissioner, was that the repeal of the confirming law constituted an annulment of a contract and did much injustice, especially to those who sought to obey the law.[15] From the time of the Decree of Trenton until the passage of the compromise act of 1799, five commissions at one time or another had acted ineffectually, and apparently there had been considerable violence in the Wyoming district.

The compromise act of 1799,[16] under the provisions of which Cooper later began his work, provided for compensation to the Pennsylvania claimants of lands within the seventeen townships of the county of Luzerne and for the granting of titles to Connecticut claimants who had been actual settlers at the time of or before the Decree of Trenton. A commission of three was appointed to carry the act into effect. The Pennsylvania claimants were to

---

[12] *Ibid.*, pp. 660-4. [13] March 29, 1788, *ibid.*, pp. 675-6.
[14] April 1, 1790, *ibid.*, pp. 682-3.
[15] "Observations on the Wyoming Controversy," *Aurora*, March 17, 1802.
[16] April 4, *Wyoming Documents*, pp. 715-20.

convey their land to the state and receive compensation in accordance with the value set upon it by the commissioners, who were to be guided by a schedule of prices given in the act. The Connecticut claimants were to be given title upon the payment to the state of a considerably smaller amount per acre than that which was to be awarded to the Pennsylvanians who were surrendering their claims. The work of the commissioners was to be primarily the division of the land into specified classes and the award of land to claimants under the prescribed conditions.

The original ₍act appointed as commissioners Isaac Whelen, Thomas Boude, and General William Irvine, and provided that vacancies should be filled by appointment of the governor. Cooper said that his commission was the third under the act, but apparently the only difference between the second commission and the first was the substitution of Andrew Porter for Isaac Whelen. The third commission consisted of Cooper, General John Steele, and William Wilson.[17] Cooper's appointment had been made, or at least definitely determined upon, by March 31, 1801, and he served until August, 1804.[18] His term of service, then, lasted slightly more than three years and during this time he seems to have been almost entirely occupied with his laborious duties as commissioner. He desired and expected earlier relief from a task which must have been exceedingly arduous; several times before his term of service was over he expressed satisfaction that his work was nearly done, only to find that it

[17] *Ibid.*, pp. 335-6.

[18] The secretary of the land office, Tench Coxe, wrote him, March 31, 1801, to give specific suggestions about the work, *ibid.*, pp. 389-90. The first letter of the commission was sent in June, 1801, and the last August 3, 1804, *ibid.*, pp. 433-5, 506-9. It appeared in 1811, at the hearings for the removal of Cooper from the judiciary, that he drew a salary as judge from August 1, 1804. *Narrative of Proceedings*, pp. 19, 22.

was again to be necessarily prolonged beyond his expectation.

The new commissioners had scarcely begun their labors when the Federalist press expressed dissatisfaction with the governor's appointments.[19] Oddly enough, in view of Cooper's violent anti-British sentiments, objection was urged on the ground that he, like one other member of the commission and the surveyor and secretary, was an Englishman. The governor was condemned for appointing Old England men to deal with New England men. The *Aurora,* in reply, naturally defended the appointments of the governor whom it had supported, and said in reference to Cooper that the hatred which his talents had excited would render it surprising that any occasion should be left unemployed to attack him.[20]

Before this time, however, the commissioners had arrived at Wilkes-Barre. In June they were writing to various officials and to other persons seeking information in regard to land surveys and titles. Where the names of all the commissioners appear in signature to communications, Cooper's name comes first and frequently he signed alone, so his chairmanship and doubtless his determining influence may be assumed. These letters indicate not only that meticulous attention to intricate detail which seems to have characterized his entire procedure in this matter, but also a spirit of most commendable fairness which he seems also to have carried through the entire service. He was trying to secure a strictly legal settlement and to obviate violence and disorder, but his sympathies seem to have been rather with the Connecticut claimants, whose position was legally weak but morally strong.

In this regard he seems to have gone somewhat beyond

[19] Philadelphia *Gazette,* July 14, 1801.
[20] July 16, 1801.

the secretary of the land office, who, on May 25, made a long public statement in which he emphasized the invalidity of the claims formerly made upon Pennsylvania lands by Connecticut settlers, and sought to evince the liberality of the government and landholders of the state as shown in the act of 1799.[21] Copies of this statement he sent the commissioners, and others he had distributed through the state and in other states, in vindication of Pennsylvania. The attitude of Tench Coxe does not appear to have been one of unfairness or of hostility to the Connecticut claimants, but he was inclined to insist upon the letter of the law in order that there might be no imposition upon the state by intruders or speculators, and was less patient than the commissioners were with violence and obstruction on the part of the New Englanders.

Cooper's attitude cannot be attributed to any predilection which he had for New England, because he was rather unfavorably disposed to that section than otherwise. Nor can it be attributed to party influence, for strong prejudice against the so-called outsiders and in favor of the natives was later expressed at least in the *Aurora*.[22] Indeed, Cooper's favorable attitude toward the New Englanders may have been the beginning of the alienation between him and his former political associates. His association with Tench Coxe,[23] however, and with Governor McKean continued close, and doubtless his conduct as commissioner enhanced him in their esteem. His attitude toward the Connecticut claimants may be naturally explained as having resulted from his own disinterested first-hand study of the situation, his sense of justice, and perhaps an unconscious sympathy for a misunderstood and seemingly oppressed minority.

21 *Aurora*, June 29, July 22, 1801.   22 Jan. 22, 1803.
23 See Coxe's letter of August 29, 1801, *Wyoming Documents*, pp. 418-21.

The attitude of the commissioners during the first months of their work was well described in a long letter to the secretary of the land office.[24] In this they expressed "some slight difference of opinion" between themselves and him, spoke in partial justification of a Luzerne publisher who had failed to publish his letter, and intimated that the effect of this letter had been to arouse a certain amount of dissatisfaction among the Connecticut claimants, who in turn had spoken of the unfairness which had been done them. The commissioners expressed the opinion that a fair and liberal, rather than a strictly legalistic, construction of the act of 1799 would win over the more respectable of the Connecticut settlers to the position of the state, but that any attempt to harass them and any duplicity on the part of the agents would cause them to reject with disgust the terms of a law of which they were not unreasonably suspicious. Cooper stated later that when the commissioners arrived in Luzerne they found no disposition on the part of the Connecticut settlers to take advantage of the law, since the futility of earlier applications and submissions and the failure of previous commissions served to deter them.[25] The policy of the commissioners, accordingly, was to be one of conciliation and scrupulous candor and patience, in order that the forces of opposition to the settlement might be divided and the influence of the speculators upon the ignorant settlers neutralized. By liberality and fairness, they hoped to avoid any occasion for violence and disorder and to obviate the necessity for the use of force by the state.

The principal supporters of the Connecticut title in Wyoming, Cooper felt, would never be induced to submit

[24] July 13, 1801, *ibid.*, pp. 447-58. *Cf.* Coxe's letters in reply, July 24, 29; *ibid.*, pp. 406-14.

[25] "Observations," *Aurora*, March 17, 1802.

except by force or by the overpowering sentiment against them among the Connecticut claimants in general.[26] Indeed, they continued to stir up trouble, not so much among the earlier settlers, who in due time generally submitted under the act of 1799, but among those who had been enticed in by speculators since the Decree of Trenton and were naturally under their influence. With settlers who had expended much effort in improving their land and whose all depended upon their being secured in possession, Cooper had great sympathy, even though they might be ignorant and easily deluded by the principals of the Susquehanna Company. His object, accordingly, was by means of a liberal policy to wean them away from the men who played upon their fears for their own personal advantage. He was influenced further by the consideration that it was highly desirable for the state to have these hardy New Englanders in this particular region, which he felt would become and remain a wilderness if left to Pennsylvanians.[27]

The policy of the commissioners seems to have been statesmanlike, and Tench Coxe made no effort to interfere but continued on terms of entire friendliness with them. Governor McKean, furthermore, in reporting to the assembly in December, 1801, the resignation of the earlier commissioners and the appointment of the present ones, said that the latter had displayed "great assiduity, abilities and fidelity for the task."[28] Subsequent communications between Cooper and the governor indicate that he retained McKean's full confidence throughout his term of service.

In March, 1802, Cooper addressed to the speaker of the

[26] See the letter of the commissioners to the board of property, July, 1801; *Wyoming Documents*, pp. 463-5.

[27] See the letter from the commissioners to McKean, July 21, 1802, *ibid.*, p. 461.

[28] Dec. 5, 1801. *Senate Journal*, XII, 16.

house of representatives a letter containing observations on the Wyoming controversy apropos of amendments to the act of 1799, which were pending.[29] He expressed the opinion that any liberal plan of conciliation steadily pursued would have been accepted by the Connecticut claimants and would probably have terminated the dispute. But since the repeal of the confirming law in 1790, difficulties had been increased by the doubts of old settlers and the influx of new ones. He felt that if a plan of conciliation was to be followed, amendment of the act of 1799, was necessary; if not, the sooner force was resorted to the better.

The supplementary act as finally passed[30] contained several changes which Cooper had approved, although not quite all of them. The most important new provision was designed to force cession of lands by Pennsylvania claimants or to provide for procedure in the absence of such cession, thus facilitating settlement and reassuring the Connecticut settlers who had been loath to submit their claims without assurance of cession by the Pennsylvanians.[31] The commissioners were authorized to survey all the land claimed by a Connecticut settler, whether released by a Pennsylvania claimant or not. A Pennsylvanian not releasing his land before August 1, 1802, should not be entitled to recover it from a Connecticut claimant, but could institute a suit against the commonwealth, the courts being authorized to award just compensation. Despite this desired change in the law, Cooper

[29] *Aurora*, March 17, 1802. This contains an excellent brief history of the entire controversy.

[30] April 6, 1802, *Aurora*, July 16, 1802, by authority.

[31] See the letter of the commissioners, July 31, 1801, *Wyoming Documents*, pp. 447-58. The form of submission to which Connecticut claimants were first asked to subscribe had been objected to as being a complete surrender of their claims, without any guarantee of similar action by the Pennsylvanians.

regarded it as yet very imperfect and hoped for further amendment.[32]

In successive lengthy letters to McKean,[33] Cooper either in conjunction with his associates or on his own authority discussed the entire situation in Wyoming, giving the governor full information about conditions and making suggestions regarding the most desirable procedure. He commented freely upon the disturbing activities of the Susquehanna principals and favored the ultimate apprehension of some of them, particularly Franklin, who was in due time elected to the legislature from Ulster where the opposition centered. With regard to the settlers in general, however, he was hopeful of peaceable acceptance of the conditions, provided there were genuine guarantees against the ruin which they feared. He emphasized the value of these industrious, if ignorant, people who were cultivating a region where Pennsylvanians would be unwilling and unable to live, and discussed the relations of the region to the rest of the state in matters of trade. He opposed the use of force until every peaceable means had been exhausted, because of the suffering which would be involved and the necessary continuance of the exercise of force after it had been begun.

Most of Cooper's work in Luzerne seems to have been practically completed by the autumn of 1802,[34] and his representations to the governor concerned themselves rather with the district as a whole than with Luzerne alone. He took the position that the violent party among the Connecticut claimants was small in number, and that if the policy of conciliation were continued another year

[32] See his letter to Gov. McKean, *ibid.*, pp. 460-2.

[33] See especially the letters of July 21, 1802, *ibid.*, pp. 460-2; Oct. 20, 1802, pp. 487-8; Nov. 15, 1802, pp. 488-92; Jan. 18, 1803, pp. 492-7; Nov. 18, 1803, pp. 500-1.

[34] Letter to McKean, Oct. 20, *ibid.*, p. 487.

the opposition would become negligible and the leaders probably be driven from the state. He was opposed to the use of force until the work of the commission had been finished, which he hoped would be soon because he was anxious to be rid of this unpleasant business. After that, he would have no objection if all intruders were forcibly ejected. But he was particularly anxious that the legislature should do nothing violent or hasty which would set back the existing peaceable proceedings. Apparently there was strong sentiment in the legislature for the Pennsylvania claimants, although no action favorable to them was taken. The *Aurora* commented in January, 1803, upon the conduct of "Connecticut intruders" whose actions, it claimed, the Federalist press did not notice.[35] Perhaps this indicates that the Federalists, with their New England affiliations, tended to support the Connecticut claimants, whereas the Republicans showed stronger local patriotism and upheld the claimants from their own state. If so, we have signs here of an incipient divergence between Cooper and one wing of his party.

In the autumn of 1803, Cooper and one of his colleagues wrote the governor that everything dependent on the personal exertions of the commissioners was finished, but that it would probably be the following May before all the certificates could be issued.[36] He stated that even the half-share men, that is, those who had been brought into the region comparatively recently and were not among the original proprietors of the Susquehanna Company, were beginning to see their true interest and were becoming anxious to secure a Pennsylvania title. The greatest obstacle was the uncertainty of the Penn-

[35] Jan. 22, 1803. *Cf.* the reference to disorder in Cooper's letter of Jan. 18, 1803, *Wyoming Documents*, p. 493.

[36] Nov. 18, 1803, *ibid.*, p. 500.

sylvania title in the regions outside the seventeen townships.

Cooper's salary as judge began on August 1, 1804, although he wrote a letter as commissioner as late as August 3. At this time, then, his services on the commission came to an end and most of the remaining work, which appears to have been largely clerical, was probably done by the clerk. Some difficulty arose, early in 1804, on the question of the form of the certificates. Thus the commissioners wrote in January to Andrew Ellicott, who had succeeded Coxe as secretary of the land office, to express surprise and indignation that the board of property had refused to grant patents on the commissioners' certificates to the Connecticut claimants.[37] According to a provision of the supplementary act of 1802, which the commissioners had proposed, it was no longer necessary to the Connecticut certificate that the land claimed by a Connecticut settler should be first released to the state by a Pennsylvania claimant. The board of property seems to have desired that the certificates state what part of the land certified had been released, but the commissioners decided that this would prodigiously increase their labors, protract the settlement, and be an entirely unnecessary expense. They felt, furthermore, that it was their function, not that of the board of property, to determine just what form should be used. So they openly expressed their opinion, to which they claimed no objection was raised, and issued a form of certificate which they regarded as strictly legal and as quite sufficient.[38] They were confident that a Connecticut claimant could put entire dependence upon the validity of his certificate and could set the board of property at defiance, but felt that

[37] Jan. 14, 1804, *ibid.*, pp. 503-6.
[38] See form of certificate, *ibid.*, p. 780.

the action of the latter body had aroused distrust and encouraged opposition to the settlement.

In due time the attorney general gave an opinion that it would be best for the patents to recite the release of the Pennsylvania claimants, but that it was not necessary for the commissioners' certificates to contain such recital. The board of property felt that the release should be cited and finally announced that it would secure the necessary information from the surveyor of the commission. Cooper resented the attitude of the board and vented his displeasure. in several letters.[39] He even went so far as to intimate in a letter to Ellicott that the land office and board of property were unfavorably disposed toward the Connecticut claimants and were not averse to treating them unfairly, and asserted that final settlement of the controversy would be impossible as long as such an attitude was maintained and so much suspicion was created.

The secretary of the land office replied most vigorously, describing the policy which he would follow, and referring contemptuously to the suspicions which Cooper had voiced.[40] So Cooper's long, arduous, and thoroughly altruistic labors for the settlement of the Wyoming controversy ended in a quarrel over a technical point and led to withering comments upon him by the state official most intimately concerned with the question. In his enthusiasm for a group of people whom he regarded as unfortunate and even oppressed, he had overreached himself by exceeding his authority perhaps, and certainly by voicing unwarranted suspicions and making reckless charges. His own services had been magnificent and fortunately the final controversy could not undo them. But here is

---

[39] To land claimants, August 3, 1804, *ibid.*, pp. 506-9; to Andrew Ellicott, August 1, 1804, *ibid.*, pp. 510-12.

[40] Letter to the commissioners, Oct. 10, 1804, *ibid.*, pp. 383-5.

another instance of the persistent tragedy of his life: splendid service was consistently marred by excess, the memory of the service was blurred if not obliterated, and only bitterness remained as his reward.

Although his main interest during these three years was in the Luzerne claims, Cooper was not so absorbed in this question as to pay no attention to public affairs. He wrote a long letter to Governor McKean, which was duly published in the *Aurora*,[41] making observations on the internal commerce of the state and urging the development of roads; he made a successful application to the legislature for an appropriation to the Northumberland Academy;[42] and sent the press vigorous communications on various matters of greater or less political importance.[43] He was kept informed of both European and American developments by Tench Coxe, and carried on a desultory but highly interesting correspondence with Thomas Jefferson.

His correspondence with Jefferson began shortly after the election with strong expressions of mutual esteem. The sufferings Cooper had undergone for the cause of political opposition and the services he had rendered the Republican party had doubtless commended him to the attention of the president, and he had been informed, erroneously as it later appeared, that the latter in a letter to Governor McKean had spoken of him in terms of high approbation. This information led to a modest disclaimer on the part of Cooper, coupled with an expression of

[41] From Wilkes-Barre, Nov. 18, 1802, *Aurora*, April 8, 1803.

[42] *Aurora*, April, 1, 1803. For the act, see *Statutes at Large*, ch. 2412.

[43] A communication of about a column and a half dealing with the Mississippi question and signed ''C'' was published in the *Aurora*, March 17, 1803, and seems unquestionably to be from Cooper. He deprecated all talk of war because of the conduct of the intendant at New Orleans and blamed the Federalists for agitating the question.

great appreciation and of the desire that Jefferson might continue to think well of him. As he put it, *"Laudari a tam laudato viro,* is too gratifying not to excite the wish for its continuance.''[44] At this time and again shortly afterwards, he interceded with Jefferson in behalf of a humble Federalist friend of his who had been deprived of his office as collector of the excise to make way for the man who was the government witness against Cooper in his trial.[45] Jefferson replied that the matter would have due consideration and made the rather ingenuous statement that Cooper's disinterested anxiety on the subject would add to the just estimate in which his character was held by the wise and the good.[46]

Indications of Cooper's dissatisfaction with one aspect of the Jeffersonian policy, however, soon appeared. A few weeks after the inauguration, he sent the *Aurora* a communication in which he discussed the question of the Barbary pirates and took the same position that he had taken earlier in opposition to the protection of American commerce.[47] He objected to the sending of frigates against the Tripolitans and Algerines, saying that national honor did not demand action against a set of sea-robbers, and that the cost of the expedition would be twice as great as the profits from the trade which was involved. He felt that merchants trading in the Mediterranean should take their own chances, and that it would be absurd to run the risk of war on account of any foreign commerce. He showed that his ideas about the desirability of a minimum of government had suffered no change when he said that in politics a good motto was, ''the least done the soonest mended.'' Dissatisfaction with any protection of the merchant at the expense of the

[44] March 17, 1801, Jefferson Papers, CX.
[45] April 2, 1801, *ibid.,* CXI.   [46] April 17, 1801, *ibid.,* CXII.
[47] May 6, 1801.

rest of the country was also expressed in a letter to
Tench Coxe, where the tone of criticism of Jefferson was
somewhat sharp.[48] This question was later to be the occasion for a spirited exchange between Cooper and Jefferson, before their greatest intimacy had developed.[49] Even
at this time, though, the admiration of the commissioner
for the president was very great.

His connection with Priestley furnished the occasion
for most of his early letters to Jefferson. In the autumn
of 1802, at the desire of his friend, he sent the president
a copy of a letter from abroad in which European conditions were described.[50] His own comments indicated a
continued hostility to England where, as he put it, "liberty so far as it is known is the mere footstool of party";
but he agreed with Priestley's correspondent that, after
all, the cause of liberty had gained much in France. He
expressed great interest in Alexander of Russia, whom
he regarded with "fearful hope" and with whom he suggested that Jefferson assume a correspondence. He reiterated his conviction that there should be as little government as possible, and gave expression to his great
confidence in Jefferson. So far as we know, no other living man, not even Joseph Priestley, ever received from
him such words of praise as these:

We have to learn even in this mildest of Governments, how
easy it is to govern too much and how prone the best of rulers,
are from the best of principles, to overact their part. Permit me
however sincerely to except from this Observation your principles and your practice. I know that I state your opinions when
I say, that wise men have just begun to suspect that the art of

48 July 13, 1801, *Wyoming Documents*, p. 459.

49 See below, pp. 190-2.

50 Oct. 25, 1802, Jefferson Papers, CXXVII. The letter to Priestley was
from J. H. Stone, who had figured in an earlier controversy in which Priestley was involved. See above, pp. 85-6.

Governing, consists in knowing how to govern as little as possible. . . .

How very gratifying it is to your friends to hear of the high regard paid to your Character among the best of men throughout the enlightened World! Almost am I persuaded that your principles are now too habitual, and your Character too fixed, for your practice to be warped, or your Conduct to waver. Almost: for looking at the Buonapartes of present and former times, who of us can say he can completely trust himself, under every vicissitude of popular favour and popular Ingratitude? My earnest prayer is that you may continue as you have begun: and that Power and prosperity may never tempt you from the honourable path that led you to them: or deprive you of the exquisite Luxury of knowing and feeling, how anxiously you are looked up to, and how sincerely you are beloved by those who love mankind.

Despite the slight reservation and the expression of anxious solicitude, such praise must have greatly commended its author to its recipient. Cooper was obviously trying to gain the approval of Jefferson for himself, but his long admiration for the Republican leader and his principles seems to have been quite sincere, and the later intimacy between the two men was founded upon essential community of interest and ideas. Jefferson was delighted to find that there were some men who still thought that all was not lost in France, although with Cooper he deplored the silencing of the press, "the only tocsin of a nation," and agreed with him that the agitations of the public mind advanced its powers.[51] Regarding domestic

51 Jefferson to Cooper, Nov. 29, 1802. *Writings* (Ford), VIII, 176-8. Jefferson in this letter promised Cooper's son, for whom the father had made application, the second vacancy at Annapolis, the first having been promised. See letter from Duane to Jefferson, Nov. 27, 1802, Mass. Hist. Soc. *Proceedings*, 2 series, XX, 279. This was Thomas Cooper, Jr., the same youth who had attacked the Philadelphia publisher in 1800. See above, pp. 133-4. In due time he received an appointment, but his experience at the naval academy was not entirely satisfactory to his father, who in July, 1804,

policy, he reassured his correspondent by saying, "The path we have to pursue is so quiet, that we have nothing scarcely to report to our legislature, a noiseless course."

There was no other correspondence between Cooper and Jefferson until the death of Joseph Priestley early in 1804. Cooper had every reason to suppose that the president would share his own grief, so informed him of the death as soon as it occurred,[52] and expressed at the same time the hope that Jefferson's life might continue to be as useful as it had been and that his end might be as cheerful as that of his old admirer. Less than two weeks before his death, Priestley had expressed his great appreciation of the president in a letter to Dr. Logan, in which he had said, "Tell Mr. Jefferson that I think myself happy to have lived under his excellent administration; and that I have a prospect of dying in it. It is, I am confident, the best on the face of the earth, and yet I hope to rise to something more excellent still."[53]

The necessity of acknowledging a letter from the president to Priestley which arrived after the death of the latter, furnished the occasion for Cooper to discuss with Jefferson the Malthusian doctrine, upon which his opinion had been asked.[54] He accepted with melancholy conviction the general truth of the theory, but thought Malthus carried it too far, especially in his failure adequately to take into account the benefits which might arise from improvements in government and in the arts contributing to the comfort of human existence, and the relief which might be secured through a system of gradual emigra-

wrote the secretary of the navy that he had learned of his son's intemperate habits and wished as a favor to himself that the commission which he was disgracing should be taken from him. See his letter to Robert Smith, July 16, 1804, Jefferson Papers, CXLII.

[52] Letter dated Feb. 6, 1804, Jefferson Papers, CXXXVIII.

[53] Jan. 25, 1804, *Aurora*, March 2.

[54] Feb. 16, 1804, Jefferson Papers, CXXXVIII.

tion. He himself seems to have favored some sort of birth-control. He wished that some of Malthus's opponents in England would consider more fully the relief which would be afforded by a regulated system of gradual colonization, for he felt that as the question stood, the whole system of human affairs was "too gloomy for a benevolent mind to rest upon." Jefferson in his reply agreed with Cooper's opinions about Malthus, and stated that the large amount of rich and uncultivated land in the United States made the doctrines of the book inapplicable to this country.[55]

The main purpose of his letter, however, was to express grief at the death of Priestley and to inquire about a syllabus giving a comparative view of the morals of Jesus and the ancient philosophers which Jefferson had sent him with a letter to Benjamin Rush. He was anxious that these should get into no other hands, because, as he put it, "if I write as a text that two and two are four, it serves to make volumes of slander and abuse." Cooper in reply stated that Mrs. Priestley had the letter and the syllabus and that they would be safeguarded for his protection.[56] He said, by way of personal reassurance, that he believed Jefferson to be a far better Christian than nine-tenths of the professors of Christianity, and that his view of the subject was highly honorable, but that he fancied that his own opinion agreed neither with that of Jefferson or Priestley. He might have said, also, that he was less fearful of exposing it, although he did not reveal it here.

One of the most amusing evidences of Cooper's support of Jefferson given at this or any other time, was a reply to the various jokes passed upon Jefferson's salt

---

[55] Feb. 24, 1804, Jefferson Papers, CXXXVIII.

[56] March, 1804, *ibid.*, CXXXIX. For the syllabus, and the pertinent correspondence, see Jefferson's *Writings* (Ford), VIII, 223-8, and notes.

mountain. In a communication to the Northumberland *Argus* in May, 1804, he first vented his sarcasm upon the Federalist wits and wiseacres for their jokes on the salt mountain and the credulous philosopher, and then sought to show—in apparent seriousness—that mountains of salt were referred to by Pliny and by various modern scientific writers.[57] He asserted that the Republicans did not laugh at Jefferson's account, since they were in the habit of reading and giving credit to common books of established authority; but that the Federalists who, as he put it, "read little and know less," monopolized all the sport for themselves, and enjoyed the exclusive privilege of laughing at distinguished votaries of science and philosophy. There is little indication here that he possessed a sense of humor!

Within a few months after his departure for Wilkes-Barre, Cooper was welcomed into the brotherhood of learning by the American Philosophical Society of Philadelphia. Jefferson had been president of this famous organization during the entire time of Cooper's residence in America, Governor McKean had been long a member, and Priestley, who was addressed by the society upon his arrival in America, and was always held in highest esteem by it,[58] had been elected to membership some years before he left England.[59] Although absorption in public affairs and practical politics and the distance of his place of residence from Philadelphia prevented Cooper's active participation in the affairs of the society for a

[57] Copied by the *Aurora,* June 12. See also the Northumberland *Republican Argus,* March 8, 1805. Jefferson, it will be remembered, thought there was a mountain of salt in the territory of the Louisiana Purchase.

[58] *Cf.* the eulogy delivered Jan. 3, 1805, at the First Presbyterian Church, Philadelphia, before the society, the governor, and others, *Aurora,* Jan. 15, 1805.

[59] Jan. 22, 1785. *Proceedings* of the Amer. Philos. Society, XXVII, list of members and officers.

number of years after his election, he was at least given public stamp of approval at this time. Through association with the society he was in due time to form valuable and enduring friendships, and during his later residence in Philadelphia was to distinguish himself by great zeal for science.

When the list of members elected in January, 1802, was published in the Philadelphia press,[60] the *Gazette of the United States* took it upon itself to state exactly who and what "Tom Cooper" was, in order that the public might know how justly to appreciate the American Philosophical Society.[61] A Republican writer hastened to the defense and gave enthusiastic description of Cooper's attainments:

> The talents and literary acquirements of Mr. Cooper are known and acknowledged by his very enemies. There are not many men in America who possess knowledge drawn from so great a variety of sources. It is a fact beyond contradiction that there are very few whose reading has been so diversified or so extensive. Whatever may have been the decision of a partial court, it is certainly novel to imagine that a judicial sentence can either augment or diminish the talents or science of any man.[62]

The writer then stated that the Federalist paper had attacked the American Philosophical Society before, the obvious reason being the election of Jefferson as its president. He admitted that although the constitution of the society forbade political discussion, it was nevertheless true that most of its members and, indeed, most scientific men, were democrats. An editorial in the *Aurora* of the same date attacked "the impudence of the

[60] *Aurora*, July 23, 1802; Philadelphia *Gazette*, July 23; *cf.* list of members and officers in the society's *Proceedings*, XXVII.

[61] Quoted by the *Aurora*, July 28, 1802.

[62] Communication signed "J. R. S." *Aurora*, July 28, 1802.

Connecticut youths'' who published ''the Tory Gazette.''[63] The Republican paper said that Cooper was
prosecuted for speaking the truth, but that he was far
superior to his persecutors.

> Among the whole of his persecutors, nay, it may be without
> risque or contradiction asserted, among the whole tory faction—
> so much learning, genius, universal science, wit, fine taste and
> love of his species, are not to be found as centred in the man
> Thomas Cooper—whom philosophy has justified against faction.

The commendation of his learning, if not of his taste,
was well deserved. His printed works, his letters, and
the catalogue of his private library reveal him as an
omnivorous reader. Probably no man of his generation in
America had read more widely or could make greater
display of erudition. His intellectual judgments were
often hasty and not uninfluenced by personal considerations, and he lacked creative originality; but the energy
of his mind was almost incredible and few of his contemporaries could compare with him either in intellectual
acquirements or in prophetic insight into the future
course of thought. He was much like the greater Jefferson in the universality and timelessness of his genius.
The American Philosophical Society did well to give him
its approbation.

The criticisms based upon the circumstances of his
trial and conviction, we may be sure troubled him not at
all. He never wavered from his conviction of the entire
justification of his conduct. A petition asking the repayment of his fine was presented by him to Congress, April
28, 1802, when it aroused discussion but suffered the
inevitable postponement.[64] He had it introduced regu-

[63] Bronson and Chauncy, editors of the *Gazette of the United States*. See
an editorial in the *Aurora*, July 30, for further defense of Cooper.

[64] *Annals of Congress*, 7 Cong., 1 Sess., p. 1251. There is no account of
the discussion. See also *Aurora*, May 3, 1802.

larly thereafter, wrote many letters about it, ever insisting that the constitutional right of freedom of speech was involved, and, if the family tradition be true, when upon his deathbed requested his wife to carry on the fight, which she did with ultimate success.[65] Far from being ashamed of his conviction under the Sedition Act, he ever gloried in it, and the effort to secure redress extended through and beyond his life.

[65] See below, pp. 374-6.

CHAPTER VI

A CONSERVATIVE JUDGE AND THE DEMOCRACY, 1804-1811

His work on the Luzerne claims completed, Cooper became in August, 1804, president judge of the third district of the state of Pennsylvania. He had long expected an appointment to the bench. Shortly after the inauguration in 1801 he had written Jefferson that Governor McKean expected to nominate him president judge under the new judiciary system which the Republicans expected to establish at the next session of the legislature.[1] A reorganization and enlargement of the judiciary was recommended by the governor at the next session,[2] but the recommendation was not carried into effect until 1806. Meanwhile, Cooper had been appointed to the Luzerne commission and by the time his work there was finished a vacancy had occurred and he received the long-promised appointment. The third district included the counties of Berks, Northampton, Luzerne, and Northumberland. In 1806, the state was divided into ten districts instead of five, and he was then assigned to the eighth district, consisting of the counties of Northumberland, Luzerne, and Lycoming.[3] So his entire service as judge was among the people of his home county and among the

[1] March 17, 1801, Jefferson Papers, CX.

[2] See his address to the legislature, Dec. 5, 1801, *Aurora*, Dec. 9; cf. *ibid.*, Jan. 1, 1802.

[3] Pennsylvania *Statutes at Large*, ch. 2646, sec. 12.

Luzerne settlers for whom he had done so much. The president judge with the county judges in each county constituted the court of common pleas and by 1806, certainly, Cooper received a salary of sixteen hundred dollars.[4]

While he was absorbed in work of an essentially judicial character in Luzerne, and was less free and doubtless less inclined to play his accustomed rôle as a member of the opposition, certain of the Republicans of the state turned upon the judiciary, where offensive Federalists and others unmindful of democracy yet lingered.[5] Alexander Addison, president judge of the fifth district, was impeached and found guilty of misdemeanor by the senate in January, 1803, removed from office, and disqualified. The *Aurora,* a few weeks later, gave a list of sixteen judges and justices of the peace against whom complaints had been preferred to the house of representatives.[6] In four cases besides that of Addison the governor had been addressed by the two houses for removal and the decision was pending in several other cases.[7]

Not only was there this direct assault upon the judges, but there were also numerous flank attacks in the agitation for the reconstitution of the judiciary so as to make it more democratic. As early as the autumn of 1803, Cooper opposed in the press certain of the proposed "hazardous experiments," and stated that he saw little

[4] Pennsylvania *Constitution of 1790,* art. V, sec. IV; Act of April 13, 1791, *Statutes at Large,* ch. 1575, sec. 3; ch. 2646, sec. 13.

[5] An admirable summary of political developments in the state during this entire period is given by William M. Meigs in his "Pennsylvania Politics Early in this Century," *Pennsylvania Magazine of History and Biography,* XVII, 462-90. For the period 1800-1805, see also McMaster, *United States,* III, 153-162.

[6] March 29, 1803.

[7] The constitution of 1790 provided both for impeachment and for removal by the governor upon the address of two-thirds of each branch of the legislature. Art. V, sec. II.

defect in the general plan of the state judiciary.[8] He admitted that the docket was crowded and the course of justice slow, and advocated an increase in the number of judges, both of the district courts and the supreme court. Beyond that he was unwilling to go. His position was assailed as reflecting upon the integrity and intelligence of the people, and reference was made to a third party composed of hypocrites who had not sufficient virtue and patriotism to be Republicans, nor strong enough nerves to be Federalists, and who planned to deceive and betray them both.

In a letter to Jefferson a few months later, Cooper expressed a similarly conservative opinion.[9] He referred there to the conflict between the legislature and the governor, which was in its beginnings, and to the charges of Federalism which had been brought against the latter. His own attitude was favorable to the governor and to the judiciary, even in its right to pass on the constitutionality of laws enacted by the legislature. His attitude toward the governor may be partly explained on personal grounds, and perhaps on the ground that he himself expected a judicial appointment, but it may be more easily explained in terms of reaction against the extremes of democracy and as the natural outcome of his own strongly intellectual emphasis.

The democratic assault reached its climax in 1804, when three justices of the supreme court, Edward Shippen, Jasper Yeates, and Thomas Smith, were impeached by the house of representatives for their action in the celebrated case of Thomas Passmore, who had been fined and imprisoned for contempt as a result of indiscreet

[8] Knowledge of Cooper's "elaborate essay" in the Northumberland *Argus*, Nov. 18, 1803, has been gained from the reply to it by "A Friend to the Adjustment Bill" in the *Aurora*, Dec. 19, 1803.

[9] Feb. 16, 1804, Jefferson Papers, CXXXVIII.

conduct on his part. This case served to draw the line sharply between the friends and foes of the judiciary and to split the Republican party in the state into two bitterly hostile factions. The lawyers almost to a man upheld the bench, although the assaulters of the judiciary interpreted this as an indication of their humiliating subservience and degradation.[10] Justice H. H. Brackenridge, the only Republican member of the supreme court, stated publicly that he approved of the action in the Passmore case, although on account of absence he had not officially participated, and wrote the legislature to ask that he also be impeached. The legislature declined to impeach him, but by joint-address asked the governor to remove him, which the latter declined to do.[11] A. J. Dallas and other prominent Republican lawyers declined to serve as counsel for the prosecution and the legislature was forced to go outside the state, finally securing the services of Caesar A. Rodney of Maryland. When the judges were acquitted by the senate, the rage of the prosecutors knew no bounds and the formation of a distinct anti-judiciary party was the inevitable result.[12]

By the spring of 1805, when the gubernatorial election was impending in the autumn, two distinct and opposing parties had appeared. The Constitutional Republicans, whom the *Aurora* referred to as "Dallas and Company" and "Tertium Quids," supported the governor and the existing state constitution and opposed "tyrannical and disorganizing schemes."[13] The Society of the Friends of

---

[10] *Aurora*, Feb. 6, 1804.

[11] *Ibid.*, March 28, 29; April 5, 1804.

[12] *Ibid.*, May 15, 16, 22; August 24, 1804.

[13] For an account of their organization in Philadelphia, see *ibid.*, April 11, 1805. Peter Muhlenberg was elected president and George Logan, vice-president. Dallas was a member of the corresponding committee. Tench Coxe had been the chief object of the fire of the *Aurora* earlier, chiefly because of his opposition to the reëlection of Dr. Michael Leib to Congress.

the People took its stand upon the principles of the Declaration of Independence and favored the calling of a state constitutional convention to alter the government so as to safeguard life, liberty, and happiness.[14] The specific amendments which they favored involved limitation of the executive power through restriction of the powers of veto and appointment, shortening the senatorial term to two years, provision for conviction by a majority vote upon impeachment, and some provision for the amendment of the constitution, for which no rule was then laid down. Some favored the taking away of the governor's appointing power and the conferring of it upon a council selected annually from the assembly, and the election of judges by the legislature for a term of years.[15]

The anti-judiciary party nominated for governor a neighbor of Cooper's, Simon Snyder of Northumberland, and issued an elaborate address "To the Democratic Citizens of Pennsylvania."[16] They bitterly denounced the officers of executive appointment, claiming that most of them had described the tried and true friends of the people as anarchists, innovators, disorganizers, and Jacobins. The governor was accused of having referred to the agitators for a convention as "geese" and "clodhoppers," and admitted that he had used terms which were equally offensive. In the case of an appointment to which certain of the extreme democrats had objected, he claimed that the appointee had been commended to him by men in whom he could place confidence and named

For an address to the Republicans of the state, June 10, 1805, see G. M. Dallas, *Life and Writings of Alexander J. Dallas*, pp. 211-33.

[14] For an account of meeting in Philadelphia, March 27, 1805, see the *Aurora*, March 29. For a circular letter addressed to the Republicans of the state, see *ibid.*, April 17, 1805.

[15] See the communication signed "Hutchison," *ibid.*, August 26, 1805.

[16] For the entire address and subjoined documents, see *ibid.*, May 20, 1805.

Cooper in this connection.[17] So the former advocate of the rights of the masses against political tyrants had become identified with the detractors of the people.

Conventionalist sentiment seems to have been very strong in Northumberland, where Simon Snyder lived.[18] The Northumberland *Argus* was strong against McKean; communications were copied from it by the *Aurora* almost every day during the campaign. Snyder ultimately carried the county by a decisive vote.[19] So the atmosphere which had been so congenial in 1800 to Cooper the martyred democrat, was oppressive in 1805 to Cooper the defender of the judiciary. And his position was rendered particularly unpleasant by the gleeful action of his present opponents in unearthing certain of his earlier writings and expressions, and then charging him with inconsistency.

Thus a writer to the *Argus* in May called for the republication of Cooper's address of 1800, because it contained stronger arguments in favor of a convention than any which had yet been published.[20] This writer assumed, doubtless with intent of irony, that the signers of the address were still favorable to a convention. He stated that the terrors of federal persecution had been unable to move Cooper to recant, and that he was sure the blandishments and perquisites of office would never cause him to retract what he had written so conclusively and eloquently. The writer said that he had heard from Federalists and *Quids* that Cooper had brought a large

[17] See letters in explanation of the governor's actions, *ibid.*, June 3, 1805. The appointment in question was that of William Brunson to be justice of the peace. Cooper had merely signed his name to the general recommendation, so his connection with the incident was rather remote.

[18] See the account of the meeting of June 14, *Argus*, June 21; and the address of the county committee, *Aurora*, August 3, 1805.

[19] Returns in *Aurora*, Nov. 21, 1805. The vote was 3202 to 1254.

[20] "A Mifflin County Mechanic," May 31, 1805. See above, pp. 147-8.

assortment of their addresses and remonstrances from Lancaster and had been distributing them over his district, but that he knew they had lied. He was sure that if Cooper distributed anything it must have been memorials and petitions for a convention.

The address of 1800, which gave such unfortunate evidence of Cooper's earlier sentiments, was accordingly published in the *Argus,* with an editorial paragraph stating that the address showed the idea of calling a convention to be neither new nor the offspring of faction, malice, or disappointment.[21] Meanwhile, the *Aurora* published a communication which enclosed the same address and the form of petition which asked a reduction in the senatorial term.[22] The writer wished this republished to show that Cooper and other present opponents of a convention were the first to criticize the form of government in 1800. He gave Cooper the credit for having been the first man in the state to publish a call to alter and amend the constitution, and pointed out the fact that he had gone much further than the present advocates of a convention were going, for no one of them was asking, "Of what use is the senate?" Nor were they comparing the legislative system to a machine with one horse (the house) to draw before and two horses (senate and governor) to drag behind.

The democratic writer then proceeded to explain the defection of the former critic of the senate. The address of 1800, he said, was from Cooper the oppressed, and the performance was worthy of him "in the days of his purity, while his heart was yet uncorrupted by the vanity and perquisites of office." But he had changed with his changing fortunes. "He has tasted of the *forbidden fruit;* he saw that he was naked and has decked himself with fig leaves. He now *persecutes* those doctrines which he

[21] June 7, 1805.   [22] June 1, 1805.

formerly preached; he proscribes those now whom he
formerly admired.'' He was a ''striking instance of
human mutability, human frailty, and human deprav-
ity.'' Because of his services in opposing proposed
changes in the judiciary, he had become the honorable
Thomas Cooper, president of the courts of six counties,
with a salary of sixteen hundred for life—if a convention
could be avoided. No wonder he could no longer see defects in the constitution! But, as this writer interpreted
it, his attachment was not to the constitution, but to his
salary.[23]

Cooper explained and sought to justify his position in
a letter to the *Argus*.[24] He acknowledged that he had
originated and composed the address of 1800, but denied
that he was a changeling, turncoat, and anti-republican.
Irritated by the obstinate action of the senate in blocking
the expression of popular preference for Jefferson in
1800, he had condemned that body. He still thought that
a term of four years was too long, but five years' experience had convinced him of the utility of the senate even
as then constituted. He regarded that body as essential
to the preservation of public liberty and republican
government.

He gave as his reasons for favoring the reëlection of
McKean the sacrifice of popularity which the governor
had made to principle, and the latter's acquaintance with
the law which qualified him to pass upon legislation. He
said he opposed the arbitration system[25] because he pre-

[23] It was pointed out that two other signers of the address, Samuel
Roberts and Jesse Moore, had also become presidents of courts of common
pleas and defenders of the constitution. The change of Dallas, Logan, and
Coxe was also commented upon. The writer felt that McKean, Barton, and
Ellicott had always been Federalists and had only worn the mantle of
democracy.

[24] June 14, 1805.

[25] The trial of causes by arbitrators outside court.

ferred the decisions of the court house to those of the tavern. He believed that the decision of controversies had better be based upon the collective wisdom of the nation as expressed in laws than left to the common sense of the common people, and thought life-tenure judges sworn to support the constitution preferable to short-term judges who would have to support the prevailing faction or be turned out. He strongly intimated that many members of the opposing party had an antipathy for law, lawyers, and judges because of the consciousness of their own deserts. He regarded a period of political ferment and almost unexampled party violence as an inconvenient time to amend the constitution, and thought it a great evil to keep the people in revolutionary ferment and foster political rancor. In this, it may be observed, he departed far from his own earlier thought and practice.

He felt that the Friends of the People were proceeding too much in the manner of the French revolutionists, ridiculing all moderate and gradual reform and denouncing all advocacy of caution based upon experience. He thought there should be some middle ground between a system of hereditary rank and privilege and a state of confusion and anarchy like that in Israel, when there were no judges in the land and every one did what was right in his own eyes; and he felt that the existing constitution came near the mark, although by no means perfect. He favored periodical revision of the constitution on the basis of experience, to be provided for by a clause in that document itself. Otherwise, the need of alteration would be urged for political purposes, and when there was a change of parties the constitution would be altered in a spirit of vengeance and ambition. He preferred that conventions be appointed for every twenty or twenty-five years, thus giving plenty of time for experiment, but would not oppose a convention to be held in five, seven, or ten years. The present time he thought inopportune, but admitted that in his irritation he would willingly have voted for a convention in 1800.

He thought his political creed unchanged in its essential features. He still renounced bishops, nobles, and kings, and believed that political authority ought to emanate from the people and that officials ought to be responsible to them. His views on details, however, were not unalterable like the laws of the Medes and Persians. He had read, observed, and reflected much and thought himself wiser than he was twenty years before. "I see things a little more distinctly, by climbing the vantage-ground of years and experience." He stated that he had made many sacrifices for principle and was not actuated by interest now. He claimed that he had nothing to gain from supporting McKean, while by opposing him he would at least safeguard himself against the vindictive injustice of his opponents in case they should be finally successful.

The charges against Cooper of inconsistency and even apostasy were reiterated in subsequent communications to the local paper. These were generally copied by the *Aurora,* which sometimes took a shot at the judge on its own account. One writer thus lamented Cooper's defection, "Alas! poor Cooper; how art thou fallen; in science sun of the morning, but in firmness and stability, weak as the weakest of the people."[26] He sought to show that there could be no reconciliation between Cooper's positions in 1800 and 1805, because that gentleman had formerly advocated speedy action, while he now counseled delay and so was "a changeling guilty of vile tergiversation." He said experience had taught the former democrat the uses of the senate in opposing popular and bene-

[26] *Argus,* June 28, 1805; *Aurora,* July 6.

ficial legislation and in enabling the governor to retain a whole host of judges and lawyers, with the liberties of the people prostrate at their feet.

The original advocate of the republication of Cooper's address returned to the attack after a few weeks and indulged in an eloquent astronomical analogy.[27] He deplored the degeneration of a splendid primary planet into a mere satellite, and said that he could hardly refrain from exclaiming, "How art thou fallen from heaven, O! Lucifer son of the morning!" He then proceeded to say that Cooper's action, and his judicial conduct in more than one instance had justified the truth of "that grand political axiom which once emanated from his pen *that power entrusted for too long a period will certainly be abused.*" In 1800, Cooper was powerless; now he was depending upon the senate to keep him in power. His talk about the present's being a time of public frenzy was ridiculous rant, for the public mind was infinitely less disturbed now than in 1800. Once he was "as rank a Jacobin as ever wore a red cap," but he had become an apostate and had made a pitiful shift to justify himself and the remarks about him had come home to his conscience.

There was little reference to Cooper in the campaign except in the communications from Northumberland. The *Aurora* entered into many elaborate discussions of the political situation, but rarely mentioned him among the chief characters who were considered.[28] In one instance, it stated that he was a candidate for the vacancy on the supreme bench upon the probable resignation, after the election, of the chief justice, and described him as a *Quid*

[27] "A Mifflin County Mechanic," *Argus,* August 9, 16, 1805; *Aurora,* August 17.

[28] *Cf.* the omission of his name in the discussions of August 7, 9, and Sept. 12, 1805.

and the first proposer of a convention.[29] But his part in the campaign seems to have been chiefly local and very much less vigorous than in 1800. The *Argus* showed no such bitterness toward him as was shown by the Federalist papers in 1800,[30] and the one considerable communication from him was much more restrained in tone than were his utterances while a member of the opposition—a position much more in accordance with his character and temper than that of defender of the existing order.

It can scarcely be said that his conduct in the two campaigns was consistent. The best explanation seems to be that in 1800 he fought an administration which he abhorred, especially because of its suppression of freedom of speech, and sought the election of Jefferson, whom he greatly admired and revered. The senate of the state threatened to prevent Jefferson's election, so Cooper bitterly assailed that body. In 1805, the issue was chiefly the upholding of the dignity of the courts against the assaults of ignorance. His English legal background and his work as Luzerne commissioner and then as judge naturally led him to side with the judiciary. Furthermore, McKean was a friend of his and had stood back of him, and Cooper was intensely loyal to his friends. In this situation, the continuance of the existing order of things seemed to him to be imperatively demanded. His personal interests were involved, it is true, and his theoretical position was accordingly weakened. But from a realistic point of view, from a consideration of actualities and not theories, he seems to have been justified in his later position or certainly as much justified as McKean,

[29] August 19, article on "The Quiddity" which extended through the issues of August 14, 16, 17, 18 and 19, and made only this one reference to Cooper.

[30] This was probably due to the friendship between him and Binns, editor of the *Argus*. See the *Recollections of the Life of John Binns*, pp. 13, 171, 176-7, 294.

Dallas, Coxe, and other former democrats were. If he had not talked so much, if he had not tried to buttress the political position of any particular moment with arguments for which he claimed universal validity, his position would have been less embarrassing. He was neither a disinterested political philosopher nor a frank opportunist, but wavered between the two positions, hence was inevitably embarrassed. And the new enemies he had made were biding their time, to strike him later a deadly blow. The election went for McKean, who carried all the counties of Cooper's judicial district except Northumberland, which went for Snyder. But three years later Cooper's neighbor came into the gubernatorial office, and the position of the judge became from that time a most precarious one.

Secure in his judicial position after the victory of McKean and the constitutionalists in 1805, Cooper remained aloof from state politics during the years immediately following. Writing to Jefferson in June, 1807, he described the various political factions and expressed his dissatisfaction with them all.[31] To the Federalists he had a traditional hostility, and with the Duane-Leib faction of the Republicans he had no sympathy whatsoever.[32] He attributed to the larger faction of the Republicans the intention of abolishing all courts and law and absorbing all executive and judicial functions in the legislative branch, and viewed their proposals with the alarm of a convert to conservatism. Their prospective candidate for the governorship, his neighbor, Simon Snyder, he thought

[31] June 23, 1807, Jefferson Papers, CLXVIII.

[32] Duane expended most of his energies in supporting Dr. Michael Leib, congressman and later senator from Pennsylvania, who was the object of much bitter attack even by fellow Republicans. See Meigs, ''Pennsylvania Politics Early in this Century,'' Penn. Magazine Hist. and Biography, XVII, 474-9, for the political situation and developments, 1805-08.

on the whole the man most eligible for the position, although he deplored his lack of education. He himself gave grudging allegiance to the *Quids,* who were the advocates of things as they were.

For my own part I am persuaded that many things may be needed in our Constitution, but the longer I live, the more cautious I am of pulling down without clearly seeing how I can build up. I cannot go with the Democrats throughout. They introduce too strong habits of insubordination: they are of opinion, that knowledge is aristocracy & that Ignorance with republicanism is competent to every political purpose that a government needs. In our state legislature, all this [abolishing courts and law and executive power and patronage] has in my presence and hearing been openly & repeatedly advocated. This is too strong a dose for me. I have pressed in vain, a vote to call a Convention at some definite time hence, four or five years, but this is a proposition too moderate. I lay by therefore, and am ranked with the quids, tho' I act with none. I begin to get weary of this incessant storm, and long for a short time of quiet, when the invaluable comforts of domestic society & social intercourse will not be exacted as the price of political reforms.

It shortly appeared that Cooper's fears for the immediate safety of the institutions of government were unwarranted. Snyder in due time announced himself as opposed to the calling of a convention and most of the constitutionalists were lured into his political fold. Judge Cooper, for reasons which do not fully appear, refused to quiet his fears and found himself in an anomalous and, as we shall see, a perilous position. Personal considerations of one sort and another may well have served to isolate him, for his temper was never conciliatory, and his temperamental unfitness for a judicial task doubtless served to increase his dissatisfaction with his lot. He was to continue restive until a new crusade should engage him.

In practical politics now perforce a conservative, he revealed himself in his theoretical writings as little more than a moderate progressive. In the discussion of Priestley's political writings, which he appended among other things to the *Memoirs* of his old friend,[33] he showed himself yet a believer in the progressive amelioration of the state of mankind and unwilling to accept in entirety the "melancholy theory of Malthus." He admitted that it was possible that war, pestilence and famine, vice and misery, might be necessary to counteract excessive increase in the human species, but was persuaded that much good might be brought about "by gradually putting into practice well-founded theories of political reform." He emphasized the word "gradually," for he was now "no friend to sudden, extensive, and violent innovations."[34] He further indicated his complete repudiation of the philosophy of revolution which he never practiced, to be sure, but which he certainly had proclaimed at the beginning of his career, by saying, "If there be any fact better ascertained than another, it is that gradual and peaceable, is in all cases preferable to violent reform."[35]

He was convinced that there had been great improvement in human conditions and that this had come as the result of increased knowledge. His hope for humanity, then, was in the spread of light, hence his lifelong insistence upon freedom of discussion and the devotion of so many later years to the work of education. Much of his old distrust of rulers had been lost, and he thought that

[33] *Memoirs of Dr. Joseph Priestley*, 1806, appendix 3. The first five appendices, dealing respectively with Priestley's scientific work, metaphysical writings, political works and opinions, miscellaneous writings, and religious opinions, were written by Cooper. The philosophical and religious opinions here expressed by him will be considered in connection with later controversy. See below, pp. 239-241, 270, and ch. XI.

[34] *Ibid.*, II, 338 n.

[35] *Ibid.*, II, 363. For his earlier philosophy of revolution, see above, pp. 12-15.

for the present it would probably be safest "to err on the side of control." One could judge only by experience, he said, for government was "as much a science of experiment as chemistry," and it was "the business of a political philosopher to deduce principles from a close observation of, and a fair deduction from, past facts."[36] These admirable definitions, prophetic of a science of politics even now unrealized, had an additional merit in that they relieved this particular philosopher, then and subsequently, from the necessity of being consistent with his past.

However disillusioned he may have been in regard to Pennsylvania politics, he was greatly pleased with the success of the experiment of government in the United States as a whole.

It is in America alone, that the sovereignty of the people, is more than a mere theory: it is here that the characteristic of that sovereignty is displayed in written constitutions; and it is here alone that the principle of federal union among independent nations has been fully understood and practised. A principle so pregnant with peace and happiness . . . that it may be regarded as among the grandest of human inventions. . . . There has been no republic antient or modern until the American. There has been no federal union on broad and general principles well understood and digested, until the American union . . . The guiding principle that pervades every republic upon this continent, is that which Dr. Priestley has so happily adopted and so well explained, *the interest or good of the majority of the individuals composing each political community.*[37]

The American states he apparently regarded as so many nations bound together in an admirable federal compact. Of such an arrangement, guaranteed by a written docu-

[36] *Ibid.,* pp. 365-6.
[37] *Ibid.,* pp. 357-8.

ment, he thoroughly approved, whatever his dissatisfaction might have been with the practical workings of democracy in an individual state.

Disgusted though he was with local politics, national problems were of great interest to him, and in numerous letters to Jefferson he discussed them, besides giving information about state affairs and his own activities. It was during this period that the relations between the two men attained that intimacy which ever afterwards characterized them, although their correspondence was somewhat more extensive after one of them had retired to Monticello and the other had been relieved of his judicial duties. The many letters which they exchanged, between 1805 and 1811, indicate not only the attitude which Cooper took toward the troubled relations between the United States and Great Britain and France, but also show that he tried to influence Jefferson and that Jefferson greatly valued and generally had his good opinion.

At the outset, however, the president and the president judge did not agree in the matter of protecting foreign commerce, and formal, if not frigid, letters in the third person passed between them.[38] Cooper was consistent with his utterances during the administration of Adams and spoke in deprecation of foreign commerce and commercial wars. Jefferson, on the other hand, wrote that it was not a question whether or not the United States should engage in commerce, but that since commerce was permitted under the constitution the government must needs protect it as any other lawful enterprise. He professed himself a lover of peace, but felt that the European opinion that the American government was run on Quaker principles and would turn the left cheek when

[38] Cooper to Jefferson, Feb. 14, 1806; Jefferson to Cooper, Feb. 18, 1806; Jefferson Papers, CLVI. Cooper sent the president an essay signed ''Vindex,'' which seems to have been published, although we have found no trace of it.

the right had been smitten, must be corrected or we should become the plunder of all nations.

Cooper did not recede from his position. No commerce, in his opinion, repaid the expense of the hostility it induced, not to speak of the misery attendant upon war. During his English days he had attributed to the ambitions of "privileged orders" the wars which had cursed mankind,[39] but he now saw greater danger in the selfishness of the mercantile interests.

I know of no body of men, so ready to postpone the interests of their Country to their own Interests, as Merchants. They are truly a swinish multitude: touch but the bristle of one of them and the whole herd cry out murder. Profess to defend your own territory and that only, and you will have no wars: profess to defend your distant Commerce, and you are never safe for a Day.[40]

In theory more pacific even than Jefferson, although personally so much more belligerent, he at this time opposed all measures of reprisal against the British, who were now struggling for existence but who were likely, he thought, ultimately to be revengeful of the ungenerous advantage taken of their perilous position by the infant republic.

He was grieved that the president did not think with him, but assured him that his heart was with the administration, for he felt that if the experiment of republican government was to succeed at all it must be under Jeffersonian auspices. Subsequent exchange of letters growing out of the publication of Priestley's *Memoirs*, a copy of which was sent the president, served to restore the friendliness between the two philosophers.[41] After the

39 See above, pp. 46-7.
40 Cooper to Jefferson, March 16, 1806, Jefferson Papers, CLVII.
41 Cooper to Jefferson, June 23, 1807, *ibid.*, CLXVIII; Jefferson to Cooper, July 9, 1807, Jefferson's *Writings* (Ford), IX, 102-3.

momentary estrangement, indeed, the note of personal regard in the letters of both men became very marked. This appeared particularly in the request of Cooper that Jefferson explain his silence about him in a letter to Governor McKean in 1801, when he had had every reason to expect active concern to be expressed.[42] He did not learn of this inexplicable disregard of him until six years later and was then deeply grieved because of it. He hoped the president had heard no report unfavorable to his conduct and character and assured him that his own sincere respect for him had always operated as an additional motive to his conduct. The tone of the letter is almost that of a dutiful son to a father who has misunderstood him. Jefferson's explanation in reply was correspondingly paternal. He expressed the highest esteem for Cooper's abilities and integrity and stated in effect that he would have appointed him to public office upon his accession to the presidency had he not known that he wished to remain near Priestley. His failure to refer to him in the letter to McKean was entirely due to the press of other more immediately necessary affairs.[43]

After the original clash over commerce, the attitude of the judge was more favorable to the policy of the government. Thus he approved of the efforts of the president to secure the surrender by the British of the practice of impressing American seamen and seems to have had high hopes of Monroe's diplomatic mission in 1807.[44] He subsequently approved of the embargo and was considerably embarrassed in his efforts to cultivate a favorable sentiment in Northumberland toward the administration

[42] Cooper to Jefferson, August 9, 1807, Jefferson Papers, CLXIX.

[43] Jefferson to Cooper, Sept. 1, 1807, Jefferson's *Writings* (Ford), IX, 103-4 n.; (Memorial edition, 1903-4), XI, 351-4.

[44] Cooper to Jefferson, June 23, 1807, Jefferson Papers, CLXVIII.

by the repeal of this measure, which he felt would be interpreted by the Federalists as a victory.[45] The embargo, he felt, was just beginning to affect the British seriously. In this, Jefferson unquestionably agreed with him. Such was Cooper's personal regard for and confidence in the president that he allowed his own scruples to be overborne and supported the administration at every stage of its tortuous policy.

It is a matter for some surprise, in view of the violence of Cooper's attacks upon the tariff while in South Carolina, that as early as December, 1808, he favored congressional action for the protection of infant manufactures. He expressed his continued adherence to the doctrines of Adam Smith, but looked upon the measure as one of defense in a time of danger.

It will be a horrible fraud to entice our citizens to embark in the troublesome and hazardous speculation of new manufactures, and then on a sudden peace leave them to all the malignity of british competition in our own market. I well know that Adam Smith's general doctrine is true that bounties and protecting duties to encourage the raising at home at a dear rate, what can be purchased abroad at a cheap one, is neither more nor less than picking the pockets of one class of the Community to support the monopoly of another. But there may be cases where necessity will call for this. With us, it will be, not a measure of economy, so much as a measure of protection and defence. Our markets ought to be more at home; more under our command: & this will call for permanent not temporary regulations.[46]

He expressed the same opinion immediately at the close of the war of 1812, when he publicly urged the passage of a protective tariff.[47] For this he was in due season accused of inconsistency and of time-serving, since he

---

[45] Cooper to Jefferson, Feb. 5, 1809, *ibid.*, CLXXXV.
[46] Cooper to Jefferson, Dec. 4, 1808, *ibid.*, CLXXXIII.
[47] See below, pp. 215-16.

favored a tariff while in Pennsylvania and opposed it when in non-industrial South Carolina. His attitude in 1808 was at least consistent with earlier utterances, however, in that it favored home trade and home merchants against the commercial interests.

In this connection, he suggested to Jefferson that action in protection of domestic manufactures would commend the administration to industrial New England, against the commercial interests who would separate from the union and join England if they could. Thus opposition in those states to the mercantile predilection for British goods, politics, and government would be strengthened and the contemplated schemes of disunion would probably be frustrated. He even suggested that the president call some of the New England manufacturers into consultation. No action in favor of manufacturing was taken by Jefferson, but such action was taken later, although not soon enough to prevent the separatist movement in New England.

Opposed as he was to the protection of commerce by warlike measures, Cooper viewed with no complacency the violation of American commercial rights by Great Britain and France, and in a notable judicial opinion threw himself against the weight of British and even American authority by denying the entire conclusiveness of the decision of a foreign court of admiralty. He sat as a member of the high court of errors and appeals of the state in July, 1808, and presented a dissenting opinion in the case of *Dempsey, Assignee of Brown, v. The Insurance Company of Pennsylvania.*[48] The immediate ques-

[48] The act of Feb. 24, 1806, provided for the discontinuance of this court but permitted it to hold two terms in order to determine all causes yet pending. Pennsylvania *Statutes at Large*, ch. 2646, sec. 11. It consisted of the judges of the supreme court, the president judges of the five districts created by the act of 1791, and three appointees of the governor, any five judges to constitute a quorum, and had authority to examine errors in judg-

tion at issue was the recovery of insurance upon a vessel confiscated by the British, and this court, like the federal supreme court shortly before, decided that condemnation by a British court was conclusive evidence of breach of blockade and precluded recovery by the insured.[49] Cooper, in an able opinion, after an historical analysis of the principal cases bearing upon the point, held that a sentence of a foreign court of admiralty or vice-admiralty was evidence only that the captured property was condemned, and that such a sentence was examinable in all its parts.[50] He denied the binding force of foreign interpretation of the law of nations, especially in a time of strife when there was much manifest injustice, and spoke both for American judicial independence and for justice to individual citizens.

The official adoption of the British doctrine by American courts was to the obvious disadvantage of American shippers, and was not unnaturally objected to both by the latter and by partisans of the administration.[51]

ments of the supreme court. *Ibid.*, ch. 1575, sec. 17. This particular case had been before the supreme court in December, 1804, where verdict favorable to the defendants had been rendered. It had been argued before the appellate court in July, 1807, and was further argued in July, 1808, when the decision of the supreme court was upheld. Cooper alone dissented. See Horace Binney's *Reports of Cases Adjudged in the Supreme Court of Pennsylvania*, I, 299-300 n., and *The Opinion of Judge Cooper on the effect of a Sentence of a Foreign Court of Admiralty*, pp. xii-xiv.

[49] *Croudson and Others v. Leonard*, March, 1808, William Cranch, *Reports of Cases Argued and Adjudged in the Supreme Court of the United States*, IV, 434-43.

[50] For the general considerations which influenced him, see his *Opinion*, pp. 64-79.

[51] See Charles Warren, *The Supreme Court in United States History*, I, 319-20 and notes. Peter S. Duponceau, writing in 1824, said that the discussions of this doctrine ''drew forth the talents of Judge Livingston, Judge Cooper, Mr. DeWitt Clinton, the late Mr. Dallas, and several others,'' and attributed the change in sentiment in England, beginning in 1808, to the effect of the writings of American jurists. *Dissertation on the Nature and Extent of the Jurisdiction of the Courts of the United States*, pp. 124-5.

Cooper's position, the sincerity of which need not be questioned, was accordingly acceptable both to home interests and to an administration which was struggling heroically to uphold these interests by peaceable endeavor. The opinion was published in 1810, with the consent of the judge, by his old friend, A. J. Dallas, who hoped that the question might be taken up again and felt that "so comprehensive, analytical and clear" an opinion would be "sufficient to preserve all the requisite information for any future judicial or legislative inquiry." Even if the public object should not be attained, the profession, he felt, would be thankful for "so valuable a present."[52]

Jefferson, to whom Cooper apparently sent a copy of the opinion as soon as it was published, wrote in August, 1810, to thank him for it and to say that he had read it with great pleasure and entire conviction.[53] He said that he had no respect for courts acting under the arbitrary orders of the British and French governments, which had disregarded all the rules of intercourse which had hitherto governed nations in their relations, and that he saw no reason for American courts to heed their decisions. He expected little, however, from old judges.

Those now at the bar may be bold enough to follow reason rather than precedent and may bring that principle upon the bench when promoted to it; but I fear this effort is not for my day. It has been said that when Harvey discovered the circulation of the blood, there was not a physician of Europe of 40 years of age, who ever assented to it. I fear you will experience Harvey's fate. But it will become law when the present judges are dead.

52 *Opinion of Cooper*, pp. xi-xii.
53 August 6, 1810, Jefferson's *Writings* (Memorial ed.), XII, 402-3.

He felt that Cooper was fighting the battle of reason against bigotry in law and supported him, as he did later in his struggle against bigotry in religion.

Madison, who was now president, expressed equal approbation and wrote to ask Jefferson if he had seen this "masterly opinion," which he himself regarded as an "irrefragable disproof of the British doctrine on the subject."[54] The judge was greatly gratified at Madison's approval and entered upon a correspondence with him which was long to continue.[55] He sought to aid the administration by furthering the efforts of the census officials in Northumberland,[56] and shortly afterwards solicited the president's assistance to secure recent scientific treatises from France.[57] Madison responded cordially and the two men became and continued to be very friendly, although their relations were always more impersonal and less intimate than those between Cooper and Jefferson.

The ex-president had meanwhile called his Pennsylvania friend to the attention of Joseph C. Cabell, who was to hear much of the learned gentleman later in connection with the University of Virginia. The judge had written to ask his friend to secure a mineralogical correspondent for him in Virginia, and Jefferson forwarded the request to Cabell in a letter in which he gave Cooper most extravagant praise.

[54] June 22, 1810, Madison's *Writings*, VIII, 103-4. Warren, *Supreme Court in U.S. Hist.*, I, 320 n., refers to this letter, but does not clearly indicate that Madison's comment was upon Cooper's opinion.

[55] Cooper to Madison, July 9, 1810. Madison Papers (Library of Congress), XXXIX, 6.

[56] His address to his fellow citizens was published in a local newspaper, July 31, 1810, and is now pasted upon the back of his letter of July 9, 1810. *Ibid.*, XXXIX, 6.

[57] Cooper to Madison, August 19, 1810, *ibid.*, XXXIX, 62; Madison to Cooper, Sept. 4, 1810, *ibid.*, VII, 1.

He is one of the ablest men in America, and that in several branches of science. The law opinion which he mentions, I have received, and a more luminous one has not been seen.[58] It will produce a revolution of opinion on the question treated; not in the present day, because old lawyers, like old physicians, and other old men, never change opinions which it has cost them the whole labors of their youth to form; but when the young lawyers get on the bench, they will carry Cooper's doctrine with them. The best pieces of political economy which have been written in this country were by Cooper. He is a great chemist and now proposes to resume his mineralogical studies; on this subject, you will perceive that he wishes a correspondent in our state. I know nobody to whom I can so advantageously commit him as to yourself. My information in Mineralogy dates with Linnaeus, and like other old men I have lost the ardor of science; and permitted egoism to qualify all its pursuits. I add another word to Cooper's 'mihi cui bono?' but at your time of life I should have jumped at such a correspondent as Cooper; will you accept him? You will be of mutual value to each other.[59]

Cabell wrote that he lacked the *sine qua non* of a sufficient knowledge of mineralogy and leisure to explore the country and make the necessary collections, so asked that Cooper be referred to someone else.[60] Apparently Jefferson was unable to secure the desired correspondent, and Cabell subsequently showed himself disinclined to accept in its entirety the highly favorable opinion of the jurist-chemist which the sage of Monticello held.

Within a year Cooper was free to devote himself entirely to mineralogical investigation, if he chose, for on April 2, 1811, he was removed from his judicial office by

58 *Dempsey v. Insurers.*

59 June 27, 1810; N. F. Cabell, *Early History of the University of Virginia, as contained in the letters of Thomas Jefferson and Joseph C. Cabell,* pp. 1-2.

60 July 23, 1810, *ibid.,* pp. 2-5.

the governor upon joint-address of the two houses of the assembly.

Contemporary comments upon his conduct as judge, except such as were brought out in the hearings in the assembly, are almost entirely lacking. In 1805, when the question of the judiciary was so heated, there was at least one favorable newspaper comment.[61] His close attention to the duties of his office, the unusually expeditious procedure, and his established abilities and talents were spoken of. Even this writer, however, while complimentary of the judge was critical of the judicial system.

Within three years Cooper had become, so far as state politics were concerned, a man without a party. Following the reassuring announcement of Simon Snyder that he no longer favored the calling of a constitutional convention, most of the constitutionalists supported for governor in 1808 the man whom they had opposed in the previous election.[62] The contest was between him and James Ross, a Federalist. John Spayd ran as a "constitutional," but received a very small vote, while Snyder had a decisive majority.[63] Cooper publicly stated that he would not vote for his neighbor and he probably voted for Spayd, although he played no active part in the campaign.[64] In 1811, factional divisions seem to have reappeared,[65] and although this particular president judge had long ceased to be a significant factor in state politics,

[61] Communication signed "A Bystander," *Aurora*, Nov. 6, 1805. The records of the courts of common pleas for the period of Cooper's service have not been printed.

[62] Meigs, "Pennsylvania Politics," *Penn. Magazine of Hist. and Biog.*, XVII, 474-8.

[63] Returns in *Aurora*, Nov. 11, 1808.

[64] *Narrative of Proceedings against Thomas Cooper, Esq., President Judge of the 8th Judiciary District of Pennsylvania on a charge of official misconduct*, p. 50. There was no reference to him in the *Aurora*, July 1-Nov. 2, 1808.

[65] Meigs in *Penn. Magazine*, XVII, 481.

the government of the commonwealth was in the hands of
the faction he had opposed and the stage was set for
action against him.

According to his own account, petitions against him
which had been printed in Lancaster with the idea of
circulation in his district, began to arrive in Sunbury in
the latter part of January, 1811.[66] These recited charges
against him, to which he replied in the Northumberland
Argus in February, and asked consideration and action
by the assembly. He claimed that his enemies found it
impossible to secure the signatures of moderate men, especially because of the injustice of proceeding by address
rather than impeachment, and that they accordingly
brought forward what was called the "gull-trap" petition, which merely asked for an investigation. To this
they obtained one hundred and ninety signatures. According to his own statement, more than two thousand
names altogether were attached to the various petitions,[67]
so it would appear that the device to ensnare the moderates was not absolutely necessary. He claimed, to be sure,
that there were signatures of boys as well as men and
that there were forgeries and duplicates. He was unable
to examine the list closely, but spoke positively of
seventy duplicates and intimated that there were more.
Apart from the question of the genuineness of signatures, he felt that the petitions did not accurately represent the sentiments of the sixty-five thousand people in
his district. The dearth of contemporary comment makes

[66] *Narrative of Proceedings*, pp. 3-4. This account was prepared by
Cooper himself after his removal, and is a defense as well as a narrative.
It contains, however, more documentary material than the journals of the
house of representatives and the senate, and is the most important single
source of information. The Philadelphia *Democratic Press*, Snyder's organ,
described the course of events at Lancaster in some detail, but we have
gained from it little information beyond that given by the journals and the
Narrative. The *Aurora* showed no interest in the proceedings.

[67] *Ibid.*, p. 7.

it impossible to determine with any certainty whether they did or not, but it cannot be denied that the movement against him was far stronger than the movement in defense, which was largely confined to his professional associates.

He attributed the opposition to him to unjustifiable personal enmity and political prejudice. He said that the petitions were circulated by certain young members of the bar who bore him resentment because of decisions against them or merited personal rebuke,[68] and that the seven or eight movers against him called, one or another of them, at almost every house in the entire district and did everything possible to inflame the minds of the ignorant. He said the matter was taken up by "the political description of citizens usually called democrats" on two grounds, that he was a foreigner and that he had gone over to the Federalists.[69] His personal and political foes doubtless initiated the movement against him, and they probably sought to arouse the prejudices of the people, as he claimed, but the success of their appeal indicates that dissatisfaction with his services must have been widespread. Many of the inhabitants of his district perceived that he was out of sympathy with them and their point of view and wanted to be rid of him. He had lost much of his faith in the people, and there is every reason to believe that they had lost interest, if they had not lost faith, in him.

The house of representatives was flooded with petitions against Judge Cooper, some fifty of which were presented between February 21 and March 13. On the former date, the first of these, ten in number, were referred to a special committee, as were the later petitions

[68] He named Bellas, Greenough, Maus, Marr, and Billington, and gave specific explanation of the hostility of each, *ibid.*, pp. 4-5 n.

[69] *Ibid.*, p. 5.

when they were presented.[70] The committee drew up
articles of accusation including fifty-one distinct items,
and Cooper stated that testimony was permitted on two
others, making fifty-three. These included charges of
wanton and cruel tyranny in the fining and imprisoning
of citizens without cause and hearing, violent abuse of
suitors and their counsel from the bench, contempt for
and disobedience of acts of the legislature, the passionate
setting aside of a jury verdict, partiality and favoritism,
the use of office for personal advantage, ridicule cast
upon the doctrines of the Presbyterians and Quakers as
"damn'd hypocrisy and nonsense," personal intemperance and immorality, and many other things more or
less reprehensible.

The hearing of testimony began March 7, and continued for almost two weeks.[71] Cooper, as we should
naturally expect, asked a public hearing for the witnesses
for the defense, but his request was denied. Some of his
opponents regarded the committee as liberal and indul-
gent in allowing the accused and his witnesses to be
heard before them, and in allowing him the assistance of
counsel, Thomas Duncan of Carlisle.[72] The Philadelphia
Democratic Press, Governor Snyder's organ, which gave
the proceedings full publicity and remarked upon the
great interest which was shown in them, referred frequently to the faithfulness, diligence, and impartiality
of the committee.[73] There were forty-two witnesses for

[70] *Journal of the House of Representatives of Pennsylvania,* 1810-11,
pp. 522, 525, 559, 564, 570, 583, 602, 606, 611, 637; *Narrative of Proceedings,* pp. 14-9.

[71] *Narrative of Proceedings,* pp. 20-3. The *Democratic Press,* beginning
with the issue of March 8, gave an account of the proceedings almost every
day.

[72] House *Journal,* 1810-11, p. 717. The petitioners were also represented
by counsel, Greenough of Sunbury, *Democratic Press,* March 9.

[73] See especially, March 13, 14.

the prosecution, and seventeen, almost all of whom were associates of Cooper's in the judiciary or practitioners in his courts, for the defense. Eight of the nine associate justices of his district sent letters "in the hope of stemming the torrent of public abuse,"[74] and Cooper is said to have spoken for four and a half hours before the committee in his own defense.[75]

The committee reported, on March 23, that they were of opinion that Cooper's official conduct had been "arbitrary, unjust and precipitate, contrary to sound policy and dangerous to the pure administration of justice," and submitted a resolution asking that a committee be appointed to draft an address to the governor requesting him to remove him.[76] They upheld eight charges of the original fifty-three. The charges of intemperance and immorality were disproved by testimony both for the prosecution and the defense, and particularly by that of Joseph Priestley, with whom Cooper had lived for some ten years. The son and namesake of the latter's old companion testified that never, except for one evening, during this period had he seen his friend the judge so affected by liquor as not to be in full possession of his powers, and that upon this single occasion his condition was not perceived by the rest of the family.[77] Cooper himself expressed horror at the "infinite industry" which was employed to foster this charge upon him. Of the eight charges which were upheld, five had to do with fines

[74] The letters of Judges William Montgomery, William Wilson, John Macpherson, William Hepburn, James Davidson, Samuel Harris, Matthias Hollinbach, and Jesse Fell are quoted in the *Narrative*, pp. 7-14. All of these men, together with the two senior practitioners in the district and a few other citizens, either gave oral testimony or made deposition, *ibid.*, p. 22; House *Journal*, 1810-11, pp. 602-3.

[75] *Democratic Press*, March 22.

[76] For the report, see House *Journal*, 1810-11, pp. 707-9; *Narrative*, pp. 24-5.

[77] *Narrative*, p. 23.

inflicted upon offenders against good order in the court, once in the case of a Quaker who would not remove his hat. One had to do with the arbitrary and passionate imposition of a fine on the supervisor of highways, one with the increase in the sentence of a boy horse-thief after his imprisonment had begun, and one with his engaging in the purchase of a tract of land at a sheriff's sale levied on by an execution issued by his own court. The committee regarded this latter as unbecoming, though not an actual violation of the statute. The letters of Judges Montgomery, Wilson, and Macpherson showed that Cooper acknowledged his connection with the sale, and that the other judges ordered the land sold over again, as it was at an advanced price.[78]

The letters of the associate judges in general absolved Cooper from the charges of arbitrariness and brow-beating, although Montgomery thought that he exercised considerable freedom in summing up testimony. Wilson and Macpherson thought him justified in the case of John Hanna the Quaker, and stated that he had established order in court from a state of disorder and tumult. The other judges bore essentially the same testimony, although they recognized the unpopularity of his actions in some cases. All attested his high abilities.

Being confident that an unfavorable report was not warranted by the testimony and desirous of the greatest possible publicity, Cooper asked leave to be heard by counsel at the bar of the house.[79] Although this request was regarded by some as unreasonable, in view of the privileges and time which had already been granted him, and as a reflection upon the integrity of the committee, it was finally agreed to by a close vote.[80] Accordingly, David

[78] *Ibid.*, pp. 8-11.
[79] House *Journal*, 1810-11, pp. 709-10; *Democratic Press*, March 26.
[80] House *Journal*, pp. 714-19. The final vote was 49 to 41.

Watt and Thomas Duncan, the senior members of the bar of the district, who gave Cooper three weeks of their time in connection with the case, occupied about two hours each on March 26.[81] They were unable to go into the surrounding circumstances of the whole movement, as they would have done in an impeachment trial, but had to confine themselves to the accusations adopted by the committee. According to the judge himself, his counsel showed the absurdity of the charges against him in the case of Hanna, the Quaker, and explained the circumstances of his other actions against disorder, showing that he had greatly improved procedure in the court. It appeared that his predecessor, Judge Ross, had sometimes been compelled to leave the bench, unable to proceed because of the disorder. As to the case of the boy horse-thief, Cooper gave him one year instead of seven in the first place and extended the sentence upon the remonstrances of the neighbors of the boy and the other judges. As to the Galbraith land, he never sat in judgment on the sale. Cooper claimed that only six of the sixteen witnesses produced in support of the charges adopted by the committee were free from legal objection, most of them being men who had been fined by him and were not competent witnesses to criminate the magistrate, but that, on the other hand, the evidence in his favor was given by men of the highest standing.

The address to the governor which was finally adopted made no direct reference to the charge that Cooper had used his office for personal advantage, but asserted that he had committed many acts of official misconduct and abuse of authority.[82] It declared that public confidence

[81] *Ibid.*, pp. 722-3; *Narrative*, pp. 20, 28-34. Cooper gives the date as March 25.

[82] Senate *Journal*, 1810-11, pp. 535-6; *cf.* House *Journal*, 1810-11, p. 735 for the amendment which was adopted. See also *Narrative*, pp. 36-7.

in his decisions had been destroyed and that his usefulness as a judge had been much diminished, if not totally
destroyed. This was probably true. Cooper's own comment was that, upon such charges, he should have had
the opportunity to defend himself. This seems a justifiable position, although it should be noted that he managed to make a strong defense, even as it was.

Two dissenting opinions were entered upon the journal. The first, which bore five signatures, took the position that the charges against the judge were such as could
be dealt with only by impeachment, and that the proper
procedure would have been to proceed by that method at
the next session.[83] The second opinion, which bore thirteen signatures, including that of Nicholas Biddle with
whom the now harassed judge was in a later day to carry
on an extensive correspondence, took the same position
regarding the necessity for impeachment when such
charges had been made, and presented the additional
argument that the ninth section of the Bill of Rights was
violated by the action, since Cooper was to be deprived of
the emoluments of office, that is, property, without the
judgment of his peers.[84]

The house agreed to the address on March 27,[85] and
transmitted it to the senate the following day. On the
same day Cooper sent a letter to the upper house asking
the privilege of being heard on the subject before that
body. He claimed that the accusations, if true, were mis-
demeanors and justified impeachment but did not give
ground for removal by address, as in a case where no
official conduct was involved. His request was denied by
a vote of nearly three to one and the address was adopted

[83] House *Journal*, 1810-11, pp. 729-32; *Narrative*, pp. 38-40.

[84] House *Journal*, pp. 738-9; *Narrative*, pp. 40-1.

[85] The final vote was 72 to 19, House *Journal*, pp. 735-6.

by almost the same vote.[86] An opinion dissenting from the address was signed by five senators, on the grounds that impeachment was the only constitutional procedure in the case and that it was not in accord with the dignity and justice of the senate to act on evidence taken wholly by the house without a proper hearing for the accused.[87]

The yet resourceful judge presented a remonstrance to the governor, April 1, in which he made the same objection as previously, namely, that the charges justified impeachment, and added that actions such as his removal would subordinate the judiciary to the legislature and prostrate the constitution itself.[88] He protested in his own name, in the name of the profession, the constitution, and the public. Throughout the affair, indeed, he left no stone unturned and endeavored in characteristic fashion to secure as much publicity for his cause as possible.

He remained in Lancaster to receive notification of his removal, but Governor Snyder had sent it to Northumberland to be served on him there.[89] Upon Cooper's request, a copy of it was sent him by the secretary of state. Cooper intimated that there was lack of courtesy on the part of the governor, and pointed out that he and Snyder had been friendly neighbors for years, that he was once Snyder's counsel, and once obligated him by a voluntary vindication of his character in an important case. He did not vote for him for governor, however, and publicly declared he would not.

In his final summary, the ex-judge said that he was removed because four or five years before he had fined

[86] The two votes were respectively 20 to 7 and 21 to 6, Senate *Journal,* 1810-11, 542-7; *cf. Narrative,* p. 45.

[87] Senate *Journal,* pp. 607-8; *Narrative,* pp. 45-6.

[88] *Narrative,* pp. 47-50.

[89] For the governor's announcement, April 2, see House *Journal,* 1810-11, p. 804; Senate *Journal,* 1810-11, p. 634; *Democratic Press,* April 4, 1811.

four or five men a dollar each for disturbing the court, and stated that if he had to act again on the cases which formed the articles of accusation he would act essentially as he had done.[90] A disinterested inquiry into the facts of the case seems at least to justify the conclusion that the charges against him were in actuality trivial, and that if they had been as serious as they were made out to be he should have been proceeded against by impeachment, as he claimed.

As has already been indicated, he felt that the success of the movement which led to his removal was largely due to prejudice against him as a foreigner and, more particularly, to the feeling that he had gone over to the Federalists. In his narrative of the proceedings, he stated that he would not condescend to reply to the charge that he was a foreigner, although he might well reply that he had lived in the country seventeen years, that his son and daughter were both married to native Americans, and that he had been conspicuous in his efforts for the public good ever since his arrival. "I have been either the original promoter or the active supporter of every scheme of public benefit that has taken place in my town or county from my first inhabitancy there to the present time."[91] It is probable that this was an essentially correct statement, which made the lack of appreciation all the greater tragedy. Whether he was too superior a person to be appreciated in a somewhat primitive community, or whether the trouble lay rather in his own unbalanced personality, is another question. The vehemence, impetuosity, and reckless outspokenness of the man served ultimately to turn a large number against him in every community where he ever lived.

The comments which he made on the charge of Federal-

90 *Narrative*, preface; *cf.* pp. 52-4.
91 *Ibid.*, p. 5.

ism are even more interesting and significant. Thus he said, and we should not otherwise have suspected it, that he had been in the habit of living chiefly with Federalists from the beginning of his stay in America, and stated that he could not help being attached to persons who had so long had intimate social intercourse with him despite the fact that his political principles and conduct were decidedly opposed to their own. It would appear that his personal and intellectual attainments had led him inevitably to associate with the more aristocratic group, and that his democracy was essentially theoretical. In no accurate sense can he be said to have been personally a man of the people.

The modification of his theoretical democracy resulted from more extended observation of the democrats. He stated that he had learned from long observation, and had not hesitated to say, that the Republicans were no more disinterested than the Federalists and no less intolerant.

I have long found it impossible for me to go all lengths with the party to which I belonged, and of course I have shared the common fate of all moderate men. I have influence with no party, and have willingly and deliberately incurred the decided hatred of the most violent and thoroughgoing of my own. I went over to France in 1792, an enthusiast, and I left it in disgust. I came here; and seventeen years experience of a democratic government in this country, has also served to convince me that it may have its faults; that it is not quite so perfect in practice as it is beautiful in theory, and that the speculations of my youth do not receive the full sanction of my maturer age: nor do I feel that justice and disinterestedness, wisdom and tolerance, are the necessary fruits of universal suffrage, as it is exercised in Pennsylvania; for these are not always the qualifications that procure a man to be sent as a representative of the people. There are many good and some wise men in the legislature; but no one can say, that the wisdom and moderation of the community at large, are exclusively represented at the seat of government.[92]

He said that the precise meaning of Federalist and Republican was not clear to his mind. He was opposed to hereditary monarchs, peers, and judges and to primogeniture, but deplored the perversion of sacred governmental institutions to the ends of vengeance. The insubordination, ignorance, intolerance, and persecution of the present Republican party in Pennsylvania he felt would bring the party ultimately into detestation and contempt. They vented "their most bitter execrations on the aristocracy of talents,"[93] to which he unquestionably felt that he belonged. So long as he had used his intellectual gifts to further the designs of the democrats, they had given him honor; but when he came to mingle with them in actual political life he found them uncongenial companions, and at length they turned to rend him.

The report of the proceedings and the account of the circumstances leading to his removal, he published for the satisfaction of his friends, and with a particular view to the moderate men of all parties who, he intimated, might be led to doubt "whether our republican institutions present a sufficient barrier to the despotic and vindictive spirit of political party, or furnish any protection to individuals who take shelter under their authority."[94] So he protested in the name of freedom and individualism against despotism in democratic guise. Perhaps he was consistent after all!

[92] *Narrative*, p. 6. [93] *Ibid.*, p. 47.
[94] *Ibid.*, preface.

CHAPTER VII

SCIENCE AND LEARNING, 1811-1819

CONVINCED that his removal from the judiciary reflected no discredit upon him and had lost him no friend on the bench or at the bar, Cooper seems speedily to have recovered from any depression which it may have occasioned him. The attentions of the former governor, McKean, who appreciated independent judges, and of his old friend, Alexander J. Dallas, shortly to become Madison's secretary of the treasury, he said were increased and flattering. And in June, 1811, the trustees of Carlisle (later Dickinson) College made him a voluntary offer of the chair of chemistry in that institution.[1] His former professional associates among the trustees probably initiated the movement to bring him to the college,[2] and when some of the trustees hesitated to vote for so heterodox a person Benjamin Rush, the chemist, himself a member of the board, insisted upon Cooper's election.[3] Thus a place was found for the former judge by appreciative friends who thought he had been unjustly treated.

The new position was never satisfactory from a finan-

[1] Cooper to Madison, Oct. 4, 1811, Madison Papers, XLIII, 22.

[2] Among the members of the board of trustees in 1815 were Justice H. H. Brackenbridge of the state supreme court, President Judges James Hamilton and Jonathan Walker, and Thomas Duncan and David Watts, who had served Cooper during the proceedings for his removal. Some or all of these men may have been upon the board in 1811. See the address of the trustees upon Cooper's resignation from the college, Port Folio, 3 series, VI, 512-13.

[3] Edgar F. Smith, Chemistry in America, p. 128.

cial point of view. The college apparently guaranteed
Cooper only eight hundred or eight hundred and fifty
dollars, although he succeeded in supplementing this to
an equal amount by means of his many contributions to
contemporary periodicals.[4] None the less, the current of
his life during the four years he served the rather obscure little Pennsylvania institution was relatively
smooth. He got into no violent controversy and left the
college in September, 1815, with the plaudits of the trustees ringing in his ears. His pen was unusually active
during this period, although not always fruitfully employed, and he made real contributions to science, despite
inadequate facilities for experiment. It was during these
years that his correspondence with Jefferson reached its
highest point. However uneventful the period may have
been, it is pleasant to contemplate, a peaceful interlude
in a tempestuous life.

The summer of 1811 was spent with Joseph Priestley
at Northumberland, and in August the new professor
began his work with an introductory lecture on chemistry, really a history of that science, which was shortly
afterwards published at the request of the trustees and
widely commented upon.[5] Here he referred with equa-
nimity to his removal from the judiciary and said that he
had cheerfully accepted the post at Carlisle. He stated
that, in his opinion, the reasons assigned for his removal
ought to entitle him to the thanks of the community, and
that from the beginning of his judicial career he had
given it to be understood that he cared little for popularity. He admitted that at first he had been resentful of

[4] Cooper to A. J. Dallas, Dec. 22, 1814, Madison Papers, L, 35; cf.
Cooper to Madison, Sept. 3, 1813, ibid., L, 38.

[5] *The Introductory Lecture of Thomas Cooper, Esq., Professor of Chemistry at Carlisle College, Pennsylvania.* 1812. The date of the preface, April
1, 1811, must be a misprint.

the treatment which he had received from the legislature, but stated that he now realized that if the legislature had not followed the just course it had followed the speedier one, and "had cut the knot which it could not venture to untie." His election to Carlisle College he regarded as an honorable addition to the proofs he had already received that he had not forfeited the good opinion of that portion of society which was best qualified to judge him.[6] So he turned from law and politics to science, in which he had never relinquished interest; he did so of necessity, but apparently without bitterness, and he launched upon his new career with great enthusiasm. This illustrates the extraordinary resilience of his temperament and the vast resourcefulness of his nature.

A writer in the *Port Folio,* reviewing this lecture and commenting upon the circumstances of its author's removal from the bench, stated that Cooper had just cause for complaint, but that good had resulted from evil. He said that as a consequence of injustice and persecution Cooper had been elevated to a station which was more honorable and conspicuous and better suited to his talents, and in which he could render himself more extensively useful. So this writer declared that the friends of science would be inclined to forgive the legislature for the act which resulted in converting a "respectable judge into a much more respectable teacher of chymistry.'"[7] While there was an obvious effort here to make a virtue of necessity, there is much to be said in favor of this opinion. Cooper might have been a dominant figure in science, learning, and education, had he been able to refrain from practical politics.[8] But if he had resisted the

---

[6] *Ibid.,* preface, pp. vi-vii.

[7] *Port Folio,* new series, I, 129.

[8] Edgar F. Smith, former provost of the University of Pennsylvania, has commented upon Cooper's scientific work in his *Chemistry in America,* VI,

lure of political controversy, his life would have been much less interesting and political history would lack a most enlivening figure.

The reviewer spoke also of the significance to the college of the acquisition of this new professor. After the death of President Nesbit, the very existence of the institution had been precarious, he said, but the election of the Rev. Dr. Atwater of Connecticut had brought "brightness out of gloom." Other arrangements for the benefit of the institution had followed the election of a new president and he felt that the establishment of a professorship of "chymistry" was the most important of these. The appointment of Cooper to this important chair, he claimed, could not be "amended" in the United States.[9]

We shall not endeavor to discuss the introductory lecture, highly interesting as it is even to a layman, and we shall not describe in detail Cooper's other scientific writings during his last years in Pennsylvania. This period of his life was characterized by a whole-hearted devotion to science and learning. Baffled in his quest for freedom and disillusioned as to democracy, he resumed his quest for truth and did what service he could toward public enlightenment. The utilitarian motive now dominated his work. Indeed, his special interest in chemistry was probably due to his conviction of the utility of this science. Thus he said, "I think it can be shown, without much difficulty, that chemistry is of more immediate and useful application to the every day concerns of life—that it

and his *Chemistry in Old Philadelphia*, pp. 62-81, and is at present making further investigations into this side of Cooper's life. He has stated to the present writer in conversation that Cooper was a great investigator and might have been eminent in chemistry had he devoted himself more exclusively to it.

[9] *Port Folio*, new series, I, 111.

operates more upon our hourly comforts, than any other branch of knowledge whatever.''[10]

Early in 1813, Cooper became editor of the *Emporium of Arts and Sciences* and during the next year and a half he sought to give practical value to this periodical.[11] In his prospectus he announced that he would continue the plan originally proposed by the former editor and publisher, John Redman Coxe. The *Emporium* was to contain a judicious selection of practical papers on science and the arts taken from foreign publications, and be a repository for original papers furnished by American scientists. The new editor promised that he himself would contribute a series of essays on manufacturing processes, which he had previously prepared for separate publication. He desired to write a ''classic book'' on the subject, but made no pretense at originality. His chief object was to stimulate and aid American manufacturers. ''Having been much occupied in chemical pursuits, and much conversant with manufactures and manufacturers,'' he considered himself qualified for the task he had assumed.[12] He made no mention of disastrous experiences at Manchester and apparently no one annoyed him by recalling them.

His discussion of the encouragement of manufacturing was later used against him when he was so boldly preaching free trade in South Carolina.[13] Even in 1813, he regarded bounties and protective duties as taxes upon the rest of the community for the benefit of manufacturers and in general opposed governmental attempts to direct

[10] *Introductory Lecture,* p. 90.

[11] His prospectus was issued under the date of February, 1813; *Port Folio,* 3 series, I, 399-403; *Emporium,* new series, I, 1-10. The first number was issued in June of that year, and publication was suspended in the autumn of 1814, because of financial difficulties. Cooper to Madison, Nov. 16, 1814. Madison Papers, LIII, 95. Cooper edited vols. 1-3, new series.

[12] *Emporium,* new series, I, 4.   [13] See below, pp. 293-4.

the employment of capital. But considerations of defense, home market, economic independence of England, and the stimulus to science which would result from industrial development, led him to favor the initial encouragement of manufacturing by means of protective duties. Some of these points he had previously discussed with Jefferson and Madison,[14] and he later discussed them at great length in letters to the former.[15] He frequently paid tribute to Adam Smith, so was able afterwards to claim that he had made no surrender of his economic principles. His attitude toward protection was directly due to the international situation and his continued suspicion of the British, which seems largely to have disappeared by the time of his residence in South Carolina. Thus he stated that he would be perfectly willing to see America remain agricultural if any reliance could be placed upon Great Britain, but that the mercantilist policy of that nation made her undependable.[16] He continued to manifest considerable hostility to foreign trade and the commercial class in general. "Commerce, ever clamorous for protection, is never worth protecting."[17] He favored agriculture, manufacturing, and domestic trade—indeed, a sort of "American System." He did not urge the abandonment of foreign commerce, but was opposed, as heretofore, to the protection of speculation.[18]

The articles and notes in the *Emporium* reflected the practical purposes which Cooper announced. The editor gave iron and steel particular prominence because of their importance and, with profuse display of scientific information and homely wisdom, himself discussed the steam engine, the bleaching of paper, cookery, weights

14 See above, pp. 193-4.
15 See especially the letter of August 17, 1814, Jefferson Papers, CCII.
16 *Emporium*, new series, I, 161.
17 *Ibid.*, I, 162.   18 *Ibid.*, II, 123-4 n., 137 n., 150 n.

and measures, wines, mineral waters, the uses of a dead horse, manures, dyeing, coverings for roofs, not to mention various matters of economic theory. And occasionally he made casual reference to some events in his own past life of which otherwise we should have been ignorant.

Cooper's work did not lack for praise. A fellow editor, who had greeted his original prospectus with enthusiasm,[19] later spoke of him and one of his numbers in terms of eulogy:

In the estimation of those acquainted with the vast and varied resources of the editor, conjoined with his attention and never-tiring industry, his name alone must stamp a value on every work in which he is concerned. In furnishing materials for that which we are now considering, he appears to move peculiarly within his own province. For the extent and correctness of his knowledge of the principles and processes of the arts and manufactures, in Great Britain, France, and elsewhere, perhaps Mr. Cooper is inferior to no man of the present or any former period. His sources of information appear to have been books, correspondence by letter, and personal observation; and he has evidently profited most amply of them all. His business now is merely to empty on paper a part of the rich and multifarious store-house of his mind, and a volume is formed.[20]

The enthusiasm of the editor of the *Port Folio* may have been partly due to the fact that the Carlisle professor had already begun to contribute to that periodical, but words of praise were also given him by others.[21] There seems little doubt but that Cooper was regarded by his contemporaries as exceptionally qualified for his editorial task and as performing a genuine public service.

19 *Port Folio*, 3 series, I, 399.
20 *Ibid.*, 3 series, III, 480 (May, 1814).
21 See the *Analectic Magazine*, III, 350. Jefferson and Madison expressed appreciation several times in their letters.

The *Port Folio* was a monthly magazine of rather promiscuous but primarily literary character published in
Philadelphia. Charles Caldwell, who became its editor in
1812, states in his autobiography that in 1814 or 1815
Cooper and another were employed as assistant writers
for a "liberal compensation."[22] He also says that
Cooper's finances were unusually low when he removed
to Philadelphia in 1815, so the professor doubtless wrote
to supplement his meager salary.[23] His numerous and
diverse contributions to this periodical must have taxed
even his extraordinary ingenuity, but their value to
society was doubtless slight.[24] He wrote on Indian her-
aldry, Homerian mineralogy and the sensibility of vegetables; he ventured into philology to set forth the fantastic theory that the modern Irish language was identical with the ancient Carthaginian and closely related to
the Hebrew; he entered upon literary criticism to the
discredit of Shakespeare, commented unfavorably upon
Pope, and promised to write in similar fashion of other
English poets, all of whom he regarded as greatly over-
estimated. Several of his contributions led to violent literary controversy, which this veteran of the political
arena who had attacked Burke, threatened Hamilton and

[22] *Autobiography of Charles Caldwell, M.D.*, pp. 321, 8. From January,
1812, the *Port Folio* was conducted by Oliver Oldschool, but apparently
under the editorship of Caldwell. The other "assistant writer" was Judge
Workman. Cooper had contributed to the magazine before he was regularly
employed by it.

[23] *Ibid.*, p. 341.

[24] A mere list of his contributions would require several pages. Among
the more interesting may be mentioned, "Homerian Mineralogy," 3 series,
III, 409-22; "On Vegetable Life," 3 series, IV, 59-74, 176-191; "On the
Irish Language," 3 series, IV, 409-18, 480-5; V, 528-42; 4 series, I, 480-2;
"Freron's Critique on Shakespeare," 3 series, V, 8-18. His "Copy of a
Letter to a Friend on University Education," 3 series, V, 349-59, has real
value, but reflects the same point of view as that indicated in other letters
to Jefferson, of which this was probably one. See below, p. 227.

defied John Adams, must have found mildly diverting. All his writings are interesting, however fantastic; they reveal an extraordinary catholicity of interest, however superficial; and they all make magnificent display of learning. He frequently overreached himself and sometimes made a fool of himself, although he never admitted it, but he appeared to be having a delightful time.

The many letters which Cooper wrote Madison and Jefferson while he was at Carlisle are of much greater importance than his often trivial, although always interesting, communications to contemporary periodicals. He wrote the president in regard to foreign scientific treatises,[25] discussed possibilities in the manufacture of explosives,[26] spoke of the work of Madison's nephew at Carlisle,[27] where he had probably been sent because of Cooper's membership in the faculty, described his own affairs and troubles, and upon one occasion sought appointment to petty offce.[28]

The most important product of Cooper's pen which was sent Madison during this time was a private pamphlet entitled *Extract of a Letter to a Student at Law*, which had resulted from the request of a student that the versatile professor outline for him a course of reading in politics. Only a few copies were printed because the author felt that his political sentiments were very unlike those of any party and because he thought many of his remarks unsuited to the public eye. Upon the sympathy and discretion of Madison, however, he could rely, so he sent him a copy,[29] as he doubtless did Jefferson also. In

[25] Oct. 4, 1811, Madison Papers, XLIII, 22; Nov. 16, 1814, *ibid.*, XLIII, 95.

[26] Feb. 18, 1813, *ibid.*, XLVIII, 43.

[27] Nov. 16, 1814, *ibid.*, LIII, 95; August 8, 1815, *ibid.*, LVI, 53.

[28] See below, p. 228.

[29] A copy is preserved in the Madison Papers, LXXVII, 4. See the letter to Madison, August 8, 1815.

outlining the reading he set forth many of his own political doctrines and gave his interpretation of recent political developments in Europe and America. It is one of the most conservative of all his writings and shows how far from radicalism the pendulum of his thought had swung.

He reiterated the conviction so often expressed by him earlier that power intrusted has a natural tendency to encroachment and abuse, and ought accordingly to be submitted to periodical revision and control, and that government should be for the benefit of the people, to whom governors should be held responsible. But beyond that he found a realm of perplexity and uncertainty which must be painfully explored by political experiment.

But under what limitations political power should be entrusted to produce the proper effect—how the mischiefs of popular ignorance, injustice and caprice, are to be prevented on the one hand, and the usurpations of entrusted authority controuled on the other—are problems yet to be solved. The science of politics is yet in its infancy; many experiments must be made, and much evil endured, before we arrive at accuracy in the result; neither pure monarchy nor pure democracy will answer the purpose; . . . they are equally proud, insolent, unfeeling, tyrannical, cruel, revengeful, and unjust. All these bad qualities are exemplified more strongly under the Greek democracies, than under the monarchy of Persia. . . . I think we have gained in America a glimpse of the true path, but our practice is very imperfect as yet.[30]

He had come to doubt the right and expediency of universal suffrage and at this time thought the vote should be subject to limitations dependent upon property.[31] He said that after the triumph of the *theory* of republican government, he had been disillusioned as to the wisdom of the populace, and now thought that all appointments

<hr>

[30] *Letter to a Student at Law*, p. 2.   [31] *Ibid.*, p. 6.

should be made by persons one or two removes from the multitude.[32] He regarded parties as unavoidable in a republican community, but felt that talents on the whole amounted to a disqualification in politics, and that with parties of all descriptions the sin against the Holy Ghost was lukewarmness.[33] He stated that men like himself who were disinclined to go the length of either of the prevailing factions, were considered on both sides as half enemies and were viewed with a kind of hostile contempt. Such lamentation doubtless disclosed also some dissatisfaction with a position which was one of practical impotence at the same time it was one of philosophical detachment.

Although yet persuaded that republican forms of government possessed many and great advantages over any form of monarchy or aristocracy, Cooper now thought that the American executive should be somewhat stronger and that elections should be less frequent and offices less rotatory.[34] To provide for necessary changes in the instrument of government he favored either a revision of the constitution every twenty-five years,[35] or better still, a council of revisors or censors appointed decennially.[36] He felt that such a body had served well in Pennsylvania and that its abolition in the state was to be regretted. The whole matter, however, he regarded as uncertain because of the lack of adequate experiment.

In his historical discussion of American political controversy[37] he disclosed a more critical attitude toward the Republicans than would have been expected of one who had participated so vigorously in their crusade. He admitted that the democratic societies, while useful agencies of protest against oppression and tyranny, were,

[32] *Letter to a Student at Law*, p. 8.   [33] *Ibid.*, p. 9.
[34] *Ibid.*, p. 10.   [35] *Ibid.*, p. 7.
[36] *Ibid.*, Errata and Addenda, p. 1.   [37] *Ibid.*, pp. 11-19.

in Washington's time at least, "violent, turbulent, and perhaps mischievous." He felt that such organizations were liable to factious use, and that it was better to consider the constitutional authorities as fully competent to redress all such grievances! Though he regarded the establishment of the Bank of the United States as unwarranted by the constitution, he felt that when a measure had been acted upon as constitutional and acquiesced in for twenty years, an attack upon its legitimacy would shake the foundations of property itself. He maintained a consistent attitude on this question in subsequent controversy when he staunchly supported Nicholas Biddle. Here his regard for property and his training in economics manifested themselves, to the disregard of purely political considerations. During his term as judge and professor in Pennsylvania he unquestionably experienced a strong anti-democratic reaction. No longer content with theories he had once proclaimed, he was groping after a science of politics based upon experience.

The correspondence with Jefferson during these years was more extensive and is more interesting than that with Madison.[38] Cooper's friendship with the Sage of Monticello had now come to its full flower. He sent his correspondent a copy of everything he wrote and rarely failed to arouse the enthusiasm of that eminent patron of learning. Upon receiving the introductory lecture in chemistry, Jefferson said he perceived that he had a feast in store for him. He wrote at great length upon Cooper's edition of Justinian, commented approvingly upon the *Emporium,* asked and received advice about the University of Virginia, sent a sample of his commonplace book,

[38] In addition to the letters specifically referred to below, may be mentioned those of Jefferson to Cooper, July 10, 1812, *Writings* (Memorial edition), XIII, 176-8, and Feb. 10, 1814, *ibid.*, XIV, 85; *Writings* (Ford), I, 360-1 n.

and discussed with his friend metaphysics, religious prejudice, the state of affairs in Europe, and many other subjects which suggested themselves to a mind which, like that of his correspondent, roamed with joyous interest over the entire field of intellectual endeavor.

With his edition of the *Institutes of Justinian,* Cooper ventured into the field of legal scholarship. He undertook the work that he might not entirely renounce his accustomed studies, and sought merely to give the public a useful translation with the best notes which the limited sources of his information permitted him to add.[39] His modesty in matters of scholarship in his days of maturity stands in striking contrast with the overweening confidence of the controversial utterances of his youth, and even of his old age. In this particular instance he had labored under great difficulties, for his first collection of notes and references was destroyed by fire while he was proceeding from Northumberland to Carlisle. Furthermore, he suffered greatly from his eyes for a considerable period thereafter and his lectures on chemistry occupied most of his time. None the less, he produced a work which Jefferson at least highly appreciated, and of which probably no great number of his American contemporaries would have been capable.

Jefferson wrote that he had read the notes, the addenda and corrigenda, and especially the parallels with English law "with great satisfaction and edification." He felt

[39] Preface. He first thought merely to republish the edition of Harris, now become scarce, and he used Harris's translation as a ground-work, condensing it about one-fifth to avoid diffuseness. He added notes of his own and, among other things, a bibliography. His original purpose to give a brief history of the Roman law had to be abandoned because of his inability to secure the books desired. His personal opinions are reflected in the notes, and some incidental information about his past life may be found there. So far as we have been able to discover, there was no earlier American edition of the *Institutes.*

that the edition would be very useful to American lawyers, some of whom needed the translation as well as the notes. Perhaps the most interesting of his comments, however, is the expression of regret that the editor had not put the same time and research instead upon a translation of Bracton's *De Legibus Angliae*, with notes. This treatise, he said, was less well known because of the technical character of its Latin, and to give it in English with a glossary of its old terms was a work for which he knew nobody but Cooper who possessed the necessary learning and industry, so he suggested that it be considered as a possible undertaking.[40] Cooper replied that he realized the utility of such a work, but that it was necessary for him to benefit his pocket as well as his reputation, and that he could not afford to publish a book which no one would buy.[41] We are by no means sure that his Justinian was among the best sellers. In this same letter Jefferson sent a word of encouragement to one who despite public expressions to the contrary seems to have felt that he was not adequately appreciated:

> Go on in all your good works, without regard to the eye "of suspicion and distrust with which you may be viewed by some" and without being weary in well doing, and be assured that you are justly estimated by the important mass of your fellow citizens, and by none more than myself.

The disillusionment and discouragement of the Carlisle scholar over the political situation in Europe and the general state of affairs in America, which stand in such striking contrast with his earlier confident enthusi-

---

[40] Jan. 16, 1814, Jefferson's *Writings* (Memorial), XIV, 54-61. This suggestion is the more interesting in view of the fact that Bracton has had to wait a century for a competent editor and conditions suitable to the publication of his great treatise. See George E. Woodbine's *De Legibus et Consuetudinibus Angliae*, the first volume of which was published in 1915.

[41] March 20, 1814, Jefferson Papers, CCI.

asm for democracy, are nowhere better illustrated than in his frank discussions with Jefferson. As he contemplated the European situation in 1814, he feared that royal dynasties were destined to continue as they had done through all the ages.[42] Several weeks later he wrote more fully:

I brood over the events of Europe, with melancholy forebodings of what may be the case here, and with no violent predilection in favour of this best of all possible worlds. It seems to me as though "Chaos were come again." I shall doubt hereafter about all wise "saws" and moral and political axioms. I shall no longer unhesitatingly agree that *Magna est Veritas et prevalebit*. I shall no longer declare it as my opinion that in political opinions "no effort is ever lost." Heretofore I have enlisted under Leibnitz and Candide, but *Le disastre de Lisbon,* and the French Revolution, have shaken my Optimism. Doubtless I am bound to acknowledge that the Manichees were sad heretics; but their mistakes might happen to minds no stronger than mine.[43]

He proceeded to speak of his doubts as to human perfectibility and of the limits of amelioration. He questioned even the advantages resulting from a state of tolerable equality, and expressed reluctant praise for England, where despite great inequality and misery there was a wider range of ideas, greater mental and physical energy than in America and perhaps as much happiness as here. The American people, lacking the stimulus of poverty, were an idle lot, he said, and lacking manufactures, which at this time he was so anxious to encourage, they had no science but only the faculty of making long speeches.

It is not true that (with as much natural capacity at least as any people) we are the most enlightened people on the face of

42 May 31, 1814, *ibid.*, CCI.
43 August 17, 1814, *ibid.*, CCII.

the earth, as some very ignorant and silly orators were pleased to call us; we are a people of whom political wrangling, and political speech making are as food of the first necessity, and sufficient to satisfy all other mental cravings.

Science and learning had not developed in America as he had so hopefully predicted in 1794. Jefferson was more optimistic than his friend, whose whole philosophy at this time was colored by the depression growing out of personal financial difficulties and lack of adequate opportunities to realize upon his talents. The older man, now in honorable retirement, expressed the conviction that there was greater happiness in America than in Europe.[44]

The Carlisle professor could not refrain from intimating to so trusted a friend that he was dissatisfied with his position. He had not been in it a year when he mentioned a recurrent notion of moving to New Orleans to practice law, to which despite his attachment to chemistry he considered himself married.[45] Later he wrote that Priestley's library and apparatus had been left with him for disposal and that he was looking for a purchaser. He had offered them to Jefferson's old college, William and Mary, which had invited him to the chair of chemistry there. Although he did not accept the position he was strongly inclined to do so, for he was "looked at with great suspicion and distrust by a body of parsons" who formed a large part of the trustees at Carlisle. He said that he had done and said nothing to irritate in the slightest degree this *genus irritabile*. He had even gone to church with tolerable regularity, but he thought they hated him the more cordially because he had furnished them no cause for complaint.[46]

---

[44] Sept. 10, 1914, Jefferson's *Writings* (Memorial), XIV, 179-90.

[45] Cooper to Jefferson, July 25, 1812, "The Jefferson Papers," *Collections* of the Massachusetts Historical Society, 7 series, I, 171.

[46] Nov. 8, 1813, *ibid.*, pp. 184-5.

Jefferson by this time had definite educational projects of his own and he naturally thought of his learned and non-theological friend in connection with the prospective University of Virginia. Early in 1814, he suggested that if the institution should be established it would offer Cooper a place both worthy and deserved.[47] While this prospect remained nebulous, he asked Cooper's advice about subjects of instruction and received in reply elaborate suggestions in regard to the three grades of grammar school, college, and university.[48] Cooper thought that institutions of the first grade should give training in everything a citizen ought to know, that those of the second grade should give instruction in everything a well-educated gentleman should know, while universities should provide instruction in those branches usually pursued with a view to subsistence. He emphasized the classics as of fundamental importance in college, regarded French as essential, recommended mathematics, chemistry and mineralogy, physics, logic, metaphysics, the theory of government, statistics and political economy, and suggested historical reading by way of amusement. He thought training for the professions of engineering, medicine, and law should be provided in a university, but rejected technology, which he regarded as impracticable for teaching under existing conditions, and theology, because there was no available criterion of the various conflicting systems. Jefferson expressed great appreciation of these suggestions. He agreed that theology should be excluded, as one would expect, but was not quite so zealous as Cooper for the classics.[49]

This enlightening correspondence, which was doubt-

[47] Jefferson to Cooper, Jan. 16, 1814, *Writings* (Memorial), XIV, 58.
[48] Jefferson to Cooper, August 25, Sept. 10, 1814, *ibid.*, XIV, 173-5, 179-90; Cooper to Jefferson, Sept. 22, 1814, Jefferson Papers, CCII.
[49] Jefferson to Cooper, Oct. 7, 1814, *Writings* (Memorial), XIV, 199-202.

less not without influence upon the Father of the University of Virginia, brought with it no prospect of immediate solution of Cooper's personal difficulties, and he continued to seek elsewhere for a better place. In 1813, thinking to supplement a meagre salary, he had made application to Madison for appointment as collector of the assessed taxes of the district of which Cumberland county formed a part.[50] For some unknown reason he had been spared the indignity of this petty appointment, so had turned to literary activity for supplementary revenue. Of promiscuous writing he doubtless soon wearied, and a year later he made inquiry of his friend Dallas, then in the Cabinet, in regard to a possible election to a professorship at West Point.[51] A member of the faculty there had written Cooper that he thought he would be highly pleased with a place where everything was "regulated by the drum,"[52] which seems to us highly improbable.

In August, 1815, Cooper wrote Madison that he thought he would not remain at Carlisle longer than the present session and that if he could find an opening to practice law he was inclined to go to New Orleans with Madison's nephew.[53] In September he resigned his position, although not yet to move to a southern clime. An address of the trustees, September 25, expressed their deep regret at his departure and their great appreciation of his service to the college.[54] This address implies that financial considerations had proved the chief obstacle to his continuance at Carlisle. It was said by a later writer

[50] Cooper to Madison, Sept. 13, 1813, Madison Papers, L, 38; A. J. Dallas to Cooper, Sept. 1, 1813, ibid., L, 36.

[51] Cooper to Dallas, Dec. 20, 1814, ibid., L, 35.

[52] Andrew Ellicott to Cooper, Dec. 12, 1814, ibid., LIII, 108.

[53] August 8, 1815, ibid., LVI, 53.

[54] See the Port Folio, 3 series, VI, 512-13, for the text of the address and editorial comments upon it.

that there was a connection between Cooper's resignation and a rebellion in the college which he aided to quell and which was followed by a slight change in the government and the resignation of some of its officers.[55] Financial considerations would doubtless have brought about his resignation in any case. The plaudits of the trustees may have been conventional and perfunctory, but they seem to have been sincere. The important services which Cooper had rendered the institution were remarked upon, and the trustees stated that they could not expect to fill his place with a man of equal talents. Upon the face of it, it would appear that he left the institution in high favor, which cannot be said of his other changes of employment. But it is by no means certain that there was not rather serious maladjustment even here!

To Philadelphia the itinerant scholar now came, although as yet without definite academic appointment there. In earlier days he had known the city well, first as a lieutenant drawn to the seat of Republican counsels, then as a prisoner of political war. After his election to the American Philosophical Society in 1802, he had had occasional opportunity to consort there with the learned. Late in 1814, he had been elected a councilor of this society and beginning with January, 1816, was very active in its deliberations.[56] By this time he was undoubtedly a resident of Philadelphia.

Before his election to the faculty of the University of

---

[55] Charles Caldwell, *Autobiography*, p. 341. He wrote from memory and his other comments upon Cooper have led us to doubt his accuracy.

[56] *Early Proceedings* of the American Philosophical Society, 1744-1838, p. 450. His election was for a term of three years and he was reëlected in 1817, *ibid.*, p. 468. The accounts of the meetings show that he attended occasionally until 1816, and from 1816 until his removal from Philadelphia in 1819 attended practically every meeting and read a number of papers. Some of the latter were published and will be referred to subsequently.

Pennsylvania, he carried on at long range another of his many academic flirtations. In the autumn of 1815, the medical college of Transylvania University in Kentucky was reorganized and he was offered the chair of chemistry, mineralogy, and natural history there. It is said there was a movement on the part of certain local citizens, whom we should term unwary, to make him president of the institution. In the spring of 1816, however, a Baptist clergyman was chosen for the presidency and Cooper declined the proffered professorship "in a letter which deprecated sectarian control of the institution."[57]

The chair at the University of Pennsylvania to which he was elected December 6, 1816, was that of applied chemistry and mineralogy in the college department.[58] During the next two years he delivered several courses of public lectures within the two general fields assigned him and seems to have aroused considerable popular interest.[59] A professorship of chemistry in the medical school seemed more attractive, however, probably because more remunerative, and in 1818 he made application for this place. Perhaps he had not labored more to promote the science in the United States than any other man, as he boastfully claimed in his letter to the trustees, but he had done much. He had read numerous papers on chemical subjects before the American Philosophical Society and had published as author or editor a number of

[57] Robert Peter, *Transylvania University, Its Origin, Rise, Decline and Fall*, pp. 95-6.

[58] Minutes of the Trustees of the University of Pennsylvania. This information was obtained through the kindness of Dr. Edgar F. Smith, former provost. Charles Caldwell in his *Autobiography*, p. 350, speaks of a new faculty of physical sciences which was created and to which he also was elected.

[59] These lectures, seem to have been supported by subscription. See Cooper to Jefferson, April 19, 1818, *Collections*, Massachusetts Historical Society, 7 series, I, 271. Three of Cooper's lectures and a general syllabus were published in the *Port Folio*, 4 series, III, 187-201, 405-17; VI, 117-20.

works, generally dealing with the more practical aspects of chemistry.[60] Meanwhile, in recognition of his achievements and merits as a scientist, the University of New York had conferred upon him the honorary degree of Doctor in Medicine.[61] This was the first academic degree of any sort which he had ever received and from December, 1817, whether he wrote on science, politics, economics, religion or law, his medical title invariably appeared in conjunction with his name. He delighted in being called "Dr. Cooper," and it is thus that history has best remembered him. His New York friends also secured him an invitation to a professorship in chemistry which was to be established in connection with a state board of agriculture, but he preferred to stay in Philadelphia or join Jefferson in Virginia.[62] In the meantime, he was nothing loath to take full advantage of his bargaining position.

The vacancy in the medical school resulted from the resignation of John Redman Coxe as professor of chemistry. Numerous candidates for the position immediately appeared and doubtless no one of them presented his claims more strongly than did Dr. Cooper, who wrote the trustees as boastful a letter as remains on record.[63] With entire absence of modesty, he referred to his distinguished services for chemistry, to which science he claimed that he had been longer devoted as a lecturer and author than any man in the country. It had been stated that theoretical knowledge of medicine and experi-

[60] For a complete list of his chemical works, see Bibliographical Note.

[61] See the note of dedication of his pamphlet, *A Discourse on the Connexion between Chemistry and Medicine,* to the trustees and professors of the University of New York, November, 1818. The degree was used by Cooper at least by December, 1817; see *Port Folio,* 4 series, IV, 482. The registrar of the institution has no record of the degree, but there can be no question of its genuineness.

[62] Cooper to Jefferson, April 19, 1818, Massachusetts Historical Society *Collections,* 7 series, I, 270. The invitation was doubtless provisional.

[63] This is quoted in full in E. F. Smith's *Life of Robert Hare,* pp. 58-61.

ence in its practice were highly desirable qualifications for the particular position which he sought. Cooper accordingly informed the trustees of his attendance upon anatomical lectures in England, his assistance in medical practice in Manchester and his open and avowed practice as a physician in America for twenty years, a longer time, he claimed, than any present member of the medical faculty of the university had practiced. He referred to his appointment by the medical society of Philadelphia to deliver the annual report of the progress of *materia medica* for the year, and recognized, indeed, but one sense in which he was not a regular physician: having been trained to pursue the law as a profession, he had always deemed it improper to act for profit in a double capacity, so had consistently refused to take fees for medical services.

The election, however, went to another. Robert Hare, who lacked the very medical experience of which Cooper boasted and whose rival candidacy he despised, was given the place. Hare's biographer feels that the election was eminently wise.[64] Cooper, not without personal resentment doubtless, publicly expressed his disapproval of the indifference of the medical profession to chemistry which this action and subsequent actions indicated. The newly elected professor was persuaded to relinquish what Cooper regarded as his duty of passing on the qualifications of medical students for the degree and to confine himself to the examination in chemistry. In *A Discourse on the Connexion between Chemistry and Medicine*,[65] delivered in the university in November, Cooper emphasized the importance of medical chemistry, which he felt

[64] *Ibid.*, p. 62.

[65] Published as a pamphlet, Philadelphia, 1818. See preface. A presentation copy of this, together with his pamphlet *On the Tests of Arsenic*, was sent to Benjamin Silliman in New Haven.

was as little realized as the importance of the classics in education in general. The tendency in America as he saw it was not only to neglect ancient erudition, but the most useful parts of modern science as well. He felt that the undervaluation of chemistry was due to the failure of the medical professors to appreciate the progress made in the science in the twenty years which had elapsed since they had received their education. He recognized that chemistry as applied to medicine was in its infancy, but was confident that this was "the infancy of Hercules." His hope was that the trustees would not support the medical professors in their opinions, but would require a full share of chemical knowledge of every candidate for the degree. How immediately successful his efforts were we do not know, but it is apparent that here, as in so much else, he was forward-looking.

Before he left Philadelphia, the indefatigable scientist who yet retained his interest in the law published a volume of *Tracts on Medical Jurisprudence*,[66] consisting chiefly of the most useful English tracts on the subject but including notes and a digest on the law relating to insanity and nuisance, prepared by himself. The work was published for the benefit of both the medical and legal professions, with doubtless the additional purpose of contributing to the income of the needy editor. It furnishes another example of Cooper's pioneering spirit. His interest in insanity was subsequently to bear fruit in South Carolina in the establishment there, in large part through his efforts, of a state hospital for the insane.[67]

[66] Philadelphia, 1819.

[67] See below, pp. 279-80. The encyclopedic character of his knowledge and interest was further indicated by the publication under his direction of the second American edition of Willich's *Domestic Encyclopedia*. This was announced in the *Port Folio* in October, 1817, 4 series, IV, 351, but was not published until 1821.

Definite negotiations with Jefferson in regard to a position in the University of Virginia were begun several months before Cooper's formal candidacy for a professorship in the medical school of the University of Pennsylvania.[68] Jefferson hoped to draw from Europe to the new institution the "first characters in science," and naturally thought, in this connection, of his learned friend, who was of European birth and training and who held views which were in general so harmonious with his own.[69] So he wrote Cooper at Carlisle to say that there might be a place for him and asked and received detailed suggestions regarding the organization of instruction.[70]

Dr. Samuel Knox of Baltimore was the first professor elected by the visitors of Central College, out of which the university was to grow, but upon information that he was "withdrawn from business" Cooper was elected, October 7, 1817, professor of chemistry and law.[71] He was to receive a salary of one thousand dollars, to be supplemented by tuition fees of twenty dollars from each of his students, and was to be reimbursed for the expense of transporting his library and apparatus, which were to be rented or purchased by the institution. Jefferson somewhat prematurely congratulated Joseph C. Cabell upon Cooper's acceptance and suggested to Madison that the solitary appointee should at first exercise also the func-

[68] Cooper's candidacies were not solely academic. He had written Madison, Jan. 17, 1817, in regard to a possible appointment as commissioner of bankruptcy, in case a general law should be enacted. Madison Papers, LIX, 106.

[69] In addition to the specific references given below, see Philip A. Bruce's *History of the University of Virginia*, I, Second Period, chs. XIV, XV; and H. B. Adams's *Thomas Jefferson and the University of Virginia*, ch. VIII.

[70] See above, p. 227.

[71] Minutes of the visitors of Central College, Oct. 7, 1817, *Early History of the University of Virginia as contained in the letters of Jefferson and Cabell*, N. F. Cabell, editor (hereafter referred to as Cabell), pp. 396-9.

tions of classical professor,[72] which so versatile a scholar would have been nothing loath to do.

When it appeared that Cooper had a chance to secure a much more remunerative position in Philadelphia, Jefferson generously stated that he should not be prevented from accepting it, much as he himself would deplore his loss.[73] The founder of the University of Virginia was greatly exercised over the matter, despite the fact that the position to which his friend had been elected through his agency existed only upon paper. By August, 1818, when the commissioners agreed that the university should grow from Central College, it was definitely known that Cooper had failed of the opportunity in Philadelphia and was available for Virginia.[74]

Meanwhile Joseph Corrèa de Serra, the Portuguese botanist, who had lived in Philadelphia since 1814, and had there become acquainted with Cooper, probably through the American Philosophical Society to which both belonged, had planned to bring his friend with him upon the occasion of his annual visit to the Sage of Monticello. He was thoroughly disgusted at the injustice done his friend by the preference to him of "a man poor in science," but congratulated Jefferson upon an event which would contribute so much to the fulfillment of the latter's hope.[75] He stated that Cooper would bring to Virginia "an immense store of useful knowledge accompanied with much philosophy and a great zeal for the dis-

72 Jefferson to Cabell, Dec. 18, 1817, *ibid.*, p. 88; to Madison, Dec. 30, 1817, Jefferson Papers, CCXII.

73 Jefferson to Madison, Feb. 6, 1818, Jefferson Papers, CCXII; *cf.* Cooper to Jefferson, April 19, 1818, Massachusetts Historical Society *Collections*, 7 series, I, 269-72.

74 Report of the commissioners, Cabell, p. 433; Jefferson to Cooper, August 7, 1818, Jefferson Papers, CCXIII.

75 Corrèa to Jefferson, Sept. 26, 1818, Jefferson Papers, CCXIII. Frequent reference to the proposed visit was made in earlier letters of Jefferson and Cooper.

semination of true science,'' and predicted that his settlement in the state would ''prove a remarkable epoch in the history of the literary advancement of Virginia.'' The pilgrimage to Monticello which had originally been planned for the preceding spring and in which presumably Mrs. Cooper participated, took place in September or October. Jefferson had looked forward to it very eagerly and apparently found no cause for dissatisfaction with Cooper,[76] whom he had probably not seen for years.

The Pennsylvania paragon of learning was destined never to be an actual member of the faculty for which Jefferson hoped so much. For one thing, it was decided to apply all the available funds to buildings. Jefferson felt embarrassed at the temporary inability to live up to the agreement with Cooper, but Cabell seized the opportunity to claim that the obligation to him existed no longer and to say that much criticism of his appointment had been aroused.[77] He stated that while Cooper's talents and acquirements were unquestioned, the impression was very general that either in point of manners, habits, or character, he was defective. Cabell was certain that he was ''rather unpopular in the enlightened part of society,'' although he admitted that this unpopularity might be due to the fact that Cooper was not so well known to the world as he was to Jefferson and Madison. In the latter statement Cabell was nearer the truth than perhaps he knew. In public life, Cooper gave a most irritating impression of contentiousness, omniscience, and contemptuous disregard for the opinions of others, whereas in his personal association with intimate friends, in so far as one can judge from his correspondence, he was

76 See Jefferson to Cabell, March 1, 1819, Cabell, pp. 167-9.

77 Jefferson to Cabell, Feb. 19, 1819, *ibid.*, pp. 164-5; Cabell to Jefferson, Feb. 22, 1819, *ibid.*, pp. 165-6.

more modest, exceedingly genial, delightfully facetious and apparently sincere.

Jefferson, in reply to Cabell, made strong defense of his protégé.[78] He described the circumstances of the election and the subsequent developments and stated that Cooper had not only had the chance of a better place in Philadelphia, but also opportunities to go to New York, William and Mary, or New Orleans under very favorable conditions. Cooper preferred Virginia, however, to any place except Philadelphia, and Jefferson had informed him that he would be expected in the spring of 1819. So Jefferson concluded that they were bound legally as well as morally if Cooper accepted. Then followed the paragraph of extravagant praise which has been more often quoted than anything else Jefferson ever said about his friend.

And why should we wish otherwise? Cooper is acknowledged by every enlightened man who knows him, to be the greatest man in America, in the powers of mind, and in acquired information; and that, without a single exception. I understand, indeed, that a rumor unfavorable to his habits has been afloat, in some places, but never heard of a single man who undertook to charge him with either present or late intemperance; and I think rumor is fairly outweighed by the counter-evidence of the great desire shown at William and Mary to get him, that shown by the enlightened men of Philadelphia to retain him . . . the anxiety of New York to get him, that of Correa to place him here, who is in constant intercourse with him, that the state of his health permitted him to eat nothing but vegetables, and drink nothing but water, his declarations to me at table, that he dared not drink ale or cider, or a single glass of wine, and this in the presence of Correa, who, if there had been hypocrisy in it, would not have failed to tell me so.

[78] March 1, 1819, *ibid.*, pp. 167-9; *cf.* letters to Madison, March 3, *Writings* (Ford), X, 124; March 8, 11, Jefferson Papers, CCXV.

Greatly exercised over this matter of alleged intemperance, Jefferson wrote Corrèa, and in reply the botanist
attested Cooper's temperate habits and high abilities and
ascribed to jealousy the opposition to him.

I was very glad you had thought of Mr. Cooper, to whom you
could find no equal in America, in point of science and zeal to
spread it, and in point of sound and manly morals too, fitter
perhaps for the Virginian climate, than for that in which he now
lives, but from my knowledge of mankind, as far as it goes, I
am apt to believe that since the news of the spirited acts of your
legislature have been made known, as well as your intention
which is not a secret, all the aspiring mediocrity has been specu-
lating, and their first step will be to try by all means to put him
out of the way. The first three years of my residence in America,
it is incredible the *but* with which such people particularly of a
certain description mixed when they spoke of him to me, the
praises which they could not well deny to his superior talents
and knowledge. I have passed the past four years in acquaintance and intimacy with him, remarking the direct opposition,
between his real character and all the *but,* I had heard before.
They had represented him as nearly an infidel, of a violent
temper, and of intemperate habits, and I have found him only
a bitter enemy of hypocrits, no violent man, but by no means an
enduring one, and have not seen a single solitary instance of
intemperance. He will always have the cordial hatred and interested too, of all the Litterary fire-flies who shine only in the
dark, and whom he has seldom the prudence to manage. God
grant you may get over all the snares that will surround your
new born university.[79]

Apparently there was common report in Philadelphia
that Cooper's temper was unaccommodating and that his
temperance was questionable. The confidential investigations of another of Jefferson's friends revealed that the

[79] Jefferson to Corrèa, March 2, 1819; Corrèa to Jefferson, March 22;
Jefferson Papers, CCXV.

report of intemperance prevailed formerly when there might have been some foundation for it, owing to some domestic infelicity then existing, but that for many years Cooper had been most sober and temperate, in fact a mere water-drinker. The appearance of his face, it was said, gave a contrary impression and may have kept the report alive after there was no longer justification for it.[80] It was only during the period of conservatism in Pennsylvania that the charge of intemperance was brought against Cooper, and it may be that he became careless of his morals as disillusionment came and old ideals were abandoned.

Jefferson's influence prevailed over the opposition and Cooper's appointment to Central College was confirmed for the University of Virginia. He was formally elected, March 29, 1819, professor of chemistry, mineralogy, and natural philosophy, and was temporarily to serve also as professor of law. His permanent salary, which was to begin a year later, was to be fifteen hundred dollars, with a guarantee of additional income from tuition fees to bring the total to three thousand five hundred dollars.[81] Jefferson, now nearly seventy-six, rode on horseback from Monticello to Montpelier to be present at the meeting of the board and support his friend.[82]

Although the question of Cooper's alleged intemperance was satisfactorily disposed of, a fundamental cause of hostility yet remained, which Jefferson was powerless to remove. The philosophical and theological views of his friend had ever offended the orthodox, and criticism of them would not down. In the name of a legitimately interested religious public, Dr. John H. Rice, a Presby-

[80] William Short to Jefferson, May 25, 1819, Massachusetts Historical Society *Collections*, 7 series, I, 278-9.

[81] Minutes of the visitors, Cabell, pp. 454-5.

[82] Bruce, *History of the University of Virginia*, I, 201.

terian clergyman and the editor of the *Virginia Evangelical and Literary Magazine,* strongly disapproved of the appointment and offered for the consideration of his countrymen certain quotations from Priestley's *Memoirs* and his own remarks upon them.[83] In this work Cooper had said with characteristic recklessness, "the time seems to have arrived, when the separate existence of the human soul, the freedom of the will, and the eternal duration of future punishment, like the doctrines of the Trinity and transubstantiation, may no longer be entitled to public discussion."[84] Such all-comprehending heterodoxy was likely to antagonize practically all the sects, and Dr. Rice had reason to expect a hearing from others than Presbyterians. He objected to Cooper's frank materialism, to his declaration that religious opinions were immaterial, to his condoning even of atheism. He felt that the direction of the youth of the state should not be committed into the hands of a man who obtruded such views upon the public, and who himself lacked some of the most important requisites in the character of a philosopher. His comment upon Cooper's temperament, indeed, was very acute and not inaccurate. "Dr. Cooper," he said, "appears in his book, rash, dogmatical, and peremptory. The intrepidity of his conclusions is really appalling; his hardihood is fearful. At the same time his prejudices appear to us violent; and all his liberality is reserved for his own party."[85]

Rice felt that the placing of such a man in a prominent

[83] Rice expressed his opposition in the issue of January, 1820, and gave in detail his reasons in February. *Virginia Evangelical and Literary Magazine,* III, 49, 63-74.

[84] Priestley's *Memoirs,* I, 335. It will be remembered that Cooper wrote appendices 2 and 5, in which he described Priestley's metaphysical and religious opinions and made many independent comments indicative of his own views. See above, p. 188.

[85] *Virginia Literary and Evangelical Magazine,* III, 72.

position in the university would alienate from the institution many who wanted to support it, and that it would become "a mere party affair, countenanced and supported only by a particular class of persons." Under the conditions of religious and theological opinion which then prevailed, his objections to Cooper were entirely natural, and both his earlier efforts in behalf of the university and his influence in a denomination whose support was particularly important, especially since old William and Mary was Episcopalian, entitled him to a hearing.[86] The Presbyterians, as Cooper discovered both in Virginia and South Carolina, were more zealous for theological orthodoxy than the Episcopalians, whose emphasis was more upon ecclesiasticism, and their influence had increased with the growth of the southern piedmont and with the waning of French philosophical ideas. Rice did not refer to Cooper's specially abusive remarks about Calvinistic theology, and "its horrid criterion, the doctrine of election and reprobation,"[87] but he was unquestionably aware of them. The Presbyterians, both in Virginia and South Carolina, thought that Cooper deliberately went out of his way to insult them, and their hostility to the new professor naturally caused the promoters of the new enterprise serious concern.

Before this hostility had been publicly expressed, the delay in the opening of the university provided a sufficient reason why the professor-elect should not assume his duties. In October, 1819, the visitors, while reaffirming the appointment of Cooper, stated that the time for the commencement of his functions was not yet fixed, and that it was inexpedient either to elect more professors

[86] For general accounts of this episode, see Cabell, 234-6 n.; Bruce, *History of the University of Virginia*, I, 204 ff.; H. B. Adams, *Thomas Jefferson and the University of Virginia*, p. 107 and note.

[87] Priestley's *Memoirs*, II, 476.

or to pay any salaries to professors before buildings had been provided.[88] This was entirely sensible from the point of view of the institution, but the visitors themselves intimated that an injustice had been done Cooper, since it had been originally stipulated that he should enter upon his office in April, 1820.

The communication of this decision to the expectant chemist by Jefferson elicited from him expressions of surprise and regret and a somewhat pathetic description of the dilemma in which he now found himself. He stated that he had trusted to the fulfillment of the contract and had induced Dr. Patterson to give a course of lectures in chemistry in Philadelphia that winter, since he had felt that he could not give it himself. He had packed up his minerals and was unable to give the lectures on mineralogy which people were inquiring about and asking for.

Thus I am thrown completely on my back; I have given up my usual occupations and I have not a single employment left for the support of my family. It is true the difficulties of the times and the general pecuniary embarrassments, here as well as elsewhere, would be felt by me, as indeed they have been, in common with others. But relying on what has passed I have placed myself in a *cul de sac* and I see no way out.

However I shall look about me and seek for employment somewhere or other until the period arrives when you propose to commence the business of your institution. My wife and myself have confined our views and wishes to your state, which I still hope I need not ultimately renounce.[89]

A year of depression like 1819 was no time to be without a position, and Cooper lost no time in looking about him. He learned of a vacancy in the South Carolina Col-

[88] Minutes of the meeting of Oct. 4, 1819, Cabell, pp. 457-8.

[89] Oct. 22, 1819. A copy in the library of the University of South Carolina was made by the late Colyer Meriwether from the original in the possession of Mrs. S. J. Hanna, a descendant of Cooper.

lege at Columbia, made application for it, and on December 3 was elected professor of chemistry there for one year.[90] His services were so satisfactory to the trustees that by the spring of 1820 they were negotiating with him to accept a permanent appointment, contingent upon a combination of some other department with that of chemistry so as to provide a suitable salary.[91]

Meanwhile, the visitors of the University of Virginia had voted Cooper an indemnification of fifteen hundred dollars.[92] Jefferson could not conceal from his trusted friends his disgust at the attacks on Cooper which the clergy of the state, and particularly the Presbyterian clergy, continued to launch. In a letter to William Short, in whose discretion he doubtless had fullest confidence, he stated that the most serious enemies of the university were "the priests of the different religious sects, to whose spells on the human mind its improvement is ominous."[93] He described the Presbyterians, who were "loudest," as "the most intolerant of all sects, the most tyrannical, and ambitious; ready . . . to put the torch to the pile, and to rekindle . . . the flames in which their oracle Calvin consumed the poor Servetus." In their attitude toward Trinitarianism, the clergy in general, and the Presbyterians in particular, Cooper and Jefferson were essentially agreed. The greatest difference between them was that one expressed in public print what the other wrote only in confidence to comprehending friends; one proclaimed from the housetop what the other murmured in the closet.

To the visitors of the university, though, Jefferson

[90] Minutes of the Board of Trustees of South Carolina College, Nov. 24, Dec. 3, 1819.

[91] *Ibid.*, April 28, May 1, 1820.

[92] Jefferson to Cabell, Jan. 22, 1820, Cabell, p. 178; Minutes of the Visitors, Oct. 3, 1820, *ibid.*, p. 460.

[93] April 13, 1820, Jefferson's *Writings* (Memorial), XV, 246.

expressed himself boldly. In a letter in May to two of them who had been absent from the last meeting,[94] he referred to the embarrassment which had been caused by the "hue and cry raised from the different pulpits" on the appointment of Cooper, and stated that he himself "was not disposed to regard the denunciations of these satellites of religious inquisition," but that the other visitors, who were better judges of public feeling, thought they ought not to be altogether neglected, and that it might be better to relieve Dr. Cooper, the visitors, and the institution from this crusade. He stated that he had received a letter from Cooper in which the latter offered to resign if it were felt that the persecution would prove embarrassing. It had accordingly been decided to relieve him, and to arrange a suitable indemnification. Jefferson had written him, and in reply he had described the arrangements which were in prospect for him at Columbia and had stated that he would be satisfied with the balance of the fifteen hundred dollars which had been voted him, which however was not more than enough to cover his actual losses of time and expenses.[95] In his letter, Cooper had also said:

It is right I should acknowledge the liberality of your board with thanks. I regret the storm that has been raised on my account; for it has separated me from many fond hopes and wishes. Whatever my religious creed may be and perhaps I do not exactly know it myself, it is a pleasure to reflect that my conduct has not brought, and is not likely to bring, discredit to my friends. Wherever I have been, it has been my good fortune to meet with or to make ardent and affectionate friends. I feel persuaded I should have met with the same lot in Virginia had it been my chance to have settled there, as I had hoped and

[94] May 16, 1820, to General Robert Taylor and Chapman Johnson, *ibid.*, 254-6.

[95] Letter not discovered, but largely quoted by Jefferson.

expected, for I think my course of conduct is sufficiently habitual to count on its effects.

Jefferson then proceeded to say, by way of valediction:

I do sincerely lament that untoward circumstances have brought on the irreparable loss of this professor, whom I have looked to as the corner stone of our edifice. I know no one who could have aided us so much in forming the future regulations for our infant institution: and altho we may perhaps obtain from Europe equivalents in science, they can never replace the advantages of his experience, his knolege (sic) of the character, habits and manners of our country, his identification with its sentiments and principles and the high reputation he has obtained in it generally.

Jefferson's estimate of Cooper's abilities, while extravagantly expressed, was more justifiable than has generally been supposed, for, in versatility of scholarship and zeal to advance the cause of learning, the latter deserves to be regarded as one of the outstanding men of his generation in America. It seems probable, however, that if he had come to the University of Virginia he would have endangered the success of Jefferson's cherished project more than he would have contributed to it; and even the cause of religious toleration would perhaps have suffered more from his presence in the university than it would have gained by it, for it is doubtful whether the cause of toleration gains more than it loses by that "collision of opinion" which Jefferson always advocated in theory and which Cooper invariably incited.

The extraordinary friendship between these two apostles of learning and protagonists of freedom continued until the death of Jefferson. In subsequent letters to him, Jefferson expressed his continued hope that after the University of Virginia should be opened, Cooper might

somehow become connected with it.[96] The latter in turn
kept himself uncommitted in South Carolina as long as
possible; when at length he did make a permanent arrangement there he wrote Jefferson and Madison at considerable length to explain his action;[97] and once, at a
later date, when the Presbyterians in that state were
troubling him, he tried to reopen the whole question of
his appointment to the University of Virginia.[98] Personal
connections were maintained by correspondence, Cooper
visited Monticello in the autumn of 1820,[99] and pending
the opening of his own institution Jefferson sent his
grandson, Francis Eppes, to be under the tutelage of his
friend.[100] Although Cooper, after the death of Jefferson,
publicly repudiated the social philosophy of the Declaration of Independence[101] and thus came to terms with his
new social environment, he ever cherished the memory of
the intellectual friendship which, with the sole exception
of that with Priestley, was the most important of his life;
and in South Carolina he championed the rights of a
sovereign state and the cause of intellectual freedom with
a vigor which even Jefferson might have regarded as
unnecessary.

Cooper's removal to South Carolina in 1820 marked
the end of the second great period in his public life. This
migration, like the one which had marked the beginning
of the period, took place under conditions not devoid of

96 August 14, 1820, *Writings* (Memorial), XV, 264-9; April 8, 1821,
Jefferson Papers, CCXX.

97 To Jefferson, March 12, 1821, Jefferson Papers, CCXX; to Madison,
March 12, 1821, Madison Papers, LXIII, 29.

98 See below, pp. 273-4.

99 Jefferson to Cooper, August 27, 1820, Jefferson Papers, CCXVIII;
Cooper to Jefferson, March 12, 1821, *ibid.*, CCXX.

100 Jefferson to Cooper, August 14, 1820, *Writings* (Memorial), XV, 264.

101 See below, pp. 289-90.

controversy. But there were mitigating circumstances, as there had been before, and the sixty-year-old wanderer was far from the end of his resources. Indeed, whether he realized it or not, twenty almost incredibly vigorous years lay before him, and these were to prove the most significant in his life. And, despite all the controversies which befell him there, South Carolina was to prove the most congenial of all the many places where he lived.

PART THREE: SOUTH CAROLINA

CHAPTER VIII

THE TROUBLES OF AN EDUCATOR, 1820-1826

During almost fifteen of his twenty years in South Carolina, Thomas Cooper was a teacher and an educational administrator, although he by no means confined his versatile talents and superabundant energies to academic circles. He felt it to be his mission to instruct the public as well as his youthful charges and he exerted greater political influence in South Carolina than anywhere else he lived, but it was his academic position which gave him prominence and secured him a ready hearing. The particular form which his contributions to thought, science, and learning assumed during this very fruitful period of his intellectual activity was determined or suggested by the requirements and conditions of his professional life. His difficulties as an administrator form an instructive chapter in American educational and social history, and the religious controversies which raged around him as an eminent figure in public education serve to give concrete illustration not merely of his personal limitations but of contemporary religious and philosophical opinion as well. The echoes of those controversies yet linger in the state and their influence was felt throughout the section. His career as an educator, therefore, has more than personal, or even local, significance.

In January, 1820, he assumed his duties as professor of chemistry in South Carolina College, and within a few weeks his family, which then consisted of his second wife and her three children, joined him in Columbia.[1] By spring he had so established himself in the graces of the trustees that they expressed their unanimous desire that he hold this position permanently.[2] In order that adequate financial provision might be made for this distinguished but needy scientist, a professorship of geology and mineralogy was soon created and committed also to his care, at a total annual cost to the state of three thousand dollars.[3] In May, 1820, before this arrangement had been consummated by legislative action, President Maxcy died and the title of president *pro tempore* was unanimously conferred by the trustees upon the new professor, although the presidential duties were divided between him and two other members of the faculty.[4] Convinced that there was no immediate prospect for him in Virginia, Cooper accepted these successive appointments, although he felt it necessary to explain fully to Jefferson and Madison why he had done so. Meanwhile, negotiations were begun for the purchase of his much-heralded collection of minerals, which at length resulted in favorable action by the legislature.[5]

He wrote Jefferson that he suspected that he would have no occasion to remove from the position of president *pro tempore* unless he himself should desire it and so indeed it proved, for in December, 1821, he was elected

[1] Elizabeth Pratt Hemming, like her husband, was born in London. Their marriage had occurred either during his stay at Carlisle or shortly before. Two children, Frances Hemming and Thomas Priestley, were born there and a third, Ellen Connelly, was born in Philadelphia in January, 1820. Information gained from letters to Colyer Meriwether and now in the library of the University of South Carolina.

[2] Minutes of the Trustees, April 28, 1820.

[3] *Ibid.*, May 1, Dec. 20, 1820. The legislature acted Dec. 20, *Acts and Resolutions* of the General Assembly of South Carolina, 1820, pp. 17, 87.

[4] Minutes of the Trustees, Dec. 15, 1820, Nov. 28, 1821.

[5] Dec. 20, 1821, *Acts and Resolutions*, 1821, pp. 35-6.

president.[6] Of the nineteen trustees present, however, he received the votes of only ten, the rest of the votes probably being scattered. There was not unanimity in his choice, but he had every reason to be gratified at the recognition which he had received and at the evident concern of the authorities to minister to his needs and comforts. As president he was to continue to act as professor of chemistry and he subsequently stated that he taught *belles lettres,* criticism, and logic until 1824.[7] He remained at South Carolina College until 1834.[8]

Cooper's first public utterance as a professor in the college was of a character to commend him to all lovers of scientific learning. In his introductory lecture on chemistry, which was published at the request of the trustees and dedicated to them, he sought to show the incalculable service which had been rendered humanity by men of science, whose work had seemed remote from human life and who had been often derided.[9] This lecture showed his acquaintance with the whole range of discovery and invention, and its wealth of allusion must have made it most delightful and stimulating to his hearers. Some of the passages, indeed, as in the contrast between what science and ignorance see in nature, possess genuine beauty.[10] Scientific men, he said, have generally received little immediate recognition and have pursued science for its own sake. But, as he declared, in reflection

[6] Minutes of the Trustees, Dec. 1, 1821.

[7] In the preface to his *Lectures on Political Economy.*

[8] The present writer is indebted to Professor Edwin L. Green, who describes the period of Cooper's connection with the college in his *History of the University of South Carolina,* pp. 31-43, not only for the valuable suggestions made there but for many others made in person. There is much that is interesting in Maximilian La Borde's *History of the South Carolina College* (edition of 1874), pp. 121-77.

[9] *Introductory Lecture on Chemistry,* delivered at the College of South Carolina, in Columbia, Jan. 1820.

[10] *Ibid.,* p. 7.

doubtless upon his own experience, "the acquirement of knowledge, and the discovery of truth, is often attended by a too seductive and infatuating pleasure, which induces us sometimes to throw aside that prudent attention to competent fortune which it is every man's duty to bestow."[11]

He felt that scientific knowledge should be of equal interest with literature to gentlemen. Indeed, he disparaged fiction and poetry.

What should make the knowledge of those laws on which all useful manufactures depend, less interesting than a knowledge of the licentious poets and dramatists . . . ? It is in the infancy of society chiefly, that works of mere fiction receive an inordinate share of public attention. It is in our boyish years, that the poets and novellists, the writers who are disgracefully employed in furnishing stimulus to appetites that require to be bridled, engage our attention. When experience has taught us wisdom, we begin to estimate *utility* as the criterion of desert, and look back with some regret at the time misemployed in mere amusement. It is so with the progress of civilized society; in the infancy, and the ignorance of all communities, the great objects of intellect in peace are poetry and oratory; as nations advance in knowledge, science gains a rightful ascendancy.[12]

Here he appears to have been hopelessly mature and entirely utilitarian, but this advocate of science and utility found time during his first year in the college to read Horace with Jefferson's grandson for an hour every day.[13]

Cooper's first address to the graduates was likewise published at the request of the trustees, and well deserved it.[14] It was a very able address, sane in point of

---

[11] *Ibid.*, p. 11.
[12] *Ibid.*, pp. 13-14.
[13] Cooper to Jefferson, March 12, 1821, Jefferson Papers, CCXX.
[14] *Address to the Graduates of the South Carolina College*, Dec. 1821.

view, fatherly in tone, and indicative of an extraordinary appreciation of the various forms of human learning. In accordance with the custom and doubtless in the effort to be conciliatory, he delivered a religious exhortation at the outset and stated that he did not see how society could dispense with religion. He implied a personal belief in the superintendence of a moral governor of the universe and a future state of rewards and punishments. As he put it, the great use and end of all religion, socially considered, is to make men better citizens, and the religious group which most effectually promotes that great end is to society the best. Society is concerned with conduct, he said, not opinions. He urged each of his hearers to do honor to his denomination, to show charity toward the views of others, and to adopt the criterion laid down by Christ himself, "By their fruits shall ye know them."[15] Bigoted sectarians may well have been disquieted at the emphasis, but even they could have made little serious objection to so sane a position.

By way of fatherly counsel, Cooper urged the young graduates to be thrifty and frugal and to seek only the best companionship. He then took up specifically the different callings which they would probably follow and pointed out how their past studies had helped them and what remained to be done. Thus he considered agriculture, commerce, manufacturing, law, medicine, and the ministry, and gave specific suggestions for further study in preparation for each of the three last professions.[16] He urged the continuance of classical studies and particularly decried mere eloquence without matter. For the prospective minister he outlined a course which corresponds surprisingly to the practice of the best seminaries today, although his emphasis upon liberality, charity, and

15 *Ibid.*, pp. 3-4.
16 *Ibid.*, pp. 6 ff.

the critical study of sacred literature was doubtless unusual then.

He had made an admirable beginning and it might perhaps have been predicted that this extraordinarily
learned man whose wisdom had been ripened by the
arduous study and wide experience of an already long
life, would end his days in peaceful benevolence in this
sunny southern land. So it was not to be. His first serious
difficulties, however, did not arise from the persistent
belligerency of his own nature; they came from the irrepressible deviltry of his youthful charges. With this the
old apostle of *laissez-faire* never learned just how to
cope.

Jefferson's grandson wrote his grandfather in the
spring of 1821 about disturbances in the college,[17] and
the president himself wrote, the following February, to
describe a much more serious college rebellion, which is
exceedingly interesting to read about and has aspects
both pathetic and amusing.[18] The devotion to duty on the
part of the professors and the unfailing regularity of
their attendance upon classes had not been fully appreciated by their young pupils. Cooper said that the students, despite the kindness, respect, and indulgence which
had been shown them, had adopted it as an unwritten law
that they should have no personal dealings with their in-
structors, lest it should be thought they were currying
favor. Jefferson's grandson had no further dealings with
Dr. Cooper and felt himself prevented from even paying
a call upon the president's wife.

Furthermore, the students felt themselves bound to
conceal any offense against the laws of the land or the
laws of the college. So when hen-roosts were robbed and

<hr/>

[17] See Jefferson's reply, April 8, 1821, Jefferson Papers, CCXX.

[18] Feb. 14, 1822. Quoted in full in Green's *History of the University of South Carolina*, pp. 336-7.

Thomas Cooper in Old Age in South Carolina
Silhouette done from life by William H. Brown and first published
in his Portrait Gallery of Distinguished American Citizens, 1846

turkeys were stolen at night from the houses in the neighborhood, no evidence whatever could be secured from any member of the student body. When efforts were made by the faculty to prevent such lawlessness and the trustees had been summoned by the governor to settle the difficulty, the students were guilty of even greater outrages. Professors were threatened, pistols were snapped at them and guns fired near them, the president's windows were shattered and he himself was burned in effigy, and whether upon this or another occasion, his horse was stolen from its stable, to be bereft of tail and mane and ridden about in the night until the poor beast was nearly exhausted.

Severe measures in the matter of suspension and expulsion were taken, but Cooper felt that there could be no adequate solution of the difficulty until some means could be found to make the students testify against one another. He felt that parental indulgence in the South rendered the problem of student discipline more difficult than in northern colleges.[19] The trustees seem to have been as much at sea as the distressed president was, but they at least proceeded to revise the laws,[20] although in a way which Cooper felt to be inadequate. He has been criticized by South Carolinians for his lack of appreciation of the sense of honor of southern boys, and has been accused of favoring a system of espionage.[21] It should be noted, however, that he advocated what we should today term student-government and opposed the rigid faculty supervision which the trustees favored. His general

[19] He quoted President Dwight to this effect, but it is interesting to note that in March, 1823, there was a serious riot in New Haven between Dwight's own Yale students and certain townsmen; see Charleston *City Gazette*, March 22, 1823. Apparently student disturbances were not confined to South Carolina College or the region south of the Potomac.

[20] Minutes of the Trustees, April 25, Nov. 27, Dec. 9, 1822.

[21] See Green, *History of the University of South Carolina*, pp. 34-5.

policy seems to have been one of very great kindliness and generosity to the students, and his failures are rather to be attributed to administrative limitations and to a certain hopeless maturity in his point of view.

The following spring witnessed a disturbance, the like of which apparently occurred every year, growing out of the requirement that students board at the college commons which, it will not surprise us to learn, they resented.[22] The faculty advocated the abolition of the compulsory system, but the trustees negatived their suggestion. More trouble grew from an indescribable indignity committed upon the college chapel. The students would not testify, the trustees refused the grant of power to make them do so, and the matter was finally settled by an inadequate compromise. The affair was evidently a serious one and discipline was unquestionably poor, whether this was due to lack of skill on the part of Cooper and his colleagues, to the meddlesomeness of the trustees coupled with their failure to provide some means of compulsion, or to local conditions over which the authorities could exercise no control. The question of student discipline was a permanent feature of the president's report.[23] There was serious disorder or less serious disorder, and occasionally no disorder at all. Only a few weeks before the death of Jefferson, Cooper wrote him that he was "weary and worried" out of his life and would gladly quit the job if he had any alternative.[24] During the last few years of Cooper's presidency the matter of discipline was much less frequently referred to, so it may be assumed that during the excitement of

[22] Minutes of the Trustees, April 28, 1823.

[23] *Ibid.*, Nov. 26, 1823, Dec. 3, 1823, Nov. 30, 1825, Nov. 28, 1827, Dec. 3, 1827, Nov. 25, 1828. It should be noted that there was serious disorder during the administration of President Maxcy. Green, *History*, p. 28.

[24] May 18, 1826, Jefferson Papers, CCXXI.

the controversy over the tariff and nullification, the young South Carolinians found other ways to expend their energies than in more or less serious school-boy pranks.

It should be noted also that the learned president ultimately gained a strong hold upon the respect and affections of his students. According to the classic college story, he was always referred to as "Old Coot," "coot" being short for "cooter," a common southern name for terrapin.[25] The term was applied to Cooper perhaps because of its similarity to his name, perhaps because of the rotundity of his person. It is said that he used to ride a white pony about Columbia and that his bald head, round and jolly-looking face, and twinkling eyes, were known to everybody.[26] A bust of Cooper in the library of the University of South Carolina which is generally regarded as a caricature shows an enormous head, almost square. A silhouette of a later date shows a short man with a thick body and big head.[27] There are ruffles around the bottoms of the pantaloons.

A much more serious situation than that which resulted from undergraduate irresponsibility grew out of the controversy between the philosopher of materialism and certain of the religious groups of the state, especially the Presbyterians. This raged during 1822 and the following year, then died down to burst forth in even greater fury in 1831. Despite the discretion of Cooper's public utterances and conduct during his first years in South Carolina, his general theological and philosophical position

[25] J. Marion Sims, *The Story of My Life*, p. 82. Sims graduated in 1832.

[26] Letter of J. G. Gibbes to Colyer Meriwether, quoting his father, Dr. R. W. Gibbes, a colleague and warm friend of Cooper's. Meriwether Collection.

[27] Wm. H. Brown, *Portrait Gallery of Distinguished American Citizens*, 1846, p. 81; reproduced in the *Outlook*, Oct. 6, 1900, p. 332. See above, p. 256.

must have been fairly well known because of his earlier publications. And doubtless in personal conversation, although apparently not yet in the classroom, he indicated something of that contempt for the clergy, or as he called them, "the priesthood," which he expressed so freely in his letters to Jefferson and to which he later gave public expression.

The Presbyterians had led the attack on his appointment to the University of Virginia and for them in particular he cherished no friendly feelings. Theological doctrine meant more to them than to any other prominent sect, and Cooper and Jefferson felt that their aggressive orthodoxy was chiefly responsible for the growth of intolerance in the country as a whole. After a visit to Pennsylvania during the summer of 1822, Cooper wrote Jefferson to give him some idea of the "progress of fanaticism" as he had observed it there and elsewhere.[28] The old harmony of social life which he had known at Northumberland had given way to the bitterness and intolerance of theological hatred, and for this he chiefly blamed the Presbyterian ministers. He felt that in Columbia the "mutual tolerance and harmony" in which irrespective of their denominational affiliations the professors lived, had caused the college to be "openly and publicly denounced as void of all religion." Yet, he said, prayers were "enforced" twice a day among the students and were attended regularly by the faculty, including himself. Tolerance may indeed have been interpreted as indifference, as he implied, for the two are often confused and are in fact not unrelated; but the local religious devotees doubtless suspected the president on general principles, despite any regularity of formal religious

[28] Oct. 18, 1822, Massachusetts Historical Society *Collections*, 7 series, I, 315-18.

observance on his part and even though he may not at this time have deserved their censure.

Cooper accused the Presbyterians of more than the cultivation of intolerance, although that charge was serious enough. In New York state he had received information, which he had accepted without question, that there was an avowed attempt among the members of this denomination to establish a system of tithes, and he was convinced that the movement had come all the way to South Carolina. If it had, it must have terrified this former foe of the English Establishment. Of greater immediate concern, however, was the alleged design of the Presbyterians to secure control over education. Cooper's remarks on this subject cannot be paraphrased without loss of flavor but must be quoted.

Equally decided and persevering is the attempt of the same sect to acquire the command over every seminary of education, and finally to establish, in favour of the Presbyterians, a *Church establishment*. Of these designs on the part of that sect I am as fully persuaded as I am of my own existence; and what is worse, I greatly fear they will succeed. The people, not aware of the frauds committed, are the gross dupes of missionary societies, Bible societies, and theological seminaries; and every head of a family of a religious turn, or in any way connected with that sect, must submit to the power these parsons have acquired,— acquired by making the females of the families which they are permitted to enter the engines of their influence over the male part. I foresee another night of superstition, not far behind the Inquisition; for so rancorously is every opponent calumniated that the persecution becomes gradually irresistible, and the men who hate these impostors & their frauds are actually compelled to bow down to them. I look around me, and knowing, as I do, the general prevalence of liberal opinions on religious subjects among well educated men, I regard with absolute horror the system of simulation and dissimulation which they are compelled to adopt; and I cannot help exclaiming with Lucretius: "Tantum haec religio potuit suadere malorum!" In the college here, the industry of the faculty is *exemplary*, their competence undeniable, but the cry is gone forth, "There is no religion among them," & I greatly fear it will make the college totter to its fall; for utterly false as it is, the want of prayer meetings and religious revivals will be accepted as undeniable evidence of the charge.[29]

Jefferson's point of view was essentially the same as that of his friend, although he was less easily affrighted, less prone to hysteria, and much more discreet in his public utterances. He also particularly disliked the Presbyterians and their doctrines, and was equally convinced that they were trying to gain control of education.[30] He felt that the spread of genuine education was the only cure for fanaticism and saw a more immediate remedy in the spread of Unitarianism, which he doubted not would soon be the religion of the majority throughout the country. Although Cooper felt that even the Unitarians were sectarian in spirit, he also thought more highly of them than of any other religious group, and he predicted that within twenty years they would be the prevailing sect among the better informed people. They "would gradually eat out the more ignorant fanatics, except the Methodists" who, addressing the passions, would hold fast upon the multitude, more especially from the erotic language of their devotional poetry which carried a special appeal to women.[31]

Cooper felt strongly that education and denominational religion should be entirely divorced, but approved of the practical expedient which had been suggested by the visitors of the University of Virginia that the various

29 Massachusetts Historical Society *Collections,* 7 series, I, 317-18.

30 Jefferson to Cooper, Nov. 2, 1822, *Writings* (Ford), X, 242-4.

31 Cooper to Jefferson, Nov. 22, 1822, Jefferson Papers, CCXXIII.

sects should establish professorships of their own tenets. Jefferson felt that such action would serve to silence criticism, promote toleration and make the general religion one of "peace, reason and morality." His correspondent, although agreeing, was confident that the sects would make no response to a suggestion which left no opportunity for domination. All this was private and confidential. The president of the South Carolina College was heroically restraining his insistent natural tendencies toward public criticism and opposition and for once in his life was trying to avoid controversy. Officially he attended the college chapel services every morning and on Sunday he went regularly with his family, he said, to worship with the Episcopalians, toward whom at this time he felt a benevolent tolerance.

There can be little doubt but that he was unduly fearful of Presbyterian aggression. He became hysterical whenever the name of the denomination was mentioned and could see no good in any of their efforts and proposals. That they and other similar groups were desirous of placing a definite religious stamp upon institutions of higher learning would probably not have been denied by them, for such a desire they regarded as entirely legitimate. Some of the more aggressive sectarians may have desired to gain indirect control over the policies of the state college for their particular group through domination of the trustees and the faculty. Such control has been sought and acquired elsewhere and at other times. In this particular instance, however, Cooper's critics doubtless justified their hostility to him in all good conscience on other grounds. If he regarded the Presbyterians as fanatics, they adjudged him from his written words a dangerous heretic who was exerting an insidious and pernicious influence upon the minds of impressionable youth. It ultimately appeared that their first attack was premature, that it was interpreted by others besides Cooper as due to sectarian zeal, and that it entirely failed of its immediate object.

The campaign was begun at least by the autumn of 1822. Disciplinary difficulties in the college, and more particularly the decrease in the number of students, offered a point of attack.[32] Grand jury presentments from the up-country counties of Chester and York, which were duly referred to a legislative committee, described the institution as declining and attributed this to some deficiency in the teachers, and especially to the attitude of the president toward religious questions. Subsequent developments indicate that the Presbyterians were most involved in this action. The house of representatives appointed a special committee to inquire into the condition of the college. Cooper himself made representations to this body and its report upheld him fully.[33]

The committee were in entire accord with Governor Thomas Bennett in their opinion of the condition and prospects of the college.[34] They stated that the institution now commanded the confidence of the most intelligent men in the state and might challenge competition with any other college in the country. ''In more than one instance, gentlemen whose judgment may be implicitly relied on, have removed their sons from Cambridge to

[32] Green, *History of the University of South Carolina*, p. 437, gives the following statistics of attendance during the first six years of Cooper's presence in the institution:

1820,	110.	1823,	65.
1821,	88.	1824,	108.
1822,	76.	1825,	115.

[33] See Charleston *Courier*, Dec. 4, 1822; letter of Cooper to Jefferson, May 6, 1823, and broadside containing this report, Jefferson Papers, CCXXIV.

[34] For the message of the governor, see Charleston *Courier*, Nov. 30, 1822.

Columbia.'' They said that the presentments which described the institution as declining could be easily disposed of, and expressed the hope that the grand juries would now retract their charges as unfounded and unjust. Distinct reference was made to the attacks on Cooper. ''In the presentments before your committee they recognize with regret the unhappy influence of that persecution against the president of the college to which his excellency in his message alludes.'' The committee did not question the uprightness of the intentions of the grand juries, but asked whether they were basing their objections upon vague ''reports and interested clamour,'' and whether they would continue to ''lend themselves to the purpose of sectarian zeal.'' Cooper's official attitude toward religious questions was given entire approval, and his character and conduct were spoken of in a most laudatory manner. ''In the manner in which this persecution has been met and overcome, your committee see additional reasons for confidence in the gentleman against whom it has been directed. Were his talents moderate, his character ambiguous, or his learning superficial, he could not have withstood the efforts of his opponents. That he comes triumphant from the trial, is the happiest augury of the success of the institution.''

It must have been with considerable satisfaction that Cooper sent Jefferson and Madison copies of this report and received from them letters of congratulation and encouragement.[35] Perhaps it would have been better policy if he had let the matter rest after his victory, but whether because he felt that the opposition to his administration was still too menacing to be permitted to go unrebuked, or because of sheer pugnacity, he sought

[35] Cooper to Madison, Dec. 21, 1822, Madison Papers, LXIV, 70; from Madison, Jan. 5, 1823, *Letters and Other Writings of James Madison*, 1865, III, 291; from Jefferson, April 12, 1823. Jefferson Papers, CCXXIV.

greater publicity for the affair and carried the warfare into the enemies' country. The report of the legislative committee was published as a broadside, probably at his instance, and in January he sent the press a statement regarding the situation in the college and the opposition which had arisen.[36] This apparently contained in essence the representations which he had made to the committee.

Cooper attributed the decline in attendance to the death of the beloved former president, Dr. Maxcy, the uncertainties which grew out of the interregnum, the struggle to establish discipline and the greater age and attainments now required for admission. All these he termed purely temporary influences. Then he proceeded to assert that the most powerful present obstacle to the prosperity of the institution was "the systematic hostility of the clergy generally, to any seminary of education which is not placed under their government and control." This hostility, he claimed, had been the source of "many calumnious reports injurious to the reputation of this college," and had turned many students away to northern institutions. Thus Cooper challenged the clergy.

In a dignified protest, a number of prominent clergymen of the Episcopal church denied his charge, which they regarded as erroneous and calculated unjustly to bring odium upon the clergy in general.[37] They spoke of "the very learned president," but apparently without rancor and without even implying that they were dissatisfied with his religious position. In all his long controversy over religious questions in America, Cooper never had just cause to complain of hostility on the part of the Episcopalian clergy. Either they were broader and

---

[36] Charleston *Courier*, Jan. 10, 1823, and doubtless other papers as well.

[37] Charleston *Courier*, Jan. 13, 1823. No statement of denominational affiliation was made but the names of the signers identify them as Episcopalians, *cf. ibid.*, Jan. 17, 18.

more tolerant than the Presbyterians, or matters of theology were to them of relatively less importance. The report is that after the death of the aged controversialist, sixteen years later, the Presbyterians would not permit his interment in any of their churchyards, and it is in an Episcopalian churchyard in Columbia that his dust now lies.

The Presbyterians were not slow to accept the challenge which had been issued. One of them, speaking for his fellow clergymen as well as for himself, declared that they were utterly incapable of acting under the influence of the principle imputed to them.[38] He stated, however, that it was impossible for the clergy of his church "to be indifferent to the enquiry, to what kind of tuition, in respect to both precept and example, youth are to be subjected." This feeling, he said, was common to all consistent clergymen of every name, and there was no propensity on the part of his own group to shirk from any odium which might come from such adherence to conscientious views and a sense of duty.

The campaign against Cooper was more vigorously conducted after this. In his representation to the legislature and his newspaper statement he had come into the open. He wrote Jefferson late in the year that five pamphlets against him had been published during the course of the campaign.[39] Upon one occasion at least he replied to his critics in a public letter.[40] Many inquiries about his

[38] *Ibid.*, Jan. 16, communication signed "A Presbyterian Clergyman."

[39] Dec. 27, 1823, Jefferson Papers, CCXXVI. Although these pamphlets have not yet been discovered, two of them were referred to by the Charleston *City Gazette*, April 12, 19, 1823. The Columbia papers of this year have not been preserved and those of Charleston naturally gave smaller space to the controversy.

[40] *City Gazette*, April 26, 1823, quoting from Columbia *South Carolina State Gazette*.

religious opinions had been made to him and he thought that trouble might be saved by a public statement. So he stated that his religious opinions were all deduced from the Scriptures by diligent study; that he had a perfect right to hold any opinions he might care to, so would not gratify the malignant curiosity of his slanderers by detailing or proving them; that he had a great dislike for all metaphysical theology as a source of unending discussion, envy, hatred, malice, and uncharitableness; that he was not a theologian by profession, was not paid for preaching or teaching religious opinions, had neither interest nor duty to make proselytes, and would enter into no theological discussion without much stronger motives than were likely to occur during his life. He purposed this to be his last appearance in a controversy which he did not begin and did not like to end. Thus he seems to have refused the proffered gage of battle.

This was doubtless partly due to the fact that he had become engaged in the meantime in one of the most heated and unedifying newspaper controversies of his entire career and had found that Justice William Johnson of the United States supreme court, a citizen of Charleston, was more than his match in power of invective. Justice Johnson, in a letter to a committee on public education appointed by the legislature of Kentucky, had stated that Cooper favored the withdrawal of funds from the common school system of South Carolina and their application to the college. It duly appeared that Johnson had based his opinion upon statements contained in an anonymous pamphlet which he thought Cooper wrote and of which he claimed to the very end that Cooper at least approved.[41] Without seeking a pri-

---

[41] This had been reviewed in the *North American Review*, new series, X, 301, in connection with an address of Cooper's in such a way as to lead to the natural inference that he was the author of both.

vate explanation of a statement which he felt was calculated to injure him and which he probably interpreted
as being part of a concerted move against him, the indignant president rushed into print with a most undignified
letter[42] in which he not only denied that he had written
anything against the common school system, but also
reflected upon the ability of Johnson to estimate the
value of evidence, upon his recent historical writings,[43]
and his attitude toward the recent trial of the negro
insurgents in Charleston.[44] He said that Johnson had
spoken of "Mr. Cooper," but that presumably he meant
"Dr. Cooper," and stated that so far as he himself was
concerned his reputation was the property of the people
of the United States. Johnson in reply said, among other
things, "God forbid that the public property should be
judged from this sorry sample!"

The significance of the stinging rejoinder from Justice
Johnson lies both in its overwhelming invective and in its
assault upon Cooper's religious opinions.[45] Of invective
there was more than enough. He said that he replied only
out of respect for the college, because Cooper's "foul-
mouthed publications" had divested him of every claim
to personal respect. After explaining his reasons for
making the statement which had been objected to and
expressing regret that a private communication had not
elicited immediate reparation, he said that Cooper's letter forced the friends of the college to blush with shame
and brought them a feeling of infinite disgust. The
several reflections upon himself he dismissed as bids for
popular favor in the manner of a demagogue. "Mere

[42] Feb. 28, 1823, copied by *City Gazette*, March 8, 1802, from Columbia
Telescope.

[43] *Sketches of the Life and Correspondence of General Greene*, which had
been the object of considerable attack; *cf. City Gazette*, March 14, 15, 1823.

[44] Following the famous Denmark Vesey insurrection.

[45] *City Gazette*, April 8, 9, 1823.

artifice, mere cunning is a low and animal quality. The polecat or the rat, the savage or the maniac, would far outdo a host of titular M.D.'s in this quality.'' His finest irony was vented upon the medical degree, which he said he had unintentionally neglected but which he would never hereafter deny him, for he ''would not pluck a feather from the cap of an idiot if it afforded solace to his harmless vanity.''

He dismissed as absurd the charge that he was trying to make Cooper unpopular, for his letter was not intended for publication, and stated that the best policy for an evil-wisher would be to let this particular gentleman alone to wreck himself. If he had had any such designs he would have adopted a different course from the one he did adopt. He would have turned to Cooper's attacks on oratory to show that the latter was conscious of and made a poor apology for the total lack of the divine talent which he decried;[46] or he would have turned to Priestley's *Memoirs* where Cooper had denied the separate existence of the human soul, freedom of the will, eternal duration of future punishments, and the doctrine of the Trinity, and had made statements which would be generally regarded in the state as bald blasphemy.[47] The presidential address of 1821, where Cooper had urged the cultivation of religion, Johnson described as a literary curiosity and intimated that it must be regarded as a recantation, an artifice, or a mere temporizing concession. Cooper had laid an anchor to windward, however, when he said that society had to do with actions and not opinions. Johnson stated that this was in general true but in its application to Cooper altogether incorrect, for with the opinions of the president of a college society had a

[46] *Address to the Graduates*, 1821.
[47] He cited pp. 295-6, 335, 371-2, 423-6.

great deal to do, since the sanction of his known opinions was implied in his election.

In his concluding paragraphs Justice Johnson fairly overwhelmed his opponent with contempt. ''You have written me in a style that could only have been expected from the vulgarity of a porter, or of a nymph of Billingsgate.'' He stated that Cooper, having forfeited all claim to the immunities which might otherwise have been conceded to his station, would be prosecuted for a libel. He had no fear that Cooper's ''vulgar sneers'' could injure his own public standing but would act because of his veneration for the freedom of the press. Such prostitutions of the press to purposes of private malice deprived it of public confidence and should be punished. If Cooper's elevated station were such as to bloat him with the idea that he might scoff in safety, he was more properly the object of the notice of the law. The threat of prosecution may not have been made in good faith, but it was certainly made with a menacing gesture. He said that Cooper might soon be peering through the bars of a gaol!

Cooper's reply was not so vitriolic as Johnson's letter but contained many highly derogatory expressions which need not here concern us.[48] He stated that in a contest of vulgarity and scurrility he yielded the palm to such a master of the art and retired from the field. He replied briefly to the attack upon his religious and theological opinions, declaring that these were published sixteen or seventeen years before, that he had published nothing on the subject since, and that since writing them he had reconsidered all his doctrines and was convinced that they were the doctrines of Christ. He denied that there was inconsistency between a denial of the existence of a separate immaterial soul and a belief in a future state of retri-

[48] *City Gazette*, April 19, 1823, quoting from the Columbia *Telescope*.

bution. Only preference for the truth to every other consideration could have induced him to adopt opinions so unpopular as perpetually to thwart his interest. He said that he made no living by his theology—by implied contrast with the clergy—but that on the contrary his opinions had been very troublesome and expensive to him. He asserted that neither his opinions nor those of his opponents were essential to morality and asked that he be judged by what he was in fact, not theory. He claimed that he desired no controversy but intimated that he might be "tortured and goaded" into more vigorous statement.

Cooper made no reference to the threatened prosecution for libel, of which nothing ever came. Without entering into a consideration of Johnson's fairness, discretion or taste,[49] we may say that Cooper, upon this and other occasions, did unquestionably abuse the liberty of the press and descend to scurrilous language and demagoguery. Indeed, his very belligerency and sensitiveness to criticism led him frequently into actions which injured the very cause of freedom of discussion which he advocated. More "sweet reasonableness" and less pugnacity would unquestionably have enabled him to render greater service to liberty.

There can be no question but that the public statements of the president of the College of South Carolina were somewhat inconsistent with those of the editor of Priestley's *Memoirs*. Cooper himself admitted in his letters to Jefferson that he had adopted a policy of greater discretion than hitherto. Perhaps under the circumstances this was a defensible policy. In May, however, he referred to "some pieces of his on the pretensions of the clergy to

---

[49] Madison thought Johnson had been most indiscreet and deplored his effort to invoke religious prejudices against Cooper. See his letter to Jefferson, June 27, 1823, Madison, *Letters and Other Writings*, III, 324-5.

tythes,'' which had been copied in a Columbia paper from one in Philadelphia and had combined with his earlier utterances greatly to exasperate the Presbyterian clergy, who were holding meetings in every part of the state with the avowed intent of procuring his expulsion from his position.[50] The Presbyterians by this time had a majority on the board of trustees, although the policy of the board had generally been to keep the balance between them and the Episcopalians fairly even. Cooper's fear was that the former group might yield to the wishes of their clergy and move against him. He claimed that the students had never been so well satisfied, and that no one pretended that he had failed to discharge his duties in an exemplary manner or that he had ever made any declaration of religious opinion to a student, directly or indirectly. Nevertheless, he felt that the situation was sufficiently serious to warrant his writing Jefferson to inquire about possibilities for a livelihood as a private teacher of chemistry or law, or both, in the vicinity of Charlottesville and to ask whether his Unitarian professions were so obnoxious in Virginia that he would be an obstacle to the success of the university. There is a decided pathos in the description which he gave of himself in his letters to his old friend. ''I am too old to go again to the bar and I should not like to carry my family to New Orleans, to which place however I shall write by this post, not choosing if I can avoid it, to starve with my family when turned adrift.''

Jefferson, in reply, expressed his concern and regret at the persecutions, but spoke discouragingly of the proposed coming to Charlottesville, where a private and rival school would probably be looked upon unfavorably and where perhaps the old ''clamors of tritheistical hiero-

50 To Jefferson, May 6, 1823, Jefferson Papers, CCXXIV. The articles were in the Philadelphia *Reformer*, but have not been discovered.

phants'' might be aroused.[51] Cooper's real idea, as he explained shortly afterwards, was to reopen the question of his appointment to the University of Virginia. He thought that, pending the choice of professors there, he might become a private tutor in the neighborhood and that his conduct and capacity, being under the immediate inspection of the visitors, would operate in his favor against common prejudices.[52] By June, however, he was much more hopeful in regard to the situation in South Carolina and betrayed a somewhat naïve confidence in his own powers as a controversalist. Thus he said that he had made an attack on the Calvinistic clergy which had been felt by them throughout the state and under which they would sink and be paralyzed.[53] He felt sure that the favorable opinion of the trustees, even the Presbyterians among them, was unchanged and that from them, the only practical and efficient tribunal, he had nothing to dread. The printer at Columbia, he said, had been strongly averse at first to the essays on the clergy, which were published anonymously, but within three months there had been a noticeable gain in subscribers and he was now convinced that the public was favorable to his position. His inveterate opponent in the city, the Calvinist Evangelical pastor of the Presbyterian church, would be compelled to resign, completely defeated; and another parson, who had published a pamphlet charging Cooper with atheism, had lost all his congregation, had set up as a schoolmaster, and was advertising that he would send his pupils to the college. By autumn he was even more confident, although a presentment against him

[51] May 30, 1823, Jefferson Papers, CCXXIV.

[52] June 18, 1823, *ibid.*

[53] *Cf.* the pamphlet, *An Exposition of the Doctrines of Calvinism*, published anonymously in 1830, but attributed to Cooper in the charges brought against him before the board of trustees. If not identical with the pamphlet of 1823, its character and arguments were doubtless much the same.

by the grand jury of the York district, "gotten up by the associated clergy of that bigoted quarter," would again bring him before the legislature.[54] The college was increasing and the students had become so disgusted with the clergy that he was convinced that every one of them would resign, together with the great majority of the trustees, if the legislature should act in concert with the priests.

Apparently there was no reason to fear any unfavorable action on the part of the rulers of the state. Both the message of Governor John L. Wilson and the report of the senate committee on the college breathed a spirit of genuine educational statesmanship and showed that science and learning had won the full support of the political authorities against alleged religious narrowness. The governor referred to the spirit of hostility against the presiding officer of the college which had been kept alive by a limited number of sectarians, whose motives and objects had been very evident to the community at large.[55] The public feeling which they had excited was

rapidly subsiding and concentrating in one undivided opinion in favor of a gentleman, whose whole life has been devoted to the sciences and the arts, and who stands unrivalled in that excellence which knows no superior in acquirements, the fruits of his unceasing labors. His fame is not confined to this country. If his religious tenets be in accordance with none of those that would remove him from his present situation, it is a matter of little consequence to the student. Our Constitution tolerates all religions and legalizes none; and, if that section which precludes those who have the care of souls from legislation, is wise—it is equally important that they should not be placed in a situation where any particular creed or belief should be instilled into the minds of the rising generation.

[54] Cooper to Jefferson, Nov. 23, 1823, Jefferson Papers, CCXXV.
[55] *Courier*, Nov. 26, 1823.

The senate committee spoke with similar enthusiasm, and exulted in the distinction attained by so many alumni of the institution and in the wisdom and learning of the president.[56] They felt that "the gloom of ignorance and the intolerance of fanaticism" would be dissipated under "the liberal and enlightened system of instruction now adopted in the College."

Although some communications in the newspapers indicated displeasure with the governor's intimation that clergymen should not teach in state institutions,[57] the general tone of press comment was favorable to Cooper,[58] and he was always spoken of as "learned" or "distinguished," or both. Apparently there was a general spirit of religious toleration in South Carolina, especially among the ruling class, in whose favor Cooper had strongly established himself. The studied moderation and restraint of his admirable commencement addresses doubtless continued to commend him to the favor of fair-minded men. His address of December, 1823, probably had a campaign purpose.[59] Its choice diction, sane counsel and fine spirit of paternal solicitude are noteworthy, and its large attention to the matter of religious duties indicates a design to conciliate.

Jefferson wrote to make a prediction which was justified in the event: "I will not believe that the liberality of the state to which you are rendering services in science which no other man in the union is qualified to render it, will suffer you to be in danger from a set of conjurers."[60]

[56] *Acts and Resolutions*, 1823, pp. 111-12.

[57] *Cf. Courier*, Dec. 13, communication signed "An Observer"; Charleston *Mercury*, Dec. 15, communication signed "Common Rights, Duties and Privileges."

[58] *Cf. City Gazette*, Dec. 12, 24; *Mercury*, Dec. 19.

[59] *Address of the President of South Carolina College to the Graduates*, 1823.

[60] Letter of Dec. 11, 1823, *Writings* (Ford), X, 285-6.

Before he received this, Cooper wrote to announce his victory, but at the same time expressed the opinion that it would only increase the caution and rancor of his fanatic opponents, and that the snake had been scotched, not killed. His situation was still far from comfortable, he said, for clerical influences were secretly at work in the board of trustees and his individual efforts were in many ways paralyzed. "I shall by great exertion keep them at bay, but I am weary even of being victor, and the spirit that guides the clergy never dies."[61] Shortly afterwards he wrote that in his campaign he had gone to the limit of prudence and that he would certainly be compelled to retire were he to press his opposition to the clergy any further.

One is compelled to act here, as I should act in Turkey; if an honest Musselman were to say to me, "Christian Dog, take your choice, become a follower of the prophet or be impaled," I should not put him to the trouble of the latter operation. The simulation and dissimulation which a prudent dread of public ignorance and priestly rancour, imposes on men otherwise honest and well disposed, does more harm in the world (in my opinion) than religion does good. When will the American people acknowledge practically that Truth is the offspring of unfettered discussion![62]

Jefferson was so affected by the recital of his friend's troubles that he sent some of his letters to Madison, and asked the latter whether, in his opinion, it would be feasible even then to bring him to Virginia, which he himself was perfectly willing to do.[63] Madison, in reply, while expressing his great sympathy for the persecuted scientist, suggested that the opposition in Virginia might be as unpleasant to Cooper as that in South Carolina and that the cherished new university might be imperiled by

61 Dec. 13, Jefferson Papers, CCXXV.
62 Dec. 27, 1823, *ibid.*   63 Jan. 7, 1824, *ibid.*

his presence in it.[64] With this the matter ended, and Jefferson reluctantly gave up his fond, persistent hope to gain the paragon of learning for his own university. The religious controversy in South Carolina in the meantime abated, and the president and the college appeared to be in high favor. In 1826, the senate committee on the college went so far as to say: "It would, at this time, be a libel on the intelligence of the community, to dwell upon the utility of the college or upon the wisdom of its founders. Both are already felt in every district of the state, and we may almost say in every state in our Union."[65]

Despite all the turmoil and controversy of these first years in South Carolina, Cooper was able to do much for the advancement of science, in addition to his own lectures in the college.[66] He was later given credit for having been one of those most responsible for the establishment of the first medical college in the state, and his services in connection with the state hospital for the insane came in due time also to be highly valued.

The first suggestion for the establishment of a school of medicine in South Carolina was made by certain Charleston physicians in 1821,[67] but the president of the state college was the first to attract much attention to the subject. In 1822, he read to the medical board at Columbia an address in which he pointed out most forcefully the desirability of an immediate attempt to establish a medical college in the state, preferably in connection with the institution over which he presided.[68] The address was

[64] Jan. 14, 1824, *Writings* (Hunt), IX, 174.

[65] Journal of the Senate of South Carolina, 1826, p. 103.

[66] In 1821, he published a *Syllabus of a Course of Lectures on the Elements of Geological Mineralogy.*

[67] Edward McCrady, "An Historical Address delivered in Charleston, S. C., before the Graduating Class of the Medical College of the State of South Carolina," 1885, Charleston *Year Book*, 1895, pp. 386 ff.

[68] *Ibid.*, p. 393.

communicated to the medical society in Charleston and they were so struck by it that they sent a petition to the legislature praying for the incorporation of a medical college, although in Charleston and not Columbia. This memorial was not successful, but in 1823 the power to grant degrees and to organize a school was granted, although without appropriation. The first appropriation was made in 1825.[69] Cooper failed of his immediate object to secure the college for Columbia,[70] but he unquestionably did a conspicuous service in advocating its establishment.

His interest in the treatment of the insane doubtless grew out of his studies in materialism and his conviction of the somatic nature of insanity, which he felt the clergy opposed on principle and the medical fraternity insufficiently recognized because of ignorance.[71] So his efforts along this line were part of his lifelong effort to shed light and advance the cause of truth and knowledge, as well as to minister to the unfortunate. During the almost seven years that the Lunatic Asylum of South Carolina was in process of construction, Cooper was a prominent member of its governing board.[72] He resigned in 1828,

[69] General Assembly of South Carolina, *Acts and Resolutions*, 1825, p. 104.

[70] *Cf. Mercury*, Sept. 5, 1827.

[71] See the preface to his translation of Broussais, *On Irritation and Insanity*, 1831. My attention was called to Cooper's interest in the insane and his connection with the South Carolina Lunatic Asylum by the late Dr. J. W. Babcock of Columbia, long superintendent of that institution, who very kindly gave me access to his notes on the subject, which, however, I have verified from the official records of the legislature. Dr. Babcock felt that Cooper's services in the matter of mental diseases and in medicine in general had not been sufficiently appreciated, perhaps because this side of his career had been overshadowed by his political and religious controversies, perhaps because his removal from Philadelphia to Columbia caused the scientific and medical fraternity to lose sight of him.

[72] The institution was created by act of the legislature in December, 1821, and when a board of seven trustees and visitors was created a year later Cooper's name was first upon the list; House Journal, 1822, p. 277, Senate

just when the institution was beginning its active work and greatly needed his advice and experience, but the physician of the asylum was his personal friend[73] and a professor and trustee of the college were among the regents,[74] so his personal influence was doubtless exerted even after his resignation. His continued interest in the insane was shown by his translation, in 1831, of a French treatise on the subject, the materialism of which so horrified the clergy that they were led almost to question the sanity of the translator.[75]

By his constructive services for medicine, Cooper doubtless commended himself to many, and by his tremendously vigorous activities in behalf of the rights of the state, which became conspicuous by 1823, he endeared himself to the state rights party and so established himself in political favor that his position was for a few years impregnable against the assaults of the religiously orthodox. But his political activities form a separate chapter and probably the most significant, whether for good or ill, in the long story of his stormy life.

Journal, p. 264. In 1823, he was again elected to the board which served until 1827; House Journal, 1823, p. 197, Senate Journal, p. 191. He was not elected a member of the board of regents established in 1827 until a vacancy occurred in 1828, and he resigned within a year; *South Carolina State Gazette*, March 22, 1828, and information given by Dr. Babcock. *Cf.* the latter's pamphlet, *State Hospital for the Insane, Columbia, S. C.*, reprinted from *The Institutional Care of the Insane in the United States and Canada*, Vol. III.

[73] Dr. James Davis.
[74] Professor Robert Henry and William C. Preston.
[75] Broussais, *On Irritation and Insanity*, see below, pp. 347-8.

CHAPTER IX

THE SCHOOLMASTER OF STATE RIGHTS, 1823-1826

BEFORE serious opposition to Cooper's religious opinions
again arose, he might have claimed that he was "in the
odour of [political] sanctity" in South Carolina.[1] He
established himself in the favor of the ruling class in the
state as he did in no other place where he ever lived. During his twenty years in the South, he returned in a sense
to his accustomed rôle of opposition, for he was a severe,
although at first a somewhat restrained, critic of the
clergy, and he soon became an unsparing critic of the
federal government. His championing of extreme doctrines of state rights, however, although it aroused the
hostility of the more conservative local faction, identified him with the faction which ultimately became dominant in the state. It was primarily because his grateful
political allies supported him that the assaults of the
clergy upon him failed of their immediate object in 1832,
and that he was provided with honorable and dignified
employment after his position in the college was shown
to be untenable.[2] During his last years, for almost the
only time in his life, he belonged with the political majority in his locality.

[1] He used the expression negatively, in another connection, in a letter to
Senator Mahlon Dickerson, Feb. 22, 1832, *American Historical Review*, VI,
734.

[2] See below, pp. 360, 371.

The first and probably the greatest services which Cooper rendered the cause of state rights were educational. In the preface to a pamphlet which he wrote in 1824 against the tariff, he said that he hoped that a brief statement of the arguments against the protective system might answer the purpose of a textbook in the final struggle between right and wrong;[3] and it was later claimed that his pamphlet, *Consolidation,* had become "the textbook of South Carolina politics."[4] He doubtless regarded himself and was regarded by others as the schoolmaster of state rights doctrines. He incorporated his political and economic views in his college lectures and took full advantage of his strategic position for propaganda. The influence which he exerted, directly and indirectly, through his teaching and his writings must have been enormous. As a recent writer has said, he "laid the academic foundation" upon which the doctrines of the state were built.[5]

A speaker at the centennial celebration of South Carolina College in 1905, attributed to the college the influence which had not only made the state the recognized champion of southern rights and interests, but which had also so deeply impressed her doctrines upon the heart and intellect of the entire section.[6] He said that in this connection the name of Thomas Cooper, who was in advance of the great South Carolina statesmen in his

[3] *On the Proposed Alteration of the Tariff.* See below, pp. 290-2.

[4] This claim was advanced by the unnamed publisher of his *Letter to Any Member of Congress,* edition of 1831, p. vi. He himself referred to his contributions to the political education of the state in *The Case of Thomas Cooper, M.D., President of the South Carolina College.* Submitted to the Legislature and People of South Carolina, 1831, p. 33.

[5] Colyer Meriwether in *The South in the Building of the Nation,* XI, 234. See also the comment of U. B. Phillips, *ibid.,* VII, 174.

[6] LeRoy F. Youmans, *Proceedings of the Centennial Celebration of South Carolina College,* pp. 161-3.

advocacy of state sovereignty and free trade, must never be obscured. He quoted the testimony of Langdon Cheves, the younger, who in a speech in 1860, "spoke not of his illustrious father, nor Calhoun, nor McDuffie, nor Hayne, but referred to and cited the works of Dr. Cooper as first having given that bent to his thought, which assured him of the soundness of his political views and the rectitude of his political principles, his devotion to which he afterwards sealed with his blood and life." The second president of the state college undoubtedly prepared scores of other young southerners for the civil war which he predicted but the tragedy of which he did not live to share.

It is somewhat surprising that Cooper should have identified himself so completely with the interests of the community of his last adoption. His feeling for South Carolina was very different from the native devotion of men whose lives were rooted in the soil of that gallant and passionately self-conscious state. He was as free from local attachments as one well could be, and his loyalty could not have been instinctive. It must be attributed either to far-sighted prudence, which seems improbable with such a temperament, or to the coincidence of the fundamental doctrines of state rights with the essential principles of his own political and economic philosophy. Despite his lack of entire consistency, the latter explanation seems the correct one. Democracy he had essentially discarded, because it placed too great a premium upon ignorance, but his passion for freedom remained and expressed itself in advocacy of a modified political individualism, the sovereign power of the state. Furthermore, he rejoiced in the opportunity to battle for what he regarded as an oppressed minority; and the doctrines of South Carolina, as they evolved in part through his influence, were a logical development from the eco-

nomic philosophy of Adam Smith and the political teachings of the great Virginians, whom of all American
statesmen he reverenced most.

One important feature of southern life might have been
expected to meet with Cooper's strong disapproval. In
England he had written a fervid pamphlet against the
slave trade, and when he first sought a place of residence
in America he dismissed from consideration all the southern states because of their objectionable labor system,[7]
so no one would have thought that he would later accept
and even defend negro slavery. It was later asserted that
he, like Francis Lieber, was at heart an abolitionist,[8] but
nothing could be further from the truth. His daughter,
replying to this charge, stated that one of his first acts
on settling in Columbia was to purchase two families of
slaves who, with their descendants, lived in the family
until its disruption and were then divided among the
children.[9] His faithful old body-servant, Sancho, about
whom many legends linger in Columbia, served loyally
during his master's life and, with his wife, was liberated
by a provision of his master's will. Cooper's daughter
said her father never regretted coming to the South. "Its
people and customs pleased him, and he adopted the feelings, the prejudices, if you will, of that section with all
the ardor of an impulsive nature. To the day of his death,
all the influence of his powers and talents was devoted to
her rights and interests, or what he deemed to be such.''

[7] See above, p. 76.

[8] See the letter of ''Gath,'' Cincinnati *Enquirer*, June 18, 1883. Lieber
was professor of history and political economy in the South Carolina College, 1835-55, and declared himself an abolitionist after he left the state,
although he held slaves while he lived there. See Green, *History of the University of South Carolina*, pp. 45, 60-1.

[9] Letter of Mrs. Frances Cooper Lesesne, written in reply to ''Gath'' but
never published. Meriwether Collection, University of South Carolina Library.

His daughter, a southerner by training although born at Carlisle, doubtless wrote with a certain bias, but the essential accuracy of her statements can be confirmed by other evidence.

Cooper unquestionably adopted the traditional southern attitude toward the negro. In the controversy over the state law regarding the entrance of free negroes, he strongly upheld the action of South Carolina against the protests of the federal government, and he went somewhat out of his way to express his conviction of the essential inferiority of the negro race. Presumably he had become less a theorist and more a realist as he had grown older, and with his rejection of democracy as a sufficient solution of human problems had surrendered also his former theories about human equality. At any rate, explain it how you will, he had no quarrel with his neighbors on the slavery question and seems never to have suffered from any suspicion on this score.

South Carolina was thrown into a panic of fear in 1822, by the threat of slave revolt.[10] An insurrection had been planned by Denmark Vesey, a free mulatto from the West Indies, and in the effort to prevent any further danger which might arise from the activities of free negroes, the legislature at its next session passed an act,[11] one section of which the federal government objected to as a violation of treaty obligations to Great Britain. This section rendered free negroes on board any

[10] *An Account of the Late Intended Insurrection among a Portion of the Blacks of this City.* Published by Authority of the Corporation of Charleston, 1822. *Cf.* Theodore D. Jervey, *Robert Y. Hayne and His Times*, pp. 130-6.

[11] *An Act for the better regulation of government of free negroes and persons of colour*, Dec., 1822; published in the *City Gazette*, Dec. 7, 1824. *Cf.* Jervey, *Hayne*, pp. 178-85, for an account of the controversy between the state and the Federal government, in disagreement with McMaster (*United States*, V, 199-204), who he claims is in error as regards the final developments.

incoming vessel liable to seizure and confinement while in port, and provided that the expense of detention should be borne by the captain of the ship which brought them. If he neglected or refused to comply with the law, a captain was liable to fine and imprisonment and the negroes might be sold as slaves. A case in which this act was involved was tried before Judge William Johnson, whose subsequent controversy with Cooper has already been described, in the United States district court, and in August, 1823, the third section of the act was declared by him to be unconstitutional.[12] Attorney General Wirt took the same position. The argument of Benjamin F. Hunt, who upheld the constitutionality of the law, was later given unqualified approval by Cooper.

Hunt held that the right to pass such a law was one which, under the peculiar circumstances of her slave population, the sovereign state of South Carolina had not surrendered to the federal government and could not surrender, since the right of self-preservation is perfect and inalienable.[13] It had been contended that the convention of 1818 with Great Britain interfered with the power of a state to pass such a law, but Hunt claimed that even if this were true the treaty would not be binding upon the state because the treaty-making power, like the power of Congress, was limited to what had been delegated, and permitted of no stipulation impairing the rights reserved to the states.

In a letter to Hunt in October, Cooper stated that he had received from him a copy of his argument, that he concurred with him on all points, and that he would

---

[12] *Ex parte Henry Elkison, a subject of his Brittanic Majesty, vs. Francis G. Deliesseline, Sheriff of Charleston District*, August 7, 1823. *Niles' Register*, Sept. 6, 1823, pp. 12-16; *cf.* Warren, *Supreme Court in United States History*, II, 83-7. For the controversy between Cooper and Johnson, see above, pp. 268-72.

[13] See *City Gazette*, Dec. 11-16, 1824, for Hunt's argument.

shortly give to the papers his own views on the subject, not that he could say anything new, but because he felt it important that the subject be very fully discussed.[14] Although the promised communications have not been discovered, it is apparent that he was in full accord with the state rights position and was opposed to any federal interference with the state in its efforts to cope with the racial problem.

In the course of this controversy, he wrote a newspaper article on "Coloured Marriages" in which he expressed with brutal frankness his conviction of the inferiority of the negro race.[15] After citing foreign authorities, he considered the status of the negroes in the various states and concluded that

people of colour are, in every part of the United States, considered, not merely by the populace, but by the law, as a permanently degraded people; not participating as by right, of the civil privileges belonging to every white man, but enjoying what civil privileges they possess, as a right and grant, as a matter of favour conceded by the law, and revocable by law.

One is reminded of the Dred Scott decision! His final conclusion was that a marriage between a black or mulatto and a white would be a fraudulent contract and would amount to an indictable offense against public decorum and public morals. The expression of such an opinion, supported with great learning, must have been highly satisfactory to most South Carolinians, and it is probable that the identity of the writer was generally known.[16]

14 *Ibid.*, Dec. 15, 1824, while Hunt's argument was being published in that paper.

15 Written originally for the *Telescope* under the pseudonym "Civis." A portion of the article was copied by the *Courier*, Sept. 15, 1823, and the entire article appeared in the *Carolina Law Journal*, July, 1830, pp. 92-106, over the initials "T. C."

16 *Cf.* comment in the *Mercury*, Oct. 19, 1823.

Three years later, in a discussion of the Missouri question, Cooper declared his conviction that Congress could impose no condition upon the admission of a state except that it must have a republican constitution, and expressed the hope that the slavery question was now forever freed from being tampered with by the federal legislature.[17] He attributed the agitation against slavery to sectional interest and blind sentimentalism and philanthropy, and defended the southern system of labor with a frankness which was yet most uncommon. Slavery, he said, was practically universal and was forbidden nowhere in the Bible; and the conditions under which American negroes lived compared most favorably with conditions of life in Africa and even among laborers in industrial Great Britain.[18] All of these arguments were later advanced and elaborated upon by southern apologists, such as Thomas R. Dew, William Harper and James H. Hammond, upon all of whom Cooper doubtless exerted direct influence.[19] He regarded emancipation as

[17] *On the Constitution of the United States, and the Questions that have arisen under it,* 1826, pp. 48-9.

[18] *Ibid.,* p. 45.

[19] Dew's *Review of the Debate in the Virginia Legislature of 1831 and 1832,* which has been described by Professor William E. Dodd as "the ablest of all the works treating slavery from historical and social points of view" (*Cotton Kingdom,* p. 149), was published in December, 1832, six years later than the essay of Cooper's from which we have just quoted. Dew's "new system of social science," based upon a philosophy of inequality, may well have been the outgrowth of his studies in Germany, as Professor Dodd suggests (*ibid.,* p. 49), but he was acquainted with and thought highly of Cooper's writings in political economy and may well have known of the latter's defense of the institution of slavery and been emboldened by it. See Dew's *Lectures on the Restrictive System,* p. 56, and his *Review,* p. 123 n., for complimentary references to Cooper. William Harper, whose *Memoir on Slavery,* published in 1838, carried the doctrine of inequality a step further, was a member of the board of trustees of South Carolina College, and presented the resolution in vindication of Cooper which was adopted by that body in 1832. See below, p. 360. James H. Hammond, whose *Letters on Slavery* were written in 1845, was a student at

undesirable in the South because of the worthlessness of the freed blacks, the necessity of slave labor, and the probability of a servile war in case the blacks were freed. He asserted that "a population of free blacks is the most idle, debauched, thievish and insolent that we have ever witnessed in the United States," and cited the experience of New York and Pennsylvania as an example. He said that emancipation would convert the negroes into "idle and useless vagabonds and thieves," as every southern man conversant with negro habits and propensities well knew, "the first object of every negro being, not an improvement of his condition, but a life of idleness; freedom from all kind of labour and exertion."[20]

If any further proof of his disillusionment regarding the negroes and his entire acceptance of the southern point of view be needed, the following quotation from a letter to Senator Mahlon Dickerson, in which he commented upon the Panama Congress, will supply it:

If a minister is to be sent to the Congress at Panama, I hope his hands will be well tied. If Cuba should be placed in a revolutionary State, it will at present be a black government, and the people of Cuba joined to the rascally tribe of Wilberforce's evangelical reformers, will surrender all the british west indies into the hands of the blacks.

I do not say the blacks are a distinct species; but I have not the slightest doubt of their being an inferior variety of the human species; and not capable of the same improvement as the whites.[21]

Cooper had never expressed public approval of the emancipation policy which Jefferson advocated until

South Carolina College during Cooper's presidency and was very intimate with him after graduation. See below, pp. 387-9. Cooper's right to be regarded as a pioneer in the philosophical defense of slavery seems indubitable.

[20] On the Constitution, p. 46.
[21] March 16, 1826, American Historical Review, VI, 729.

death, and he proceeded logically to a complete repudiation of the social philosophy of his old friend. He was among the first of the former followers of the great Virginia democrat publicly to deny the validity of the social doctrines of the Declaration of Independence. In 1829 he declared that he knew of no sense in which it ever was, or would, or could be true that men are "born free, equal and independent," and questioned the doctrine of "unalienable and indefeasible rights."[22] "Rights," he said, "are what society acknowledges and sanctions, and they are nothing else."[23] He felt that the conduct of government should be determined by public expedience, public utility, and the greatest good of the greatest number.[24] He opposed universal suffrage,[25] and admitted that after the experiences of nearly fifty years his opinions were not in exact conformity with those of his youth, although he hoped they were "equally in favor of the just rights of the people, against those who would abuse entrusted power."[26] Negroes were not included by him among the "people," however, and the power which he now feared was that of the central government, encroaching upon a sovereign state.

Although Cooper's contributions to southern social philosophy have been little recognized, his services in opposition to the tariff have been generally admitted. When defending himself against the clergy in 1831, he claimed that he was the first person who suggested that the system of protection was unconstitutional.[27] In the pamphlet, *On the Proposed Alteration of the Tariff*, which he published in 1823, and sent to the members of

22 *Lectures on Political Economy*, 1829, p. 360.

23 *Ibid.*, p. 361.

24 He later declared himself a Benthamite; see below, p. 370.

25 *Ibid.*, pp. 362-6. He had manifested opposition to universal suffrage earlier, see above, p. 220.

26 *Ibid.*, p. 366.   27 *Case of Thomas Cooper*, p. 34.

the South Carolina delegation in Congress,[28] he himself referred, however, to the memorial of the citizens of Charleston in 1820, which contained general arguments similar to those which he was himself advancing.[29] By 1831, he had forgotten that this memorial also raised the constitutional objection. He discussed the constitutional aspects of the question more fully than the Charleston memorial had done and could have justly claimed that he had emphasized them. His greatest service in the campaign against the tariff, however, was in providing general economic arguments to support the position which South Carolina upheld. More familiar with the literature of political economy than most of his contemporaries were, he buttressed his doctrine of *laissez-faire* with arguments drawn from European writings. In South Carolina at least, he was the recognized philosopher of free trade,[30] and the comments upon him by protectionist philosophers show that they regarded him as a conspicuous and formidable foe. Matthew Carey, replying to him in 1824, said that Cooper had collected nearly all the arguments which had been advanced in favor of free trade,[31] and that his pamphlet was "circulated with great industry, and hailed as a complete triumph" by the

[28] The pamphlet is referred to in several letters from Jefferson, Madison, and Nicholas Biddle. It went through at least three editions and according to Jefferson, was copied in Ritchie's Richmond *Enquirer*. Letter of Jefferson, Dec. 11, 1823, *Writings* (Ford), X, 285-6.

[29] The memorial may be found in the *City Gazette*, Sept. 16, 1820. Jervey discusses it at considerable length in his *Hayne*, pp. 106-13.

[30] Thomas R. Dew's *Lectures on the Protective System* were published in 1829, so Cooper anticipated this noted Virginia economist by several years. Dew was acquainted with Cooper's arguments against the tariff and thought highly of his abilities. See *Lectures*, p. 56. The doctrine of *laissez-faire* was perpetuated at South Carolina College by Francis Lieber, who followed Cooper, but the latter had no contemporary rival south of Virginia.

[31] *Examination of a Tract on the Alteration of the Tariff by Thomas Cooper, M.D.*, by a Pennsylvanian, 2 edition, 1824, p. iii.

school of economists with which he had identified him-self.[32]

Cooper took the position that commerce might be regu-lated by Congress for purposes of revenue, self-defense, and retaliation, and to ensure a constant supply of the necessities for defensive warfare, but not for the purpose of unequal protection.[33] In view of the fact that the tariff operated directly upon manufactures alone, and only affected commerce indirectly, he doubted whether the assumption of power by Congress to enact tariff meas-ures could be defended on the ground of the right to regu-late commerce. He emphasized the desirability of pur-chasing in the cheapest market and sought to prove that the burden of the proposed tariff would fall upon the consumers, who in America were predominantly agricul-turists.[34] He emphasized the necessary dependence of one nation upon another in matters of trade, and the special dependence of the South upon its exports to Europe. "Those who live without buying must live without sell-ing. If we must not purchase the manufactures of Great Britain, the latter will not purchase our cotton, rice or tobacco."[35] He said that his desire to safeguard southern staples was the main reason why he had written his pam-phlet.[36] He feared Brazilian competition in the produc-tion of cotton, and British import duties on this staple in retaliation against American duties on manufactured goods. The southern states were threatened, he said, not merely with taxation, in the form of offensive duties on articles of large southern purchase, but even with de-struction, through the annihilation of trade in their chief product.

[32] *Ibid.*, p. 2.
[33] *On the Proposed Alteration of the Tariff*, p. 5.
[34] *Ibid.*, p. 8.   [35] *Ibid.*, p. 14.   [36] *Ibid.*, p. 27.

These arguments were first attacked on their merits by the protectionists. Thus Matthew Carey challenged the fundamental principles of the free trade school, and claimed that Cooper had made many sweeping and unjustifiable statements, especially in his assertion that the prosperity of manufacturers was entirely dependent on industry and intelligence, and that failures among them were due to the artificial conditions and false hopes aroused by the protective system.[37] Carey regarded southern fears of Brazilian competition as absurd and advocated the development of a home market.[38] He said that Cooper's "abuse" of the manufacturers showed "how very unfit a temper of mind" he was in, and that his zeal had so led him astray that he was a very unsafe guide on political economy.[39] Carey regarded him, with some justification, as essentially a theorist.

A more severe attack was later made upon the consistency of Cooper's position. To certain addresses of his own published in 1829,[40] Carey added several appendices, the first of which was entitled "the irresistible arguments of Judge Cooper in favour of the protecting system." These arguments had been extracted from the prospectus of the *Emporium* in 1813, and Carey said that he hoped the "powerful arguments of Judge Cooper" would lose no weight because of the "very wonderful" recent change in his opinions.[41] The charge of inconsistency had been made earlier than this, however, and

---

[37] *Examination of a Tract*, pp. 13 ff. This pamphlet consists of nine papers, dated January 1-28, 1824, and each signed, "Hamilton." It is attributed to Carey, and Cooper's references to him in his own letters show that he regarded Carey as his chief critic and opponent. The references here are to the second edition, 1824.

[38] *Ibid.*, pp. 20, 25.   [39] *Ibid.*, p. 36.

[40] *Common Sense Addresses*. The references here are to the fourth edition, 1829.

[41] *Ibid.*, p. xi.

had been replied to by Cooper in a letter to the Charleston *Mercury*.[42] Here he stated that his position in 1813 was due to the fact that the United States was then at war, and that the dependence of the mercantile interests upon Great Britain had caused the rise of a British party dangerous to national interests, and to the additional fact that our manufactures were then in their infancy. He said President Madison had agreed with him that moderate protection of manufactures which were of prime necessity and useful in war should not be objected to. He claimed that Jefferson also had agreed with him, although he too had been misrepresented by the manufacturing interests. Cooper insisted that he himself was an advocate of *laissez-faire* then, as now, so was not inconsistent. His contention is on the whole convincing. His efforts for protection were made under special conditions, and he stated repeatedly at the time what his fundamental economic principles were.[43] Certainly he was quite as consistent as Madison, Calhoun, and the other statesmen who were involved in the tariff legislation which immediately followed the War of 1812.

In the autumn of 1824, Cooper published a pamphlet, *Consolidation,* which established beyond question his standing as a radical exponent of state rights.[44] This gave an outline of political developments from the beginning of the government, as sketched by one biased against consolidation. He wrote as an Anti-Federalist, using the term long after it had passed from the political vernacular.

42 Sept. 11, 1827.   43 See above, pp. 193, 215-16.

44 *Consolidation, An Account of Parties in the United States from the Convention of 1787, to the present Period.* Published before Nov. 1, when its republication in the *City Gazette* began. It appeared in this paper in six numbers, Nov. 1-8. A second edition appeared in 1830, with the statement in the preface that the pamphlet had been republished in various parts of the United States.

The historical treatment, which emphasized the rights of the states, was intended to prepare for a discussion of contemporary issues, especially the question of internal improvements, with a view to the presidential campaign of 1824. The author specifically stated that the renewal of the system of internal improvements had chiefly elicited his observations.[45] His object was to show that not only Adams and Clay, but Calhoun and Jackson also were really Federalists, and thus to advance the candidacy of Crawford, the most consistent advocate of state rights. The first place in the organization and direction of the early movement in South Carolina against the centralizing tendencies of the government has been commonly assigned to Judge William Smith, and Cooper has generally been considered his most valuable ally.[46] Smith led the fight for Crawford and had a personal controversy with Hayne, although his chief animus was against Calhoun. This pamphlet was Cooper's most important contribution to the campaign of 1824. The immediate political significance of the work did most to attract attention to it at the time,[47] but subsequently its general state rights position caused it to be most highly valued, leading to its republication six years later, after Crawford had ceased to be a political factor and the campaign of 1824 was almost forgotten. By that time the South Carolina statesmen whom Cooper had attacked for inconsistency and faint-heartedness had become conspicuous leaders of the state rights party, in which he had preceded them.

[45] *Ibid.*, p. 10, *cf.* p. 14.

[46] *Cf.* David F. Houston, *Critical Study of Nullification in South Carolina*, p. 56; Jervey, *Hayne*, pp. 175 ff., 186. Smith had been replaced as United States senator by Hayne in 1823, but returned to the senate in 1827.

[47] Cooper wrote Senator Mahlon Dickerson, Jan. 18, 1825, ''My consolidation pamphlet has affronted Colonel Hayne and McDuffie sadly.'' *American Historical Review*, VI, 727.

There was nothing original in Cooper's claim that the independence and separate sovereignty of the states were renounced only to the extent of the specific concessions made to the federal government in the constitution, but his emphasis was very strong.[48] He spoke of the advocacy of a "national consolidated government" at the convention of 1787, not only by Hamilton and Gouverneur Morris but by Randolph, Madison, and what was more to the point, Pierce Butler and Charles Pinckney, who represented South Carolina. These men were defeated, he said, by the friends of a real federal union who sought to make the federal government the creature of the states and to allow it only delegated powers; so the powers of Congress are "specific, limited, enumerated"; they "do not emanate . . . from any abstract principle of what the public good may require; but from the deliberate concessions and absolute will of the sovereign and independent states."[49]

His description of the Federalist and Democratic-Republican parties was essentially similar to that which he had given in many earlier writings; but he went a step further and expressed the opinion that the Republican party had forgotten its original principles and had permitted successive encroachments, "till the power of the President of the United States, the power of the Congress of the United States, and more than all, the power of the Supreme Court of the United States (the most dangerous body in the Union) *has increased, is increasing and ought to be diminished.*"[50]

After tracing the political and constitutional story through the earlier administrations, he came at length to Monroe's administration and the question of internal improvements, which had caused him to write. Here he

48 *Consolidation*, p. 2.   49 *Ibid.*, p. 3.
50 *Ibid.*, p. 6.

made an attack on Calhoun, for whom he had no words of praise. Indeed, one recent writer has said that the pamphlet should have been entitled "A Diatribe on Calhoun."[51] Cooper said that Calhoun had joined with President Monroe in advocating coast fortifications, which would afford the distribution of many jobs to contractors, and had quieted the president's scruples on the subject of the Cumberland Road, his main object being to increase the power, patronage and influence of the president and the secretary of war.[52] He particularly ridiculed the employment of part of the engineering corps of the government to ascertain the practicability of uniting the chief Pennsylvania rivers, which, he intimated, was due to political motives. "Mr. Calhoun, himself, has been lately surveying some of the creeks in the Allegany mountains, no doubt for some great national object hereafter to be explained."[53] He referred to Calhoun's "frolic to Deep-Creek, on the top of the Allegany," and asked, "Who can read the account of his journey for this purpose with gravity?"

The only sufficient ground for the defense of internal improvements, according to Cooper, was the general welfare clause, so he claimed that those who favored internal improvements were identifying themselves with the consolidating party, which made so much of this clause. He said that McDuffie confined the power of Congress to those objects which could be affected by an appropriation, claiming that Congress had unlimited discretion in this respect, but Cooper himself regarded the precedents cited as insufficient and unconvincing and denied the unlimited power of appropriation.[54] He stated that he was not opposed to internal improvements *per se,* but that he de-

---

[51] Jervey, *Hayne,* p. 175.
[52] *Consolidation,* p. 10; *cf.* W. M. Meigs, *Life of Calhoun,* I, 248.
[53] *Consolidation,* p. 11.   [54] *Ibid.*

sired them to be executed on some plan of equality among the states.[55] He was sure that Congress, in its present policy, was tyrannically exercising usurped power. The doctrine of internal improvements, with its Federalistic implications, was now the fashionable doctrine of Congress, he said, and at least half of the representatives of South Carolina favored it. So he issued a solemn warning against what he regarded as apostasy:

Fellow-Citizens, it is vain to talk of the amalgamation of parties, while the dividing line of 1787, has continued to be the dividing line from thence forward, to 1825. Is South Carolina destined to be a federalist state? Do you mean to join the ranks of that party? If you do, so be it. Things must take their course, and the friends of state rights must be content to remain in the minority. If not, the politics of Mr. Adams, Mr. Calhoun and General Jackson, are not the politics of this state; for these gentlemen supported to the utmost of their power, a principle and a measure, which, from the very moment of party difference, has decidedly characterized the federalist party.—Consolidation is the motto of their flag.[56]

He recognized that his accusation would involve some of the most able, zealous, and useful sons of South Carolina, who had with most praiseworthy zeal defended the rights of the South in the matter of the tariff, but he thought that even Hayne, Poinsett, and McDuffie had neglected to emphasize the constitutional aspects of this latter question. In 1824, he was a more thorough-going advocate of state rights in opposition to internal improvements, as well as the tariff, than the more conspicuous younger statesmen who were later to come over to the uncompromising position which he had assumed.

The Charleston *City Gazette,* a strong Crawford paper,

republished *Consolidation*[57] and commended it by saying
that it contained "a statement of important truths, arguments of irresistible force, and a display of talents and
reasoning which ought to convince all who are open to
conviction." The *Mercury,* a strong Jackson paper,
stated on the other hand that the want of candor in the
pamphlet showed that it could not have been written by
the "learned and truth-loving gentleman" to whom it
was attributed, and asserted that the real design of the
work was to promote the election of Crawford by showing
that South Carolina could not support any of the other
candidates without becoming a Federalist state.[58] The
Mercury charged the author with disingenuousness in
not openly and manfully avowing the true object of his
work by putting Crawford's name on the title page, and
then sought to show that, by the standards of *Consolidation,* Crawford was as liable to the charge of Federalism
as any of the other candidates. It asserted that he had
concealed his opinions, and was being supported in the
North as an advocate of internal improvements and the
tariff, and defended in the South as their opponent.

With all due recognition of Crawford's political ob-
scurantism, there can be little doubt but that he was the
most thorough-going advocate of state rights among the
presidential candidates,[59] and that Cooper's support of
him was consistent with the political convictions he was
himself now expressing. As good a characterization of

[57] Nov. 1-8, 1824.

[58] Nov. 24, 1824. The comments were continued Nov. 25 and 26. A similar
criticism was made by McDuffie, who also questioned the historical accuracy
of Cooper's account of the constitution. See the *Speech of Mr. McDuffie on
Internal Improvements with a few Introductory Remarks in answer to a
pamphlet entitled Consolidation,* 1824.

[59] *Cf.* Jervey, *Hayne,* p. 173, who states that Crawford was opposed by
Calhoun's followers on the ground that he was dangerous to the Union. For
a general characterization of the points of view of the candidates, see F. J.
Turner, *Rise of the New West,* pp. 245-6.

Cooper's attitude as can be found is that which was made for itself by the *City Gazette,* when it stated that it favored Crawford as the man whose administration would promise to approximate nearest to that of the illustrious Jefferson.[60] At this time Jefferson was still, more than any other statesman, Cooper's political ideal, and in *Consolidation* he had cited him in support of his own contentions. Crawford was generally regarded as the heir apparent of the Virginia Dynasty, so Cooper's support of him was consistent with his loyalty to Jefferson.

The vote of the state went for Jackson, who was later to prove a great disappointment to many of the men who now favored him. Cooper had put himself at the forefront of the state rights party. He never entirely approved of Calhoun, who was so lukewarm at the beginning of the fight and whose inconsistencies were never explained to his full satisfaction. Calhoun voiced unionist sentiments at a time when the clash between the interests of his beloved state and those of the national majority had not appeared so clearly, and became an extreme advocate of state rights only when the clash had become apparent and he had been disappointed in his own presidential ambitions. Cooper approached the whole question from a more theoretical point of view and accordingly maintained a more theoretically consistent position.

Two years after the publication of *Consolidation,* Cooper gave expression to even more pronounced state rights views in his essay, *On the Constitution of the United States and the Questions that have arisen under it.* He had drawn up some lectures on "general politics," to be delivered to his students at the close of his lectures on political economy, but felt that the decided tone which he adopted on disputed points rendered them improper

60 Nov. 3, 1824.

for the classroom, so he published them to the world instead.[61] At the same time he republished his *Propositions respecting the Foundation of Civil Government* of 1787,[62] stating that his interest in the philosophy of politics had continued nearly forty years, and that he was still convinced of the necessity for vigilance against usurpations of power. Though he had continued to be an implacable foe of tyranny, as he claimed, his emphasis had shifted from the rights of man to the rights of the sovereign states, and the safeguard he now advocated was not the spread of democracy but the strict interpretation of the constitution, which he regarded as a bulwark against usurpation.

In his description of the constitution as "power of attorney,"[63] he manifested a more advanced opinion than any which he had yet expressed. He flatly denied that the constitution was the work of the people of the United States, as had been claimed since the days of Hamilton, he said, to hide the agency of the states. He claimed that the doctrine of general welfare implied despotic power, asserted that the states were becoming petty municipalities controlled from Washington, and proposed as a remedy "the constant pruning away [of] the luxuriant growth of executive power and patronage."[64] He felt that the American government was better designed than any other to assure the people's rights and happiness, but that perpetual superintendence and control were necessary, and he favored a half-centenary revision of the constitution to profit by past experience.[65] As a good Jeffersonian, he viewed with alarm the extensions of the

[61] Preface, 1826.   [62] See above, pp. 12-13.

[63] Essay *On the Constitution*, p. 21. John Taylor of Caroline had earlier used the term "trustee" in his *Construction Construed*, pp. 50, 57, etc.

[64] Essay *On the Constitution*, p. 29.

[65] *Ibid.*, p. 30. For an earlier similar suggestion, see above, p. 221.

power of the federal judiciary.[66] His suggested solution
of the difficulty was not that a change be made in the
method of appointment to something more popular, nor
merely that the right of impeachment be exercised, but
that the house of representatives should receive petitions
for the redress of grievances and act upon them as circumstances warranted.[67] He cited cases where the house
of commons had exercised authority over the decisions of
courts, without formal impeachment of judges. He
claimed that it was only true in theory that the three
departments of the government were so distinct that one
could not encroach upon the others, but that, as a matter
of fact, the judiciary encroached upon the legislature.

His attitude toward the judiciary may appear to have
changed considerably from that which he had manifested
during his own judicial service in Pennsylvania, but it
should be noted that he there defended the state courts,
and that he did not even now approve of interference
with the orderly processes of justice by the ignorant and
undiscriminating populace. The check upon federal judicial usurpation which he advocated would be exercised
by a regularly constituted branch of the national government acting in an orderly and, as he felt, not unconstitutional manner. So his positions were not necessarily inconsistent, although he was undoubtedly influenced by
pragmatic considerations both in Pennsylvania and
South Carolina.

His claim to be ranked as a pioneer in the formulation
of the doctrines of South Carolina was strengthened by
his general writings on political economy,[68] the signifi-

---

[66] *Ibid.*, pp. 50-60; *cf.* pp. 61-6.

[67] *Ibid.*, p. 56.

[68] *Lectures on the Elements of Political Economy*, Columbia, 1826; 2
edition with additions, Columbia, 1829; 3 edition, Columbia and London,
1831; *Manual of Political Economy*, Washington, 1833. For a contemporary

cance of which lies rather in their relation to subsequent
political developments than in their relation to the history of economic thought. As early as 1799, he had expressed his great interest in the subject and his anxiety
that the scattered facts of economics and statistics might
be collected and compared in order that men might get
at the important inferences which they afforded.[69] In all
his writings on commerce and the tariff, and in many of
his letters, he had shown an acquaintance with the literature of economics and an interest in economic theory such
as was doubtless rare among his American contemporaries. He had recommended that the subject be taught
in the University of Virginia, and himself became the
first academic lecturer on political economy in the South
and may have been the first in the entire country.[70]

Soon after his election to the presidency of the college
it was suggested that he lecture on metaphysics, rhetoric
and *belles lettres,* in addition to chemistry. In his report
to the board of trustees in April, 1823, he stated that he
was disinclined to teach metaphysics, although he had
"devoted much more time to that very unsatisfactory
study than most men: so much so as to be fully persuaded, it is not worth the time required to be bestowed
upon it."[71] He asked that he be permitted to offer a
course in political economy instead and the board shortly

review of the first of these, see *North American Review,* XXV, pp. 408-25.
Regarding the second edition, J. R. McCulloch, in his *Literature of Political
Economy,* 1845, p. 17, says, "This work, though not written in a very
philosophical spirit, is the best of the American works on political economy
that we have met with." For a favorable comment on the *Manual,* see Philadelphia *Examiner,* March 19, 1834.

[69] *Political Essays,* 1 edition, pp. 39-42, see above, p. 98 n.

[70] *Cf.* W. E. Dodd in *The South in the Building of the Nation,* V, 567.
It was the contemporary opinion in South Carolina that Cooper was the
first regularly appointed professor of political economy in the country. See,
for example, *Telescope,* Jan. 1, 1830.

[71] Minutes of the Trustees, April 28, 1823.

agreed, but he was unable to do this until relieved of rhetoric and *belles lettres* in 1825.[72]

The lectures which he first delivered were published in 1826. They do not represent an original contribution to economic thought; they were prepared for beginners and the published work was intended as a textbook, although the author undoubtedly expected to exert an influence beyond the limits of the classroom. Only George Tucker of Virginia had preceded him in the South as a writer on general economic questions,[73] and Cooper's work was considerably more comprehensive than Tucker's. Although the influence of Cooper upon southern economic thought may have been less than that of Thomas R. Dew,[74] it was exercised earlier than that of this well-known Virginia writer. Cooper stated that his interest was not in the "metaphysics of political economy," but in the application of the principles of the science to state-craft.[75] He confined himself largely to matters which had definite bearing upon contemporary political questions, and was accused of omitting doctrines in which he did not believe but which none the less should have found a place in a comprehensive textbook.[76] He made his lectures the means of communicating his own ideas on current problems both to his students and the general public, and through them he unquestionably exerted great influence.

[72] *Ibid.*, Nov. 27, 1823, Dec. 3, 1823, Dec. 7, 1824.

[73] See Tucker's "Thoughts of a Hermit," published first in the *Port Folio* in 1814, and later in a book entitled, *Essays on Various Subjects of Taste*, 1822.

[74] *Cf.* W. E. Dodd's comment on Dew in *The South in the Building of the Nation*, V, 568.

[75] *Lectures on the Elements of Political Economy*, preface.

[76] This criticism is made in an unsigned review which is on the whole very complimentary, *North American Review*, XXV, 413-4. Special reference is made to his omission of arguments in favor of the tariff.

He stood with the classical school,[77] and strongly advocated the doctrines of *laissez-faire*. The government, he felt, should guard the community against hostility from without and fraud and force within, but should leave agriculture, manufactures and commerce to the free pursuit of individuals.[78] He was convinced that unfettered commerce through free ports would do most to make one family of the nations of earth,[79] and specially commended the growing appreciation of sound economic principles by the statesmen of Great Britain.[80]

He gave in outline what he regarded as the requirements of a popular government: a system as plain and simple as possible, with the avoidance of mystery and complication; the universal responsibility of agents to the people; the absence of sinecures and exorbitant emoluments; little expense and patronage; rare war and as low taxes as possible; a free press and free discussion; and not too much government.[81] He saw the hope for humanity in the work of the scientists, who had made the most priceless gifts to mankind and before whom the "tribe" of poets and orators and rhetoricians would in due time sink into "merited insignificance."[82] He stated that mankind had been unduly prodigal in rewarding unproductive classes, and repeated with grim humor the observation that men pay best those who murder, cheat and amuse them, and least well those who instruct them.[83]

He did not, and would have had no right to, claim that his own services as the schoolmaster of state rights lacked for appreciation, or that the rulers of South Caro-

---

[77] Note the references to Adam Smith, Ricardo, Mill, and others in the introductory chapter.

[78] *Ibid.*, chs. 12, 17, especially pp. 117, 123.

[79] *Ibid.*, p. 168.

[80] Lord Liverpool, Huskisson, and Canning, *ibid.*, pp. 5-6, 14.

[81] *Ibid.*, pp. 51 ff.   [82] *Ibid.*, p. 182.

[83] *Ibid.*, p. 107.

lina denied him the honor to which his more general educational work entitled him. He was soon to suffer from the slings and arrows of outraged unionists, but only because he himself invited them.

CHAPTER X

CALCULATING THE VALUE OF THE UNION, 1827-1830

No one familiar with Cooper's temperament and career would have expected him to be content with an academic influence, but doubtless few anticipated for the last years of his life a newspaper notoriety even greater than that of the days when he inveighed against John Adams. In 1827, he stated publicly that it was time for South Carolina to "calculate the value of the Union." Upon this expression the changes were rung for years not only in the state but throughout the nation, and reference was made to it by Webster and Hayne in their famous debate. Its author immediately became one of the two or three most conspicuous agitators for the rights of the state and continued such until the nullification controversy passed into the legislative stage, by which time the excessively advertised college president was being pursued so relentlessly by his old Presbyterian foes that he had to exert his strongest efforts in his own behalf. The two or three years immediately following this radical and prophetic utterance may be regarded as the climax of his life in South Carolina.

On July 2, 1827, a meeting was held in Columbia to protest against the proposed increase in the tariff.[1] Although the speech of Colonel W. C. Preston was regarded

[1] *The South Carolina State Gazette and Columbia Advertiser,* July 7, 1827, gives a description of the meeting, but does not give Cooper's speech.

by some as the greatest made upon the occasion,[2] that of Cooper has greatest historic significance. Two professors of the college figured prominently in the proceedings, and the president not only spoke but also moved the adoption of the resolutions of protest, and was made a member of a committee of five to devise the best means of opposing the proposed woolens bill. His speech, which contained a historical sketch of the tariff from the beginning of the government, was not so much an abstract discussion of the rights and wrongs of the question as a portrayal of the present dangers to which the state and section were exposed.[3] He felt that the situation had become acute because of the combination of various manufacturers, as shown by meetings at Baltimore and Boston and by the prospective national convention at Harrisburg. He said that northern views might be honestly intended but were distorted by self-interest, and that the present tax on South Carolina amounted to at least half a million a year. Throughout his speech he appealed to southern sectional interest, if not to prejudice, and painted a gloomy picture of the prospect for the section:

Wealth will be transferred to the North, and wealth is power. Every year of submission rivets the chains upon us, and we shall go on, remonstrating, complaining, and reluctantly submitting, till the remedy now in our power, will be looked up to in vain . . . It is in vain that the force of argument is with us; the hand of power is against us and upon us; we are within its grasp, and nothing but determination and decision can prevent our being prostrated.

Because of the greatness of the danger and the advantages of the present opportunity he advocated immediate and vigorous resistance.

[2] *Cf.* letter to the editor, *Mercury*, July 3, 1827.

[3] *Mercury*, July 18, 19, quoting from the Columbia *Telescope*.

He said that the tariff was primarily due to the activities of the manufacturers and their representatives and incidentally voiced insinuations against Webster and Clay. Then he launched into an extravagant tirade against the American System, which must have been exceedingly effective at a mass meeting, unworthy as it was of a scholar and disinterested seeker after truth.

I am now sir to learn for the first time, that in the canting, cheating, cajoling slang of these monopolists, the American System, is a system, by which the earnings of the south are to be transferred to the north—by which the many are to be sacrificed to the few—under which powers are usurped that were never conceded—by which inequality of rights, inequality of burthens, inequality of laws and unequal taxes are to be enacted and rendered permanent—that the planter and farmer under this system, are to be considered as inferior beings to the spinner, the bleacher and the dyer—that we of the south hold our plantations under this system as the Serfs and operatives of the north, subject to the orders, and laboring for the benefit of the master-minds of Massachusetts, the Lords of the spinning-jenny, and Peers of the power loom! . . . To call this system of fraud, robbery and usurpation, the *American* system, will sound to your ears as it does to mine, a base libel on the American character.

After a reference to southern trade with Great Britain and a statement of his own attitude toward manufacturing which contained nothing new, he came to the paragraph, a part at least of which was destined to become famous:

I have said that we shall, before long, be compelled to calculate the value of our union; and to inquire of what use to us is this most unequal alliance? by which the south has always been the loser, and the north always the gainer? Is it worth our while to continue this union of states, where the north demand to be our masters, and we are required to be their tributaries? Who with the most insulting mockery call the yoke they put upon our necks the *American System!* The question, however is fast approaching to the alternative, of submission or separation. Most anxiously would every man who hears me, wish on fair and equal terms to avoid it. But, if the monopolists are bent upon forcing the decision upon us, with themselves be the responsibility. Let us, however, apply to the feelings of truth and justice, and patriotism among our fellow citizens, while there are hopes of success. I would fain believe it is not yet in vain. But at all events we must hold fast to *principle:* if we compromise our *rights,* and act from motives of expediency, we trust to a broken anchor, and all that is worth preserving will be irretrievably lost.

It was to be expected that such expressions as these would arouse a tempest of protest. With the possible exception of a few leaders, no one in South Carolina before this time had considered disunion as a possible measure of resistance to the protective policy of the federal government.[4] Two days later, Congressman George McDuffie, in a speech to certain of his constituents, went so far as to say that the Union could not last twenty years under a policy which invaded the rights and affected the distribution of property,[5] but such an expression was most exceptional. Almost everyone in the state resented the tariff, but few questioned its constitutionality, as indeed Cooper had himself complained. The threat of secession was destined to be made many times during the next thirty years, but the idea of the withdrawal of the South from an unprofitable Union certainly received its first extensive advertising as a result of this speech of Thomas Cooper's. The southern public was to become more familiar with the term disunion as a result of the writings of Robert J. Turnbull, whose *Crisis* was

[4] *Cf.* C. S. Boucher, *The Nullification Controversy in South Carolina*, p. 3.
[5] *Mercury*, July 20, 21, 1827.

published that same year.[6] He and Cooper were the prophets and pioneers of secession in South Carolina.

The comments in the newspapers of the state upon Cooper's speech would alone fill a very long chapter.[7] The character of these comments varied with the politics of the paper in question. The Charleston *Mercury*, a strong Jackson paper and bitterly opposed to the administration, although not yet so radical for state rights as it became later, served as a medium for his defenders. The Columbia *Telescope* unquestionably supported him, but its file for this particular year has not been preserved. The *Courier* and *City Gazette* of Charleston, both of which were strong union organs throughout the nullification controversy, fairly teemed with hostile communications and editorials. The indignant protests quoted from papers outside the state show the intense irritation which had been created throughout the country.

Cooper's attitude was opposed on the ground of loyalty to the Union and was described as extreme and absurd. Most of his critics, however, emphasized the personal note. They stated that his foreign birth and his recent coming to the state made it preposterous that he should have attacked the Union. A "learned renegade" from England had presumed to attack the country which had provided him refuge, speaking in the name of his recently adopted state with a violence such as no native South Carolinian had shown! There was scarcely a vulnerable point in his armor that his critics did not find. His long career of controversy, his incessant trouble-making, his

[6] See below, p. 325.

[7] The following list of references in the Charleston papers during 1827 alone will show in some measure the excitement which was created by Cooper's speech: *City Gazette*, July 21, August 10, 14, 15, 16, 17, 18, 23, 24, Sept. 10, 14, 17, 25, 26, Oct. 11; *Courier*, July 20, 21, August 21, Sept. 1, 4, 6, 10, 13, 15, 20; *Mercury*, July 7, 18, 19, August 11, 15, 28, 29, Sept. 3, 4, 5, 6, 8, 11, 20, 25, Nov. 1, 19.

numerous and not entirely voluntary migrations, the inconsistency of his successive attitudes toward the tariff, the amazing heterodoxy of his religious opinions, not one of these was overlooked.

One of the most significant of the condemnations of Cooper, because of its relative moderation and its strong expression of devotion to the Union, was contained in an editorial in the *Courier*. After stating that meetings of the people to present real grievances were entirely legitimate, the editor proceeded to say:

But whenever such meetings are perverted to the purposes of faction; when, instead of facts and arguments, the passions of the people are whetted by those who are either seeking their own personal elevation, or are uninterested in the welfare of the state; when, upon a question of policy merely, a man but recently arrived in the state, undertakes to violate the injunctions of Washington, and assault the permanency of the Union, it is time for all good men to give the alarm. . . .

For ourselves, we call "disunion" *treason*—We believe it fully; and should it ever occur, we doubt not it will end in ruin, irretrievable ruin.[8]

It is interesting to note that many of the attacks upon Cooper as a foreigner described his attitude as pro-British and interpreted his violent opposition to the tariff as designed to favor British merchants and manufacturers against American. Cooper's references to British trade and the commendation which he had earlier given the British statesmen for their economic policy[9] furnished an additional pretext, although the charge was entirely preposterous. Thus one writer, after stating that there was a natural difference of opinion as to the amount

8 Sept. 15, 1827.
9 *Lectures on Political Economy*, 1826, pp. 5-6, 14.

of protection that should be given American manufacturers, said:

But in its discussion and determination, we neither ask *foreign* advice nor *foreign* interference. Politically independent of Europe, we ought to be mentally so. Of her experience we may indeed profit, but we ask not to be instructed or advised by emigrants from her shores in matters of which we feel fully competent to judge. . . .

British merchants as well as American manufacturers have *private* ends to attain; and it cannot be a question among us, who are the most willing to make sacrifices for the union and prosperity of the country, her native sons, or the adopted citizens and aliens among them. We have not only the exclusive right to adopt what policy we please, but to give it such *appelation* as we please, and shall not consult Dr. Cooper or any of his countrymen, to know whether it sounds pleasantly in their ears or not.[10]

After making a spirited defense of the American System, this writer said of Cooper's "political exhibition" at Columbia, that no grosser insult to the American people had been offered by any foreigner since the days of Genêt.

A quotation from a North Carolina paper presents a particularly strong expression of the patriotic American reaction:

It is bad enough to see a native American so destitute of principle, so steeped in faction, as to speak with complacency of so deplorable an event as a separation of the Union; but in a foreigner, whether naturalized or not, it is insufferable. Dr. Cooper has found an asylum in this country; but if he is now dissatisfied, if he dislikes our laws or government, let him go where they are better; let him not stay here to preach up sedition and treason.[11]

[10] "Querist," *City Gazette*, August 14, 1827.
[11] Quoted by "Querist," without giving the name of the paper.

The comments in the northern press were prevailingly hostile. The speech was published in *Niles' Register,* because it had been much spoken of and might be sought after, and the opinion was there expressed that the distinguished and learned gentleman had indulged his feelings more than he had exerted his powers of argument.[12] Surprise was subsequently expressed that excitement in South Carolina had grown so great as to tolerate a proposition to calculate the value of the Union, and the author of the proposal was referred to as an avowed advocate of disunion and the leader of the restless spirits who supported this policy.[13] The New York *American,* which upheld the same general economic principles as Cooper, denounced his presumption, ingratitude, and intolerable audacity, and described his suggestion as ''moral treason.''[14] The Boston *Courier* declined to believe that his language represented the sentiments of the people of the state,[15] but the New York *Evening Post* published communications both of approval and condemnation.[16]

Cooper did not lack for local defenders although apparently only the *Mercury* and *Telescope* officially supported him.[17] It was asserted in defense that he had given a fair description of the deplorable situation of the state, and that the attacks upon him were part of a campaign of abuse against all who fearlessly supported the state's best interests. In general there was little reference to his expression, ''calculating the value of the Union,'' although the *Mercury* toned this down somewhat and stated that it would approve of such a threat, if there were an

---

[12] Sept. 8, 1827, XXXIII, 17, 26-32.

[13] *Niles' Register,* XXXIII, 49, and 69, quoting *City Gazette.*

[14] *Courier,* Sept. 1, 1827.   [15] *Mercury,* August 15, 1827.

[16] *Mercury,* August 22, 1827, Sept. 20, 1827.

[17] Apparently the only papers acceptable to the radical party, cf. *City Gazette,* Oct. 5, 1827.

increase of oppressions.[18] Not even this radical sheet was willing to go with him all the way, but it was primarily concerned to bring about the election of Jackson[19] and approved of violent language against the administration. The editors of the *Mercury* and the *Courier* indulged in personal accusation and recrimination and almost came to blows as a result of the Cooper episode.[20] Most of the communications endeavored to defend the learned doctor against personal attacks and said little about disunion. They referred to his great reputation, his lifelong services to science and freedom, and his irreproachable personal character, and described the attacks upon his English birth as an unworthy appeal to prejudice. It seems sufficient to quote from an editorial in the *Mercury*:

Throughout the whole of his career, he has been distinguished by an ardent attachment to liberty; and has ever asserted the rights of the people against tyranny and oppression. Few men in this country equal him in genius—none, perhaps, surpass him in the extensiveness and variety of his acquired information. . . . We rather apprehend that had the opinions of Dr. Cooper been other than they are, he would have escaped the tempest which has been aroused against him. But unfortunately he is a republican in his principles, and that is odious to Mr. Adams— he is a South Carolinian in his feelings, and that is wormwood to Mr. Clay—he is a foreigner by birth, and that is utter abomination to the Kings of New York[21]—and he is all these put together, and that constitutes his crime with the Courier of Charleston.

[18] Sept. 4, 1827.

[19] *Cf.* Boucher, *Nullification*, p. 31, who states that the prevailing northern opinion was that the violent talk in South Carolina was primarily designed to elect Jackson. Cooper strongly opposed Jackson later, although he probably preferred him to Adams in 1828. *Cf.* Van Buren, *Autobiography*, p. 160, however.

[20] *Mercury*, Sept. 3, 4, 5; *Courier*, Sept. 4, 6.

[21] Referring to an attack in the New York *American*.

A general proscription of our adopted citizens has gone forth. From one end of the union to the other, they are reviled and abused in the administration prints.[22]

Sentiment in Columbia was particularly favorable to a vigorous assertion of the rights of the state, but a second anti-tariff meeting there, August 21, was characterized by relative moderation of temper.[23] In this meeting Cooper played little active part and was conspicuous chiefly as an object of attack by the unionists. One writer in the *Mercury* said that the people of the community had been sceptical of the extreme dangers which the "virtuous, knowing sentinels of liberty" had proclaimed, and that their fears had been somewhat lulled by the newspapers, three-fourths of which had promoted good feeling. The committee appointed by the previous meeting reported that hostility to the protective policy was practically unanimous both in the state and section, but that the South was strongly attached to the Union. The committee accordingly recommended nothing more drastic than a solemn appeal to the constituted authorities. A memorial to Congress, asking for the repeal of all laws intended to protect manufacturers, and a memorial to the state legislature, submitting the grievances of the state for consideration, were adopted by an almost unanimous vote. Cooper did not enter into the debate, but moved the adoption of the report of the committee, whereupon Alfred Bynum arose to protest against certain "seditious phrases" and to twit Cooper, "the mighty Hector of the first meeting," for his silence during the discussion. In his own report of the proceedings, Bynum said

22 *Mercury*, Sept. 4, 1827.

23 The meeting is described briefly in the *State Gazette*, Sept. 1. For references to Cooper, see the letter from Columbia in the *Mercury*, August 29, and Bynum's own account, copied from the *State Gazette* by the *Courier*, Sept. 10.

that "the colossus of light and knowledge sat unmoved, like the immortal Franklin, when in a similar situation." Cooper was either restrained by his friends or voluntarily remained silent as a matter of prudence. Bynum stated that he himself "was disposed to look with a degree of excessive distrust, upon the candour and sincerity of the motives of those politicians and political economists, whose principles would sympathize and freeze with the inhabitants of a northern latitude, and when transported to the 'line' melt down into a plastic compliance, with any thing that would run parallel with self-interest."

There are other indications that Cooper's radical sentiments were by no means agreeable to all of his Columbia neighbors. Thus a writer to the *Courier* who approved of Bynum's protest stated that the threat of disunion was "treasonable madness."[24] After the second meeting many threats were thrown out against the extremists, and scandalous lampoons were put up at night even earlier. These were particularly abusive of Cooper, who was called a *drivelling fool, traitor, renegade Englishman,* etc. But, it was stated, all this greatly amused the Doctor.[25]

The protests of moderate men against Cooper's extreme position were entirely natural, and the charges of inconsistency and demagogy which were made against him were partially justifiable. Nevertheless, there is sufficient reason to believe that he thought the situation very serious, that he felt the Union to be of little present value to South Carolina, and that he was convinced that an increase in the tariff would probably lead to disunion. This he clearly showed in several letters to Martin Van Buren,

24 "A Disciple of Washington," *Courier*, Sept. 12, 1827.
25 Letter from Columbia, published in the *Mercury*, August 29.

whom he was seeking to induce to take a stand against the tariff and thus aid in saving the Union.

Cooper seems to have made the acquaintance of this astute New York politician upon the occasion of a visit to the North in 1825.[26] He immediately sought to persuade him of the insidious designs of the clergy against political freedom and of Jefferson's consistent opposition to the tariff.[27] Three days after the meeting in Columbia where he made his famous speech, he wrote Van Buren to describe the strong anti-tariff sentiment in South Carolina.[28] He stated as his opinion that by the time the legislature met, the members would be ripe for a motion to order the representatives of the state away from Congress if the woolens bill should be passed. The next step, which he thought would be taken within a year if the American System should be extended, would be to separate and declare Charleston a free port. This he stated as his *firm persuasion* at the time, although he could not be sure about the future.

A few weeks later, Cooper wrote to express his regret that Van Buren was, as he understood, supporting the principle of a protective tariff, and to say that he regarded such a position unworthy of his good sense and political firmness.[29] Because of personal regard, he took the liberty of saying this, for Van Buren was "treading on the crust of a lava not yet solid." He believed that the

[26] After July 15, see a letter of that date, written apparently from Albany, Van Buren Papers (Library of Congress), VI. The very interesting remarks about Cooper made by Van Buren in his *Autobiography*, pp. 159-60, 183, show the many inaccuracies which are to be expected in the reminiscences of an old man, so it seems necessary to depend upon the correspondence of the two men for reliable information. Van Buren certainly supported Cooper's efforts to secure the repayment of his fine and thus gained his esteem. See below, p. 376.

[27] July 19, 1825, Van Buren Papers, VI.

[28] July 5, 1827, *ibid.*, VII.   [29] July 31, 1827, *ibid.*

woolens bill would be passed, although possibly with
some slight modification as to the quantum of impost,
and said that he counted "with full assurance" upon
South Carolina's becoming an independent state with
free ports within a twelvemonth thereafter. He then described the effect this would have upon New York and
the North.

> Your wealth and consequence depends on being the factors
> and agents of the South. You sell for us, you buy for us, you
> are our carriers. The South furnishes in value ¾ or at least ⅔
> of all the commodities furnished to Europe by the United States.
> Reflect for a moment, if Charleston be a freeport, admitting
> without impost of any kind, European vessels of every nation,
> where will New York in that case derive her trade from? Will
> not Charleston when a freeport, not merely entice but in fact
> compel all the South to deal with her? Is not this unavoidable?
> We shall separate in all amity; and assume conscientiously our
> share of the national debt; we have and shall have with you, no
> quarrel or dispute: we construe the term of our present pact,
> differently: we cannot exist under the construction you give it:
> we are compelled to separate. Let your own manufacturers tax
> your own consumers as much as you choose to permit: we cannot
> stand under the System that transfers our money into y[ou]r
> pocket without an equivalent. The authors on international Law,
> which I *have* consulted . . . are clear, explicit, unequivocal in
> our favour as to the right.
>
> I again take the liberty of saying to you, that the events I
> have stated as probable, appear to me inevitable.

He predicted that if Van Buren should strongly oppose
both the woolens bill and the principle of protection, his
present popularity would sink but would rise with re-
doubled strength and full permanence. By appealing to
Van Buren's personal ambition, as well as to his concern
for the ultimate well-being of his section, Cooper sought
to arouse his opposition to the tariff, and thus to preserve

the Union. He brought influence to bear also upon DeWitt Clinton, he said, so the New York political leaders would be unable to claim that they had not been informed of South Carolina opinion and forewarned of the probable outcome if the protective policy were continued.

By November, he was apparently not so confident that disunion would come. The severe attacks upon him in the national press and the charge that he had urged that the Union be dissolved in any case, led him to address a letter to the editor of the *United States Telegraph* in which he explained his statement and described his position.[30] He commented most vigorously upon the various epithets which had been applied to him, but denied that his expressions were the effusions of a speaker in the warmth of debate or that they were so violent as not to be approved of by any one else. He begged leave deliberately to readopt every syllable which had been complained of, but insisted that he had advocated a *consideration* of the value of the Union, not disunion, which he was anxious to avoid.

The true meaning of what I said, is what a plain man of common sense would put upon the words in their usual acceptation; namely, that although neither I, nor any man who heard me, is desirous of separating from the Union; but, on the contrary, we are strongly disposed to think of it with all reverence and affection, yet, systematic encroachments upon the bounds prescribed by the Constitution, perpetual perversions under its authority, by means of which one section is made rich and powerful by the impoverishment of another, will, at length, if they be persevered in, force us to consider whether the benefits we receive, are not more than counterbalanced by the evils we suffer. Now, if it be treason to believe and assert this, I am undoubtedly guilty, and

[30] *Mercury*, Nov. 1, 1827. He referred specifically to attacks by the *National Journal, National Intelligencer*, Richmond *Whig*, and Charles King (New York *American*).

am likely to continue so. I am so ''ineffably stupid,'' that I would not choose to be bound to an union, such as Mr. J. Q. Adams and Mr. H. Clay would impose.

He claimed, as he had done so many times before, that opponents of investigation showed that they feared it. If the North were so valuable to the South, her value could be proved. The people of the South loved the Union, he said, but they would not be deterred from considering the question of separation from it by the senseless clamor of men who cared no more about the real constitution of the United States than they did about the constitution of Turkey.

The attitude toward the Union which Cooper had manifested was referred to and disparaged in due time by the greatest of all the unionists of the period. Webster paid his compliments to it in both his first and second replies to Robert Y. Hayne. The great South Carolinian answered with words of heated defense, but the vainglorious president of South Carolina College, who we may be sure was more pleased than otherwise at the advertisement he had received at such distinguished hands, could not rest content until he had himself replied to the famous New Englander.

In his first reply to the senator from South Carolina, Webster spoke of the fantastic fears of consolidation which had been expressed by persons outside the capital and now by Hayne within it, and then made more specific reference to threats of disunion.

I know that there are some persons in the part of the country from which the honorable member comes, who habitually speak of the Union in terms of indifference, or even of disparagement. . . . They significantly declare, that it is time to calculate the value of the Union; and their aim seems to be to enumerate, and magnify all the evils, real and imaginary, which the Government under the Union produces.

Such a spirit of local selfishness and petty calculation Webster deplored. The Union was discussed by these men

as a mere question of present and temporary expediency; nothing more than a mere matter of profit and loss. The Union to be preserved, while it suits local and temporary purposes to preserve it, and to be sundered whenever it shall be found to thwart such purposes. Union, of itself, is considered by the disciples of this school as hardly a good. It is only regarded as a possible means of evil. They cherish no deep and fixed regard for it, flowing from a thorough conviction of its absolute and vital necessity to our welfare.[31]

This thinly veiled allusion to Cooper, a citizen of his state, Hayne could not allow to go unnoticed. He said that if Webster had merely intimated that there was a party of disunion in the country, he would not have heeded him. "But, when he goes on to give to his accusation a local habitation and a name, by quoting the expression of a distinguished citizen of South Carolina [Dr. Cooper] 'that it was time for the South to calculate the value of the Union' . . . it is impossible to mistake either the allusion or the object of the gentleman."[32] He asserted that Webster had crossed the border and invaded the state of South Carolina, that he was making war upon her citizens and endeavoring to overthrow her principles and institutions. Hayne defended his state and sought to prove her devotion to the Union, speaking only incidentally of Cooper. He doubtless referred to the latter when he said, in his peroration, "You must pardon something

31 *Register of Debates in Congress*, VI, 38, Jan. 20, 1830; *cf.* VI, 71-2, Jan. 27, 1830.
32 *Ibid.*, VI, 50. Cooper's name was supplied by the editor.

to the spirit of liberty.''[33] In his own reply to Webster, Cooper said that General Hayne seemed rather to apologize for his expression, "as among the pardonable ebullitions of patriotic feeling," but that he himself, undeterred by considerations of prudence, could defend his recommendation in its full significance.

Both Cooper's reply and the editorial paragraph in the *Telescope* which introduced it[34] implied that Webster had bestowed greater attention upon him than he actually had done. With characteristic vanity, Cooper said that he found himself repeatedly alluded to, on account of his pamphlet, *Consolidation*, on account of a toast he had recently delivered, and chiefly on account of his suggestion that it was time to calculate the value of the Union. Webster's attack was in reality much more general, and he made no specific reference to the pamphlet or the toast. Cooper appropriated to himself more criticism than was probably intended, and in turn abused Webster unfairly. The latter deserved to be twitted with the inconsistency of his attitude toward the tariff, but Cooper himself lived in a glass house and should have thrown no stones. Even had his own position been unassailable, he would not have been justified in saying that Webster, "like a hackney lawyer," was "openly in the market— to be hired, by the merchants last year, by the manufacturers this."

Cooper claimed that there was no necessity of defending his attitude of "calculation," which he regarded as the "obvious dictate of reasonable caution" and a mere matter of common sense. He expressed the wish that some advocate of the American System would make a

[33] *Ibid.*, VI, 58, quoting Burke.
[34] *Telescope*, March 19, 1830. The reply fills more than four columns. Certain paragraphs were quoted, with favorable comment, by the *Mercury*, Nov. 24, 26, 1830.

detailed statement of the benefits the South had gained from the Union, instead of confining himself to sneers and declamations. He himself pointed out certain ills which necessary submission to a "despotic consolidated government" had brought upon the section. He referred particularly to the likelihood of being drawn into quarrels growing out of northern commercial and manufacturing interests; to heavy direct and indirect taxation, most of the revenue from which was expended in the North; and to the constant danger of congressional interference with the race question. He felt that the depressed condition of South Carolina required her to adopt a policy of calculation. His own attitude toward the Union was entirely unsentimental, and his appeal to the state was defended solely on the ground of local self-interest. His frankness is commendable, but such unabashed utilitarianism is not attractive. Webster spoke for his section in speaking for the nation, but he breathed a spirit of lofty patriotism which Cooper utterly failed to comprehend, and Hayne defended his native state with a passionate and unselfish devotion the like of which Cooper never knew.

Hayne himself said that Cooper's letter was well received in Washington, and that its moderation had commended it.[35] He hoped and trusted that Cooper would be equally temperate in all his writings, because nothing was to be gained by violence or by shocking men's prejudices. He felt, however, that it was desirable that excitement should be created in the state. For that task the author of the *Reply* was superbly qualified. His function in the campaign for the rights of the state, indeed, was primarily that of economic philosopher and agitator, and his greatest service to the cause was rendered during

[35] Hayne to J. H. Hammond, March 29, 1830, *American Historical Review*, VI, 738.

these early years of agitation. He did nothing significant after 1830, although his personal difficulties provide a partial explanation for this.

There was no definite nullification party in the state until after the passage of the Tariff of Abominations in 1828,[36] but the nucleus of one existed somewhat earlier. In August and September, 1827, a series of essays under the title, *The Crisis,* written by Robert J. Turnbull, or "Brutus," appeared in the *Mercury.*[37] In these, disunion was openly advocated as preferable to submission, and nullification of the South Carolina brand was first formulated.[38] With the name of Turnbull, who had been born in East Florida and was frequently stigmatized as a foreigner, that of Cooper was repeatedly associated in the press, and as late as June, 1830, they were described as the principal leaders of "disorganization and misrule."[39] Turnbull manifested his approval of Cooper in a toast in which he referred to the attacks upon the latter as a foreigner and commended his labors for the cause of constitutional freedom.[40] With them and the group of the extreme left were associated in the public mind the *Mercury* and the *Telescope.* The former paper was chiefly concerned to bring about the election of Jackson,[41] which was a matter of indifference to Cooper, and strongly denied the charge of advocating disunion.[42] With the *Telescope,* which was probably the most radical paper in the state, Cooper was intimately associated, and through it he exerted a considerable influence between the time of

---

[36] *Cf.* Boucher, *Nullification,* p. 13.

[37] August 17-Sept. 22. Eleven essays were added in the pamphlet, which was published the same year.

[38] *Cf.* Houston, *Nullification,* pp. 72-3.

[39] *City Gazette,* June 16, 1830; *cf. Courier,* June 21, Sept. 4, 1830; *Mercury,* June 25, 1828, June 19, 1830; *City Gazette,* July 27, 1830.

[40] Charleston State Rights Meeting, July 1, 1830; *Proceedings,* p. 48.

[41] *Cf.* Oct. 6, 1827.   [42] *Cf.* June 27, 1828.

his famous speech and the rise of the second and fateful clerical movement against him.

There can be no question of the position taken by the Columbia paper. The editor himself said in 1829, "Our paper is one of decided politics. For many years we have been devoted to the cause of state rights, literally *radicals* of the Smith school."[43] Even before this, a correspondent from Colleton said that for years he had regarded the *Telescope* as the strongest paper in South Carolina on the subject of state rights, "the paper from which we, in this part of the state, imbibed our first and purest notions of state rights."[44] Since he spoke for the low-country where the *Mercury* was most widely circulated, his statement is of special significance; there can be no question but that the *Telescope* was the most influential state rights organ in the middle of the state and the up-country. One writer, in 1830, said that it was the most widely circulated journal in South Carolina.[45]

In 1829, and again in 1830, Cooper was charged with being, to all practical purposes, editor of this paper. Although the charge was denied, the personal relations between him and the editor were so close, and the defense of him and his position by the latter was so strong, that it may almost be said that the *Telescope* was his personal organ. In 1823, David James McCord, who was later to succeed Cooper as editor of the *Statutes of South Carolina*, probably because of the earlier intimacy between the two men, became editor of the *Telescope*. It was intimated by the *National Journal* in September, 1829, that the paper was edited by Cooper. McCord in reply stated that it was a pity that the paper was not in such able

---

[43] Oct. 9, 1829; *cf.* Oct. 16.

[44] Quoted by the *Mercury*, July 9, 1828.

[45] Article signed "Veto," *Southern Times and State Gazette*, August 23, 1830.

hands, but that the charge was entirely false.[46] The following month, in reply to an article in the *Edgefield Carolinian* in which it was said that Cooper's famous statement was "uttered at an improper time, and by an improper person," the *Telescope* not only expressed its approval of the utterance but at the same time gave the most eulogistic description of Cooper's services to the state that we have yet discovered.[47] He was given credit for having been the pioneer exponent of all the chief doctrines, except nullification itself, which later came to be described as South Carolinian. Probably no more was claimed for him than he himself felt that he deserved.

The charge of Cooper's dominance of the *Telescope* was revived, with a most extraordinary addition, in a communication, presumably from a South Carolinian, to the New York *Courier and Enquirer* the following year. The article was headed "President Cooper and His Plenipotentiary," that is, McCord, whose trip to Europe at the time, it was claimed, was that of a plenipotentiary to England, sent by Cooper and the nullifiers in order to ascertain British sentiment and to learn what South Carolina might hope for from Great Britain in case of civil war in the United States. It was asserted that rupture between South and North was being urged, and that Cooper, who was an Englishman and actuated by pro-British motives, was the chief agitator for it. McCord was described as a man of limited fortunes, who could not well meet his own expenses. He was also spoken of as a man of still more limited intellect, as an ordinary man in all respects save one, but in that the most extraordinary man of his age: he had evinced "a most extraordinary, total, absolute, devoted subserviency to all the

[46] Sept. 11, 1829.
[47] Nov. 6, 1829; *cf.* reply of *Edgefield Carolinian* and reply of Cooper, *ibid.*, Nov. 20.

dictates, to all the moral, political disunionist principles
and purposes of that two-legged library of all knowledge,
and all science—the president of the college of South
Carolina.'' It was asserted that for the past seven years
the *Telescope* had been Cooper's instrument.[48]

The other Columbia paper, which was moderate in its
politics, described the attack as malignant and reckless
and entirely condemned it. The *Telescope* itself was content with praising the absent editor and his alleged domi-
nator,[49] while Cooper himself defended McCord's patriotism and stated that the latter went to Europe entirely
without political motive. He said that he himself had
been in this country thirty-seven years and hoped to die
here. His political position he described as follows, ''For
my own part I think with Mr. Jefferson that disunion is
a bad thing, but consolidation is worse.''[50] It is worthy
of note that Calhoun was criticized by the extremists because he, in a public toast, had made the two evils equal.[51]
The charge that the nullification party was pro-British
was subsequently repeated many times and the charge
that McCord had gone on a mission to England was at
least once referred to afterwards.[52]

During the years 1828 and 1829, Cooper did not confine
his efforts to the propagating of what he regarded as
sound constitutional doctrines in the state, and to the
exciting of his fellow citizens to a sense of the iniquities
which he thought were being practised against them; he

---

[48] Article signed ''Veto,'' copied by *Southern Times and City Gazette*,
August 23, 1830.

[49] August 27, 1830.

[50] Letter to the New York *Courier and Enquirer*, August 20, 1830, quoted
by the *Telescope*, Sept. 10, 1830. The New York paper published the entire
correspondence and made a practical disavowal of the charge; cf. *Telescope*,
Oct. 15, 1830. Cooper's reference was to Jefferson's letter to Giles, Dec. 26,
1825.

[51] *Telescope*, Sept. 10, 1830.   [52] *City Gazette*, March 29, 1831.

also sought to bring influence to bear upon at least one statesman of national prominence, whom he expected soon to see in a position of more commanding influence. He had already corresponded with Martin Van Buren and was not disposed to neglect the opportunity to exert any influence which he might have had upon him. His prophetic instinct had already led him to foresee that Van Buren would some day be president. Even before Jackson's election, he had written to express this prophecy: "I hope you will choose your course so as to arrive with the full aid of public opinion, at the ne plus ultra. I think the path is open to you, if you go on steadily, straitly."[53]

During his last years, Cooper was destined to indulge considerably in the sport of president-making.[54] The significance of his attitude toward Van Buren lies primarily in the unquestionable fact that he preferred him to Jackson's other lieutenant and political ally, whom most South Carolinians expected to succeed the old general. Of Calhoun, Cooper continued to be suspicious. There was the old disagreement between them about internal improvements, for one thing, and Cooper had his own ideas about the character and ambitions of the man. He wrote Van Buren that Calhoun was "too pretending, too fond of the brilliant, the magnificant, the imposing, too calculating how all his sayings and doings will work with respect to his own honour and glory."[55] His own main objection to Calhoun doubtless was that the latter was not yet sufficiently outspoken in defense of the state against the federal government.

After Jackson's inauguration, Cooper wrote to con-

[53] April 11, 1828, Van Buren Papers, VII. In this letter he also made characteristic references to the tariff agitation, the discontent in South Carolina, and "honest construction" of the constitution.

[54] See below, pp. 381-5.

[55] April 11, 1828, Van Buren Papers, VII.

gratulate Van Buren upon his establishment in Washington as the "master mover" of the administration, and to offer paternal advice to his young friend, with a view to the future success of the latter. His hope was to win him to a favorable attitude toward southern interests by showing him the importance of the support of the South in the attainment of his political hopes.

You look naturally to succeed Genl. Jackson: be it so. You are entitled to do so. But let me give you my notions of the course that will lead you there and support you up the Steps. I think you cannot count on the support of the north eastern States: they are not and never will be your friends. You must make too many sacrifices to gain them: but their likings and dislikings are steady: they move as an united Corps, for their political importance depends on this.

If you come in you will come in by aid of the South and West. Your opponent will be Calhoun. He has talent and energy; but his improvement System will prostrate him in the South if he does not *expressly* renounce it. I think he will. But on the Tariff he will go all lengths with the South; and this they will impute to him as righteousness; if indeed the Union should continue, till the end of Jackson's administration; which I do not believe, if the Tariff continues.[56]

He then described the state of feeling in South Carolina, as he had done before. The excitement was not quite so open and noisy now, he said, but was more deep-seated, more extensive, and was daily growing more formidable. He felt that among the men of first intelligence in the state there was a deep-rooted conviction that the Union was no longer of value to the South, and this feeling extended to Georgia and Alabama. On Virginia he did not count decisively, but he thought that the secession of one southern state would necessarily throw the whole

[56] March 24, 1829, Van Buren Papers, VIII.

section into one condition. Every port would become a free port, and New York would be ruined.

I do not know whether you ever reflect upon this result: to me it is inevitable under the present policy: it may be procrastinated a year or two: not more. If you think these notions visionary, I can only regret it. A repeal of the Tariff of 1828 *will do no good*. . . . Rely on it, either the Tariff or the South must be prostrated: they cannot, will not, and ought not to exist together.

Whether or not these representations made any impression on the "master mover" of the administration, we do not know,[57] but certainly he could not claim that he had not been duly warned of the dangers of a continuation of the protective system. There is no reason to believe that Cooper ever had such high hopes of Jackson as most South Carolinians had before the president's famous toast to the Union in the spring of 1830, but of Van Buren he was more hopeful. Yet it is surprising that he should have continued to prefer him to Calhoun after the publication of the Exposition, which he must have known was from the pen of the vice-president.

By 1830, party lines were sharply drawn in South Carolina over the question of the calling of a state convention, with definite mandate to take more vigorous action against the tariff.[58] Cooper favored a convention, as we should naturally expect, and was aligned with the state rights or resistance party against the union or so-called submission party. During the year he continued

[57] No letters from Van Buren to Cooper have been preserved in the Papers of the former in the Library of Congress. The references to Cooper in Van Buren's *Autobiography*, pp. 159-60, are very friendly but do not indicate that Cooper exerted any influence upon him. The statement of Van Buren that Cooper favored the election of Adams rather than Jackson in 1828, we question, especially since it was made many years later (after 1854).

[58] See Boucher, *Nullification in South Carolina*, ch. 3.

his work of political agitation. He published a second South Carolina edition of his pamphlet, *Consolidation*, which he said was called for.[59] The following year, it was claimed that this pamphlet had become the "textbook of South Carolina politics."[60] In the preface to the new edition, Cooper spoke violently of the encroachments of the federal government upon the states and the assumption of "tyrannical power" by the majority in Congress, which had "brought this Union of independent, sovereign states, nearly to its close." All counsels of delay and patience he boldly derided.

Wait! Have we not waited these 7 long years? Patience! How has our patience aided us, except by affording time and temptation to our adversaries to heap insult upon injury, and injury upon insult? Is it not the very remedy recommended by our oppressors? The more patience we have while they rivet the yoke on our necks, the better for them.

As an appendix to the pamphlet, he published a brief summary of "South Carolina Doctrines,"[61] for which he claimed no originality. He recognized his indebtedness to Hayne but entirely ignored Calhoun. He regarded the constitutional philosophy of South Carolina as practically identical with that of the "most accredited politicians" of Virginia, of whom he named Jefferson, Madison, Giles, and Stevens Thompson Mason;[62] and was convinced that only by general acceptance of this philosophy could the "confederated republic of America" be saved from despotism.

---

59 The preface bears the date, August, 1830.

60 See the foreword to Cooper's pamphlet, *A Letter to Any Member of Congress*, by a Layman, p. vi. The claim was made by the publisher, whose name is not given. Cooper himself spoke of the significance of the pamphlet in his *Case*, submitted to the legislature and people, p. 33. For a general description of *Consolidation*, see above, pp. 294-8.

61 *Consolidation*, 2 ed., pp. 31-7.   62 *Ibid.*, preface.

Most of Cooper's activities in the pre-nullification campaign have been described. After his famous speech in 1827, he refrained from oratorical effort, and exerted his influence through personal association with party leaders and by means of a pen whose vigor was unabated. In 1830, he was seventy years old and must have found public meetings exhausting of even his extraordinary energy. He attended caucuses,[63] but contented himself with sending occasional, though always violent, letters or written toasts to public meetings or political dinners.[64] He remained a storm-center. Indeed, except for the year 1827, never during his life in South Carolina did his name figure so prominently in the press as during 1830.

It is questionable whether his association with the convention party was now of great value to it, for the unionists centered their attack upon just such extreme measures as he advocated. In the campaign preceding the election of an intendant in Charleston, the conservative party frequently joined the name of H. L. Pinckney, editor of the *Mercury* and candidate of the state rights party, with that of Cooper, in the effort to associate Pinckney and his group with dangerous radicalism,[65] and the words of Cooper were frequently cited to justify the charge that the convention party favored disunion. The attacks upon his past record and the assaults which were beginning to be made upon him again in the name of religious orthodoxy caused him to be something of a political liability. None the less, his associates in the state

[63] The correspondent of the *City Gazette*, speaking of a recent caucus of the convention party at Columbia, said, "Dr. Cooper was one of the meeting of course; for without *him nothing* could have been done." *Ibid.*, Oct. 19, 1830.

[64] See Columbia *Southern Times and State Gazette*, July 8, 1830; *Telescope*, July 9; *Courier*, Sept. 1, for examples.

[65] See especially *Courier*, August 3, and Cooper's reply, *ibid.*, August 14, 1830.

rights party were thoroughly loyal to him; they drank toasts to him on numerous occasions[66] and never failed to defend him when he was assailed. They may well have regretted certain of his indiscretions, but they never forgot his conspicuous and pioneering services to the state rights cause.

The tremendous significance of Cooper as a factor in South Carolina politics in the late twenties is shown even more strikingly in contemporary comments which were made upon him by unionists. Joel R. Poinsett, Jackson's confidential agent, stated that upon his arrival in Columbia in October, 1830, he found the public mind poisoned by the utterances of the South Carolina statesmen in Washington, "and by the pernicious doctrines of the president of the college, Dr. Cooper, whose talents and great acquirements give weight to his perverse principles, and make him doubly dangerous.'"[67] Somewhat earlier, a writer in the *Courier* had named the leaders of the movement to bring about separation from the Union.

I could name the persons. Who are they? I answer, but some six or seven Lawyers, and one of our associate Judges, headed by Dr. Cooper, President of the South Carolina College. I think I have pointed to the disturbers of our peace.

After a further reference to the lawyers, he proceeded to say:

And, finally, there is one other individual in our State, who has been unremitting in his exertions to render us dissatisfied with our Government; who has had the daring effrontery to tell us, "it was time to calculate the value of our Union," and yet he is permitted to enjoy a salary of three thousand dollars, for the

[66] *Proceedings of the Charleston State Rights Convention*, 1830, pp. 51, 83; *Telescope*, Sept. 3, 1830, etc.

[67] Chas. J. Stillé, *The Life and Services of Joel R. Poinsett*, p. 57.

purpose of rendering our sons and brothers disaffected towards our Union. Why is it, that the Trustees of our College continue such an anarchist in office? What have his renegade English notions of Government to do with the arts and sciences? He was not employed to come among us and sow the seeds of discord and disunion. We were a happy, a united people, until his arrival.[68]

After 1830, Cooper played little part in state politics. He continued to be mentioned in the papers until the very end of the nullification controversy, although much less frequently than the men actually in political life, as McDuffie, Pinckney, and Calhoun. He was described, however, as "the high priest of nullification,"[69] and once even as "the father of nullification,"[70] and the extreme aversion of the union party to him was evident. In 1832, he published a pamphlet containing suggestions for a convention, but this merely went over the old familiar ground.[71] With the compromise tariff act of 1833, which ended the controversy, he was dissatisfied.[72] He wanted the protective system to be abolished, not modified. It was reported in 1834, that he intended to reply to the decision of the appellate court which had declared the state test oath unconstitutional,[73] and it would have been quite characteristic of him to do so. He felt that consolidation had not been decisively checked by the resistance of South Carolina; that the unconstitutionality of a protec-

[68] *Courier*, Sept. 7.

[69] *City Gazette*, August 20, 1831; *cf.* Sept. 9, 1831.

[70] *Courier*, July 10, 1833. This union paper ridiculed the claim by saying that the paternity of nullification had been claimed for so many men that the doctrine might be spoken of as the child of many fathers. See also *City Gazette*, July 8, 13, 29; Nov. 25, 1831.

[71] *Hints, Suggestions and Contributions toward the Labours of a Convention*.

[72] G. W. Featherstonhaugh, *Excursion through the Slave States*, p. 157, referring to a conversation of Cooper with him in 1834.

[73] *Mercury*, June 9, 1834.

tive tariff had not been recognized, and that dishonest construction of the constitution would continue. There is a certain grim humor in the toast which the grizzled old warrior of state rights sent to a fourth of July celebration in 1836, which on account of his age he was unable to attend:

The Memory of the Constitution of the United States.[74]

[74] *Southern Times and State Gazette*, July 8, 1836.

CHAPTER XI

THE PRESIDENT AND THE PRIESTHOOD,
1829-1833

AFTER the victory over his clerical foes in 1823, Cooper predicted that opposition to him on religious grounds would again arise.[1] His forebodings were amply justified in the event, for eight years later he was the object of a far more dangerous attack than the one which he had earlier repulsed. The removal of the president of the South Carolina College from office because of his offensive religious teachings was advocated by a strong group in the house of representatives in 1831, and a resolution requesting the board of trustees to investigate his conduct and remove him from the presidency if his continuance in it should seem injurious to the college, was finally adopted by a large majority. He won a nominal victory a year later when the trustees formally upheld him, but never fully regained public confidence and in the end voluntarily retired from a position which had become untenable. His final battle with the clergy was the old warrior's last major engagement.

The fact that his removal was advocated in the legislature chiefly by members of the union party lent color to the charge that the second movement against him was political in origin. There is equal reason, however, to emphasize the political motives of his defenders. His party associates procured the modification of the original

[1] See above, p. 277.

resolution and made his ultimate vindication possible. Since the nullifiers were now in the ascendant, it was most fortunate for Cooper that the attack upon him assumed a political as well as a theological character. The violent party strife of the four previous years had undoubtedly attracted attention anew to the heterodoxy of the president of the college. In their efforts to discredit the state rights group, the moderates had frequently sought to show that this very conspicuous leader of the extremists was on many counts a dangerous person, and they had found abundant illustrative material in his writings on religious and philosophical subjects. It would be inaccurate, however, to say that the memorable attack upon Cooper which reached its climax in 1831 originated in political hostility to him. Thanks to the tolerance of the ruling class in the state, he had emerged triumphant from his first encounter with the sectarians.[2] If he had been content to let matters rest he might not have been troubled again, but he took the offensive against the hated clergy and fanned into flame their smoldering resentment. Even if he had never questioned the value of the Union, the agitation for his removal from his position of commanding intellectual influence would doubtless have been renewed.

Cooper's oft-repeated assertion that he had never sought in any way to influence the religious opinions of the students of the college probably convinced few of his clerical foes. His claim of disinterestedness and non-interference was strictly true only as applied to his public commencement addresses, to the prudent moderation of which allusion has already been made.[3] The students heard the lectures on political economy in which he questioned the social value of the clergy, and as his

2 See above, pp. 263-78.
3 See above, pp. 254, 276; and the *Address* of 1831.

critics duly pointed out, were fully aware of his general philosophical position. As long as he continued discreet in his public utterances he might have remained secure in the presidency, but he precipitated the conflict by publishing two pamphlets in which he bitterly attacked the Christian "priests," and particularly the Presbyterians.

It is difficult to explain Cooper's renewed assault upon the clergy. Probably he felt about them as he did about the advocates of the tariff; they were wrong and must be exposed irrespective of personal considerations.[4] One of his critics asserted that he had become excessively bold as he had become more and more identified with the state rights party, upon whom he counted for support.[5] This seems entirely probable; he was prudent only when he felt it absolutely necessary to be so. It is impossible to justify the reckless charges he made and the abusive language he used. He was never courteous in controversy, and in old age became hysterical. The clergy had become an obsession. One of his assailants, himself a layman, described his state of mind not inaccurately when he said:

> These Clergymen are sadly in the old gentleman's way. Whether he writes a book on Political Economy, a metaphysical tract on free enquiry—whether he is treating of Geology or Chemistry—the Clergy—the Clergy still elbow him. They are like Hamlet's ghost; *Hic et ubique*—he shifts his ground, but with ghastly pertinacity, they still haunt him. If he rides upon the highway, they confront his path—in the streets they attend him—and at every corner he comes—pop upon them;—until terrified by his own fancies, and in the warmth of his imagination, the very posts and old trees are converted into Clergymen.[6]

[4] Colyer Meriwether, *History of Higher Education in South Carolina;* p. 150; Green, *History of the University of South Carolina*, p. 40.

[5] *An Appeal to the State*, by Censor (continued), 1831, p. 19.

[6] *An Appeal to the State*, by Censor, 1830, p. 12. For a description of this pamphlet, see below, pp. 343-5.

In the year 1829, when it was expected that the stopping of Sunday mails and the enforcement of Sabbath observance by civil penalties would be urged upon the national legislature, a pamphlet entitled *To Any Member of Congress*, by a Layman, appeared in Washington.[7] One of the congressmen from South Carolina, General James Blair, suspected that this anonymous work was from the "masterly pen" of Thomas Cooper, and through the columns of the Camden *Journal* demanded that the president acknowledge or deny its authorship.[8] Standing upon the legal right of anonymity and the constitutional guarantee of freedom of speech, Cooper refused to answer the question.[9] He was generally credited with the work in South Carolina, and in his pamphlet in defense of himself, addressed to the legislature and people of the state, admitted his agreement with the opinions expressed by the writer. He later acknowledged to his old friend, Senator Mahlon Dickerson, that his efforts to conceal his authorship of the anonymous pamphlet had been entirely futile, but manifested no consciousness of the rather dubious ethics of his procedure.

I did not send you my "Layman's letter to any Member of Congress" because like other great characters, I thought proper to travel incognito; but I was it seems like the Ostrich, that wise bird that hides its little head in the sand, and being unable to see anything itself, thinks its great backside invisible to all the world. I shall republish my defense, with the Layman's letter annexed for the benefit of all pious presbyterians like General Blair. Shall I send you a copy?[10]

[7] 1 edition, Washington, 1829; 1 South Carolina edition, Columbia, 1831; 3 edition, Columbia, 1832.

[8] For Blair's letter, see *Niles' Register*, XL, 145.

[9] *To Any Member of Congress*, advertisements of the editions of 1831 and 1832.

[10] Cooper to Dickerson, Feb. 22, 1832, *American Historical Review*, VI, 735.

The pamphlet of which Cooper spoke so flippantly was little more than a tirade against the clergy, especially the Presbyterians. The anonymous layman, whose identity was so ill-concealed, denied that the United States was in law a Christian land and stated that it was very uncertain anyway just what Christianity was. "Is it that paragon of Christian meekness and mildness, John Calvin's 'sweet and comfortable doctrine' of predestination to eternal damnation, and eternal broilings on Satan's gridiron? God forgive these ignorant and rancorous bigots, who form God after man's image, and choose the very worst model they can find, themselves."[11] Convinced that Christianity could not be Calvinistic, he inquired whether it were Arminian, Unitarian, Universalist, Arian, Sublapsarian, Baptist, Hopkinsian, Quaker, Shaker, Harmonist, Moravian, Swedenborgian, Hutchinsonian, Muggletonian, or Wilkinsonian. He doubtless expected his foes to recoil in consternation before such a fusillade of denominational terminology.

So bitter an attack upon the clergy would perhaps not have been made openly by even so bold a warrior as Cooper. In his anonymous diatribe he asserted, with recklessness beyond even his own high average, that the real reason for the petitions against Sunday mails was that the priests, confident that the day would continue to offer them opportunity for gain as well as godliness, wanted to keep everybody else from making hay beneath the Sabbath sun. "Who ordained the Sabbath? Those avaricious, ambitious, fraudulent and impudent impostors, the Christian priests. For what purpose? To create business for themselves; to obtain influence; to get money; to make their services necessary to the ignorant; and by the bigoted violence of the black-heads, to terrify

11 *To Any Member of Congress*, 1831, p. 9.

and to rule the wise—and well have they succeeded.''[12]
Cooper claimed that all public prayer was forbidden by
Christ, and that the employment of chaplains to pray
during congressional sessions was a farcical practice,
recognized by Congress itself as a "mere popularity-
hunting ceremony." He felt that the members of Congress themselves should pay for the services of their
chaplains, since they alone benefited from them.[13] He saw
no necessity for oral preaching, now that the Gospels
were so widely diffused and regarded the clergy as a
useless expense to society.[14] He claimed that for fifty
years the clergy, especially the Presbyterians, had been
trying to acquire political influence, and that the priesthood in general subjugated the minds and preyed upon
the substance of the people.[15]

This pamphlet alone would have been quite sufficient
to excite the righteous indignation of the Presbyterian
clergy at least, but Cooper proceeded in the following
year to add insult to injury by publishing another, entitled *An Exposition of the Doctrine of Calvinism*, also
anonymous, but universally credited to him.[16] Here he
sought to show that no one who really believed the doctrines of Calvinism and made them the guide of his conduct could be a good citizen or a good man. He claimed
that the God of the Calvinists, predestinating men to evil,
could not be loved, and challenged his readers to produce
"from ancient or modern times, a set of tenets so absolutely, so unprovokingly cruel, blasphemous, and devil-
ish" as those of the Presbyterians. The "doctrine of the
priests of Juggernaut," he said, had nothing in it "half

12 *Ibid.*, p. 10.
13 *Ibid.*, pp. 11-12.   14 *Ibid.*, p. 13.
15 *Ibid.*, p. 14.
16 In his defense before the trustees in 1832, Cooper did not deny the
charge that he had written this pamphlet.

so absurd, so inhuman.'"[17] He admitted the worth of many Calvinists, but attributed this to their failure to inquire deeply into the teachings of their sect and to follow them literally. He asserted that the Presbyterian clergy were the most numerous, wealthy, arrogant priesthood in the country, and were trying to gain dominion over all educational institutions and to make Presbyterianism the established religion of the land.[18]

It was not to be expected that Cooper's unwarranted and hysterical attacks would pass unnoticed. One of his critics said there was scarcely a family of consequence in the state which did not have some clergyman in its number or connection.[19] Most South Carolinians doubtless were grieved, and very many must have been exasperated, by his undiscriminating condemnation of a group which the citizenry in general honored. It is no reflection upon the open-mindedness and tolerance of the community that opposition to such a man arose. The strong support which he received is more remarkable and can be best explained as due to his political affiliations.

The most severe attack upon him which we have discovered was made in an anonymous pamphlet, *An Appeal to the State*, by Censor, published in 1830.[20] The force of its argument was increased by the personal position of the author, who was neither a clergyman nor a member of the union party and was a graduate of the college, which he had probably attended during Cooper's presidency.[21] He disclaimed any personal dislike and attested the latter's personal character, geniality, and great abili-

---

[17] *Exposition of the Doctrines of Calvinism*, p. 5.
[18] *Ibid.*, p. 15.
[19] *An Appeal to the State*, by Censor, p. 3.
[20] Undated, but probably published late in 1830. Continued in 1831.
[21] *Ibid.*, p. 14.

ties. He was convinced, however, that the president was
the prime mover in a "daring and insidious scheme" to
undermine the religion of the country, and consequently
felt himself compelled to advocate his removal. Censor
did not discuss the two anonymous pamphlets attributed
to Cooper, although he termed them gross and vulgar;
he centered his attack upon writings about the authorship
of which there could be no dispute, particularly the *Lectures on Political Economy* and the *Right of Free Discussion*. The former of these he thought as undesirable for
a college text-book as the writings of Thomas Paine. He
cited several passages from it in the effort to show that
Cooper was trying to bring the clergy into disrepute and
ridicule, in furtherance of the great object of his life and
wish of his heart, the downfall of the Christian religion.[22]
He strongly defended the "priesthood" and argued the
necessity for a special religious class. He recognized the
fact that in some men of preponderant intellect, morality
and usefulness were independent of religion, but asserted
that most men needed definite religious aid for the mastery of their instincts and passions. There can be no
doubt but that Cooper disregarded, if he did not entirely
fail to perceive, this valid distinction. Himself predominantly intellectual, he exaggerated the power of reason
in the lives of other men, and in effect denied the necessity for either the restraints of traditional morality or
the quickening power of religious emotion. An extreme
individualist in social as in political and economic philosophy, he regarded the clergy as the chief obstacle to
the free progress of the human spirit. He never understood the point of view of those men who defended the
clergy as the bulwark of social order.

Censor unquestionably voiced the feelings of many

[22] *Ibid.*, pp. 2-8. He referred particularly to the second edition, pp. 119,
331, 358.

citizens of the state when he asserted that Cooper had been granted unexampled liberties of speech, which he not only failed to appreciate but grossly abused. Referring specifically to the tract, *The Right of Free Discussion,* the author of the *Appeal* said:

Who in this State has been calling in question the right of free discussion? I know of none but the presses which are under the influence of the author. He certainly cannot complain of having no means of venting his misanthropy and irreligion upon the community. No people, of any country, have ever, in the history of man, suffered their feelings and prejudices and opinions to be trampled upon, and insulted, and outraged for so long a time, and with such forbearance and forgiveness, as have the citizens of this State. They have been disposed to make every allowance for the peculiar opinions and unfortunate dispositions of the man whom they have taken into their bosom; to respect his age— his learning—his talents—and the important office which he holds. They have liberally refused to retrench his salary, when retrenchment was the order of the day. And for all this kindly respect and attention, they have been repaid by having their opinions ridiculed, their institutions undermined, and themselves abused. Does he wish now, falsely to give an impression, that he is not allowed liberty of speech and press? Is he sounding his favorite war-whoop of persecution, when he himself is the rankest, I believe the only persecutor in the State?[23]

He asserted that Cooper had published attacks upon Christianity and inculcated into his students opinions which tended to subvert all religion; he claimed that such conduct in the president of a college in a Christian community amounted to a breach of trust and high misdemeanor in office; and he appealed to the trustees to remove him from a post which many other men were thoroughly qualified to fill.[24]

[23] *Ibid.,* p. 8.
[24] *Ibid.,* p. 8.

This powerful pamphlet was replied to by two defenders of Cooper.[25] Both of these writers declared themselves opposed to the imposition of any religious test upon holders of educational positions, referred to insidious clerical designs, and claimed that the president had acted only on the defensive, which seems to us exceedingly questionable. They emphasized the fact that he had advised the students to profess the religion of their parents. His opponents, among them Censor in a second pamphlet,[26] asserted on the other hand that this recommendation was merely a nominal concession on Cooper's part, and that evidence amply sufficient to disclose his real views and the influence he actually brought to bear upon the students could be found in his writings. In his second attack, Censor emphasized very forcefully the practical aspects of the case.[27] He said that even if the opposition to Cooper were based upon prejudice, this prejudice was very real and could not be disregarded. The various sects were agreed on the great fundamental doctrines, and he was confident they would not support an institution whose president held these doctrines in contempt. He claimed that many parents were sending their sons elsewhere rather than expose them to Cooper's influence. This critic found a ground for disqualification not only in the writings and conduct of the president but also in the very spirit which his personality engendered.

There is a spirit which goes forth from his presence, communicating to society the same turbulence, and restlessness, and

[25] *Reply to Censor*, by Justice; *An Appeal to the People of South Carolina*, by Wesley. Both pamphlets are undated, but they were probably published in 1831. For access to them and to the pamphlet named immediately below, the present writer is indebted to Professor Yates Snowden of the University of South Carolina.

[26] *An Appeal to the State* (continued), by Censor, p. 5.

[27] See especially, *ibid.*, pp. 11 ff.

recklessness which distinguish himself. Even at this moment, when we have a demand for the concentrated energies of the state, he is using his utmost zeal and ability to spread discord, and disunion and jealousy among our fellow-citizens. For the purpose of sustaining himself in his unwarrantable conduct, he is setting brother against brother, and the father against the son. He is endeavouring to excite envy and hatred in the bosoms of the members of our different religious denominations among whom, have hitherto subsisted great good feeling and Christian concord. He has also become a violent political partizan, interfering in a contest which no way interests him; deeply injuring the party to which he has attached himself, and outraging the feelings of those to whom he is opposed. Destitute of sensibility and delicacy of feeling himself, he cares not how he sports with the fame, and well-earned reputation of other men.[28]

He was convinced that the recklessness of Cooper's recent attacks upon religion was due to his confidence that the state rights faction would support him, but was equally certain that they would not do so and that his allegiance was an embarrassment to them rather than a help.[29]

Cooper could have gained no favor with either his critics or his friends by publishing, during the heat of the controversy, Broussais's *On Irritation and Insanity*, translated by himself.[30] This work he termed the most recent exposition of the doctrines of physiological medicine as set forth by the French school, in refutation of the metaphysical doctrines of psychology. His prophecy that materialism would be the prevailing doctrine among physiologists and physicians within twenty years doubtless aroused the horror and indignation of most clergymen who learned of it. To the translation he added two

28 *Ibid.*, p. 10.
29 *Ibid.*, pp. 19 ff.
30 F. J. V. Broussais, *On Irritation and Insanity*, Columbia, 1831.

tracts of his own on materialism and another entitled *An Outline of the Association of Ideas*. He had published the first pamphlet anonymously in Philadelphia during the first controversy between him and the clergy;[31] now he dared to issue it over his name. Here he sought to show that materialism was the doctrine of Christ and the apostles, and that it was inconsistent with belief in a separate, immaterial, and immortal soul.[32] He avowed his belief in the resurrection, but public opinion probably did not give him credit for it. The second pamphlet was merely a republication of one written long ago in England and presented physiological arguments then advanced in denial of the material existence of the soul.[33]

The current opinion in South Carolina doubtless was that the president of the college disbelieved in immortality and thought only of this life and of things physical and economic. Had he been a mere closet-philosopher there might have been little alarm, but he was the most conspicuous figure in the intellectual circles of the state and was notorious as a controversialist. Now apparently he did not fear to proclaim his dangerous philosophy from the house-top; this supremely audacious old man was publicly asserting that his doctrines were genuine Christianity, and that the clergy were impostors.

By the middle of 1831, it must have been a matter of

[31] *The Scripture Doctrine of Materialism;* Philadelphia, 1823. A letter of approval from Jefferson, dated Dec. 11, 1823, was published with the edition of 1831.

[32] Edition of 1831, pp. 310 ff. (The pages are numbered consecutively through the translation and the appended pamphlets.)

[33] *The Metaphysical and Physiological Arguments in favor of Materialism,* cf. his *Tracts, Ethical, Theological and Political,* 1789, pp. 167-303; see above, pp. 15-16. For an admirable discussion of Cooper's doctrines by a trained student of philosophy, see I. Woodbridge Riley's *American Philosophy, the Early Schools,* pp. 407-20. Riley says that in philosophy Cooper was as much a nullifier as in politics and that his views antagonized all schools, but regards his writings as significant.

general knowledge among the leaders of the union party that a definite effort for Cooper's removal would be made at the meeting of the assembly in December. Hostile and derisive toasts were proposed to him at various patriotic and partisan dinners and were duly published in the unfriendly newspapers. In the *City Gazette* and *Courier*, we find such gems as these:

> *Doctor Cooper*—Quietude to his grey hairs and a speedy and peaceful retirement to his old age.[34]
>
> *Dr. Cooper*—He has "calculated the value of the Union to South Carolina." We will also "calculate" *his* value to South Carolina. He has been weighed in the balance, and found wanting.[35]
>
> *Cooper and Turnbull*—Their claims to patriotism resemble those who sincerely exclaimed,
>> "True patriots we, for be it understood
>> We left our country for our country's good."[36]

The nullifiers probably felt that they could not afford publicly to approve the religious opinions of their political associate, but an occasional toast indicated that they would in due time claim that the attack upon him was due to partisan motives. The following from the *Telescope* is typical:

> The *Infidelity* of the South Carolina College: It is an infidelity to Northern principles, vexations only to the *designing* recreant of the South.[37]

[34] By W. J. R. Broughton, July 4, 1831, Clarendon Academy, *City Gazette*, July 11.

[35] By William M'Gee, at a dinner given to Judge William Smith and General James Blair, at Sumter, Nov. 25, 1831; *ibid.*, Dec. 6, 1831; *Courier*, Dec. 8.

[36] By James A. Monk upon the same occasion, referring to the emigration of Cooper from England and of Turnbull from British Florida.

[37] By Robert N. Gourdin, at a supper in Columbia, given the recent delegates to the free trade convention and to Gov. Hamilton. *Telescope*, Nov. 1,

When the matter at length came before the legislature, there was more general comment in all the papers, and the political and religious aspects of the case continued to be inseparable.

When the assembly met in December, 1831, Representative Pressly of Abbeville presented to the house a resolution asking the board of trustees of the college to remove the president, because the religious tenets held and promulgated by him were dangerous to the youth and abhorrent to the feelings of most of the citizens of the state, and presented an insuperable objection to the patronizing of the institution by many good people.[38] According to the *Telescope*, the debate on this resolution was the most important one of the session in the lower house, while the correspondence of President Jackson with the union party provided the topic of greatest interest in the senate.[39] The charge that the resolution had a political motive was made immediately. The original mover was a member of the union party and had supported Senator William Smith, who had been defeated for reëlection the year before by Stephen D. Miller, whom Cooper had favored, so the general hostility of the "submission party" and the most earnest of Smith's followers could be easily claimed.[40] The defenders of Cooper

1831. See also the toast of C. O. Duke upon the same occasion, and the toast of P. Gaillard, Jr., at Pineville, July 4, *Mercury*, July 13, 1831.

[38] Dec. 2, 1831. For the text of the resolution, see *Courier*, Dec. 6.

[39] Editorial, Dec. 20, 1831.

[40] General James Blair, who had attacked Cooper for his letter, *To Any Member of Congress*, was a strong supporter of Smith and early in 1831 had charged Cooper with "unwarrantable interference and tampering, in the late intrigues" which caused Smith to be defeated. See *Telescope*, April 8, 1831. The *Telescope* asserted (Dec. 6, 1831) that the movement against Cooper had been planned at a Smith caucus, but that the leaders of that faction shrank from leading the assault, and devolved the leadership upon Pressly, an unimportant person.

were all nullifiers and the *Courier* admitted that his assailants were all union men.[41]

Cooper's political allies, claiming that the house had no jurisdiction in the matter, since the right to appoint and remove the president was vested by the college charter in the board of trustees, advocated the reference of the case to the latter. Thus the nullifiers sought to serve Cooper's cause by delay, and at the same time to avoid religious controversy and any possible alienation of support from their cherished political projects. A substitute resolution, requesting the board of trustees to investigate the conduct of the president and to remove him from office if they should find that his continuance would defeat the ends and aims of the institution, was passed by a large majority December 7.[42] The union press claimed that the size of the affirmative vote indicated that the question was not entirely a political one, but later developments show clearly that Cooper's party associates did not here desert him; they were merely playing for time, and, as it duly appeared, adopted the wisest possible tactics.

Before the passage of the resolution, Cooper himself

[41] For the debate and comment upon it, see in addition to the above, *Telescope*, Dec. 9; *Mercury*, Dec. 9, 10; *Courier*, Dec. 9, 10; *City Gazette*, Dec. 12; Charleston *Southern Patriot*, Dec. 14. The attitude of the various newspapers was just what we should expect. The *Telescope* was outspoken for Cooper; the *Mercury*, more concerned for nullification, avoided discussion at the time but later defended him; the *Southern Patriot*, a moderate journal which played little part in the political controversy, opposed but felt sorry for the old man; while the *Courier* and *City Gazette* were bitterly hostile to him. The accounts of the debate give few names and are rather unsatisfactory. Among the more conspicuous supporters of the original resolution were James L. Petigru and Daniel E. Huger; among its more conspicuous opponents were R. B. Smith (later Rhett), A. P. Butler and William C. Preston.

[42] *Journal of the House of Representatives*, 1831, pp. 32-4. The vote on the motion to table the original resolution was 67 to 51, and the substitute was adopted by a vote of 110 to 3. No action was taken by the senate.

presented his case to the legislature and people of the state in a vigorous and intemperate pamphlet.[43] He frankly admitted holding the opinions which were objected to. His doctrine of materialism apparently had figured very little in the discussion so far and was not referred to by him. He said that he disagreed with the Calvinists in theory and opposed a "hireling ministry," as did the Quakers and, by implication, the Methodists since they paid very small salaries. He admitted, furthermore, that he had denied the Mosaic authorship of the Pentateuch and that his teachings in geology did not conform to the Mosaic account of the creation. He asserted, however, that he had stated his religious views in class only when the subject under discussion rendered it unavoidable that he do so.

He claimed that he was warranted under the state constitution in holding and freely promulgating any religious opinions which might commend themselves to him, and that it was not within the power of the legislature or its creature the board of trustees to take a stand in a religious controversy, religion being a prohibited subject of discussion. He said that his contract with the trustees had been made in all good faith and could not be repudiated, and that any action in disregard of the original agreement would be in effect *ex post facto*. He asserted that the college was prospering, that no one could claim that he had neglected any of his duties, and that the whole movement against him was that of an interested group, appealing to religious and political prejudice. He

---

[43] *The Case of Thomas Cooper, M.D., President of the South Carolina College.* Submitted to the Legislature and People of South Carolina. Columbia, 1831. A pamphlet of 44 pages written in the third person. Appendices of 22 pages describe clerical designs and give Cooper's opinions of the Pentateuch. For the constitutional argument, see pp. 5-9. One of the speakers against Cooper (Speer) commented upon the "curious phenomenon" that the defense preceded the accusation. *Telescope*, Dec. 9, 1831.

felt that he was fighting for freedom against tyranny, as he had fought against John Adams and as the state rights party were contending against the Federal Administration. In an appendix he quoted editorials and other writings, in the effort to prove the existence of clerical designs upon political and intellectual freedom. Thus he sought to make it appear that any action against him would be a surrender to prejudice against fundamental American principles.

The board of trustees took up the matter immediately. A committee of five was appointed to carry out the investigation, in order to determine whether Cooper had "willfully and unnecessarily" promulgated offensive opinions, whether any injury to the college had resulted therefrom, whether the injury could be remedied without his removal, or whether his conduct had been such as to merit removal.[44] Cooper himself duly presented his case to the board in writing.[45] He claimed that the charges against him were all religious and as such were not cognizable by the board, and that the only question of investigation must be whether the college had declined under his administration, which he was sure it had not done. He declared that he had never attacked, sneered at, denied, or asserted any religious opinion whatever before the students, and remarked that religion was not connected in any way with his opinions concerning materialism, a hired clergy, or Mosaic cosmogony. He felt that he could not be blamed if his opinions were unpopular, and that he should not be held responsible for anonymous pamphlets or for publications imported from another

[44] Minutes, Dec. 8, 1831. According to the *Mercury*, Dec. 14, the committee consisted of Judges O'Neale and Johnson, and Messrs. Huger, Preston, and Wardlaw; according to the *Courier*, Dec. 12, Butler was named instead of Preston; *cf.* comment upon the sentiment against Cooper, *Courier*, Dec. 13.

[45] Minutes, Dec. 14.

state. He claimed that he had expressly forbidden the sale of his translation of Broussais in South Carolina and that his opinions on materialism were well known at the time of his election.

His political allies doubtless expected the investigation to involve delay, as it did. On December 15, the board voted that because of the necessity of securing the attendance of witnesses, the consideration of the charges should be postponed until the following May.[46] In May, a postponement was again voted, this time until autumn.[47] The small attendance was assigned as a reason for the action, but the *City Gazette* said that the purpose was to delay the matter until it had been forgotten, and thus defeat the desires of the people.[48] Cooper himself is said to have desired definite and final action, but the delay was unquestionably advantageous to him. Provision was made by the board for the taking of testimony by two men, one to be appointed by itself and the other by him. He was permitted to attend the hearings and to inspect the testimony when recorded. It was then to be sealed and delivered to the board at its meeting.

Meanwhile, in an unguarded letter to his trusted friend, Dickerson, Cooper spoke of his clerical foes with unrivaled contemptuousness:

You have heard, I suppose, that the battle rages furiously between the Ch[urch mili]tant and your humble servant, even to extermination. Bellum [internec]inum. I am not yet conquered, and expect yet to bivouac on the field of Battle. I have no objection to a moral governor of the universe, but how came he in that character to create the Priesthood? Moral! You might as well apply squareness to virtue. I wish I knew how to account for moral and physical evil, and then I should be able to account

46 Minutes, Dec. 15, 1831.
47 *Ibid.*, May 16, 1832; *Mercury*, May 21, 1832.
48 May 21, 1832.

for malaria, dyspepsia, yellow fever, the plague, cholera, rattle-
snakes, mosquitoes and faquirs of all classes and orders, asiatic
and european, papist and protestant. Can you tell me for what
good purpose that man of the milk of human kindness, John
Calvin, was ordered into the world, the counterpart of Ignatius
Loyola? Hands off: that's my trick if you please, as the devil
said of the dead presbyterian! Thank heaven, when I depart
from these gentry in this world, there is no chance of our meeting again in another; else I should have to exclaim tantaene
animis celestibus irae![49]

Before the trial in December, the question of discipline
in the college had again become acute and the enrollment
had begun to decline, indicating doubtless that the attacks upon the president had had a perceptible effect
upon the life and fortunes of the institution.[50] But the
nullification question had now reached an acute stage
and absorbed the public interest, so the newspapers had
little space for educational or religious matters. The
party with which Cooper was allied was now clearly in
the ascendant. Thanks to the delay in bringing his case
to trial, circumstances were highly favorable to him and
his victory was now to be expected.

As in every other instance where Cooper had fought
for liberty or official position, he sought the greatest possible publicity for his cause. He secured the consent of
the trustees to a public hearing, and the trial accordingly
occurred in the hall of the house of representatives, before a large audience, on two successive evenings, December 4 and 5, 1832.[51]

49 Feb. 22, 1832, *American Historical Review*, VI, 734-5.

50 President's Report, Minutes of the Trustees, Nov. 28, 1832.

51 A brief account of the trial is given in the Minutes for Dec. 4, 5; a
detailed account in the pamphlet, *Dr. Cooper's Defence before the Board of
Trustees*. The latter was published by the Columbia *Times and Gazette*,
Dec. 14, and was based upon the notes and recollections of the editor,
verified by consultation with others present and with Cooper himself. There

The substance of the charges presented against him was that in his writings he had advanced religious opinions offensive to many patrons and citizens and injurious to the college, and that in his lectures and otherwise he had interfered unnecessarily with the religious opinions of his students and had inculcated objectionable doctrines. In support of the charges, the *Lectures on Political Economy, A Letter to Any Member of Congress,* and the translation of Broussais were produced and passages from them were read, together with the testimony of the students.[52] The evidence gained from the latter was very meager. Several students stated that Cooper had made it a custom in the last lecture in the course in geology to defend his own position against that of Professor Silliman of Yale, who upheld the Mosaic account of creation,[53] and that in so doing he had attacked the Mosaic authorship of the Pentateuch, drawing his arguments from the Scriptures themselves. It also appeared that in his lectures in political economy he had attacked the system of a paid clergy, and that he had said that the Savior did not pray in public. The students recognized his hostility to the Presbyterians, but did not substantiate the charge that he had attacked the latter in their presence, or that he had sought to bring religion into disrepute. On the other hand, they said that he had urged them to persist in the religion of their parents. There was general attestation of his devotion to duty and the acceptability of his lectures. Only one student definitely claimed that his reli-

is a slight discrepancy between the dates given in this account and those given in the Minutes. We have followed the latter as the official record. The testimony of the students was reported very fully in the *Mercury,* Dec. 8, 14.

52 *Defence,* p. 1.

53 See *On the Connection between Geology and the Pentateuch; in a letter to Professor Silliman from Thomas Cooper, M.D.,* Columbia, 1833. Cooper had appended his views on the Pentateuch to his *Case* in 1831.

gious faith had been weakened by his experiences in the
college, and his testimony was not given on oath but in a
letter to a clergyman.[54] Cooper waived all technical objection, however, and this testimony formed the foundation of the whole proceeding. A hostile commenter upon
the case remarked upon the meagerness of the evidence
and stated that, although little doubt of Cooper's guilt
was entertained among the people, it was very difficult
to secure testimony since there was a hesitancy in coming out against the old man.[55] It had been admitted by the
hostile press the previous year that the students had
sided with the president and would withdraw if he were
summarily removed.[56] Most of them probably remained
loyal to him to the end.

Cooper's own defense occupied part of one evening and
all of the next. His opponents admitted that he pleaded
with signal ability but asserted, with considerable justification, that sophistry abounded in his arguments.[57] His
long absence from the bar had no more diminished his
skill as an advocate than had his scholarly activities
rendered him incapable of speciousness. Most of his
arguments were those he had already presented, and
need not greatly concern us. From his insistence upon
his legal right to his position one would judge that he
regarded the presidency as a piece of private property,
to be defended by every possible means against those who
would despoil him of it. It should be noted, however, that
he made no plea for sympathy for old age; he was brave
and self-reliant, if not always fair.

He made a more manly and very effective appeal for
sympathy by claiming that he stood accused before a

[54] Thomas H. Taylor to the Rev. Mr. Capers; *Mercury*, Dec. 8, 1832.

[55] *City Gazette*, Dec. 8, 1832, quoting the Columbia correspondent of the *Southern Patriot*.

[56] *Southern Patriot*, Dec. 14, 1831.   [57] *Ibid.*, Dec. 7, 1832.

court of ecclesiastical inquisition and that he was fighting for freedom of religious opinion and for constitutional and natural rights. In view of the fact that the nullification party were now in the ascendant, he made only passing reference to the political motives of the attack upon him.[58] He did not hesitate, however, to draw an analogy between the fight of the state against usurpations of power by the federal government and his own struggle against threatened infringement of individual rights and liberty.[59] In reply to the assertion that his unpopularity was a sufficient cause for removal, he called attention to the objections which had been made against Aristides, Socrates, and Jesus, all of whom were regarded in their day as heretical and unorthodox. He reminded his hearers that he himself had been rendered unpopular by the publication of *Consolidation* and by his recommendation that South Carolina calculate the value of the Union, and that although nullification was unpopular with many, the state did not let that fact deter her from a policy which she thought justifiable.[60] His argument from analogy is open to objection on the ground of logic, but at that time and place it must have been very effective. If his political associates had failed to support him when he was under fire, they doubtless would have regarded themselves as both ungrateful and inconsistent.

Cooper disavowed none of the opinions which had been objected to, but on the contrary declared his conviction that they would ultimately prevail.[61] He admitted that the pioneer thinker was exposed to grave dangers. Thus he said, "It is a serious misfortune to run half a century ahead of the knowledge of the day; and if a man is bent on doing this, he should make up his mind to meet the consequences, and count the cost."[62] None the less, he

[58] *Defence*, p. 10.   [59] *Ibid.*, p. 2.   [60] *Ibid.*, pp. 7-8.
[61] *Ibid.*, pp. 4-5.   [62] *Ibid.*, p. 7.

felt that differences of opinion were of small importance,
and that the objections to him were too trivial to warrant
the serious consideration of sensible men. The following
egotistical and contemptuous passage may have drawn
a laugh from the crowd, but it now seems singularly
infelicitous:

Let me now suppose a case; that you have a President of the
College, of known talents and extensive acquirements; who pos-
sesses the difficult art of communicating knowledge to others;
whose literary reputation is established; whose manners are conciliatory; whose morals are unexceptionable, and his long tried
course of conduct unimpeachable,—would you reject these qualifications, because some of his speculative opinions were unpopular to a portion, and that not a large one of his fellow
citizens? If he has a right to claim popularity for qualifications
useful and substantial, will you reject him on account of *the
color of his mule, or the cut of his cravat?* . . . If I am to avoid
unpopular and offensive opinions, which change their character
and costume every year, give me, if you please an index expur-
gatorius for the year, so that I may avoid the rocks, and shoals,
and breakers of what is called heterodoxy.[63]

His hearers, who were doubtless in sympathy with his
political opinions and no more disposed to make fine logical distinctions than crowds generally are, manifested
strong approval of his arguments and applauded his
sallies of wit with enthusiasm. It is said that during the
course of his speech, "the plaudits of the multitude who
attended as auditors and spectators, threatened to inter-
rupt the business of the evening; but they were silenced
by a remonstrance from the president of the board."[64]
Even the hostile press predicted his acquittal,[65] and in
due time it came. On December 8 the trustees met in the

---

[63] *Defence*, p. 8.   [64] *Ibid.*, p. 17.
[65] *Southern Patriot*, Dec. 7, 1832; *City Gazette*, Dec. 8; *Courier*, Dec. 8.

college library, where a portrait of him now hangs, and adopted a resolution presented by William Harper, "that no charge against Dr. Cooper shewing that his continuance in office defeats the ends and aims of the institution, or authorizing his removal, have been substantiated by proof, and that the charges against him be therefore dismissed."[66] The *Mercury* reported that there were only three or four votes against him.[67]

Thus the old heretic won his fight. It is very surprising that he should have done so, since his religious views were undoubtedly offensive to many, and probably to most, of the citizens of the state.[68] He had been somewhat restrained in his actual teaching, but the violence of his real feelings was well known. He unquestionably regarded the paid clergy as not only unnecessary but even objectionable, and had attacked them in a way which must have seemed outrageous. On the other hand, he contended for academic freedom and it would not have been statesmanlike for the trustees to remove him at the instance of a particular religious group. The precedent would have been most unfortunate for a state institution. The obvious explanation of his vindication, however, is that he was supported by his political faction, which had now become dominant. A union paper reported that the nullifiers boasted of the acquittal,[69] and there is every reason to believe that they did. Politics was the absorbing topic of the hour, not religion, and the majority faction doubtless felt that it would be base ingratitude to cast out in his old age one who had been a pioneer advocate of their principles. Whatever might be said about his religion or

[66] Minutes, Dec. 8.   [67] Dec. 11.

[68] *Cf.* the comment of J. Marion Sims in *The Story of My Life*, pp. 82-3. Sims graduated in 1832 and later expressed great surprise that in "a country as full of Presbyterianism and bigotry as that was," Cooper should have been tolerated.

[69] *Courier*, Dec. 12, 1832.

lack of it, they had no fear that he would corrupt the
political principles of the youth or teach them other than
sound South Carolina doctrines.

The controversy did not end, however, with the action
of the board of trustees. Whatever the cause which may
be assigned, the college grew steadily in disfavor with a
portion at least of the public. The enrollment in 1833
showed a decline over the previous year,[70] and by autumn
rumors were afloat that the college was or was about to
be "broken up." Cooper's friends attributed the plight
of the institution to the opposition of the union party
and the leaders of a single religious sect, obviously the
Presbyterians. The *Telescope,* in an editorial discussion
of the rumors, claimed that the college had suffered less
than might have been expected "from the settled hostility of a party forming one-fifth of the free population of
the state."[71] There doubtless was something of political
rancor still, but if we may judge from subsequent comment the main ground for suspicion and hostility was
religious. The feeling of the orthodox was well described
by the *Courier* when it stated that "Dr. Cooper was
acquitted of infidelity, though in his defence he confessed
the charge and triumphed in his guilt."[72] The trustees
had to deny as late as 1835 that their policy had been,
since the election of Cooper, one of settled hostility to
the clergy and all religious influence.[73] The perennial
problem of discipline provided a further ground for criti-

[70] Green in his *History of the University of South Carolina,* p. 437, gives
the following statistics of attendance:

1830,	115	1832,	108
1831,	114	1833,	86

See also, *ibid.,* p. 42, for a description of the state of the college.

[71] Oct. 29, 1833.

[72] Dec. 6, 1833.

[73] Address of the trustees, *Southern Times and State Gazette,* Sept. 25,
1835.

cism. Cooper referred to this matter in his report in November, 1833, although he minimized its significance and said that rumors had been propagated by those not desirous of the prosperity of the college. He thus described the "mischievous insubordination" of the students; "They make noises, and blow horns on a moonlight night. They sometimes burn the benches belonging to the college. They refrain from attending lecture on pretence of rain, by a general cry of 'Hold back!' They are seen (it is said) lounging at taverns."[74] He made a very spirited defense of the institution against its critics, asserting that the faculty were diligent, that the decrease in enrollment was slight and could be accounted for by the political excitement and the increased competition from other institutions, and that politics and religion were the main causes of trouble and dissatisfaction.

The old controversialist, however, had had enough of it; at seventy-four even he was weary of strife. On November 27, 1833, he resigned the presidency. He had won a nominal victory the previous year and circumstances had since arisen which permitted him to withdraw with dignity. He had received an invitation from a number of lawyers of high standing to deliver a course of law lectures and open a school of law in Columbia, and this he claimed he could not accept without resigning the presidency. He wished to continue as lecturer in chemistry and mineralogy at the salary of a professor. "I have been so long accustomed to convey elementary knowledge, in these departments of science, that I should be unwilling to quit that part of my profession, believing myself habitually competent to pursue it usefully as a teacher." He was reluctant to give up academic life, which he had entered as though by accident a score of

[74] Minutes of the Board of Trustees, Nov. 27, 1833.

years before; the habits of many years would be hard to break. He proposed to give up the presidency the following April.[75]

The trustees accepted his main proposition, but after conference it was agreed that he should relinquish his executive position January 1.[76] He was to receive a salary of two thousand dollars and to have an assistant, and might continue to reside in the president's house until April, if he so desired. He was repaid for the use of his apparatus, and in general seems to have been provided for as generously as possible. It was reported that his aggregate income might be increased by the change, but would at least not be diminished.[77] It was also reported that most of the board wished him to accept the position of lecturer in law in the college also, but there is no record that such a proposal was made. As a parting token of esteem, however, the trustees voted to confer upon him the degree of Doctor of Laws, which he proudly printed after his long-prized "M.D." on the title-pages of the various and sundry publications which came from his yet-powerful pen during his last years.

The comments of the newspapers which had so long been Cooper's friends showed that the religious controversy had not alienated them from him. Satisfaction was expressed that he was to be in no way a sufferer because of his retirement, and that at the same time he would now be in a place of smaller responsibility and greater quiet. His eminent qualifications to lecture upon law, or anything else, were spoken of, and the hope was expressed that as he was the acknowledged parent of the school of political economy and the school of medicine in the state, he would be also the father of the school of law. Various papers spoke of the favorable reception of his

75 *Ibid.*
76 *Ibid.*, Nov. 27, 29, 1833.   77 *Mercury*, Dec. 6, 1833.

last address to the graduates, and the *Telescope,* by way of doing justice to one who was thought to be quitting the stage of public life, gave him special editorial commendation:

Nor will we forbear to say that—be Dr. Cooper's faults of religious opinion what they may—he spoke the words of a virtuous man; and was heard, with reverence, as such, by a body of youth, who are all attached to the kindliness and simplicity of his character; who respect his high attainments and his advanced age; and who, (differ from him as they may, in matters of faith) cannot be insensible to his claims upon their respect, for his long and active career of usefulness; his services to science; his devotion (from his youth upward) to the cause of popular liberty; his many engaging qualities, in private intercourse; and the perfect irreproachableness of his long and busy life.[78]

His old friend the *Mercury,* however, saw fit to add to its words of appreciation a statement that in his new capacity he would be divested of all his power as one of the college authorities, and that the institution could no longer be said to be under his influence.[79] Despite this reassuring announcement, the attacks on the faculty continued, and the serious condition of the college during the next year led the trustees to conclude that a thorough reorganization was necessary to regain public confidence, so they asked that Cooper and the other professors resign.[80] Thus his connection with the institution which he had done so much both to upbuild and to destroy came to an end. During the next few years, the college passed through a very serious decline. Criticism on the part of the evangelical sects persisted; they disliked the new faculty almost as much as they had disliked the old.[81]

[78] Dec. 6, 1833; *cf. Mercury,* Dec. 9.
[79] Dec. 6, 1833.   [80] Minutes, Dec. 9, 1834.
[81] See the address of the trustees, *Southern Times and State Gazette,* Sept. 25, 1835.

It may be that Cooper had considerable justification for his assertion that the ambition of the Presbyterians was excessive.

Local public opinion in later years, however, did not condemn Cooper's clerical foes and uphold his position as he had expected. The triumph of Unitarianism and materialism, which he so confidently predicted, never came in South Carolina, nor have later generations there looked upon him as a persecuted prophet of an ultimate religious philosophy. Rather has he been regarded as a dangerous heretic who once greatly disturbed the peace of a Christian commonwealth and seriously injured its most cherished institution.[82] He has had fewer defenders since his death than during his lifetime, perhaps because later generations became more intolerant of religious innovators, but more probably because they remembered or valued his political services less than did his contemporaries. Hostility to state universities because of their alleged religious infidelity has been not uncommon in the South since Cooper's day and this has been sometimes attributed to the fears once aroused by him.[83] Such an explanation of an attitude by no means restricted to the section where his influence upon public education was felt is obviously inadequate, but it is not without significance. Doubtless the heresies of the second president of the South Carolina College and the secularism of the Father of the University of Virginia were soberly discussed by informal groups at many a synod, conference, and con-

[82] See Maximilian La Borde, *History of the South Carolina College*, 1874, pp. 166-76 (first edition, 1859) ; Colyer Meriwether, *History of Higher Education in South Carolina*, 1889, pp. 139, 148-53; Edwin L. Green, *History of the University of South Carolina*, 1916, p. 36. All of these writers recognize that Cooper rendered distinguished services to the state and college, but they agree that he failed as an administrator and grievously injured the institution. General opinion has been less judicious and less kind.

[83] Meriwether, *History of Higher Education in South Carolina*, p. 153.

vention, and served in part to convince many an earnest
sectarian that God was denied access to the educational
institutions of the state, and that men who feared Him
must themselves establish schools of the prophets where
He would be honored according to His due.

However men may differ in their opinions of Cooper
the religious prophet, whether they regard him as false
prophet or true, no one can justly deny his claim to be
ranked as a pioneer in southern education. By his very
presence he enhanced the reputation of the college; he
broadened and enriched the curriculum; he lectured with
unrivalled brilliance; he played a direct part in the promotion of professional training; and he probably did
more to stimulate the intellectual life of the community
than any other man of his day. Far inferior to Jefferson
in giving practical effect to his academic purposes,
Cooper is not unworthy of comparison with his great
friend as an educational philosopher. No systematic
treatise remains to bear out this claim and none of his
writings on educational matters is readily accessible, but
his letters, his commencement addresses, and his reports
to the college trustees reveal him as a philosopher and a
seer. From the manuscript minutes of the board which
was so soon to try him we resurrect a paragraph from
one of his last reports. This will serve as his educational
valedictory.

The wants of this State are many, the want of a better and
more diffused education among our citizens is by far the greatest.
I desire to leave it on record here among your documents that
my full and deliberate persuasion is that a Free College is as
necessary as Free School and that the exaction of Tuition money,
for education here can neither be defended on the ground of
justice or experience. It might and would cost the State five
thousand dollars a year more, but if it cost them twenty thousand

more, it is a pittance compared to the object in view and not worth a moment's consideration. This State in point of population is inferior to most, its present superiority in point of reputation and political standing, is owing exclusively to the talents of its leading men and a more general diffusion of information than is found among its neighbours; but I am constrained to say, that this advantage is but comparative and that the mass of population in South Carolina does not possess half the knowledge and information they might and ought to possess. Knowledge they say is power; to a nation it is wealth and to individuals it is virtue. The longer I live the more persuaded I am of these truths and the more anxious I become to advance them.[84]

The implacable foe of clericalism may have sinned in seeking to alienate the loyalties of a pious people from their accustomed religious leaders, but certainly the apostle of enlightenment counseled wisely when he urged that the blessings of education be more widely diffused, for the greater glory of the state. And the favored classes would have been wise to heed him.

[84] Report to the trustees, Nov. 30, 1831; see the Minutes for that date. It should be noted that the tendency of the board was not only to continue tuition charges, but to make faculty salaries contingent upon income from student fees; see Minutes, Dec. 3, 1831. Except during the period, 1882-1885, tuition in the institution has never been free to all; Green, *History of the University of South Carolina*, pp. 303-4.

CHAPTER XII

DIVERSIONS OF OLD AGE, 1833-1839

COOPER's resignation from the presidency of the college was doubtless thought by many to imply his virtual retirement from the stage of public life. He was then in his seventy-fifth year and there was natural reason to suppose that his days of activity were numbered. During the five years of life which remained to him, however, his intellectual vigor persisted and expressed itself in manifold activities. In one sense his public life was practically over; after his introductory lecture on law in December, 1833, which presumably was the only one of the proposed course which he delivered, he appeared little in public. Several months before his retirement from the college he had become involved in the controversy which raged around the second Bank of the United States, and his interest in Nicholas Biddle later led him into a most surprising political intrigue with that astute but somewhat baffled financier. This was carried on through personal correspondence, however, and was doubtless known to only a few people. The old pioneer of state rights displayed great interest also in the abolition question, and gave much counsel in regard to it to certain of the younger South Carolina statesmen, upon whom he doubtless exerted a considerable influence. Slightly more than a year after his resignation from the presidency, he was assigned the exceedingly arduous task of editing the statutes of the state, and was chiefly occupied with this until his death. In the meantime, he continued to write articles, chiefly on scientific subjects.[1] He was still an important person and even more interesting than usual to those who came in contact with him, but so far as the general public was concerned he was comparatively inconspicuous. Most of his time was spent in his study, where he read, labored over the statutes, and wrote extraordinarily interesting letters to his distinguished friends. So active a mind would have found idleness intolerable; fortunately there was work sufficient to support and occupy him, and there were letters and articles which might be written by way of amusement. He delighted his friends with many stories of past events and long-departed statesmen, and discussed with them the vital problems of the day, in which he maintained the keenest interest.

The lectures on law apparently did not proceed according to the original expectation. The former judge, who had elicited the warm commendation of Jefferson by one of his decisions and who had later edited the *Institutes of Justinian* in order that he might not lose touch with the field of his legal interest,[2] was well qualified to instruct the youth in law. Perhaps the fatigue of delivering public lectures proved too great; perhaps a sufficient number of students did not appear. At any rate, only the introductory lecture seems to have been delivered. It was published, to take its place with the various introductory

---

[1] These appeared chiefly in the *Southern Review* and the *Southern Literary Journal*. One or two of them will be later referred to, but they add little to our knowledge of the man and his philosophy, so require no detailed treatment. It is worthy of note that Cooper was prominently mentioned in connection with the organization of the South Carolina Society for the Advancement of Learning in 1835. See *Southern Times and State Gazette*, August 7, 1835.

[2] See above, pp. 194-7, 223.

lectures which had preceded it.[3] It is a sane, liberal, and statesmanlike address and reveals a comprehension of the nature and purpose of law which might be coveted for all lawyers.

The idea of utility was strongly emphasized by Cooper, who now avowed himself a Benthamite. In opposition to certain of his clerical foes, he denied the existence of an innate moral sense, and asserted that both morals and law arose because of their supposed utility. "The polar star of morals and law, is *the greatest happiness of the greatest number.*"[4] Men obey laws, he said, because they find it to their own best interest to do so, because they find that their own good is intimately connected with the welfare of society. His hope for the salvation of humanity through the spread of knowledge was expressed here, as elsewhere; his feeling was that all sanctions become more powerful as knowledge, experience, and civilization advance.

He felt that common law and common sense should go hand in hand, and that in law as elsewhere mystery was an object of suspicion. He was pleased that he was able to claim that the principle of utility to the many had pervaded American law as it had pervaded American institutions, and that the United States was a quarter of a century ahead of England. He said that he would seek to show that

the science of Law, with all its remaining imperfections, is a liberal science : . . . That it is not a *mechanical* art, that can be practiced merely for gain; mysterious in its form, barbarous in its language—a confused mass of insulated and contradictory decisions, by which the truth may be obscured, and any error supported. But that it is . . . that noble and necessary bond of

[3] *An Introductory Lecture to a Course of Law*, Columbia, 1834. Delivered December 11, 1833; see *Mercury*, Dec. 16.

[4] *Introductory Lecture*, p. 7.

social union, by which the maxims of individual and private right, founded on individual and public utility, and extending through all the ramifications of society, are put in force throughout the land.[5]

To a layman the description seems admirable. This implacable foe of mystery and confusion in whatever guise, with his passion for clarification, might under different circumstances have made a name for himself in jurisprudence.

He was destined to leave one monument to his legal learning, and thereby to make a significant final contribution to South Carolina. In December, 1834, the legislature recommended that the governor employ some suitable person to compile the statute laws of the state, and early in the following year Governor George McDuffie announced the selection of Thomas Cooper.[6] The tradition in the state is that the appointment was made in order to provide support for the old age of one who had contributed so greatly to the state rights cause, and there is no reason to doubt that such was the case. The need for a new edition of the statutes had been long felt,[7] however, and probably no man in the state was better qualified than he for the editorial task.

The first year was employed by Cooper in formulating a general plan, which was approved, after one slight change, by unanimous vote of the legislature in December. The editor purposed to devote one volume to acts, documents, and proceedings of a constitutional character,

[5] *Ibid.*, p. 24.

[6] *Journal* of the Legislature of South Carolina, 1834, pp. 64, 75; *Courier*, Feb. 2, 1835. The editor's salary was twenty-five hundred dollars and he was provided with a clerk. Late in the year, three commissioners were appointed to advise with Cooper in the matter of publication. *Acts* of the General Assembly, 1835, p. 10; *Reports and Resolutions* of the General Assembly, 1835, p. 54.

[7] See governor's messages, *Courier*, Nov. 30, 1822, Nov. 28, 1826.

and to publish in subsequent volumes the legislative acts, both of the province and state. He regarded it as his duty to compile the complete statutes, without eliminating those which had become obsolete or had been rescinded, since such a work would be more valuable and because only the legislature had authority to distinguish between the valid and the obsolete. The report of the committee on the judiciary was most commendatory of the editor, stating that

they are not only satisfied with the laborious research and sound judgment which are exhibited [by his preliminary report] but they cannot doubt if he is enabled to fill up the outlines which have been presented, the work will be of inestimable utility to the public, and form a lasting monument to the learning and ability of this distinguished jurist.[8]

The work proceeded according to this plan and four volumes were published before Cooper's death. In March, 1839, when he became too ill to attend to the publication of the fifth volume, D. J. McCord, who as editor of the *Telescope* had stood so close to him in earlier political controversy and who had been one of the first group of commissioners to aid him in publication, was appointed to carry on the work.[9] McCord stated that he felt "in the highest degree the delicacy of succeeding so eminent a person in a work of so much importance." The task which the old man began was thus carried on by an appreciative

[8] *The Statutes of South Carolina*, I, xii-xiii.

[9] *Ibid.*, V, 5; *Mercury*, June 3, 1839. The following volumes were edited by Cooper:

    I (1836), Acts, Records and Documents of a Constitutional Character, arranged chronologically;

    II (1837), Legislative Acts from 1682 to 1716;

    III (1838), Legislative Acts from 1716 to 1752;

    IV (1838), Legislative Acts from 1752 to 1786;

    V (1839), Legislative Acts from 1786 to 1814. Index prepared by McCord.

disciple. The most severe of Cooper's critics during the religious controversy in 1831 had said that there was something touching in the thought that a great man, who had borne up through the ills and vicissitudes of a long life, would leave the world without one memento by which to be embalmed in the hearts of his fellow citizens, but that on the contrary he would be ranked among the enemies of mankind, and his name and writings be alike forgotten, or be remembered only to be avoided or execrated.[10] Even this writer, if he were alive at the time, must have admitted that a memento was left in Cooper's *Statutes,* the utility of which has been demonstrated for more than three-quarters of a century.

Cooper, the irrepressible controversialist, could not restrain himself from leaving some record of his own opinions even upon the pages of a work of law; his personality lives on in the very notes. Thus in an editorial note following the documents relating to nullification, he briefly outlined the events which settled the controversy and in so doing indicated his own position. He said that South Carolina accepted the Compromise Tariff for the sake of peace, "not renouncing her rights or her principles, but not refusing to meet halfway the advocates of opposing interests." He hoped that this law would be a final settlement of the contest, "a contest which adds one to the many proofs that a tariff is a bad mode of raising a revenue, and that a custom house is a nuisance, and a war-breeder, both at home and abroad." He spoke of the Force Act as a disgrace to Congress and said, "Whatever binding force this act of despotism may have in Congress, it has none in South Carolina."[11] The inappropriateness of such statements in a book of statute law is obvious. Cooper was polemical to the end.

10 *An Appeal to the State,* by Censor (continued), pp. 22-3.
11 *Statutes,* I, 403 n.

The South Carolinians themselves probably had no objection to this particular note, but he has himself left record that they protested against the incorporation of certain other views of his which seemed to imply derogation of the state. Thus he devoted four pages of notes to a consideration of witchcraft, casting reflections upon the doctrine of the plenary inspiration of the Scriptures, remarking upon the inconsistency of its advocates in trying to explain away scriptural references to witchcraft, and finally quoting a letter written to himself in order to show that witches had been punished in South Carolina in fairly recent times.[12] One explanation which has been given for this extraordinary insertion is that the editor was trying to prove the existence of superstition in the state as a partial explanation of his own persecution as a heretic.[13] The tradition is that a storm of protest was aroused, and Cooper himself stated that the Presbyterians wanted to quarrel with him about the note but that the judiciary committee upheld him.[14] Perhaps he made the insertion out of sheer bravado.

One of Cooper's favorite diversions during the last fifteen years of his life was his effort to gain from Congress a repayment of the fine paid by him in 1800, and thus to secure an official vindication of his conduct in the heated campaign against John Adams. His petition asking for the return of the four hundred dollars with interest, was presented in 1825 by his old friend, Mahlon Dickerson, now senator from New Jersey.[15] The peti-

12 *Ibid.*, II, 739-43.

13 This suggestion was made to the present writer by Mr. A. S. Salley, Jr., secretary of the Historical Commission of South Carolina.

14 Cooper to Nicholas Biddle, Dec. 16, 1837, The Papers of Nicholas Biddle (Library of Congress), V, 72.

15 Feb. 11, 1825, Senate Document No. 30, 18 Cong., 2 Sess.; appended also to Cooper's *Two Essays*, pp. 66-71. The history of the petition and the various committee reports upon it has been worked out to 1850 by William

tioner reviewed the circumstances of the case, asserted that the alleged libel was a justifiable and praiseworthy publication and that the Sedition Law was unconstitutional, and emphasized in characteristic fashion the necessity for complete freedom of discussion. He pointed out that inasmuch as the law had never been repealed but had been allowed to expire by its own limitation, some doubts yet remained as to the right of citizens to discuss the character of public officers, and that the refusal to return his fine would seem a sanction of the law. He wanted the whole question to be reconsidered and some definite stand taken.

This petition was pending throughout the rest of his life and for almost a dozen years after his death. Every session he had it presented, and upon his death-bed he secured a promise from his wife that she would carry on the fight. Success came only in 1850 and it led to a very disagreeable squabble among his heirs about the distribution of the money.[16] Dickerson managed the matter in the senate for the first few years, and as Cooper came more and more into political favor in South Carolina the representatives of the state interested themselves in his behalf. James Hamilton, Jr., Hayne, James H. Hammond, and other South Carolinians of less renown, sought

Nelson, Jr., of the New Jersey Historical Society, who published ten letters from Cooper to Dickerson in the *American Historical Review*, VI, 725-36, with excellent notes. Mr. Nelson found no indication of the ultimate repayment of the fine, but an act authorizing the payment to Cooper's heirs of four hundred dollars with interest at six per cent from Nov. 1, 1800, was passed by the senate, July 18, 1850, after having been previously passed by the house. *Congressional Globe*, 31 Cong., 1 Sess., XXI, Part I, p. lxiv; Part II, pp. 1398, 2075. The amount was left indefinite; at simple interest it would have been approximately sixteen hundred dollars.

[16] This is shown by a letter from Edwin DeLeon to J. W. Lesesne, Cooper's son-in-law, Jan. 26, 1851, and by various letters from members of the family, all preserved in the Meriwether Collection, University of South Carolina.

to gratify the old man by pressing his claim; and even Martin Van Buren lent a kindly hand. Cooper must have written dozens of letters about his petition, and it was an unfailing source of interest to him until his dying day.[17] The reasons for his interest can be readily seen. For one thing, he was in need of money; he wrote Dickerson that a thousand dollars would be a "most convenient windfall." His chief object, however, was to secure personal vindication and recognition of the principle of freedom of discussion. He wrote his friends again and again to this effect, so he was merely carrying on the crusade which he had begun many years before in England. He wanted his petition to be used as an instrument to overturn "the rascally imposition on the freedom of the press." In his last years, he gave up all hope of success, but wrote his friends exhorting them "to give a good talk on the Sedition Law" and declaring that he would present his petition yearly while he lived. He said several times that he would "Amy Durden the case."

It was to be expected that Cooper's great interest in economic and political questions would lead him to participate in the controversy which centered around the second Bank of the United States. In the earlier stages of Jackson's battle with the "Monster" he appears to have been little interested. Until the nullification question was settled this bulked larger in his mind, and pressing religious matters demanded his attention during 1831 and the year following. In 1833, however, when he was momentarily secure in his position in the college, he entered the lists in support of Nicholas Biddle.

As a strict constructionist, Cooper had always questioned the constitutionality of the act creating the bank.

17 See his letter to Van Buren, June 28, 1836, Van Buren Papers, XXIII; and to Hammond, Dec. 15, 1835, Jan. 6, 1836, Papers of James H. Hammond (Library of Congress), V.

He felt that the establishment of the bank was a gross usurpation of authority by the federal government which could be defended only on the ground of expediency.[18] He had pointed out the political dangers of such an institution, and had expressed his preference that the government have absolutely no connection with banking establishments.[19] He might have been expected, then, to support Jackson in his fight. So he probably would have done but for the nullification controversy, and particularly the Force Bill.

From the time that Jackson began to use strong language against the nullifiers, Cooper began to be hostile to him, and with the passing of the Force Act, which gave the federal government power to coerce a sovereign state, his hostility became intense. Always suspicious of military men, he had never been enthusiastic for the old general, and in 1833 he went so far as to say that the government of the country was now a consolidated despotism. "You are ruled by a despot, to whom Congress is as subservient as a set of slaves need be to their master; and the majority of the people their constituents are of like description. . . . The republic of the United States is now in substance, a Russian autocracy." He described Jackson as "the man of vengeance and blood, to whose hands has been committed all power over the purse and sword."[20] It would have been a psychological impossibility for him to support any project of the executive.

Jackson's opposition to the bank Cooper interpreted as due to the desire of the former to perpetuate his power and govern the country through the control of financial operations. Jackson had tried first to exercise political

18 *Lectures on Political Economy*, 1826, pp. 143, 156.
19 *Ibid.*, pp. 143, 147, 149.
20 Cooper, *Essays on the Present United States Bank*, p. 2.

control over the existing institution, he said, and failing
that had determined to get rid of it. In Cooper's opinion,
the administration objected not to *a* bank, but to *the*
bank. He was convinced that Van Buren wanted to establish an even stronger institution in New York, and felt
that the practical question which presented itself to the
country was the choice between a bank controlled by
Jackson and the present one. Although he would have
preferred that there be no governmental banking institution at all, Cooper was confident that the mercantile
interests would insist upon one, and he greatly preferred
Biddle's to Jackson's.[21] Part of his predilection was
doubtless due to personal considerations. Years before
in Pennsylvania, Biddle had supported him in the legislature and had opposed his removal from the judiciary,[22]
and the two men had probably been associated in the
American Philosophical Society, of which both were
members. Nevertheless, Cooper was unquestionably sincere when he asserted that the bank had been faithfully
conducted and had benefited both the public and the government, and that it was not a political institution. The
constitutional question troubled him, as he stated repeatedly, but he was convinced that this objection was
going to be waived anyhow and saw nothing to do but
accept the situation. He was accused of inconsistency,
and had all the facts been known he might have been
attacked even more strongly, for he intrigued with Biddle throughout the rest of his life, and received a certain
amount of financial assistance from him in the carrying
on of his propaganda.

In April, 1833, Cooper wrote Biddle explaining his
position and expressing the desire to coöperate with him

[21] *Ibid.*, preface.
[22] See above, p. 206.

in the campaign.[23] Jackson, just returned to office by an overwhelming majority, naturally interpreted his victory as a popular vindication of his opposition to the rechartering of the bank. The case of the bank was not yet regarded as hopeless, however, and even if it had been Cooper was not the man to hesitate to support the less popular cause. Biddle was glad to avail himself of the assistance of such an economist, and in his reply gave an interpretation of the situation which was very similar to that given by Cooper himself. The Philadelphian felt that the "combination of political gamblers and gambling politicians" should be opposed by all honest men, and stated that he would be glad to furnish any ammunition he could for Cooper's battery.[24]

The battery soon fired a few preliminary rounds, in the form of communications to the press, and in June broke into a powerful cannonade which continued into August. Cooper contributed to one of the Columbia papers eight essays on the bank, in which he advanced the arguments which have already been outlined. Biddle, to whom the essays were sent by their author as they appeared, expressed a desire to make further use of them, and they were accordingly published in pamphlet form. At least one hundred copies were sent to Biddle and his representatives at Philadelphia and Charleston, and others were sent by the author to other persons and other sections. To meet the expenses of publication, the president of the bank sent Cooper one hundred dollars. The cost was only sixty-two dollars and Cooper stated that he held

23 April 27, 1833, R. C. McGrane, *The Correspondence of Nicholas Biddle dealing with National Affairs*, pp. 208-9.

24 May 6, 1833, McGrane, pp. 209-10. Subsequent letters relating to the same matter were written by Cooper, May 31, 1833, Biddle Papers, XL; July 12, 1833, McGrane, pp. 211-12; July 24, 1833, Biddle Papers, XL; August 2, 1833, *ibid*.

the balance subject to Biddle's pleasure, but there is no definite indication that he ever returned it.[25]

How much influence was exerted by Cooper's pamphlet it is difficult to determine. Nothing could avail against the will of Andrew Jackson, who felt that the public was behind him. Cooper wrote Biddle that he despaired of any combination against the tyrant, but that he thought things would gradually work for good. In his numerous letters during the year, he discussed the whole situation very elaborately and stated, among other things, that the southern democracy would find the constitutional objection to the bank almost insuperable, but that he knew of no better argument to meet this objection than the one which he had himself advanced.[26] Such newspaper comment as there was indicates that the constitutional objection was raised in connection with Cooper's essays,[27] and he himself wrote that he was accused of abandoning his principles. He defended the bank persuasively and employed skilful tactics in his assault upon Jackson, who was not very popular in South Carolina. Biddle had strong supporters in the state, among others Hayne, McDuffie, and James Hamilton, Jr.,[28] and in due time strong objection was made to the removal of the

[25] Cooper to Biddle, Oct. 2, 1833, *ibid.*, XLII; March 22, 1834, *ibid.*, XLVII; A. E. Miller to Cooper, Oct. 10, 1833, *ibid.*, XLII. The *Essays on the Present United States Bank* were first published in the *Times and Gazette*, June 21-August 2, 1833.

[26] Cooper to Biddle, July 24, 1833, Biddle Papers, XL.

[27] For criticisms of Cooper's position, see the *Telescope*, Oct. 15, 29; Nov. 5, 1833; for his reply, *ibid.*, Oct. 29. He wrote Biddle July 12, "many people here think I abandon my principles." McGrane, pp. 211-12.

[28] On the other hand, according to the *Telescope*, Oct. 29, 1833, eight of the nine members of the South Carolina delegation in Congress opposed the rechartering of the bank. McDuffie favored the charter, see his letter to Biddle, May 5, 1834, Biddle Papers, XLVIII. Hayne strongly opposed the removal of the deposits at least, see his letter of Dec. 18, 1834, *ibid.*, LII. Hamilton's later relations with Biddle were very close and he wrote him many letters in 1837.

deposits. Despite his age, Cooper participated in the discussion at a meeting of protest in Columbia in January, 1834.[29]

As the prospects for the bank grew darker, Cooper made various suggestions to its president. In the summer of 1833 he recommended that if the worst came to the worst Biddle should continue his bank as a private institution. The following spring he called attention to the possibility of borrowing money for the bank in England, and stated that he would advise the heirs of his old friend Joseph Priestley to retain their investment in the institution.[30] Alarmed at the prospect of the control of the public funds by Jackson, he expressed the hope that Congress would resolve that no appropriation bill should be passed until some safe plan of deposit had been provided by law. He suggested that in case Congress should adjourn without action, a resolution be framed in New York and Philadelphia asking that custom-house collections be stopped.[31] By this time he had become hysterical in his fear of a permanent despotism through Jackson's control of the purse as well as the sword, but the old general proceeded ruthlessly on his way without regard for the scruples and fears of the foes of either political tyranny or "wild-cat" finance.

After Jackson had returned to the Hermitage and Van Buren had been installed as his successor, Cooper first sought to exert his personal influence upon a more reasonable president, and then conspired with Biddle to compass Van Buren's ultimate defeat. He would doubtless have vigorously denied the charge of duplicity of conduct, for he wrote the president chiefly about the

29 *Mercury*, Jan. 21, 1834. The resolutions of protest were adopted. by unanimous vote.

30 July 24, 1833, Biddle Papers, XL; April 1, 1834, *ibid.*, XLVII.

31 May 1, 1834, McGrane, pp. 230-1.

abolition question and frankly stated that he opposed the financial policy of the administration.[32] He never gave Van Buren an explicit promise of support, but he implied, both at the beginning of the administration and subsequently, a friendliness which he could hardly have sincerely felt. Perhaps his persistent utilitarianism had served to dull his ethical sense; perhaps during his last years he was not entirely responsible for his actions.

The proposal which Cooper made Biddle in the spring of 1837 seems to have been entirely sincere, however fantastic it may now appear. The panic of that year and the rising tide of criticism of the financial policy of Jackson and Van Buren convinced the old economist that his Philadelphia friend might yet reëstablish himself in a position of commanding importance, and exercise his great administrative talents in the service of the country. So he suggested to Biddle that he stand for the presidency.

I enter upon my 79th year next October. By the time Mr. Van Beuren's first period has expired, I shall be dead or superannuated. I can have therefore no selfish motive in my present proposal.

The tide is turning strongly against the measures of the last and present Administration. The poor now groan under the financial follies of Gen. Jackson as well as the rich . . .

[32] See his letters to Van Buren, March 27, 1837, Van Buren Papers, XXVI; April 14, 1837, *ibid.*, XXVII; March 19, 1838, *ibid.*, XXXII. In his inaugural address, Van Buren had stated that he would veto any bill abolishing slavery in the District of Columbia unless the slave states themselves desired it. Cooper approved of this, praised the president in an anonymous newspaper article, duly informed him of this action, and urged him to stand strongly against the abolitionists. He assured Van Buren several times that South Carolina would support him if he would resist attacks upon her cherished institution and see that the policy of the tariff reduction was continued. He undoubtedly had greater interest in Biddle, but sought to influence Van Buren by argument and by a somewhat insincere profession of friendly interest.

At this moment your judicious conduct has placed you prominent as a wise and temperate man, and a public benefactor. You
can go on pursuing cautiously the same course of conduct, and
earning on all hands golden opinions.

Why not look to the Presidency?

Can your name be brought forward at a time more advantageous than the present? You are rising, your opponents are
falling; strike the ball on the rebound, and I think this is the
moment . . .

Think of this; and if needful command my services such as
they may be. . . . The present suggestion is my own; received
from and communicated to no one but yourself. And so it shall
remain until you decide.[33]

With this startling proposal the septuagenarian entered upon a chapter of intrigue which diverted his last
days. As he wrote a few months later, "I might as well
amuse myself with the interesting questions of the day,
as in any other manner." He had indulged in prophecy
about the presidency before, but his judgment was somewhat clearer when he predicted that Van Buren would
succeed Old Hickory.[34] His suggestion to Biddle, however, was not regarded by that gentleman as preposterous. In an appreciative reply he stated that he had received "similar intimations" from other quarters, that
he was convinced that the good of the country required
the removal of the present governors, and that although
the presidential office had for him no attractions, he stood
ready for the country's service. "If therefore you think
that my name can be productive of good, I am content to
place it—as I now do, at your disposal—under a conviction of the friendly and discreet manner in which alone
it will be employed."[35] From this time, Cooper was unofficially Biddle's campaign manager in South Carolina.

33 April 29, 1837, McGrane, pp. 272-3.
34 See above, pp. 329-331.   35 May 8, 1837, McGrane, pp. 277-8.

He proceeded cautiously, and before sounding out any of the leading men wrote Biddle of two possible presidential candidates from South Carolina, William C. Preston and Calhoun. Both of these men, he said, were viewed with a certain amount of suspicion in the state, "rather as looking steadily at the central government, than as guided by a purely South Carolina spirit." He thought that Calhoun, whom he regarded as a man of talent without tact and judgment, was rather borne with than supported. Preston he regarded as the abler and more popular, but as better suited to a foreign court than the presidency. "Both these Gentlemen, are like me, Nullifiers. They could not be sustained out of the State, even if they could command South Carolina. It is an unfashionable Garb. It sticks like the shirt of Nesus. I am content however to wear it as my winding sheet." Regarding both of these talented and honest men as *hors de combat,* he believed Biddle had a chance to win South Carolina. He thought that Webster would be set up as his opponent and was sure that, in this event, Biddle would have the preference.[36]

Shortly afterwards Cooper informed Biddle that all to whom he had spoken about his candidacy agreed with him in favoring it, and that he and Governor Butler were planning to set up a newspaper in Columbia. He thought that McDuffie, but for his personal attachment to Calhoun, would go with them, and that the "strange infatuation" of Calhoun as to the presidency must be counteracted.[37] He thought that skillful publicity in behalf of the bank should be begun, and discussed the premature candidacy of Webster, who had "satis elequentiae, sapientiae parvum."[38] He sent Biddle, for insertion in northern

36 May 14, 1837, *ibid.*, pp. 278-80.
37 May 24, 1837, *ibid.*, pp. 280-281.
38 June 12, 1837, Biddle Papers, LXVIII.

papers, a reply to the constitutional objections to the
bank and hopefully prophesied that this bread, if cast
upon the waters, would be found again after many days.[39]
He wrote to the papers in behalf of the bank and was
replied to by a former president, Langdon Cheves.[40] He
made many prophecies about the probable political alignment, said that Preston and James Hamilton, Jr., were
quietly for Biddle, and predicted that a motion to re-
instate the bank would be made in about two years.[41]
Ultimately, however, he grew discouraged, because the
legislature had gone for the sub-treasury and the state
had gone wild about Calhoun. Nevertheless, he was convinced that as Calhoun had gone up like the rocket, he
would come down like the stick.[42] During the last year of
his life, he concluded that Clay and Van Buren would
be the rival candidates. Now regarding the nomination
of Biddle as impracticable, he suggested that he join
forces with Clay, become his secretary of the treasury,
and use this office as a stepping-stone to the presidency.[43]
He continued to write to Biddle until the final weeks of
his life, and there is a profound pathos in his last letter,
in which he described his financial straits and asked assistance in the securing of a loan. Toward the end of
his life, his letters grew somewhat incoherent, and his
schemes for his friend appear now to have been from
the outset the fantasies of a yet-powerful but failing
mind.

The veteran advocate of state rights did not confine his
last years to efforts for what he regarded as a sound

39 July 1, 1837, *ibid.;* McGrane (in part), pp. 281-2.

40 Sept. 11, 1837, Biddle Papers, LXX.

41 Sept. 15, 1837, *ibid.;* Oct. 20, 1837, *ibid.,* LXXI; McGrane (in part),
pp. 293-4.

42 Dec. 16, 1837, Biddle Papers, LXXII, McGrane (in part), pp. 296-7;
Jan. 20, 1838, Biddle Papers, LXXIV.

43 Oct. 1, 1838, McGrane, p. 333.

financial policy, but sought, to some extent through public communications and more through private correspondence, to advance the political doctrines which he had already so strongly championed. In 1834 he published a pamphlet in continuation of his *Consolidation,* in which he defended state rights against northern centralizing doctrines.[44] "The results and consequences of the two doctrines, to the South," he said, "are independence on the one hand or subjection on the other. The northern doctrines sink us into municipalities, the southern preserve our independence as states."[45] He added little to the arguments which he had already advanced, but gave a historical sketch of the development of southern doctrines which has real value.[46] He claimed, as he had not done with such frankness before, that supreme allegiance was due the state, expressing itself authoritatively in a convention. To a hypothetical citizen of his own commonwealth, he said, "You are a Carolinian. Your allegiance, therefore, is due to the state, . . . You have nothing to do with the people of Maine or Mississippi. As to the people of the United States, they have no existence, we know them not."[47] He insisted upon the right of state interposition, and boldly declared that if a state had no negative upon an act of Congress which infringed upon the constitution, a despotism would result from which an injured state must struggle to get free as soon as possible, peaceably if it could, forcibly if it must.[48]

The thought of secession continued prominent in his mind and he referred to the possible dissolution of the

---

[44] *Consolidation,* Part Second, Strictures on an essay on the origin and character of the old parties of the United States which appeared in the *North American Review,* July, 1834. Cooper's essay appeared in the Columbia *Southern Times* during August and September, 1834, and was published as a pamphlet that year.

[45] *Ibid.,* preface, p. 3.   [46] *Ibid.,* Essay III.

[47] *Ibid.,* p. 36.   [48] *Ibid.,* p. 14.

Union in several of his letters to Biddle and Van Buren, and very frequently in letters to his former student, James H. Hammond, once editor of the *Southern Times,* now congressman, and later to be governor and senator.[49] The burden of his lament to his young friend was the agitation of the abolitionists. He was entirely convinced by now that slavery was advantageous to the slave, and abhorred the thought of federal interference with an institution over which the state exercised constitutional control. For the sentimental northern abolitionists this frank realist had no sympathy whatever.[50] Thus, after paying his compliments to William Ellery Channing, of whose theological views at least he should have approved, he said, "The idea of these New England theologians, that their notions of religious duty are to supercede all law, is quite inconsistent with the well being of civil society, and elevates every ignorant fanatic into an irresponsible dictator."[51]

So strong an advocate of complete freedom of speech could not consistently have opposed on other than constitutional grounds the discussion of slavery. While the southern representatives were seeking to exclude abolitionist literature from the mails, and a few months before they succeeded in passing the "Gag Law," whereby petitions relating to slavery were automatically tabled, Cooper suggested to Hammond a form of resolution

49 Hammond graduated at the South Carolina College in 1825. He was a member of Congress for a few months in 1835-6, but resigned on account of ill health. His attitude toward slavery, which doubtless reflected in part the influence of Cooper, is described in his *Letters on Slavery,* written in 1845. The Hammond Papers in the Library of Congress contain twelve letters to him from Cooper, practically all written during Hammond's brief term in Congress.

50 See his article, "Slavery," in the *Southern Literary Journal,* I, 188-193 (Nov. 1835), in defense of the institution against the arguments of the abolitionists.

51 Cooper to Hammond, Feb. 12, 1836, Hammond Papers, V.

which stated that Congress had no right to interfere with, or in any manner to regulate, the system of domestic servitude adopted by any state, territory, or portion of territory constituting the United States.[52] He had no expectation that the anti-slavery group would permit such a resolution even to be debated, but felt that the sooner the issue was made clear, the better it would be. "If they persist in their right to interfere, because the North and the South are equally parts of one common system of government, the sooner we separate the better; for we shall be kept in hot water till the fanatics become (as they will become) powerful enough to influence the vote of the federal legislature."

Cooper urged opposition to abolitionist agitation not only upon Hammond but upon others of the younger South Carolina statesmen as well,[53] and participated in local efforts to support the uncompromising and rebuke the compromising representatives.[54] He belonged with the pioneers in this, as in the other efforts he made to defend what were spoken of as southern rights. E. W. Johnston, a Columbia publisher, condemned McDuffie because of his failure to exert leadership and Calhoun because of his popularity-seeking and said that he had no one to consult with except "old Cooper whose reasons are always worth listening to, even when wrong."[55] Cooper never trusted Calhoun, and the group to which he himself belonged felt that they first agitated and popularized

---

[52] Dec. 30, 1835, *ibid.*, V.

[53] He referred several times to letters to Waddy Thompson and Pickens.

[54] E. W. Johnston to Hammond, March 9, 1836, *ibid.*, VI, referring to a proposed meeting in Columbia to commend the action of Hammond, Pickens, Waddy Thompson and others, and, by implication, to condemn H. L. Pinckney, who it was claimed was playing politics. Johnston and Cooper prepared the resolutions, but the meeting was blocked by the actions of certain union men. See the letter of Cooper to Hammond, March 20, *ibid.*

[55] Johnston to Hammond, Feb. 28, 1836, *ibid.*, V.

doctrines which Calhoun later appropriated. As advocates of almost unlimited state rights, they were unquestionably in advance of him. He would certainly never
have gone so far as to say with Cooper:

I disapprove of the eternal panegyrics on our union, which as
construed, is worse than good for nothing; and is at its best,
worth little but for imaginative declamation; that is, to the
South; to the North, it is the widow's cruise of oil, a fountain of
living waters, an inexhaustible pretence for solemn cheating
under the forms of Law; and protected by grave exclamations
about the inestimable value of our national compact, which the
rogues well know, is made only to be broken for their benefit.
These canters talk also about their religious feelings! A never
failing mark of innate deliberate rascality; . . . The Yankees
put me in mind of Shakspear, "He is a Knave; a very Knave;
a worsted-stocking Knave!" Their construction of the Union
will fit any northern leg. However, the end approaches. A con-
summation in my opinion, devoutly to be wished for by every
Southron.[56]

To Van Buren, shortly after the inauguration, Cooper
wrote more moderately and with the apparent hope of
influencing the president to adopt a policy which would
prevent the secession of the southern states.[57] He assured
Jackson's successor that the South would continue to
demand that domestic servitude be unmolested and that
the principle of the Compromise Tariff be adhered to.
Disregard of southern demands in these two matters he
thought would lead to inevitable separation, which would
injure both sections at first but would more permanently
injure the North. In the last letter he wrote Van Buren,
the year before his death, he predicted that the slavery

56 Cooper to Hammond, March 2, 1836, *ibid.*, VI.
57 April 14, 1837, Van Buren Papers, XXVII. For his earlier discussion
of secession with Van Buren, see above, pp. 318-20, 330-1.

question would "ultimately like Aaron's rod, swallow up" all other questions,[58] as indeed it did.

Cooper seems to have carried to his grave the conviction that the Union would not endure. He sought to encourage Van Buren in a conciliatory policy in order that disruption might be prevented, but to the very end his chief concern was to arouse the citizens of South Carolina to a consciousness of their own rights and a determination to resist every infringement of them. This passionate utilitarian, who regarded sentimental attachment to the Union as ridiculous, unquestionably did much to convince the state that the Union was useless to her and thus played a not inconsiderable part in preparing South Carolina for secession. The seeds of dissatisfaction which he sowed fell upon a soil fertile in discontent and were destined to bear an abundant and bitter harvest. But if this great prophet of secession could himself be present to make rejoinder to any reproachful accusation, we have no doubt but that he would say that had his warnings been heeded earlier, and had the issue been tested sooner, the outcome would have been different.

The days of his calculating, denouncing, and intriguing were almost over. In July, 1838, he wrote Biddle that he was becoming feeble, asthmatic, and dropsical, that his machine was fast falling to pieces, but that he hoped that his head would yet remain in a tolerable state and that he might still be useful. His last letters were not written in his customary close, neat script, but the writing was spread large on account of his failing vision. One letter he said he could not read with "large magnifyors," although all the letters in it were the size of capitals. Some months before his death, he amused himself by making a catalogue of the more than two thousand five hundred

58 March 19, 1838, *ibid.*, XXXII.

volumes in his library, and this remains in the library of the college as a memento of him.[59] Painstaking as the work was, the cataloguer with true scholarly spirit was chiefly aware of its imperfections, its inadequate and imperfect classifications. No better indication of the interests of the man remains than this list of volumes. His library was rich in science, history, political economy, theology, and especially the classics. It contained thirty volumes of Dr. Priestley, and eleven of Voltaire. It contained more than a hundred volumes dealing with voyages and travels, and a surprising number of works on curiosities of all sorts. There were volumes treating of hieroglyphics, witchcraft, Chinese writing, and Egyptian monuments; there were works in Latin, Greek, French, and Spanish; there were Hebrew lexicons and grammars. But there was practically no fiction or English poetry.[60] Amusement he found elsewhere chiefly; sentiment he did not value.

In March, 1839, he was forced to give up his work on the *Statutes*, and reports of his death appeared in the Charleston papers, to be hastily corrected. He lingered on for almost two months more, until the end came on May 11. His old journalistic foes referred to his services to science and literature, without mentioning politics, but the *Telescope* published a long account of his life, which

---

[59] Meriwether Collection.

[60] Years before, he had contributed several articles on poetry to the *Port Folio*, and in January, 1836, an article of his entitled ''Sonnets'' appeared in the *Southern Literary Journal*, I, 313-18. In the latter he commended the sonnet because of its brevity, which rendered it more suitable for an age which asked only temporary amusement from poetry. He quoted an Italian sonnet—although not in conventional sonnet form—with a very respectable translation by himself under the title, ''On Helen Contemplating Herself in a Mirror.'' Professor Yates Snowden called this to the attention of the present writer. So far as we know, Cooper never elsewhere ventured into verse, and even here he damned verse with faint praise.

was duly copied by the *Mercury*[61] and even the *Courier*. This is the best brief summary of his long career which we have yet discovered. It is sympathetic and highly appreciative, without being excessively eulogistic or sentimental. The writer was evidently one who had known Cooper intimately. The comments which he made upon his intellectual character and social life are particularly illuminating.

The predominant qualities of Dr. Cooper's intellectual character were intrepidity and activity. His mind coursed the whole field of learning with untiring rapidity. It incessantly sought for knowledge; not with any apparent drudgery or toil, but, up to the last moments of his life, with that youthful and fresh alacrity which belongs to the pursuit of pleasure. He did not hesitate to follow his reasoning wherever it led, and what he thought he said. Authority had but little weight with him. He always endeavored to apply the touchstone of reason to every proposition, and to judge of it by that test alone.

His multifarious studies, and his uncommonly wide observation of society, had enriched his memory with vast stores of useful and agreeable topics; and these, combined with a cheerful temper, a social spirit, and a most pleasant style of conversation, rendered him a most delightful companion. He was an admirable talker—terse, epigramic, gay and instructive. He was rarely in a company in which he did not say the best thing that was uttered. His conversation was illustrated by well turned anecdotes, ornamented by sparkling classical allusions, and enriched by sensible and judicious remarks. His temper was most agreeable, and his whole *maniere d'etre* distinguished by a pervading *bon hommie* and kindliness of nature. He was benevolent, friendly and impulsive, prompt to do a good turn, "to spread friendships and to cover hearts." He was fond of children, addicted to pets, and kind to servants. Throughout his whole behavior there was a winning simplicity and directness; always agreeable, but in one of his age, learning and abilities, peculiarly

[61] May 21, 1839; *Courier*, the same date.

captivating. He resided amongst us for the last twenty years, and we doubt whether he has ever been known to manifest a feeling of personal unkindness towards any individual.

Not all his fellow citizens had such pleasant memories of Thomas Cooper, for many of them had known him in controversy. There is a grim significance in the inscription which one can yet read on his tombstone in the Guignard plot, Trinity churchyard, Columbia. It is stated that the stone was erected in his memory by a *portion* of his fellow citizens.

CONCLUSION

JUDGED by the standard of immediate results, the long, varied, and tempestuous career of Thomas Cooper appears to have been one of persistent failure. Baffled in his efforts for reform and unsuccessful in business, he abandoned Great Britain to the tender mercies of the "privileged orders" and sought to erase all memories of a land where he had been unappreciated. Many of the causes for which he fought so valiantly while a citizen of Manchester—the abolition of the slave trade, the repeal of the Corporation and Test Acts, and parliamentary reform— were ultimately crowned with success, but too long after his emigration for him to exult greatly in the victory or to attribute it directly to any efforts of his own.

For the success of the Jeffersonian party in the election of 1800, Cooper could rightly claim a very respectable share of credit, but, significantly, he contributed to the Republican cause in part through personal misfortune, for during six months of the election year he lay imprisoned, a victim of the Sedition Law. After the victory of Jefferson, he failed to receive a political reward which was commensurate with his abilities or his contributions to the success of his party, and he failed even to realize fully upon such opportunities for constructive public service as were now presented to him in Pennsylvania. His admirable work as Luzerne commissioner was marred in the end by unseemly controversy, resulting in part from his own indiscretions, and seems never to have been adequately valued. His former political associates, convinced that he had lost faith and interest in democracy, finally repudiated him and removed him from a judicial position which he was temperamentally unqualified to fill. Neither of his professorial appointments in Pennsylvania was satisfactory to him, and clerical opposition made it forever impossible for him to become a member of Jefferson's academic family at the new University of Virginia. The end of the Pennsylvania period of his life found him thwarted and dissatisfied, suspicious of democracy as he had formerly been suspicious of aristocracy, convinced that his unusual talents were insufficiently appreciated, perhaps even convinced that his superabundant energies had been misdirected.

He was the target of criticism during his entire term of office at the South Carolina College, and was ultimately forced to retire before the fire of his ecclesiastical foes, leaving in a most precarious position the institution of learning for which he had so greatly labored. The political faction with which he allied himself in South Carolina came into the ascendancy during his lifetime and never deserted him, but he himself felt that the state rights cause had failed of complete success, since the nullification controversy ended in a compromise. His friend Nicholas Biddle, despite the support that he gave him, fell before the mighty onslaught of Andrew Jackson. The religious and philosophical doctrines which Cooper so daringly proclaimed were not generally accepted during his life, and have made less headway in the region where he last lived and taught than almost anywhere else in the country. The principle that was dearest to his heart is not even yet fully established, for entire freedom of speech on all subjects whatsoever remains an ideal rather than a reality. Further examples of the failure of his projects and his hopes could easily be given, but enough has been said to show that there is considerable justification for the claim that his brilliant career was extraordinarily unsuccessful.

No one would be quicker than Cooper himself to deny that the immediate results of a life provide an adequate criterion of its success or its social value. He always regarded himself as a prophet and a pioneer and looked for ultimate, not immediate, vindication. Colossal egotist though he was, causes were dearer to him than personal fortune. After the brief period of financial independence in England he was several times forced to defend himself against those who sought, for one reason or another, to deprive him of his means of livelihood, and he always identified himself with the particular cause that he advocated, but few men have fought more persistently than he did for ideas and abstract principles. He laid himself open to the charge of inconsistency when, as his political philosophy evolved, he frankly repudiated many of his earlier doctrines, but his religious opinions remained essentially unchanged throughout his public life, and he always championed freedom of speech—on all subjects save abolition. Many of his failures and personal misfortunes were undoubtedly due to the irritating combativeness of his nature, but his willingness to suffer for the right and the truth, as he saw them, cannot be denied. From the vantage point of a later century we can judge this doughty, yet oft-defeated, warrior more dispassionately than his contemporaries could do, and can give him credit for services to his own generation greater than his contemporaries realized, and for a prophetic vision which they could not have been expected fully to perceive.

Cooper's political activities have received greatest attention in this study, and of their significance we can speak with confidence. Although the story of his public life in England has chief interest as an introduction of the man and his philosophy, it is deserving of more than passing reference in the history of British reform. In his enthusiastic and unselfish crusade against ecclesiastical and political privilege, he exemplified the spirit and purpose of the group to which he belonged, manifesting at the same time a passionate recklessness that was peculiarly his own. Although his efforts failed of their immediate object, they 'can hardly have been entirely futile. Manchester ultimately became the home of the causes which in Cooper's day were so unwelcome there, and the spirit which dominated the community during the great era of reform must have derived from that of the unsuccessful patriotic societies of the revolutionary period, in the activities of which he was, next to Thomas Walker, most conspicuous.

In the movement against the Federalists in America, Cooper was an outstanding and important figure. As a pamphleteer, he was second in notoriety and influence only to Duane and Callender, while as a political and economic philosopher, he is not unworthy of comparison with the most eminent leaders of his party, Jefferson, Madison, and Gallatin. Throughout the campaign which resulted in victory in 1800, he fought for the recognition of the legitimacy of political opposition and for the broader principle of freedom of speech with all the passionate earnestness that characterized his lifelong crusade, and he deliberately invited punishment under the Sedition Act in order to prove that the law was unjust and tyrannical. The intimate and enduring friendship which was then established between him and Jefferson has an abiding interest and would alone entitle him to remembrance. The letters which passed between these two men of such kindred spirit deserve high rank among the intimate political and personal documents of the generation. As Luzerne commissioner in Pennsylvania, Cooper showed himself unselfish, just, and statesmanlike, and furthered the solution of an exceedingly difficult and perplexing problem. He fought a valiant, though not entirely disinterested, fight in the state for an independent judiciary and for decorous court procedure, and despite the victory of the anti-judiciary faction and his own ultimate discomfiture, did something to check the tide of fanatical democracy.

His political activities in South Carolina were the most significant of his entire career. No adequate history of the development of the doctrines which became dominant in the South and which played so fateful a part in the movement that reached its tragic climax in secession, can ignore the teachings and the agitation of this Englishman who showed the path of sectional self-interest before Calhoun had clearly perceived it, and who calculated the value of the Union at a time when such action was accounted traitorous by the majority of people in the state and out of it. There was scarcely a characteristic doctrine of those which came to be termed South Carolinian that he did not favor, and in advocating very many of them he was a pioneer. History cannot afford to disregard this prophet of secession, who valued union too little because he loved liberty too well.

In the history of American philosophy, Cooper is unquestionably deserving of respectful recognition. Perhaps a majority of the people of the United States still regard the doctrines of materialism and utilitarianism which he championed as incompatible with the religion which they profess, but, in one form or another, these doctrines are now widely held. There is much in modern thinking that would be congenial to Cooper's spirit, and there is much in it that he may be said to have anticipated. Indeed, the evolution of his philosophy may perhaps be regarded as an epitome of the process through which liberal western thought has gone during the last century and a half: at first he was doctrinaire, sentimental, and highly optimistic, as liberals so generally were at the beginning of the French Revolution; ultimately he became a realist, an utilitarian, an empiricist, and something of a pessimist, as so many disillusioned liberals are today. He rested his hopes upon the triumph of science, which has come as he predicted; he looked for an extension of the empirical methods of science into other fields of investigation, which has begun within our generation.

Even if it be granted that he was not the originator of the doctrines that he championed, it must be recognized that he proclaimed them with extraordinary ability and vigor, and that he stamped them with his own unique personality. Regardless of the intrinsic merit or demerit of his philosophical position, his advocacy of the free discussion of all subjects whatsoever entitles him to a conspicuous place in the history of intellectual liberty in America. His fears of the designs of the clergy were often hysterical, and at times he was himself intolerant, but his implacable hostility to all forms of bigotry and his insistence that the march of mind be unimpeded have left humanity his debtor.[1] His emphasis upon the historical method as applied to the sacred writings was noteworthy for its day, and strikingly prophetic. Many others may have thought as he did, but very few showed equal courage in expressing their opinions.

Perhaps no man of Cooper's generation did more than

[1] Cooper is not mentioned in Andrew D. White's, *History of the Warfare of Science with Theology in Christendom,* but might well be.

he to advance the cause of science and learning in America. His intellectual interests were too diverse for him to become an eminent specialist in any single field, and, although a lifelong lover of the classics, he emphasized the utilitarian subjects. But he was characteristically scholarly in his emphasis upon thoroughness and, when not involved in controversy, illuminated with a broad social philosophy every subject that he touched. In chemistry, geology, and economics, he was distinctly a pioneer in America, and his formal and informal discussions of educational aims and problems reveal a statesmanship which would have made him conspicuous in any generation.

The most interesting side of his versatile personality is disclosed by his correspondence, of which unfortunately only a relatively small portion remains. The personal influence that he exerted upon the public men of his day must have been considerable, and one can afford to be enthusiastic in speaking of his letters to them. They are vivacious and witty, and abound in literary and historical allusion; they vividly portray the particular conditions under which their author lived and reveal his own rich thought-life and extraordinary personality as do none of his more formal writings. In them we see the man at his best.

Unquestionably he was seen at his worst in controversy. His age, unfortunately, knew him best as a controversialist, and primarily as such his contemporaries judged him. They saw in him many apparent inconsistencies, much demagoguery, and an irrepressible combativeness, but despite the fact that he frequently injured the causes that he supported more than he aided them, he could hardly have failed to be highly stimulating to his contemporaries. To those who can view him dispassionately, he will be often an amusing, usually an appealing, and always an interesting personality. He sought truth and endeavored to spread light, and he fought passionately for freedom. Surely it cannot be that such a life was lived in vain.

BIBLIOGRAPHICAL NOTE

THE letters and other personal papers of Thomas Cooper, which after his death were turned over to his son-in-law, Dr. John Manners, in order that the latter might write an authoritative biography, were destroyed by fire during or after the Civil War while in the possession of one of Cooper's daughters and before any use had been made of them. The late Colyer Meriwether, who made a careful inquiry into the fate of this material, printed letters from Cooper's descendants in the *Publications* of the Southern History Association (1907), XI, 339-342, and there stated that it was "almost safe to say that the bulk of everything in the shape of correspondence, diaries or other personal data" had been lost. Other letters, bearing equally negative testimony, are now preserved in the collection of fugitive material left by Dr. Meriwether to the library of the University of South Carolina. Although my own investigations have disclosed the existence of a considerable number of Cooper's letters in various repositories, the lack of a definite body of readily accessible personal material has made it impossible for me to begin where biographers generally begin, and has made more indirect procedure necessary.

A very large body of printed material from Cooper's own hand is available in his published writings, which however are collected in no single work and in no single library. From this source alone one can gain knowledge of his philosophy and of many of his controversies, but one can learn little of his personal activities or of contemporary opinion regarding him. Fortunately, it has been possible to recover from the papers of other men a relatively small but very important portion of his private correspondence. A considerable number of letters written to him have been published in the writings of various statesmen and others are preserved in the manuscript papers of the latter. Relatively few of his own letters have been printed, but I have been able to resurrect a considerable number of others from the manuscript collections where they have so long lain buried. Official records of various sorts have afforded much authoritative and valuable information about his trials and official acts. Contemporary newspapers teem with references to him and from these alone a fairly adequate account of his more important controversies could be given. Contemporary pamphlets have served to supplement the newspapers, and numerous incidental references to Cooper have been found in memoirs and other nearly contemporary writings. So, despite the lack of a definite body of personal material, it has been possible to reconstruct the story of his major activities and to restore the picture of the man himself.

THE PUBLISHED WRITINGS OF THOMAS COOPER

Cooper's writings consist of both books and pamphlets and cover a vast diversity of subjects. A large part of this study has been given over to a discussion of the more important of them, so I shall here content myself with listing them chronologically within several topical groups and commenting very briefly upon their form and relative importance.

POLITICAL AND ECONOMIC

Propositions respecting the Foundation of Civil Government, 1787. Published in the *Memoirs* of the Manchester Literary and

Philosophical Society, III, 481-509; also with his *Reply to Burke's Invective,* 1792, and with his essay *On the Constitution of the United States,* 1826. This brief work gives a summary of his political philosophy during the first stage of his career.

Letters on the Slave Trade. First published in Wheeler's *Manchester Chronicle,* 1787 (file not preserved); reprinted, with additions and alterations, Manchester, 1787. *Supplement,* Warrington, 1788. This pamphlet has slight intrinsic value, but shows Cooper's early humanitarian zeal and early hostility to slavery.

Reply to Mr. Burke's Invective against Mr. Cooper and Mr. Watt in the House of Commons, on the 30th of April 1792. Manchester, 1792. Very valuable as an expression of Cooper's early political philosophy and an illustration of his power of invective.

Editor of J. B. d'Aumont's *Narrative of Proceedings relative to the Suspension of the King of France on the 10th of August, 1792.* Manchester, 1792. Indicates the attitude of Cooper toward this event.

Political Essays, originally inserted in the Northumberland *Gazette,* with additions. Northumberland, 1799. Second edition, with additions and corrections, Philadelphia, 1800. The most important philosophical contribution of Cooper to the campaign of 1800.

Memoirs of Dr. Joseph Priestley, appendix 3. Northumberland, 1806. An account of Priestley's political works and opinions in which Cooper acknowledges his indebtedness to his friend and incidentally describes his own opinions.

An Appeal to the Government and Congress of the United States, against the Depredations Committed by American Privateers, on the Commerce of Nations at Peace with Us. By an American Citizen. New York, 1819. Listed with Cooper's works in the second edition of his *Lectures on the Elements of Political Economy,* 1829.

On the Proposed Alteration of the Tariff, submitted to the Consideration of the Members of South Carolina in the Ensuing Congress of 1823-24. Appended: "Prohibitory Duties." Remarks on them by Thomas Cooper, M.D., from the *National Intelli-*

gencer, January, 1822. Charleston, 1823; second and third editions, Columbia, 1824. Very important.

Consolidation, An Account of Parties in the United States from the Convention of 1787, to the present Period. Anonymous pamphlet, Columbia, 1824. Reprinted in the Charleston *City Gazette,* Nov. 1-8, 1824. Second edition, with Cooper's name, Columbia, 1830. Appended to this edition: "South Carolina Doctrines." Part Second appeared in the Columbia *Southern Times* in August and September, 1834, and was published as a pamphlet the same year. The original pamphlet is very important because of its relation to the campaign of 1824 in South Carolina and to the development of state rights doctrines there.

Lectures on the Elements of Political Economy. Columbia, 1826. Second edition, Columbia, 1829; London, 1831. A pioneer American work on the subject.

On the Constitution of the United States and the Questions that have arisen on it. Columbia, 1826. A pamphlet, not so well known as *Consolidation,* but comparable with it in importance. The "Petition of Thomas Cooper on the Sedition Law" is appended.

On the Tariff. A pamphlet containing Cooper's famous speech at the Columbia meeting, July 2, 1827, and the resolutions then adopted. The only copy that I have seen is now in the Madison Papers (Library of Congress), LXXVII, 5. The speech was also published in several newspapers.

The Right of Free Discussion. Appended to the second edition of the *Lectures on Political Economy,* 1829.

Hints, Suggestions, and Contributions toward the Labours of a Convention. Columbia, 1832. An anonymous pamphlet, but the copy in the library of the University of South Carolina bears Cooper's autograph and acknowledgement of authorship. He made no suggestion that had not already been made.

A Series of Essays on the Present United States Bank, Columbia, 1833. Originally published in the Columbia *Times and Gazette,* June 21-August 2, 1833. Cooper defended the bank and endeavored to quiet the constitutional scruples of the South Carolinians.

A Manual of Political Economy, Washington, 1833.

The two following anonymous works have been commonly attributed to Cooper, but in my opinion without justification:

Strictures addressed to James Madison on the celebrated report of Wm. H. Crawford, recommending the intermarriage of Americans with the Indian tribes. Signed "Africanus." Washington, 1816. Bears no marks of Cooper's style.

Memoirs of a Nullifier, Written by Himself. By a Native of the South. Columbia, 1832. Cooper was not a native of the South, and this rambling story of adventures, interspersed with poetry, shows no similarity to anything else he wrote.

LEGAL

The Bankrupt Law of America, compared with the Bankrupt Law of England. Philadelphia, 1801. A treatise written by Cooper during his imprisonment in Philadelphia.

The Opinion of Judge Cooper on the Effect of a Sentence of a Foreign Court of Admiralty. Philadelphia, 1808. Dissenting opinion of Cooper, sitting as a member of the Pennsylvania High Court of Errors and Appeals, in the case of Dempsey, Assignee of Brown *v.* The Insurance Company of Pennsylvania.

Narrative of the Proceedings against Thomas Cooper, Esquire, President Judge of the Eighth Judiciary District of Pennsylvania, on a charge of official misconduct. Lancaster, 1811. This personal account needs to be supplemented by the journals of the assembly.

Institutes of Justinian, with Notes. Philadelphia, 1812. Apparently the first American edition of this work. Highly praised by Jefferson.

Extract of a Letter to a Student at Law, 1815. A privately printed pamphlet. A copy, sent to Madison, is preserved in his Papers, LXXVII, 4.

Tracts on Medical Jurisprudence. Philadelphia, 1819. Various tracts, with notes by Cooper, and a digest of the laws relating to insanity and nuisance made by him.

"Coloured Marriages." Originally published in the Columbia *Telescope,* Sept., 1823, and copied by other papers. Republished in the *Carolina Law Journal*, I, no. 1 (July, 1830), pp. 92-106. Important as an expression of Cooper's mature judgment upon the negroes.

Treatise on the Law of Libel and the Liberty of the Press; showing the Origin, Use, and Abuse of the Law of Libel. New York, 1830. A small book wherein Cooper discusses his favorite subject, freedom of speech, in its legal aspects.

An Introductory Lecture to a Course of Law. Columbia, 1834. Delivered by Cooper in the South Carolina senate chamber in December, 1833, and apparently the only lecture of the proposed course that was delivered.

Editor, *The Statutes at Large of South Carolina*, vv. I-V (1682-1814). Columbia, 1836-1839. The final work of Cooper's life and the chief monument to his legal learning.

PHILOSOPHICAL, THEOLOGICAL, AND RELIGIOUS

Tracts, Ethical, Theological and Political, v. I. Warrington, 1789. Cooper's first book and an authoritative statement of his early philosophy.

To the Right Honourable Edmund Burke (regarding a meeting of Dissenters at Warrington), Manchester, 1790, 6 pp. London Library *Pamphlets*, XVIII, no. 16.

Memoirs of Dr. Joseph Priestley, appendices 2, 5. Northumberland, 1806. An account of Priestley's metaphysical writings and religious opinions as given by his disciple.

The Scripture Doctrine of Materialism. An anonymous pamphlet, published in Philadelphia, 1823. Acknowledged by Cooper and appended to his translation of Broussais' *On Irritation and Insanity,* Columbia, 1831. Important because of its bearing on his religious controversies in South Carolina.

To Any Member of Congress, by a Layman. Washington, 1829; first South Carolina edition, Columbia, 1831; third edition, Columbia, 1831. Perhaps the most bitter of Cooper's attacks upon the clergy.

An Exposition of the Doctrines of Calvinism, 1830. An anonymous pamphlet attacking the Presbyterians, the authorship of which Cooper never denied.

Translation of F. J. V. Broussais' *On Irritation and Insanity*, to which are added two tracts on materialism and an outline of the association of ideas by Cooper himself. Columbia, 1831.

The Case of Thomas Cooper, M.D. President of the South Carolina College. Submitted to the Legislature and the People of South Carolina. December 1831. Appendices: "Plans and Schemes of the Presbyterian Clergy," and "Pentateuch." Columbia, 1831. Second edition, Columbia, 1832.

Dr. Cooper's Defence before the Board of Trustees. From the Columbia *Times and Gazette,* Dec. 14, 1832.

On the Connection between Geology and the Pentateuch: in a letter to Professor Silliman. Columbia, 1833. On this question, Cooper was a "modernist" and Silliman a "fundamentalist."

The Fabrications of the Pentateuch proved by the Anachronism in those Books. Second edition, Middletown, N. J., 1840. A brief pamphlet.

SCIENTIFIC

Memoirs of Dr. Joseph Priestley, appendix 1. Northumberland, 1806. An account of Priestley's scientific discoveries and writings.

The Introductory Lecture, of Thomas Cooper, Esq. Professor of Chemistry at Carlisle College Pennsylvania. Published at the request of the trustees. With notes and references. Carlisle, 1812. Practically a history of chemistry.

The Emporium of Arts and Sciences, new series, I-III. Philadelphia, 1813-14. Conducted by Cooper.

F. C. Accum, *System of Theoretical and Practical Chemistry.* With an appendix, containing a view of the late doctrines and discoveries in chemistry. By Thomas Cooper. Philadelphia, 1814. Second American edition.

A Practical Treatise on Dyeing, and Callicoe Printing. Philadelphia, 1815.

Some Information concerning Gas Lights. Philadelphia, 1816.

F. C. Accum, *Chemical Amusement.* Second American edition, from third improved London edition. With additions, by Thomas Cooper. Philadelphia, 1818.

Thomas Thomson, *A System of Chemistry,* in 4 volumes. From

the fifth London edition, with notes by Thomas Cooper. Philadelphia, 1818.

Jane Marcet, *Conversations on Chemistry*. Revised and corrected by Thomas Cooper from the fifth London edition, considerably enlarged. Philadelphia, 1818.

A Discourse on the Connexion between Chemistry and Medicine. Philadelphia, 1818. Delivered by Cooper in the University of Pennsylvania, Nov. 5, 1818.

On the Tests of Arsenic. Philadelphia, 1818. Read before the American Philosophical Society, Sept. 18, 1818, and published separately before its insertion in the *Transactions*.

Introductory Lecture on Chemistry, delivered at the College of South Carolina, in Columbia, January 1820. Columbia, 1820.

Syllabus of a Course of Lectures on the Elements of Geological Mineralogy. Columbia, 1821. 8 pp.

Willich's *Domestic Encyclopaedia*. Philadelphia, 1821. Second American edition published under Cooper's direction.

Treatise of Domestic Medicine with a System of Cookery. Reading, 1824.

MISCELLANEOUS

Observations respecting the History of Physiognomy. Memoirs of the Manchester Literary and Philosophical Society, III, 408-62 (1790).

Observations on the Art of Painting among the Ancients. Ibid. III, 510-597.

Some Information respecting America. Dublin and London, 1794. 2 edition, London, 1795. French edition, Hambourg, 1795.

Address to the Graduates of the South Carolina College, December, 1821. Columbia, 1821. Published at the request of the trustees.

Address of the President of the South Carolina College, to the Graduates, at the Commencement, December 1, 1823. Columbia, 1823.

Address to the Graduates of the South Carolina College, at the public commencement, 1830, published at the request of the senior class, May 1831. Columbia.

THE PRIVATE CORRESPONDENCE OF COOPER

PUBLISHED LETTERS

Only a small number of Cooper's letters to his more distinguished correspondents have been published. Several letters to Jefferson, written between 1812 and 1822, may be seen in ''The Jefferson Papers'' (*Collections* of the Massachusetts Historical Society (1900), 7 series, I, 1-377). A few letters to Jefferson and others have been published by Edwin L. Green in the appendix to his *History of the University of South Carolina* (1916), pp. 332-343. Ten letters written by Cooper to Senator Mahlon Dickerson of New Jersey in regard to the repayment of his fine were published in the *American Historical Review* (1901), VI, 726-36; and approximately a dozen of his letters to Nicholas Biddle have been printed, entire or in part, in Reginald C. McGrane's *The Correspondence of Nicholas Biddle dealing with National Affairs (1919)*. A considerably larger number of the letters written to him have been published. Most of those from Jefferson may be found in Paul Leicester Ford's edition of the former's *Writings* (1892-99), and in *The Writings of Thomas Jefferson*, Memorial Edition, Albert Ellery Bergh, Editor (1903-4). Letters from Madison have been published in Gaillard Hunt's *The Writings of James Madison* (1910), and in the *Letters and other Writings of James Madison*, published by order of Congress (1865). Letters from Biddle may be seen in McGrane's collection.

UNPUBLISHED LETTERS

Most of the letters from Cooper that I have discovered and approximately half of those to him are preserved (generally in the form of copies) in the manuscript collections of Jefferson, Madison, Van Buren, Nicholas Biddle, and James H. Hammond in the Library of Congress. The Jefferson Papers have proved most fruitful and next to them the Nicholas Biddle Papers. In the former, which are incompletely calendared, I found thirty-four letters from Cooper to Jefferson, twenty-eight from Jefferson to Cooper, and fifteen others bearing more or less directly upon Cooper. In the latter, which are uncalendared, there are thirty-five letters from Cooper to Biddle, five from Biddle to

Cooper, and two others written to Cooper by A. E. Miller, a South Carolina publisher. In the Madison Papers, there are twelve letters from Cooper to Madison, four from Madison to Cooper, and several others from Cooper to other men and from other men to him. In the Van Buren Papers there are ten letters from Cooper, but none to him; and in the James H. Hammond Papers, twelve letters from Cooper. Other isolated letters, found elsewhere, have been referred to in the notes; and official letters have been found in certain of the collections named below.

OFFICIAL PUBLICATIONS AND MANUSCRIPTS

Since Cooper held no public office in England but was chiefly a philosopher and a relatively obscure agitator, his name occurs rarely in British official publications. For the attack on him by Burke, Cobbett's *Parliamentary History*, XXIX, XXX, was consulted, and for the general campaign against the radicals the same work, the *Annual Register*, 1792, 1793, and Howell's *State Trials*, XXIII, XXV, were used. In the United States, Cooper rarely came into contact with the federal government, but important brief reference is made to him in the *Annals of Congress*, 1801, the *Register of Debates in Congress*, 1830, and the *Congressional Globe*, 1850. The House *Journal* and Senate *Journal* of the General Assembly of Pennsylvania have proved valuable, especially from 1800 to 1805, and in 1811. The "Documents relating to the Connecticut Settlement in the Wyoming Valley," edited by William H. Egle (Pennsylvania *Archives*, 2 series, XVIII), are indispensable for his work as Luzerne commissioner. He was more important as a public official in South Carolina than in Pennsylvania, and the publications of the General Assembly have accordingly proved much more valuable. The *Reports and Resolutions* for the entire period of his life in the state are available in printed form, but the published *Journal* of the House of Representatives and that of the Senate begin with the year 1831. The earlier journals are in manuscript form in the office of the state historical commission in Columbia. The manuscript Minutes of the Board of Trustees of South Carolina College during the period of Cooper's connection with the institution are of the highest value.

PROCEEDINGS OF SOCIETIES AND UNOFFICIAL COLLECTIONS OF DOCUMENTS

The several publications of the Manchester Literary and Philosophical Society, especially the *Memoirs,* give authoritative information about Cooper's connection with that organization. No formal records of the Manchester Constitutional Society have been preserved, but in 1792 the society published its *Declaration of Principles* and *Correspondence with the Jacobins,* both of which are important, as is *A Collection of Addresses transmitted by certain English Clubs and Societies to the National Convention of France* (1793). Cooper's own account of his relations with the Jacobins can be verified and supplemented by the authoritative collection of F.-A. Aulard, *La Société des Jacobins, Recueil de Documents,* III, IV (1892). The account of the trials at Manchester given in Howell's *State Trials,* XXV, seems to have been taken from the *Proceedings of the Trial of Thomas Walker and Others* (1794). The contemporary *Account of the Trial of Thomas Cooper, . . .* on a charge of libel against the President of the United States; taken in shorthand, with a preface, notes, and appendix, by Thomas Cooper (1800), seems also to have been followed in Francis Wharton's *State Trials of the United States during the Administrations of Washington and Adams,* although Wharton's notes are disinterested and valuable. The *Early Proceedings* of the American Philosophical Society, and the *Proceedings,* XXVII, give interesting information about Cooper's connection with that organization.

WORKS AND PUBLISHED CORRESPONDENCE OF PUBLIC MEN

In addition to the works already referred to in connection with Cooper's correspondence, the following have been particularly useful: William Cobbett's *Porcupine's Works,* I, IX, XII (1801); John T. Rutt's *Life and Correspondence of Joseph*

Priestley (1831) ; Priestley's *Letters to the Inhabitants of North-umberland* (2 edition, 1801) ; N. F. Cabell's *Early History of the University of Virginia, as contained in the letters of Thomas Jefferson and Joseph C. Cabell* (1856) ; and "Letters on the Nullification Movement in South Carolina, 1830-1834," *American Historical Review,* VI, 736-765.

CONTEMPORARY PAMPHLETS AND MEMOIRS

Thomas Walker's *Review of Political Events in Manchester during the last five years* (1794) is a valuable contemporary account of events of which there is little other record, and reflects the point of view of the group to which Cooper belongs. Joseph Priestley's *Memoirs* (2 v., 1806) reflect the same point of view, but, except for the appendices written by Cooper, are less valuable. Priestley's own narrative ends, and that of his son begins, with 1795. The various pamphlets called forth by Cooper's attack on the tariff when in South Carolina have been sufficiently described in the notes and need not be referred to here. The important pamphlets of "Censor," "Justice," and "Wesley," attacking and defending Cooper's position in the religious controversy in South Carolina, also require no further mention. Most of those that I have used are in the personal possession of Professor Yates Snowden of the University of South Carolina or in the Charleston Library Society.

NEWSPAPERS AND PERIODICALS

Contemporary newspapers have proved invaluable in connection with this study, for Cooper was himself an extensive contributor to them, and many of the controversies in which he played a part are described in them more completely than anywhere else. They serve as an index of public opinion, though the point of view of a particular editor must always be taken into account, and their concurrent testimony is frequently the best available source of information in regard to events. Fortunately, I have been able to discover newspaper files covering the most important periods of Cooper's public life, and I have used these critically, but extensively.

British papers, in comparison with American, have proved relatively unfruitful sources of information but three Manchester papers are important. The conservative *Chronicle* and *Mercury* reflect the prevailing sentiment in the locality during Cooper's residence there, and the organ of the reformers, the *Herald* (March 31, 1792, to March 23, 1793), reflects the hopes and opinions of the group to which he belonged. Matthew Falkner was the publisher of the latter paper, but Cooper was credited with some share in the editorial labors. The Free Reference Library of Manchester has the *Herald* (as has the British Museum) and, for most of the years from 1784 to 1793, the *Chronicle*. The Chetham Library of Manchester has a complete file of the *Mercury,* 1786-1794.

In America, Cooper began to play an active part in politics in 1799 and attained great local prominence in 1800. For the Republican campaign in Pennsylvania during these years and his connection with it, three Philadelphia papers, the *Aurora General Advertiser,* edited by William Duane, an intimate political associate of his, the Federalist Philadelphia *Gazette and Universal Daily Advertiser,* published by Andrew Brown and Samuel Relf, and the Federalist *Gazette of the United States,* published successively by John Ward Fenno and C. P. Wayne, have proved invaluable. The Library of Congress and the Pennsylvania Historical Society have files of all three, partial or complete, for the campaign period, 1799-1800. The *Aurora* continues to be an important source of information in regard to Cooper's career in Pennsylvania until 1805, and the Philadelphia *Gazette* has some value, but the Northumberland *Republican Argus* (file for 1803-1805 in the Pennsylvania Historical Society) has proved most useful in connection with the antijudiciary movement, which it supported. Its editor, John Binns, a friend of Cooper's despite their political differences, later became editor of Governor Simon Snyder's organ, the Philadelphia *Democratic Press* (Pennsylvania Historical Society), which describes more fully than any other paper the proceedings against Cooper in 1811 and reflects the attitude of the dominant democratic faction toward his removal from the judiciary. During the period 1811-1819, Cooper played little part in politics and accordingly figured little in the newspapers, but he contributed very extensively to periodicals. He edited the *Emporium of Arts and Sciences* during 1813-1814 (Philadelphia, new series, I-III), and between 1811 and 1815, wrote regularly for the *Port Folio* (Philadelphia). The *Virginia Evangelical and Literary Magazine* (Richmond, vol. III, 1820) is important because it served as the medium through which his clerical foes opposed his appointment to the University of Virginia.

In South Carolina, Cooper was a prominent public figure from the outset and during his more important controversial years in the state received an enormous amount of attention from the local press. The files of Columbia papers unfortunately are incomplete, but the Charleston papers, of which complete files exist for our period, contain a vast amount of necessary material. The *Columbia Telescope,* edited by D. J. McCord, a disciple of Cooper's, was commonly regarded as the latter's personal organ and the most aggressive state rights newspaper in South Carolina. Its file for 1829 is preserved in the library of the University of South Carolina, and its files for 1830, 1831, and 1833 are in the Library of Congress. The former library has also the *South Carolina State Gazette and Columbia Advertiser* for 1827 and 1828, and its successors, the *Southern Times* and the *Southern Times and State Gazette,* for 1830 and part of 1831. The Columbia *State* has the latter paper for 1835-1836. The three most important Charleston papers are the *Mercury,* published by H. L. Pinckney, an aggressive champion of state rights, and the two unionist papers, the *Courier,* published by A. S. Willington, and the *City Gazette and Commercial Daily Advertiser,* published after 1826 by James Haig. Except for six months of the *Mercury,* the Charleston Library Society has complete sets of these papers, and the single gap is filled by one of the volumes in the library of the College of Charleston. For my purpose, the most important years are 1823, 1824, 1827, and 1829-1832. The Charleston *Southern Patriot* is also available and was used to some extent. *Niles' Weekly Register* (Baltimore) is not indispensable; but during the years 1827-1831 it contained a number of

South Carolina items quoted from various papers and some important comments on Cooper. During his last years in South Carolina, Cooper contributed numerous articles to periodicals of one sort and another, especially the *Southern Review* (Charleston) and the *Southern Literary Journal* (Charleston), but these add little to our knowledge of the man and his philosophy and merit slight attention.

LATER WORKS

In general, I have made little use of recollections, but the following are not without value: *Autobiography of Charles Caldwell, M.D.* (1855); G. W. Featherstonhaugh, *Excursion through the Slave States* (1844); Edwin J. Scott, *Random Recollections of a Long Life,* 1806-1876 (1884); J. Marion Sims, *The Story of My Life* (1884); and "Judge Cooper's Table-talk," said to have been recorded by D. J. McCord, in E. A. and G. L. Duyckink's *Cyclopedia of American Literature,* II (1855). References have been given in the notes to such monographs and other secondary works as have proved useful in connection with the various movements in which Cooper participated, and acknowledgement is here made of the detailed and extremely valuable information about South Carolina newspapers contained in Chauncey S. Boucher's *Nullification Controversy in South Carolina* (1916).

INDEX

ter Literary and Philosophical Society, 9; writings of, at Manchester, 10-18; activities against slave trade, 19-22; opposition of, to Corporation and Test Acts, 23-5; rejected by Royal Society, 26; connection of, with Manchester Constitutional Society, 27-30; resigns from Literary and Philosophical Society, 30; association of, with Horne Tooke, 31-3; association of, with Jacobins, 34-40; attacked by Burke, 38, 41-2, 69; proposed for membership in Society of Friends of People, 43; commended by Society for Constitutional Information, 45; reply of, to Burke, 45-53; attacks first proclamation against sedition, 54-6, 70; tribulations of, discussed by Jacobins, 58-9; edits narrative of suspension of Louis XVI, 59; protests against calling out militia, 62-3; escapes molestation in riot at Manchester, 66; disapproves of French excesses, 67-8; assists in defense of Walker, 69-70; legitimacy of conduct of, in England, 70-1; failure of firm of, 71; disillusionment of, in England, 72; prospecting trip of, to America, 75-6; *Some Information respecting America*, of, 76-9; arrives at Northumberland, 80-1; family of, 81 (note 25); occupation of, at Northumberland, 81-2; intimacy of, with Priestley, 82-3; obscurity of, 84; reasons for identification of, with Republicans, 87-91; unsuccessful application to Adams for office, 87-9; edits Sunbury and Northumberland *Gazette*, 91; *Political Essays*, of, 92-103; attracts attention of Jefferson, 101; advocates election of McKean as governor of Pennsylvania, 103-4; perverted account of application of, to Adams, appears, 104-5; replies, 105-6; upholds right of expatriation, 108-10; attacked by Federalist press, 110-12; associated with Duane in clash with senate, 112-15; attacked by Federalist press, 116-18; tried for seditious libel, 118; charges against, 119-121; efforts of, to vex prosecution, 122-3; defense of, 124-5; hostility of Chase to, 126-7; makes statement of financial condition, 127-8; denies charge of support by party, 128-9; sentenced, 129; fairness of trial of, 129-30; gloated over by Federalist writers, 131; supported by friends, 132-3; son of, attacks Philadelphia editor, 133-4; unwillingness to accept pardon, 134; in prison, engages in scholarly activity, 135; released from prison, 136; death of wife of, 136; settles score with C. P. Wayne, 137; learns of Hamilton's attack on Adams, 138; visits New York to prosecute Hamilton, 139-40; writes Hamilton, 141-2; is denied controversy, 142-3; explains abandonment of prosecution, 143-5; attacks senate of Pennsylvania, 146-8; services of, in campaign of 1800, 148; appreciation of, by Republicans, 149; loyalty of, to Republican cause in Pennsylvania, 150; counsel for Duane, 150-1; unsuccessful candidate for chief clerkship of Pennsylvania senate, 151-2; Luzerne commissioner, 150, 154-163; attacked by Federalist press, 155; interest of, in state affairs, 164; correspondence of, with Jefferson, 164; opposes protection of foreign commerce, 165-6; praises Jefferson, 166-7; writes Jefferson of death of Priestley, 168; of Malthusian doctrine, 169; discusses Christianity of Jefferson, 168; replies to jokes on Jefferson's salt mountain, 169-170; elected to American Philosophical Society, 170; attacked by Federalist press, 171; commendation of learning of, 172; attitude of, toward conviction, 172-3; appointed to Pennsylvania judiciary, 174; defends judiciary, 175-6; attacked for inconsistency, 179-180, 183-4; defends position, 181-3; explanation of conduct of, 185-6; aloofness from state politics, 186-7; conservatism of, 188-9; disagrees with Jefferson over commerce, 190-1; approves of embargo, 192; favors tariff, 193-4; condemns violation of American rights by Great Britain and France, 194-6; judicial opinion of, praised by Jefferson, 196; and Madison, 197; called to attention of Cabell, 197-8; political isolation of, in Pennsylvania, 199; petitions for removal of, from judiciary, 200-1; charges against, in legislature, 202-4; defense of, 204-5; address asking removal of, adopted, 206-7; discussion of removal of, 207-10; becomes professor of chemistry, Carlisle College, 211; peacefulness of life of, at Carlisle, 212; reconciled to removal from judiciary, 212-13; good results of change of occupation of, 213-14; introductory lecture on chemistry, 214; editor of *Emporium*, 215-17; contributor to *Port Folio*, 218-19; corresponds with Madison, 219; letter of, to a student at law, 219-22; correspondence of, with Jefferson, 222-3; edits *Institutes of Justinian*, 223; praised by Jefferson, 224; discouraged over political situation, 224-26; dissatisfied with position, 226; advises Jefferson about University of Virginia, 227; seeks a position, 228; resigns from Carlisle, 228-9; removes to Philadelphia, 229; carries on academic flirtation, 230; becomes professor at University of Pennsylvania, 230; seeks chair in medical school, 230-2; discusses connection between chemistry and medicine, 232-3; publishes *Tracts on Medical Jurisprudence*, 233; elected to faculty of Central College, 234; attacked, as intemperate, 236-7; defended, 238; elected to faculty of University of Virginia, 239; attacked by Presbyterians, 239-41, 243; University of Virginia unready to receive, 241; finds position in South Carolina, 242, 251; resigns from University of Virginia, 243-4; Jefferson laments loss of, 245; continued friendship of, with Jefferson, 245-6; significance of career of, as educator in South Carolina, 251; elected president of South Carolina College, 252-3; introductory lecture on chemistry, 253-4; address of, to the graduates, 254-6; troubled by disturbances in college, 256-9; gains strong hold upon students, 259; attacked by Presbyterians, 260, 264-5; attitude of, toward Presbyterians, 260-3; vindicated by legislature, 264-5; assumes offensive against clergy, 265-7; engages in controversy with Justice William Johnson, 268-72; danger of position of, 272-4; upheld by political authorities, 275-6, 278; still uncomfortable, 277-8; suggests school of medicine, 278-9; influential in establishment of insane asylum, 279; significance of political activities of, in South Carolina, 281-3; acceptance of slavery by, 284-5; against federal interference with racial question, 286-7; convinced of inferiority of negroes, 287; defends southern system of labor, 288-9; repudiates social philosophy of Jefferson, 290; opposes tariff, 290-2; attacked by protectionists, 293-4; publishes *Consolidation*, 294-300; publishes essay *On the Constitution*, 300-2; general writings of, on political economy,